WARMACHINE

PRIME MKII

STEAM-POWERED MINIATURES COMBAT

CREDITS

WARMACHINE created by
Matt Wilson

Project Director
Bryan Cutler

Game Design
Matt Wilson

Lead Designer
Jason Soles

Additional Development
David Carl
Brian Putnam

Art Direction
Kris Aubin

Lead Writer
Douglas Seacat

Additional Writing
Simon Berman
Rob Hawkins
Ron Kruzie
Jason Soles
Matt Wilson

Continuity
Jason Soles

Editing
Darla Kennerud
Sheelin Arnaud

Cover Illustration
Andrea Uderzo

Illustrations
Daren Bader
Chippy
Matt Dixon
Illich Henriquez
Andrew Hou
Imaginary Friends Studios
Luke Mancini
Slawomir Maniak
Karl Richardson
Brian Snoddy
Greg Staples
Andrea Uderzo
Chris Walton
Eva Widermann
Matt Wilson
Drew Wolf

Concept Illustration
Chris Walton
Matt Wilson

Graphic Design & Layout
Kris Aubin
Kim Goddard
Sean Jones
Josh Manderville
Stuart Spengler

Studio Director
Ron Kruzie

Miniature Sculpting
Sean Bullough
Gregory Clavilier
Christian Danckworth
Brian Dugas
Roy Eastland
Chaz Elliot
Will Hannah
Jason Hendricks
Mike McVey
Ben Misenar
Jerzy Montwill
Paul Muller
Jose Roig
Ben Saunders
Steve Saunders
Kevin White
Jeff Wilhelm
John Winter

Resin Caster
Sean Bullough

Miniature Painting
Matt DiPietro

Hobby Manager
Rob Hawkins

Terrain
Ambrose Coddington
Alfonzo Falco
Todd Gamble
Rob Hawkins
Pat Ohta

Photography
Kris Aubin
Matt DiPietro
Rob Hawkins

Development Manager
Erik-Jason Yaple

Development
David Carl
Michael Faciane

Product Line Coordinator
Rob Stoddard

Creative Manager
Ed Bourelle

President
Sherry Yeary

Chief Creative Officer
Matt Wilson

Executive Assistant
Chare Kerzman

Marketing Coordinator
William Shick

Customer Service
Adam Johnson

Convention Coordinator
Dave Dauterive

Community Manager & Staff Writer
Simon Berman

Volunteer Coordinator
Jack Coleman

NQM EIC
Eric Cagle

Licensing & Contract Manager
Brent Waldher

Production Director
Mark Christensen

Technical Director
Kelly Yeager

Production Manager
Doug Colton

Production
Trey Alley
Max Barsana
Alex Chobot
Doug Colton
Joel Falkenhagen

Joe Lee
Michael McIntosh
Jacob Stanley
Benjamin Tracy
Clint Whiteside

Sys Admin/ Webmaster
Daryl Roberts

Infernals
Jeremy Galeone
Peter Gaublomme
Brian Putnam
Gilles Reynaud
John Simon
Donald Sullivan

Playtest Coordinator
David Carl

Playtesters
Greg Anecito
Kris Aubin
Alex Badion
Simon Berman
Ed Bourelle
Dan Brandt
Erik Breidenstein
David Carl
Kevin Clark
Jack Coleman
Our Player Community
Dave Dauterive
Michael Faciane
Joel Falkenhagen
Rob Hawkins
Field Test Participants
Adam Poirier
Douglas Seacat
William Shick
Jason Soles
Rob Stoddard
Chris Walton
Erik-Jason Yaple

Proofreading
Ed Bourelle
David Dauterive
Darla Kennerud
William Shick
Rob Stoddard
Brent Waldher

WELCOME TO STEAM-POWERED MINIATURES COMBAT!

WARMACHINE is a game of cunning strategy, brutal tactics, and epic clashes between armies of steam-powered warjacks, battle-hardened soldiers, and elite battle mages. The game is set in the Iron Kingdoms, where you'll find deft swordsmen fighting alongside skilled riflemen and powerful magic is just as present as cannonballs or battle axes. The Iron Kingdoms are rife with conflict where the boldest heroes will reign supreme.

This book is the first step toward entering this war-torn land. It begins by throwing you right into the conflict, as a Cygnaran warcaster behind enemy lines attempts his mission of sabotage while unknowingly walking into a trap. It then continues with a historical account of the land's history and varied nations and peoples before diving into the nuts and bolts of how to play out the conflict on your tabletop battlefields.

Then, with a firm understanding of the game rules, the book moves into descriptions of four nations of the Iron Kingdoms among whom the most bitterly contested battles are waged: Cygnar, Khador, Cryx, and the Protectorate of Menoth. Each has its own history and viewpoint, and each is looking to dominate its foes on the fields of battle.

Finally, WARMACHINE is more than just a game. It's also a hobby where players collect and paint finely detailed miniatures representing the warriors, machines, and creatures of this steam-powered fantasy world. To support that effort, *Prime* offers not only inspiring photography of our studio models but also helpful instruction on how to get started yourself with the miniatures hobby.

We sincerely hope you'll enjoy WARMACHINE as much as we do. With this book and a few miniatures, you'll be on your way to ultimate steam-powered miniatures combat.

Your tabletop will never be the same!

TABLE OF CONTENTS

FAILURE IS NOT AN OPTION 6
THE IRON KINGDOMS, A HISTORY 14
THE GAME 26
    MODELS 31
    PREPARING FOR WAR 38
    GAMEPLAY 42
    COMBAT 50
    ANATOMY OF A UNIT 70
    WARJACKS 73
    WARCASTERS AND FOCUS 74
    ADDITIONAL RULES 80
    COMMAND 84
    TERRAIN 86
    SCENARIOS 90

THE FACTIONS OF WARMACHINE 94
CYGNAR 96
PROTECTORATE OF MENOTH 122
KHADOR 148
CRYX 174
MERCENARIES 200
MODEL GALLERY 210
HOBBY AND PAINTING GUIDE 235
APPENDIX A: TIMING 244
APPENDIX B: BONDING 246
RULES INDEX 250
TEMPLATES 255

Visit: www.privateerpress.com

Privateer Press, Inc. 13434 NE 16th St. Suite 120 • Bellevue, WA 98005
Tel (425) 643-5900 • Fax (425) 643-5902

For online customer service, email frontdesk@privateerpress.com

Fourth printing: April 2013. Printed in China.

WARMACHINE: Prime Mk II . . . . .ISBN: 978-1-933362-53-3 . . . . PIP 1021
WARMACHINE: Prime Mk II Hardcover . . . .ISBN: 978-1-933362-54-0 . . . . PIP 1022

FOREWORD

Rarely is a first draft the best draft; as the saying goes, "writing is rewriting." In our own world's history, there are times new information comes to light—discovered from new sources, concluded after deeper scrutiny, or revealed through more enlightened interpretation. So it goes for this next era of WARMACHINE. We, the creators, have approached this as a second draft, an opportunity to improve on that which we felt did not fully meet our original vision or stand solidly among the ranks of our otherwise esteemed work.

While some details have changed, the spirit of WARMACHINE remains intact, both in game and chronicle. Histories have been adjusted to fit a more cinematic paradigm, with an eye to epic storytelling that will allow us to spin this convoluted yarn more eloquently and through broader narrative media. We have approached the game rules in a similar fashion, ruthlessly lopping off unnecessary material, streamlining the gaming experience, and rebuilding frameworks to better support the engine and the components of the game.

Each and every cut, every new join in the materials of our effort, every new feature introduced has been done with meticulous examination and maternal care and is toward one single, overriding goal: to make the WARMACHINE experience better for you.

Those seasoned in the art of WARMACHINE may at first look upon these pages with trepidation, for what immediately draws attention are the differences, those aspects that were known so well and now have transformed into something unfamiliar. We are confident that upon further exploration the true connoisseur of WARMACHINE will realize these changes are for the good of the whole and will deliver a much more satisfying experience. For it is from a studious and laborious examination of community feedback that we approached the renovation of this game, heeding a clarion call for reform sent from the breast of those who in the same breath avowed their unabated love for WARMACHINE.

Here begins a new epoch for WARMACHINE, forged with the same passion as the original but guided by nearly a decade of experience developing the game and interacting with our community. Looking back, it is amazing to see how far we have come, and whether you are a veteran of our inaugural publication or are experiencing WARMACHINE for the first time, we can only hope you are as excited by the prospects of this game's future as we are.

With enduring thanks to our dedicated players,

Matt Wilson

THE FIVE RULES OF PAGE 5—MK II

In keeping with a tradition as controversial as it is revered, Page 5 continues as a manifesto of our disposition, the philosophy with which we have created WARMACHINE. Contained in these paragraphs is the doctrine of our players and the common ground upon which we do battle. Whether a grizzled vet or fresh meat, here are a few things you need to know if you're going to survive in the unforgiving arena of steam-powered warfare.

1) THOU SHALT NOT WHINE

This game is not suitable for wussies. If you cry when you lose, push off—'cause you're *going* to lose. If it hurts your fragile sensibilities to see your favorite character get pounded unmercifully by a rapid succession of no-holds-barred iron fury, you'd better look the other way. If you've ever whined the words, "That's too powerful," then put down the book and slowly walk away. Now.

This is a game about aggression. This is metal-on-metal combat. This is fuel-injected power hopped up on steroids. This is WARMACHINE.

2) COME HEAVY, OR DON'T COME AT ALL

In every dark alley is a ruthless bastard waiting to carve another notch in his bat with your face. And across every table, in his unassuming faded black T-shirt, is a cold-hearted killer mentally tearing you limb from limb.

WARMACHINE favors the aggressor. You've got to throw the first punch if you want to land on top. If you wait for your opponent to come to you, you're going to get steamrolled. You've got to have big [metaphorical] balls to play this game. You've got to charge your opponent and hang it all out there! You've got to break his formations. You've got to be relentless with your onslaught. You've got to go for the jugular and latch on like a rabid dog that hasn't eaten in days.

Anything less, and you'll be hamburger.

3) GIVE AS GOOD AS YOU GET

The proof is in the punishing—the one you give *and* the one you take. There's no honor in clobbering the smallest kid in the yard, and there's no pride to be won by blazing a path to the well for your fail-safe formula. The real bragging rights come from taking down the big dog with a move that jams his pizza hole open like a he just had a Juggernaut in a tube sock applied vigorously to the back of his skull. Damn the status quo. Defy convention! Tempt defeat, then wipe that food-trapping snaggletoothed grin off its face with a wrecking ball.

If the fight is easy, you're not challenging up the ladder.

4) WIN GRACIOUSLY AND LOSE VALIANTLY

Page 5 is about honesty. It's a self-awareness of what we're doing, why we're doing it, and who we're doing it for. It's about the kind of people we are and the kind of people we want to face across the table. Page 5 is a cultivated attitude designed to get the most out of the gaming experience. It's about showing up, playing your hardest to win, feeling satisfaction in a game well lost, and respecting your opponent for the accomplished competitor he or she is, no matter what the outcome.

5) PAGE 5 IS NOT AN EXCUSE

Most importantly—and let's state this loud and clear for the record—Page 5 is not permission to be a jackass in the name of competition. It's not a shield to hide behind when you're playing like a sissified cheeseball, running down the clock, gaming a scenario, or rules lawyering your hapless opponent to death. Page 5 doesn't discriminate between genders. And Page 5 is never, ever, EVER a license to diminish another player so you can inflate your own vertically challenged self-esteem.

Remember, we all come here to battle out of a common love. Respect Page 5. Respect each other.

And now that we're all on the same page . . .

PLAY LIKE YOU'VE GOT A PAIR.

FAILURE IS NOT AN OPTION
SUMMER 603 AR, EAST OF THE BLACK RIVER

The distinctive shriek of incoming rockets split the air, one blending into the next to be followed by explosions that shattered rock and packed earth. The weapons were extremely inaccurate but compensated with sheer quantity. Leaning against the rough surface of a tall, craggy boulder, Lieutenant Allister Caine shielded his face as debris and a spray of dust spilled over him. He held a magelock steel-alloy revolver in each hand, their barrels inscribed with arcane runes—priceless custom-crafted prototype weapons worthy of a gun mage warcaster. He was wearing light warcaster armor and a reinforced leather overcoat backed by a small coal-fed arcane turbine. The Cygnus on his left shoulder and lieutenant stripes on the right identified him as a Cygnaran officer.

The incessant blasts were enough to put anyone on edge, even someone protected by the thrumming energy of an active power field. To his men, Caine looked calm and self-assured, completely in control of the situation. Meanwhile, his mind was frantically concocting and discarding potential plans to prevent them from getting killed here amid the lifeless sands on the fringes of the Bloodstone Marches.

His men lay in firing positions between the rocks, protected by helmets and armor but also by their position atop the hill. They were all trenchers of the 2nd Army, a squad from the 211th who were no doubt starting to regret volunteering for this "simple little operation" across the Black River. Caine suspected his colonel had placed him in charge of the mission as punishment; earlier in the week he had reported to duty still nursing a severe hangover after a late night spent with the attractive daughter of one of Corvis' many bureaucrats. Even so, it was lucky he was there. Otherwise, these soldiers would already be dead.

"What are we dealing with here, sir?" Sergeant Kiel Cartway shouted as he peered down the bore of his rifle into the shifting sands. Between the strong winds that had kicked up clouds of dust all around their position and the need to keep under cover, visibility was poor.

"More Menites than should be in this godforsaken dust bowl. I could do with a few less, so get cracking!" Caine had the advantage of being able to see through the eyes of his warjacks in addition to his own, giving him a slightly better perspective. What he saw did not reassure him.

Several figures dressed in flowing white and sanguine robes with cloth wrapped tightly across their noses and mouths were advancing through the dunes. The sergeant's rifle barked as he fired, but his shot sank harmlessly into the sand behind the lead figure. Cartway cursed under his breath even as his fingers automatically started reloading, opening the breach and sliding another silk-wrapped cartridge into place with practiced ease. Most of the Menites, including those launching rockets onto their heads, were staying safely out of rifle and pistol range.

"You got a plan to get us out of this, sir?" Cartway asked. Something in his voice reminded Caine how young the sergeant was. It was easy to forget; Cartway was a thick-necked, broad-shouldered man who looked like a brawler, his tanned face dirty from sweating under the unrelenting sun besides. He seemed tough enough to chew shoe leather, but he wasn't more than twenty.

The situation reinforced Caine's preference for working alone rather than being shackled to a bunch of kids barely old enough to shave, however well trained they happened to be. The worst part was the complete faith they had in him; he was a warcaster of the Cygnaran Army, the battle-wizards whom young soldiers viewed almost as living gods. If he told them to charge the deliverers, they would run straight into the rocket fire. Some officers savored that sense of power, but holding other men's lives in his hands gave Caine no joy.

Caine showed no sign of these thoughts as he answered, "Keep your shorts on, son, I'm working on it." He was distracted, looking through the eyes of the two light warjacks linked to him. Through force of will warcasters could mentally connect to a warjack's cortex, the artificial mind inside the torsos of their metal chassis. His 'jacks included a Sentinel he had sent to guard the only approach up the crag and a Charger firing from an exposed position at the edge of the rocky promontory. While battered by unrelenting impacts, it had yet to sustain severe damage.

Considerably louder than the intermittent rifle fire was the deep report of the Charger's cannon, each shot followed by the crisp metal clank of its reloading mechanism. Its glowing eyes scanned the surrounding ground for targets, and occasionally its cannon bucked. Earlier Caine had sent arcane energies to bolster its long-range accuracy. Caine mentally helped guide its fire, feeling satisfaction as several of the hurrying figures below fell to the sand, unmoving.

Caine had considered their position well chosen just a few minutes before, but now he suspected his men were stuck in an elevated deathtrap. The crag had excellent cover and only a single route of easy approach, up the gentler slope behind them, but they would be exposed the moment they left cover. Caine's Sentinel stood down below to shred any foe that got too close from that direction. Caine heard the clanking buzz of its chain gun barrels spinning up to speed followed by the ripping sound of bullets fired in

rapid sequence. Plunging his mind into the Sentinel to peer through its eyes, he saw several emboldened zealots fall to the dirt in a ragged line after trying to make an abortive run toward the incline. These appeared to have broken from the main group, though; It seemed they were waiting for greater numbers before rushing the crag.

Sergeant Cartway shouted over the noise to Caine, "I thought they said no one was guarding this place, sir!"

"At a guess, I'd hazard we got some bad intelligence." Caine gave a grim smile.

Suddenly the sergeant yelled, "Incoming! Get down!" Everyone except Caine hunkered down as a larger volley of rockets pounded the boulders and sprayed them with shrapnel and rock fragments. Unfazed, Caine continued to scan his surroundings like a bird of prey, seeking an opportunity.

To the east through the choking dust and debris, Caine saw the tantalizing sight of rig towers above the sandstorm haze. This was an extraction site for Menoth's Fury, the volatile oil the Menites pulled from the desert wastes and

refined for many of their weapons. Cygnaran generals were concerned about increased weapon production by the Protectorate, which was technically prohibited by law from producing weapons of war. The order had come down to take out several of their weapons facilities. As far as the Menites should have been concerned, this location was secret. The ranger who had located the site two weeks prior had reported minimal protection. Clearly something had changed.

With the dust, they couldn't even see the deliverers whose rocket barrage had initiated this ruckus, although smoke trails from the continuing rocket fire indicated they had taken a position atop a dune to the northwest. What worried Caine was the fact that the last volley had come from the *opposite* direction. Warjacks were coming from the southeast—Redeemers, he'd guess. In that direction was a low wall of unnaturally thick black smoke. Several hulking shapes moved within the smoky depths. Caine felt a faint but familiar itch in the back of his mind that confirmed the approach of another warcaster. At any other time he might have enjoyed the prospect of pitting his skill and speed against such an enemy, but pinned down as they were, another warcaster was the last thing he wanted to see.

"Look!" The warning came from Niels, one of the younger trenchers who knelt with his rifle pointing east. Out of the black haze a single light warjack had emerged, running toward them at top speed. Its stacks were pouring smoke as it pushed its engine to its limits.

Caine's keen eye recognized the distinct profile of a Revenger. Like all Protectorate light warjacks this one was heavily plated with layers of iron and steel; the armor made them slower but also more durable than their nimble Cygnaran counterparts. With its left arm, the Revenger carried a large shield displaying a Menofix, the holy symbol of the Menite religion. It carried a long halberd with its right arm. The gun mage's gaze slid over these weapons to rest on the much bigger threat: just above the machine's shoulders and connected to its protected cortex was an arc node, by which a warcaster could channel his magic to deliver death at a distance.

Impelled by Caine's focused will, his Charger fired its cannon twice in rapid sequence. The first shot tore a ragged hole in the Revenger's shield and the second exploded one of the pistons in its left arm, but the running 'jack did not falter. Caine left his position, counting on his speed, reflexes, and power field to keep him safe. He scrambled down the steep incline while raising his pistols to fire at the approaching 'jack. He shot with an expert's precision, his bullets glowing blue with sorcerous power as they struck the arc node housing. Sparks flew as one bullet tore a chunk off the outer metal bands, but it failed to penetrate the casing to the arc node's delicate internal workings. The machine was battered but could still channel.

Caine glanced over his shoulder and saw several trenchers emerging from behind the boulders to bring rifles to bear on the incoming 'jack. He felt a presentiment of dread as one moved completely into the open to take his shot. "Niels, for the love of— Get down, you idiot!"

It was too late.

From the black haze a heavily muscled man in blackened armor strode forward. He was carrying a weapon that looked like a massive torch shod in iron and bronze. A blazing fire between its bladed flanges poured dense smoke into the air. His face was obscured behind a thick metal mask with tubes extending to a furnace strapped to his back.

This Menite warcaster raised his right hand and pointed toward the crag. A yellow light ignited between the battered slats of the Revenger's arc node with a crackling hiss like wet wood thrown on a fire. Caine felt a deep thrumming sensation in his chest while some tremendous pressure squeezed his head like it was caught in a vice. A wave

of heat surged from the Revenger to strike Niels, whose body glowed suddenly with orange radiance before fire consumed him. In an instant his flesh and bones were transformed into an ash statue. This began to disintegrate in the wind as if the air itself were chewing away the man's face and arms before exploding the column that was once his body. Flames leapt in quick sequence to the four nearest trenchers, who were similarly obliterated. The air around the survivors filled with the choking ash of their comrades. Caine smashed his gloved fist against the nearest rock and clenched his teeth. "You goddamned fool!"

They heard the sound of the Sentinel's chain gun whir to life behind them as zealots below the incline rushed their position.

The High Reclaimer felt deep satisfaction as he watched unbelievers burn to ash by the powers he invoked. Faith filled him with an implacable resolve, and his eyes were intense and unwavering. Those who had stared into them said they were lit from within, like a reflection of the Eternal Flame of the Temple of Menoth.

Dozens of zealots and deliverers pressed in on the enemy without his command. The High Reclaimer did not function like most leaders of men, for he had taken a vow of silence and his mind was focused on a higher calling. In the absence of spoken orders, those who followed him relied on faith and instincts, heeding impulses they did not fully understand. This gave his forces the appearance of a chaotic mob, but one that moved at times with uncanny coordination.

As the High Reclaimer had passed towns and villages on his march north, zealots had poured from nearby churches to join him. None of those gathered could have explained what compelled their steps. A number of Temple Flameguard had similarly abandoned their posts to join the throng as they witnessed his march. They brought their shields and spears, knowing they would soon be hurled as weapons against the faithless. Other volunteers had also joined him, including village youths tasked with driving the wagons laden with coal and water.

Their long march had been nearly silent except for the endless prayers chanted by the choir priests and acolytes following behind his warjacks. The machines had been borrowed from Tower Judgment without explanation. Those who maintained them had either joined him or watched him go without protest; the High Reclaimer answered only to Menoth and it was not their place to question his actions.

Periodically during their trek the High Reclaimer allowed a short reprieve. This allowed those behind him to refuel the warjacks, water the horses, and make quick meals for themselves. The High Reclaimer afforded them only one night's sleep out of three, during which he stood tireless vigil. No one had seen him sleep or rest.

Those who followed him were united by both overpowering faith and an unspoken fear. This silent man was no priest. He was not one for words of encouragement to ease their spirits and inspire them with reminders of the greater cause. He was an ominous figure from an old and terrifying order, a man who was perhaps the greatest of those who had taken the Oath of the Reclaimer's Last Breath. That he had no name beyond his title reinforced how far removed he was from humanity.

He could recall any of the faithful to Urcaen at any time, rendering their bodies in holy fire. Their souls were more important to him than their flesh. To reclaimers, life was transitory, a brief lull when the soul hid in skin and bone to do the work of the Creator. It was said that a reclaimer's gaze laid bare the soul with all its myriad sins, doubts, and inequities. To such a being even the greatest man was no more than the sum of his failings.

Because the High Reclaimer did not speak, no one who joined him knew his destination or purpose. They could not comprehend that he answered a divine call that impelled him north. He marched toward a confrontation that offered the opportunity to annihilate an enemy who, if left alive, would become an impediment to the Protectorate of Menoth in the years to come. Receiving such mandates was the reason the High Reclaimer and his order existed; they were conduits for the will of the divine. The knowledge of where he must travel to confront this foe seared into the High Reclaimer's mind.

Now, amid the dunes and with the oppressive heat of the sun bearing down upon him, the High Reclaimer felt righteous anger stir. Here were interlopers: a Cygnaran warcaster with pistols in hand, and behind him a pitiful handful of soldiers. These were clearly enemies of the faith, but this was not the foe he had seen in his vision. This was not his true adversary.

This fact did not deter him. Menoth had sent him to this place with the faithful and his blessed machines of war. He would eliminate this enemy and then seek out the other. Opportunities to annihilate enemies of the faith must be embraced.

A Crusader marched alongside its master, hefting its smoldering mace as if eager for battle. The High Reclaimer mentally bade it stay near his side and wait and then closed his eyes in prayer. Without warning, a young zealot behind the High Reclaimer suddenly wavered on his feet and collapsed. His skin shrunk upon itself as though all liquid was being pulled from him. A harsh orange glow covered his body and then moved to imbue the High Reclaimer's warjacks. The Menites around the youth looked fearfully at their master but said nothing as they collected their comrade's body. The nearest village priest whispered a brief prayer, his hands shaking.

The High Reclaimer beckoned to his three Redeemers, directing their attention to the warcaster below the crag. These 'jacks strode forward and their underslung Skyhammer rocket pods pivoted toward the enemy. Numerous small metal hatches along the conical forward sections of these tubes sprung open, followed by the roar of launching rockets. The chanting voices of the choir behind them swelled to add majesty and spiritual power to this attack.

Caine had shouted his warning too late to stop Niels, and now he found himself in the same predicament. There were dangers that could not be easily dodged. Redeemers emerged from the black smoke to unleash a barrage. Time seemed to slow as the rockets spun like a nest of angry hornets toward him in an expanding cluster.

Their very inaccuracy made predicting their flight difficult. He sprinted to the left and leapt into a tumble. He knew the power field generated by his arcane turbine was ebbing after he had expended so much sorcerous energy trying to shoot down the approaching Revenger.

> **OPPORTUNITIES TO ANNIHILATE ENEMIES OF THE FAITH MUST BE EMBRACED.**

His Charger moved without prompting to intercept that same Revenger by jumping heavily and awkwardly down from the crag. This was a risky maneuver given its weight, and it landed poorly. The weight of its chassis partially buckled the strut comprising the lower half of its left leg, but it managed to limp forward while raising its hammer to strike the Menite 'jack. With a metallic clang its swing hit into the Revenger's already damaged shield, partially buckling the steel along its upper edge and knocking it aside. The force of the blow was sufficient to shatter the repulsor mechanism in the shield, which otherwise would have knocked the Charger back.

Caine ducked into a roll even as the first explosions began to erupt around him. A close blast made the world temporarily go white, and his ears filled with ringing as he felt himself blown into the nearby sand. Something solid tore into his left side just below the ribs, but he was almost numb to it; he felt the wetness of his own blood but no pain. His armored breastplate and power field had absorbed a portion of the impact and likely kept it from being a more grievous injury. For now he ignored it. Coughing, he regained his feet and stumbled to the cover of a nearby outcropping of reddish sandstone.

A few dozen yards behind him, Caine heard his Sentinel firing continuously. By his mental link to the machine he knew it was dealing with a mob of zealots rushing the trenchers' crag. Its merciless chain gun tore through them but not fast enough to prevent several from hurling powder-packed bombs. It used its assault shield to protect the more vulnerable elements of its chassis, such as the connecting rods above its hips that transmitted the power of its steam engine down to its legs.

> ## FOR EVERY MENITE THEY SHOT DOWN, SEVERAL MORE ARRIVED TO TAKE HIS PLACE.

Other zealots and Flameguard advanced from several directions toward the remaining trenchers firing on them from the elevated crag. Ignoring the blood seeping down his side, Caine raised his pistols and leaned past the stone to unleash deadly shots into the nearest Temple Flameguard. His Charger, having beaten the damaged Revenger to scrap, limped closer to keep watch behind him. He felt a sense of futility as more black smoke rose to hide the Menite warcaster and his Redeemers. For every Menite they shot down, several more arrived to take his place.

Caine heard the sound of a 'jack bearing down at full steam toward his position. Wincing against the pain in his side he leaned out to see an approaching Crusader. It was a slow machine, but one hit from its tremendous mace would end him. "Bloody hell!" Caine cursed as he mustered his arcane energy, preparing to teleport to a new position out of desperation. He knew retreating would leave his Charger to face the Crusader alone and would buy only a little more time. He had no problem sacrificing the 'jack, but right now that would just leave his men even more vulnerable to the enemy that so greatly outnumbered them.

He was stopped from flashing away by an unexpected sight. From between two dunes behind his position emerged a warjack sprinting toward the Crusader. It was a Lancer, Cygnar's equivalent to the Menite Revenger, armed with a bladed spear and a shield and outfitted with a Cygnaran arc node. Well before the Lancer reached the Crusader, its node flickered to life with a gleam of bluish-white light. The ground beneath the Protectorate 'jack suddenly heaved and buckled to topple the top-heavy Crusader mid-stride. It fell back heavily and sank partway into the packed sand. Even as it labored to regain its feet, the Lancer finished its charge to open a deep rent in the armored chest of the downed machine with the tempered point of its war spear.

Looking back in the direction from which the Lancer had come, Caine saw an Ironclad rushing forward as quickly as its mass allowed. Running ahead of the warjack was a familiar figure, a Cygnaran with red hair and heavy warcaster armor. In one hand the man held an enormous sword, its pommel alight with a blue glow and thrumming with mechanikal power. In his other he brandished a similarly augmented pistol, occasionally taking shots at the nearest Menites. Caine groaned, his relief turning to chagrin. *Why couldn't it have been anyone else?* He would rather take on another entire Menite army than endure being saved by Commander Coleman Stryker.

Caine reacted with instinctive speed, turning on the nearest Menites with pistols blazing to cover Stryker's advance. The Ironclad ran past the gun mage's position to stand like a metal wall between Caine and the enemy beyond. It peered left and right while holding its quake hammer in hand. It eyed the clash between the Lancer and the Crusader as if eager to join that fray, but clearly it was being kept on a short leash. Commander Coleman Stryker was breathing hard and scowling as he stopped alongside Caine. The gun mage leered and asked, "What's wrong, Cole? Shouldn't you be somewhere else right about now?"

The senior warcaster frowned but did not bother to rebuke the lieutenant for addressing a superior officer so casually. The two had known each other too long to expect anything else. "Our rangers spotted a large force heading this way. I came to pull you out."

Caine looked past him, hoping to see more Cygnaran soldiers, but all he could see were Menites closing the gap Stryker had temporarily opened. A number of bodies littered the sands in that direction. "Where are your people?"

"It's just me." Stryker answered. Seeing Caine's blank stare, he added, "It's a long story, and we don't have time for it. You're surrounded and outnumbered. Get your men and let's withdraw before anyone else gets killed."

Caine's temper flared at the thought of being pulled off his mission by someone as insufferably arrogant as Stryker, a man who could do no wrong in the eyes of the generals. "We don't need your help."

Stryker did not seem amused. "This mission is over!"

"I have it under control." He was too angry to recognize the absurdity of his statement. "Go play hero somewhere—"

Caine's next words were rendered inaudible by a fresh volley of Redeemer rockets even as the deliverers on the further dune renewed their own assault on the crag, blanketing the entire area in explosions. Stryker extended a hand toward the crag and Caine could sense his gathering of arcane power as a ring of glowing runes encircled his fist and was mirrored by a brief manifestation above the trenchers who were hunkered down in fear for their lives. This was an additional layer of protection that might help preserve them once they were on the move. Several Redeemer rockets exploded against Stryker's Ironclad, and it staggered back a step.

Once their ears stopped ringing, Caine shouted, "I'm here to take out that extraction rig . . ." He jabbed a finger in the direction of the exposed towers, just past the smoke concealing their adversary. ". . . And I'm not leaving until that thing is ablaze!"

The Crusader regained its feet and began hammering its mace into the Lancer's upraised shield with armor-crushing force. It suffered cortex-burning feedback from contact with the Lancer's shield but still managed to knock the smaller 'jack to its knees. The Lancer's shield arm finally gave way with a screech of tormented metal. Amid this clash the High Reclaimer approached once more, emerging from a wreath of obscuring smoke behind his Redeemers and flanked by several clusters of Temple Flameguard and zealots.

Stryker stared at Caine, his face implacable. "We can get the rigs later. Saving the lives of these men is more important."

Caine sent his Charger to help the Lancer deal with the Crusader, hoping they could finish it quickly enough to respond to the other threats closing on their position. His Sentinel was nearly ruined, its chain gun firing in fits and starts as it struggled to aim after enduring sustained punishment. The trenchers on the crag had noted Stryker's arrival and were giving up their position. They scrambled down the nearest incline and fired their rifles at the approaching Menites as they joined the warcasters. This in turn prompted the deliverers on the hill behind the crag to advance, likely hoping to wipe out the exposed soldiers with their next volley.

Caine's jaw clenched. "I have a mission, and I'm completing it." What angered him most was how blind Stryker was to the fact that his trenchers wanted to complete the mission as badly as he did. They were willing to put their lives on the line to get the job done. Pulling them out now would be an insult to those who had died to get them this far. He pointed toward the enemy warcaster. "Keep him busy! I have an idea."

With his nostrils flared in obvious irritation, Stryker looked beyond his Ironclad, nicknamed Ol' Rowdy, to the approaching High Reclaimer and his 'jacks. The Cygnaran heavy was standing in the way of another rocket salvo, but already the Redeemers were spreading out to gain better angles. Stryker's Lancer was not quite demolished, but it was badly damaged. The rigs loomed just behind the Menites. The winds and swirling sand had momentarily died down, and he could see massive rusting metal tanks at the base of the towers, likely filled with explosive Menoth's Fury. He turned back to Caine and scowled. "If whatever you're planning doesn't work, you'd better beg Morrow for a merciful crossing before I catch up to you." He had hardly spoken before Caine sprinted away.

Stryker holstered his pistol and hefted his blade Quicksilver in both hands, turning toward the High Reclaimer. He exchanged a quick look with Ol' Rowdy and then they both began to move. As his pace increased, he unleashed a battle yell. Coleman Stryker and his Ironclad charged at the enemy, running headlong into a steadily closing ring of Menites.

The High Reclaimer felt the familiar sensation of the world aligning with his divine imperative. The enemy he was sent to intercept was before him. More remarkably, the foe ran straight toward him as if rushing to meet his own death.

A sudden and unexpected explosion of light and motion behind his quarry managed to break the High Reclaimer's focused concentration. The other warcaster, the gun mage, had swung into action. After running away as if fleeing the fight, he turned to point a pistol toward the nearest Redeemer. A ring of blinding runes surrounded the pistol's barrel, which immediately disgorged a wave of raw, concentrated force. The five-ton Redeemer crumpled as if hit by a train and flew back several yards. It crashed into a second Redeemer to topple both in an ear-splitting crunch of colliding machinery.

This same warcaster became an impossible blur of motion as he leapt into the air to fire his pistols in every direction. He launched glowing rounds of screaming lead with impossible speed and unerring accuracy as the barrels glowed with heat and arcane power. The advancing deliverers were annihilated in a cascade of blazing death. An entire squad of Temple Flameguard met a similar fate. Zealots fell by the handful. It was such an amazing display of sorcerous gunplay that it took even the High Reclaimer by surprise, and he was a man well accustomed to the miraculous.

There was a howling only the High Reclaimer could hear as the souls of the dead were shaken from their bodies. Those

nearest to him swept inward, crying out in rage. They swept around him with such power that they became visible as a dark tornado filled with howling faces. The High Reclaimer took these souls into his embrace to deliver them to Urcaen, meanwhile gaining power from the turbulent storm of their spiritual energy.

In moments those souls would pass through him, but in their wake he would have the strength to annihilate all his enemies in a single, great outpouring of vengeance. For now he must endure. The High Reclaimer received Commander Stryker's charge and fell back several steps along the ridge of the dune as he tried to block the sword's blows with his mace. The Cygnaran blanched when he entered the swirling tornado of souls that sucked the warmth from his blood, and the Menite leader took delight in his enemy's suffering. One of the enemy warcaster's strikes sliced a deep gash through the muscles of the High Reclaimer's left

arm, but he stubbornly refused to relinquish his hold on his ceremonial torch Cremator. He ignored the pain of his shattered shoulder when the Ironclad's blow penetrated the field of his turbine. Soon his power would be redoubled and his injuries erased by the reclaimed souls of the faithful.

The High Reclaimer did not realize how close he was to the reservoirs of Menoth's Fury behind him. He was focused on siphoning energy from the souls he bore as they crossed through the barrier to the afterlife. His injuries began to mend as he lifted his great mace to annihilate this enemy of Menoth.

Caine did not have time to observe the clash between Stryker and the High Reclaimer. Nearly exhausted from blood loss as well as the outpouring of energy, he pushed on. Adrenaline kept his legs from collapsing as he rushed past a dozen Menite corpses to where the deliverers had fallen.

He was too far from the rigs to hope to hit them with pistol fire. He awkwardly lifted one of the loaded deliverer tubes and turned back to face the towers, simultaneously calling on his remaining reserves of arcane strength. Runes erupted along the rocket tube as he augmented the weapon's range and accuracy as he had done earlier for his Charger. Caine held the rocket tube awkwardly, never having fired one before, but it was a simple, almost crude, piece of hardware designed for easy operation. With a little prayer to the scion of luck, he yanked the self-igniting fuse and aimed at the rigs.

With a jolt he realized that Stryker was closer to those towers than he had anticipated, but there was nothing to be done now. He decided grimly that if worse came to worst the man would probably enjoy going out in a blaze of glory. With a hiss and belch of flame, the rocket flew from the tube and soared forward in an erratic spiral. He held his breath and swore as he saw it swirl up as if about to veer off in the wrong direction before it suddenly fell straight down toward the tanks of Menoth's Fury.

There was a dull thump and a sound like a gigantic indrawn breath. Caine barely had time to teleport away, vanishing in a flash of light and reappearing behind a half-buried boulder. An enormous fireball consumed the eastern horizon, settling into a wall of roaring flame that sounded like an enraged dragon. Searing heat washed over him.

Ol' Rowdy had broken off to intercept the one Redeemer left standing while the other two labored to regain their feet. Coleman Stryker was facing the extraction rigs as he pressed forward with his sword locked against the shaft of the High Reclaimer's blazing torch. His eyes were watering, and he could barely breathe from the strange wind that whipped around his enemy. He thought he could hear the howls of angry ghosts. That unnatural vortex suddenly extinguished to be replaced by a palpable aura of mystical strength as the High Reclaimer's entire body shimmered with a protective halo.

Something moving quickly in his peripheral vision caught Stryker's attention: a descending projectile heading straight toward the rusting metal tanks. His eyes widened.

In that instant he unleashed a surge of protective energy, sending arcane runes over himself and Ol' Rowdy. They stretched far enough to reach the surviving trenchers hunkered behind cover a couple dozen yards behind him. The world was erased in an explosion of fire and heat,

and he felt himself thrown backward and away from the High Reclaimer. His throat filled with smoke and ash as he tumbled head over heels down the opposite slope of the rise where they had battled. He lost sight of the High Reclaimer entirely. Around him he heard the anguished screams of Menite soldiers and zealots caught in the inferno.

Commander Stryker knew all too well the High Reclaimer would gain enough power amid such carnage to become nearly invincible. His loathsome order thrived on death. Stryker slapped at the flames running along the armor of his left arm as he stumbled back toward the bewildered trenchers, who seemed to have emerged unscathed. Spotting the gun mage behind a boulder, he shouted, "Caine! Let's go! Move it or I'm leaving you for the crows!"

For once Allister Caine had no ready retort, and he ran painfully toward the others without protest. He looked dazed and blinked against the light of the raging fire. Behind them the blaze showed no sign of relenting; the air shimmered with waves of raw heat that tore at their throats and stung their eyes. There was no sign of the High Reclaimer, but both Cygnaran warcasters were certain he had survived. Caine held his side, which was still bleeding, and staggered as he came near. Stryker grabbed his arm to steady him and allowed the gun mage to lean on him as they hurried west. Ol' Rowdy—the only 'jack left standing—followed protectively, occasionally checking behind them for signs of pursuit.

Caine gave one look over his shoulder as they went and grinned at Stryker, his face pale. "Looks like I earned a medal. I'll trust you to put in for that." His voice shook.

Stryker grimaced. "Just be happy we can't demote you any further."

"Don't worry, I'm sure we can talk them into giving you a medal too, so you can add it to your extensive collection." Caine's sarcasm prompted Sergeant Cartway to chuckle, but he stopped at a glare from Stryker, swallowing nervously.

With the fire behind them pouring black smoke into the sky, the Cygnarans limped toward home.

THE IRON KINGDOMS
FORGING A WORLD IN BLOOD AND METAL

From the journals of Rhupert Carvolo, an Ordic mercenary and chronicler also called "the Piper of Sorrows"

REFLECTIONS ON WESTERN IMMOREN ON THE LAST DAY OF 607 AR

I am a traveler.

I earn my coin in battle and move constantly from one field of strife to another. I call no land my home, yet I confess a sentimental attachment to every plot of ground on which I have marched, fought, or sought shelter. It seems inevitable some peril will end my journeys one day, as is the fate of a man such as I in times such as these. With this in mind, I have collected my recent thoughts and assembled them in the hopes that these words might outlast me and prove an adequate description of our varied lands and peoples.

As I travel these embattled lands I speak of what I have seen to those who will listen. I have walked the length and breadth of western Immoren, this beautiful and rugged land split from the unexplored east. Even were the world limited to this region, there would be more places to see and people to meet than could fill a dozen lifetimes. I find it difficult to fathom the rest of Caen, the little-explored wider world beyond our shores. It is no doubt filled with countless wonders, but here I will speak only of what I have seen, read, or heard described in tales.

The kingdoms of this land are both young and old, a paradox that creates some of the tension within and between them. Each is rich in culture, tradition, pride, and the potential for bitter enmity.

In the north stands the vast nation of Khador, its lands noted mostly for the frozen bite of its ice-encased mountains and less for the milder plains, rivers, lakes, farmland, and hills of its southern expanses. A few years ago Khador declared itself an empire and I should probably speak of it as such, but old habits are hard to break. Khadorans have a long history as warriors and conquerors, having arisen to dominate any rivals they encountered as well as their rugged land.

East of Khador and enjoying its share of rugged and frozen peaks is the dwarven nation of Rhul. Their unbroken civilization predates all human claims. Politically, they seem to lack the desire for war that consumes our human nations, although recent battles have lured many individuals forth to test their mettle.

In the west is Ord, the land of my own birth. It is a small kingdom boasting hardy people but not blessed with an abundance of resources. Ord is a land of fog-shrouded moors, imposing hills, and a stretch of coastline where our proud ports seek to dominate the seas.

Northeast of Ord and south of Rhul was Llael, once famed for its vineyards and clever merchants but recently fallen to foreign invasion. Llael has been swallowed up by Khador, churned by the boots of Cygnaran soldiers, and exploited by zealots of the Protectorate of Menoth. Some few Llaelese resist their occupiers, and there are those who still dream of freedom.

Just east of war-torn Llael and long isolated from the affairs of mankind is the enigmatic nation of Ios, home to the elves. Unlike Rhulfolk, who are seen often in cities abroad, the Iosans have kept to themselves. I have heard rumors they are stirring behind their well-fortified borders: witnesses say their soldiers are on the march. Given their fearsome reputation, I pity any who stands in their path.

South of Ord and Llael is the mighty nation of Cygnar, long Khador's hated enemy. Cygnar is a large kingdom and one particularly rich in resources and fertile lands. Accordingly it boasts the largest population and one of the mightiest militaries in western Immoren. It holds the southern peninsula along the Broken Coast and thereby has the longest stretch of shoreline of any of the Iron Kingdoms, with a powerful navy to match. As large as the kingdom appears on a map, it is worth noting how much of its southern and western lands are covered by the dense mountains of the Wyrmwall, uncivilized and treacherous peaks never tamed by man. It is a diverse nation with a strong-willed and well-educated populace, but because of this its leaders sometimes become distracted by internal disagreements, impeding their ability to commit to decisive action.

For all Cygnar's power and wealth, I do not envy them. They are surrounded by enemies and in recent years have been beset on every side. In addition to their Khadoran rivals to the north, they must guard against the Protectorate of Menoth to the east and Cryx to the west. Even the wasteland called the Bloodstone Marches that occupies much of their northeastern border has recently become a menace, disgorging a race called the skorne to assail them. That Cygnar still stands against so many is a testament to the resolve of its people as much as to its strength of arms.

Cryx exists apart from the rest as a collection of horrors and abominations that barely qualifies as a nation. Southwest of Cygnar, across the Broken Coast, amid the swampy and rank Scharde Islands, dwell immortal and unimaginably powerful creatures that are a plague upon the living. There are people who live in Cryx as well, horrible as that thought might be, but their lives are not the same as ours. There the

WESTERN IMMOREN CIRCA 607 AR

dead walk alongside the living and the land itself is tainted by the unholy radiance of the dragon who rules that empire and forces his vassals to worship him as a god.

The only way for Cryx's citizens to rise above the misery and misfortune of their squalid lives is to serve the dragon in any capacity he demands. Many become brutal pirates and raiders and spend their lives preying on others. The place would be foul enough were its denizens confined to the islands, but they scour the main coastline on countless ships geared for war and slaughter. In recent years they have become more brazen in their attacks and have begun to send armies onto the mainland, a development I fear our nations are not taking seriously enough.

> **SOME DISTINGUISH BETWEEN FACT AND LEGEND, BUT I KNOW THE TWO ARE INSEPARABLE.**

That is the general lay of the land, but what does it mean? To even begin to understand the current state of affairs we must consider how it came to be. The flow of battle can change with each decision on the field, but a surge cannot be undone completely. The past is the foundation for the present in all things.

REFLECTIONS ON ANCIENT HISTORY

Though Ordic born, I have no living family there and few remaining ties to that land. I must confess I feel more comfortable outside its borders, as its murky hills and moors remind me of tragedies I have struggled to forget. In these times of increasing strife it seems Cygnar is the only place I can still find warm and inviting pubs where I can reflect in peace. Even Caspia, the City of Walls, is a haven for me now, although its warren of towering bulwarks and clustered humanity unsettles my mind with countless reminders of the ancient past. My writings from the public houses of that city invariably plunge into examinations of history rather than accounts of the present.

How many bloody wars have unfolded in sight of Caspia's great gates? How many swords and spears have pierced human flesh to purchase another few yards of land? Everywhere reminders of fighting remain, remnants of buildings destroyed by Menites during recent clashes. It is the city that forged the colossals, the giant war machines that fought off the Orgoth invaders four hundred years ago. Too often in studying the past many look no further back than the Rebellion, as if our history began with our freedom from the Orgoth.

For an era long beyond reckoning mankind roamed Immoren in wild and savage tribes, incapable of recording their deeds. Menoth, our Creator, left us in this state to test our strength. After a time we drew his attention when we put forward the rudiments of civilization. The first priests rose, chosen by the Lawgiver to bind us together and teach us law. Menoth is our first and eldest god, the Shaper of Man. I am not deeply religious, but even a wine-sodden pipe-blower and teller of tales gives deference to him who created us.

I live to chronicle man's endless appetites for destruction and strife and his search to redeem bloodshed through heroics. Some distinguish between fact and legend, but I know the two are inseparable. That Menoth once strode Caen is to me a fact as solid as the count of those who fell in the Boarsgate Massacre. Menoth's priests shaped our earliest villages and farming communities into towns and cities.

Some of our oldest buildings today stand on the bones of those ancient structures. Though I myself find most of the city rather oppressive, the simplest peasant can recognize Caspia as among the grandest of man's works. Its ancient streets mark the entire course of our history brick by brick. In another time it was named Calacia and was the home of the priest-king Golivant, who beat back the Molgur tribes and erected a great wall against them and who also gave us our first taste of true order.

Such accomplishments—great cities, statues of ancient kings, libraries with walls stacked high with weighty tomes—pale before man's unquenchable thirst for war. During the Warlord Era, the people of western Immoren fought endless battles. I am inclined to believe it was Menoth's will, a means to test the strength of both rulers and ruled.

Even between vast cycles of history, some events are so significant they forever change the shape of the world. It was in Caspia that the Twins were born, and their rise to enlightenment was one such moment. The Twins were originally mortals, but they transcended their flesh to become gods. They defined their paths in a time when all men were slaves to their gods and kings. They left their footprints across Immoren and drew thousands of followers to learn from their example. We always speak of Morrow before his sister Thamar, as her legacy is as dark as his is bright, but their destinies were joined. One need not be a theologian to appreciate the complexity of the philosophies they birthed. Their ideas shook the very foundations of civilization.

Morrow taught there was more to life than battle and blind obedience to law. He claimed a good man must think of others before himself. Thousands followed his example and looked inward for answers. He said that leading a good life required the will to protect the well-being of others, to right injustice, and to fight honorably in war. Morrow was a warrior-philosopher such as the world has yet to see again. His ideas spread faster than the Menites could contain them.

The insidious and subversive Thamar was as selfish as her brother was selfless and as fascinated by the darkness as he the light. She felt true power was boundless and came from the strength of the individual to exert his will over the masses. Thamar taught that morality was the prison of truth and freedom. She delved into forgotten occult lore and profane secrets in the pursuit of illimitable power. She ascended by freeing her mind from the shackles of conscience. As a divine being she became the goddess of temptation, indulgence, dark magic, and deception.

The rise of these ascended gods marked the beginning of the Thousand Cities Era. After the Twins rose and crossed over to Urcaen—the realm of the gods and the afterlife of the dead—the shaping of mortal history was left once again to mortal hands.

Like a stained glass window fallen from its casing to shatter on the ground, the map of western Immoren fractured. City-states of various sizes arose, each with its own warlord or petty king. Tavern-born treaties and back-alley allegiances lasted only long enough to muster men-at-arms for countless murderous wars. The suffering of these bloody days extended beyond humanity. We battled trollkin and ogrun tribes, and we foolishly encroached on the ancient lands ruled by the dwarves of Rhul and the inscrutable elves of Ios, who pushed us back with fierce decisiveness. They punished us for these violations but did not commit to conquest outside their lands.

Though warfare never ceased, the claims of kings began to consolidate as they seized the lands of their rivals and brought more people under their control. Caspia expanded. Thuria rose and Tordor consumed it. The Midlunds unified. The vast Khardic Empire stretched from the north to absorb the Kos, Skirov, Umbrean, and Ryn peoples. Caspia experienced a flowering of thought and reason exemplified by the consecration of the Archcourt Cathedral in the Sancteum. Khardic engineers invented the steam engine and began to realize its potential. Ships fueled by coal plied the rivers without relying on currents or winds. Among my ancestors, the dirgenmast captains of Tordor formed an armada stronger than the world had ever seen, and the sails of a thousand ships spread across the ocean from horizon to horizon.

Who can say what heights we might have reached had we been able to capitalize on these achievements? Alas, such was not to be. Across the ocean came a fleet of black

ships that fell upon our shores. The arrival of the Orgoth would eclipse even the ascension of the Twins and leave an indelible stain across our history. We were thrown into an even darker age, and all the progress hard won through so many bloody quarrels was undone.

The Orgoth possessed a rapacious hunger for slaughter and enslavement. They seemed human enough but proved crueler and more calculating than any race our ancestors had ever encountered. Although it is true we were also warlike, our old warlords had fought for understandable goals, obeyed codes of behavior, and sometimes heeded priestly advice. In contrast, the Orgoth embraced slaughter and cruelty with dreadful enthusiasm. The Tordoran armada sailed to meet the Orgoth ship to ship, but they sent our proud vessels to the deep, spawning the Sea of a Thousand Souls. Countless longboats then spilled cruel warriors onto the beaches of Immoren. The once-warring tribes and towns of the Thousand Cities fought valiantly together for the first time, but the disorganized resistance failed to stop the invaders.

The Orgoth consorted with dark powers. They boasted infernal magic and wielded weapons terrible beyond reckoning. Our Menite war priests and Morrowan battle chaplains brought the power of their gods and fought as best they could, but we were undone. The Orgoth subdued us with rivers of our own blood in a slow but inexorable conquest consuming two centuries.

The Orgoth did not seek to destroy western Immoren. No—they subjugated and enslaved us instead. Camps of starving men and women compelled by the whip and the threat of torture pounded out the fine roads we still use today. Thousands of stone-torn hands erected the basalt fortresses and towers of our conquerors. Of all our cities, Caspia alone held them at bay, kept safe only by her towering walls. Despite this small victory, Caspian armies were soundly defeated every time they ventured forth to meet the Orgoth in battle. For four centuries the Orgoth occupied our lands all but uncontested, plunging our people into enduring darkness.

Our eventual revolt against the Orgoth proved to be as painful and excruciating a time as our initial defeat, requiring the span of two centuries to succeed. A tide of bitter hatred rose in our ancestors and restored the fire in their eyes. This spirit of resistance was not enough in itself. Every rebellion requires weapons and carries a cost payable only in blood. While some do not like to speak of it, evidence suggests the dark goddess Thamar played a part by giving us *the Gift*, humanity's first manifestation of sorcery.

The arcane power and mechanikal wonders we take for granted today were unknown before that time. Miracles had been the sole province of gods and the priests who became living vessels of the divine. The magic afforded by the Gift of Thamar was something else again: the ability to manipulate the very laws of nature through the application of will. It would be long centuries before arcanists understood the extent of this power, if they do even today, but it quickly proved to be a formidable weapon for the Rebellion.

We learned the study of alchemy and produced the first firearms when survivors of the Battle of the Hundred Wizards fled east, but not even guns could turn the Orgoth aside. The tyrants had their own weapons, wicked and unholy, as well as warwitches capable of tearing a man's soul from his flesh.

It was the development of mechanika, coupling the old principles of engineering with the new sciences of magic, that provided the key to eventual victory. The early practitioners of this nascent science conceived the first colossal as a steam-driven, war-ready construct of gears, iron, and smoke standing fifty feet tall or more. It only remained to find the means to build several of these iron monsters without detection by the Orgoth.

Man's commitment and resourcefulness so impressed the dwarves of Rhul that they pledged their aid. The Orgoth had never conquered that northern people, having been rebuked from the great southern fortress of Horgenhold after a single massive assault. They had thereafter ignored that nation, leaving them isolated amid their remote mountains. Rhul did not send armed forces to confront the Orgoth directly, but their supplies of iron ore, fabricated steel, and mechanical expertise helped transform the colossals from an engineering dream to a towering reality. This heralded a new age of mechanika.

The colossals built from Rhulic materials in the factories of Caspia were truly monumental achievements: towering, smoke-belching, steam-powered constructs that walked on legs of steel and wielded weapons so powerful even the gods would envy them. As impressive as they were, their successes in battle relied on the warcasters who learned to control them. Shortly after the first colossal was created,

some few battle wizards awakened to their potential to communicate mentally with the cerebral matrixes that served as artificial minds inside these machines. By an effort of will, these battle wizards guided the colossals in battle.

This sharing of minds between man and machine was something the Orgoth could not match, and over the next few years their fortresses fell one by one to the Rebellion armies that brought together soldiers from each of the future Iron Kingdoms to fight alongside the colossals. Every giant footstep pushed the enemy further west. They fled back to the sea but did not go quietly. As they retreated, the Orgoth razed cities, poisoned wells, salted fields, and otherwise defiled the lands in an act called "the Scourge."

> **THE COLOSSALS WERE TOWERING, SMOKE-BELCHING, STEAM-POWERED CONSTRUCTS THAT WALKED ON LEGS OF STEEL AND WIELDED WEAPONS SO POWERFUL EVEN THE GODS ENVIED THEM.**

Following the defeat of the Orgoth, we rediscovered what it meant to govern ourselves. The leaders of the victorious armies, called the Council of Ten, met in Corvis, Cygnar's City of Ghosts. This council hammered out the map of the new Iron Kingdoms on their political anvils. Deliberations lasted weeks. The negotiations resulted in the Corvis Treaties, which drew the borders for the newly formed territories and created the kingdoms of Cygnar, Khador, Ord, and Llael. These four great nations were briefly united by peace—but soon enough, old rivalries set them once again at one another's throats.

REFLECTIONS ON THE KHADORAN EMPIRE

Every year I try to return to Midfast on the Day of Markus. I look north and consider the rugged and cruel men who dominate the expanse called Khador. At Midfast the people of Ord beat them back in 305 AR. From those walls our tired soldiers witnessed the ascension of Markus to join Morrow. He sacrificed his life to buy time for reinforcements to reach the city and proved that few can defend against many if courage holds.

I will make plain my feelings. I loathe the descendants of the Khardic Empire, and I find in them little to praise. Such men ruined my family, and the blood they have spilled in their unrelenting drive for conquest stains the pages of history. I prize truth and scorn those guilty of dangerous rhetoric, so I will attempt to restrain my distaste and write of the northerners with what measure of neutrality I can muster.

Without question Khador's people are tough, irascible, weathered, and proud. They learned well from those ancient days when man endured through strength and cruelty and see no reason to temper those qualities now. The north keeps deep and ancient customs derived from the time when barbaric horselords roamed and ruled the Khardic Empire alongside their pompous, gold-laden Menite priests. The Khadorans took to Morrow's message later but heeded only select words of his teachings. They lauded the wise philosopher-god's advice on nobility in battle while ignoring his condemnation of unrestrained aggression.

To understand these cold northerners, consider that much of Khador is frozen five months out of the year. There strong winds snap trees in half, and sudden snows sweep in so fast that entire wagon trains have vanished in mere seconds. Only a harsh people could hope to survive in such a harsh place. Khador's military personifies this strength, with huge warjacks thundering along next to steel-hearted men and women armed to the teeth with axes and guns.

Perhaps in such a frozen place the concept of freedom becomes meaningless. Khador has conscripted its soldiers since the time of the old empire. Every adult male and any woman who wishes and is not with child serves their "Motherland" for at least one period of duty. Their mastery of mechanika is nearly the equal of Cygnar's. Even I who loathe them will admit there are many Khadorans as shrewd and cunning as they are implacable.

Morrowans form the majority of this nation, but not an overwhelming one as in Cygnar, Ord, and Llael. The Menite faith is stronger in the north than anywhere outside the Protectorate of Menoth. Whether Menite or Morrowan, however, Khadorans love their sovereign above all. They are as patriotic a people as you will ever find—and that is part of why they are so obnoxious to outsiders.

Khador has always chafed at the compromises made in the Corvis Treaties, for they glorify the days of the old Khardic Empire and seek every opportunity to restore its power. Every generation a new sovereign ascends the throne and declares the time ripe to reclaim lands "stolen" from the Khadoran people. It is unfortunate the Kossite and Skirov tribes no longer remember that they once stood as their own kingdoms, free of the rule of Khards. Now all Khadorans are alike in their blind devotion to the rebirth of the old empire and heedless of the consequences of their savagery.

Recent events have shown that the desire to restore that empire is more than an idle dream. Following the recent occupation of Llael, Queen Ayn Vanar named herself empress of the Khadoran Empire to the tremendous approval of her people. She will surely never be satisfied until all of western Immoren bows before her. After the successes in Llael, Khadoran forces swept on to batter the Cygnaran northern border. They have since claimed the entire Thornwood Forest. Its capture presages bitter battles to come between these two great nations.

REFLECTIONS ON THE MIDDLE KINGDOMS OF ORD AND LLAEL

I like to compare my homeland of Ord to a walnut: it presents a tough exterior that is difficult to crack but holds nourishing meat at its center. My land lacks the resources of some great kingdoms, being a moody realm of foggy bogs, wet marshes, and difficult farmland. Land-owning castellans maintain themselves on herds of cattle and horses, aloof from the masses struggling to put food on the table. We are a tough people not easily discomfited. We find diversion in song, gambling, and ale rather than dwelling on life's inequities.

Ord's coastal cities are a sailor's paradise, and we boast the best mariners ever to live. The sea has brought a bounty of riches the peat bogs lack but is filled with Cryxian pirates and other hazards. The Ordic Royal Navy is counted a peer among the greater powers of western Immoren. Our army does not have similar acclaim, but make no mistake, they are tough as trollkin and have courage to spare. Talk to the men serving at Midfast and you will find soldiers the equal of any. Despite our resolve, however, Ord lacks the modern weapons and engineering necessary to battle on equal terms with our neighbors. Khador has often come snapping at Ord's heels like a wolf after a famished deer, but we have held. The number of Khadorans we have sent to their graves speaks to their underestimation our defenses. I hope my kingdom can maintain the security of her borders in the days ahead, but I fear the rabid northern beast will come to consume us just as they did Llael.

Llael's primary geographical advantage turned out to be its greatest weakness. It shared its borders with four kingdoms with few natural barriers to inhibit trade—or the movement of armies. This served to line the pockets of certain entrepreneurial nobles and merchants who exploited the shipping along the Black River flowing from Rhul to the Gulf of Cygnar. Llael's merchants were centrally located to serve as middlemen for a variety of lucrative exchange routes, leaving its farmlands to the east of Khador almost unprotected and making them a very inviting target. Cygnar allied themselves with Llael three centuries ago, and with their protection the smaller nation weathered Khadoran assaults for many generations. In 604 AR, however, it was finally overrun. That this was

perhaps inevitable does nothing to reduce the sting of Llael's loss among the survivors of those who fought to preserve it.

Ord cannot afford to take any joy in the misfortune of Llael, though my countrymen shed few tears over its fall. Its fate is an abject lesson on the danger represented by Khador: just as Llael was consumed yesterday, Ord could follow tomorrow. Ord's peril is all the greater now that Khador has pushed Cygnar out of the Thornwood that comprises Ord's eastern border. My former homeland stands more vulnerable than ever.

REFLECTIONS ON CYGNAR, THE GOLDEN SWAN

At the southern extreme of the Iron Kingdoms lies Cygnar, where I often find myself for one reason or another. Cygnar emerged from the Corvis Treaties as the strongest and wealthiest nation of western Immoren. They were able to unite the diverse and powerful peoples of the ancient lands of Caspia and the sweeping Midlund farmlands as

well as those in the heart of ancient Thuria and the wily Morridanes of the Thornwood Forest, inheritors of the bloodlines of Morrdh.

Cygnar has no lack of iron, gold, timber, food, gems, quarries, or any other resource coveted by a modern nation. Coming as I do from poorer lands, I view these people as overly fortunate and do not believe they properly appreciate their many blessings. Cygnar's technology and alchemy is superb and improving daily, yet it is their mechanikal engineering that gives them the edge. Their warjacks boast inventive armaments and bow to the will of their warcasters, who are trained by the finest military academy in the Iron Kingdoms.

From the time of the Corvis Treaties, Cygnar bordered each of the original Iron Kingdoms. These included Ord to the northwest, Khador to the north, and Llael to the northeast. The Bloodstone Marches made up their entire eastern border until the Cygnaran Civil War. The end of that war resulted in the establishment of the Protectorate of Menoth, their newest eastern neighbor and enemy. While they marched bravely to defend Llael during Khador's recent invasion, the fight proved futile and in the end Cygnar could not keep Khador from its northernmost lands. The subsequent loss of the Thornwood has separated Llael from its southern ally and further diminished any hopes for that small kingdom to regain its freedom.

I have mixed feelings about Cygnar. I prefer them by far to the Khadorans, and Ord has reason to appreciate their support. But they do seem to enjoy putting their head into the bear's mouth. I wonder if the rivalry between Khador and Cygnar will consume all lesser nations in a funerary pyre. Would it not be better if these two powers focused on the greater threat of Cryx in the southwest? It is my opinion that Cygnar has been short-sighted about the dark enemy off their shore. Furthermore, every Cygnaran king since the Civil War has failed to keep the Protectorate of Menoth in check, and this has led to the rise of that nation as a significant threat to peace abroad.

Cygnar endured political upheaval in recent times when Leto Raelthorne, "the Younger," ousted his tyrannical brother King Vinter IV, "the Elder." The deposed king managed to escape before being put to trial for his crimes, only to reappear from the Bloodstone Marches after almost a decade with strange allies: an inhuman race from eastern Immoren called the skorne. Since his return these inhuman invaders have been a constant peril on Cygnar's eastern border, including a failed attempt to seize Corvis in 603 AR. While it has never been easy to wear the Cygnaran crown, King Leto has borne more burdens than any sovereign deserves.

Giving a proper accounting of Cygnar's victories and defeats would fill a lengthy tome, so I must gloss over them. Suffice it to say that even diminished by the loss of its ally Llael and its territories in the Thornwood, Cygnar remains among the mightiest powers of the region. They have suffered the invasion of their own capital by the Menites but drove the enemy from their lands. Their northern border has been compromised, yet their soldiers stand at fortresses along the Dragon's Tongue River ready to fight and die for their king. A more stubborn people I have yet to meet, and I think Khador may have underestimated the Cygnaran fighting spirit. I hope that to be true, as I am not eager to see these lands crushed under Khadoran boots.

REFLECTIONS ON THE PROTECTORATE OF MENOTH

I am not a comfortable guest in Sul, and they watch me with mistrust. Still, I have friends among the alleyways of that battered and bloodied city, and a mercenary can find employment there. It is impossible not to be reminded of the strength of faith in such a place, where all facets of everyday life are steeped in religious ritual and symbols.

For years historians and politicians both have pretended the Protectorate was not a nation of its own because the agreements that ended the Cygnaran Civil War left them technically beholden to Cygnar's crown. Over time those obligations proved to be a farce, and now it is clear the Protectorate of Menoth stands as the youngest of the Iron Kingdoms. Indeed, they have now outlasted Llael, and their survival seems more certain with each passing year.

Caspia was divided in the aftermath of the Cygnaran Civil War, with the eastern portion becoming Sul, the capital of the Protectorate at that time. This placed bitter enemies in close proximity, a powder keg awaiting a spark. The rest of the Protectorate stretches east and southeast into an arid and resource-poor region adjacent to the dangerous Bloodstone Marches.

Sul-Menites practice a strict form of worship and believe endless punishment awaits them in the afterlife if they do not obey the True Law. Priests and scrutators instill a terror of the clergy in the population from an early age, and they teach the people to obey without question and to expect the lash for expressing the slightest doubt. Nowhere except the Protectorate are the priests of Menoth obeyed so completely and unflinchingly, hearkening back to the time of the priest-kings of old. Perhaps because of these harsh measures, the Menite faith has been in slow decline for many centuries, and it was clear the ruling priests sought some means to rise back to prominence.

The recent emergence of the Harbinger has provided the spark the Menites have long sought to revitalize their faith. This young woman emerged from an obscure town on the fringes of the Protectorate and displayed clear signs of miraculous contact with the divine, including most notably the fact that her feet refuse to touch the unclean earth. It is said she sometimes communes directly with Menoth and can speak his words.

While violence between the Protectorate and Cygnar has long threatened the security of both powers, these tensions erupted into open war following Khador's invasion of Llael. The leadership of the Protectorate took advantage of Cygnar's distraction to initiate a great crusade against unbelievers, one that succeeded in inspiring the people. The Harbinger's endorsement of this campaign filled the hearts and minds of the Sul-Menites with unprecedented fervor and a frightening willingness to sacrifice their lives for the cause.

Violence between Cygnar and the Protectorate escalated to a crescendo that exceeded any even in the old Civil War. The Protectorate besieged Caspia in 605 AR but were repelled.

Cygnar counterattacked and Sul's walls were breached, allowing Cygnaran soldiers to pour into the streets of Sul. Following a year of grueling battles throughout the city, eventually Protectorate forces drove the Cygnaran invaders back and in turn spilled through Caspia's gates to march on Castle Raelthorne. Cygnar's home garrison narrowly achieved victory, for a time quieting the constant warfare between the two nations—a tenuous situation that could flare back to open war at any time.

While the fighting in Caspia and Sul resulted in a stalemate, efforts elsewhere have strengthened the Protectorate of Menoth. Its Northern Crusade has met with great success brazenly marching through Khadoran-occupied Llael and seizing lands to the north, including the fortified Llaelese city of Leryn, a center of alchemical production and one of the greatest fortresses ever built.

One thing that must be remembered about these people is that the manifestation of divine power gives them unpredictable strength beyond their raw numbers. No one would have predicted a year ago that the Protectorate could seize territory from Khadoran hands. What further miracles lie in store?

REFLECTIONS ON THE NIGHTMARE EMPIRE OF CRYX

From the crow's nests of steamers crossing the heaving Meridian waters I have seen the slender watchtower called Hell's Hook on the eastern tip of the island once called Scharde—now the heart of Cryx. Only a few outsiders, myself included, have walked the black soil amid the undying hordes and necromechanikal constructs that call this place home. Even venturing close to it invites destruction. I consider myself fortunate to have avoided that dark fate and plan never to return.

The Nightmare Empire is made up of the sweltering and malignant Scharde Islands off the Broken Coast of southern Cygnar. Skell is its capital, and I fear that place more than the hellish wilds of Urcaen where the gods wage their War of Souls. There Lord Toruk landed sixteen centuries ago to claim the islands as his own. He is the father of all dragons, and he rules Cryx without question. Toruk's ancient talons have ground entire towns to dust, and thousands heed the merciless orders of his undying generals. Still more fail to escape the call to war even in death.

Cryxian raiders sail from their island home in search of plunder and spill thousands of bloodthirsty pirates and marauders, along with fiendish bonejacks and helljacks, onto mainland shores. Innumerable slaves end up conscripted into Cryxian armies, where they become undead thralls fused with mechanika or else have their souls stripped to feed the dark appetites of the Dragonfather's lich lords.

Through necromancy Lord Toruk boasts an eternal army that grows with each victory.

The full scope and strength of Cryx's potential to wage war has long been underestimated, a fact I consider now with growing apprehension. For many centuries Cryxian attacks were isolated and random, limited to piracy and terrorizing villages along the shores of western Immoren. Yet as battles erupted elsewhere, Cryx stretched its unliving claws to reach places we thought safe from its clutches. Cryxian soldiers and necromancers were ready with tools of war deep within the mainland. They emerged in great numbers following the outbreak of the conflict in Llael. Though none know Cryxian motives or goals, it is clear the Dragon has interest in the wars of men. Perhaps all they seek is carnage; if so, they have devices enough to accomplish that end. I fear their designs are both more ominous and more profound.

> **TORUK'S ANCIENT TALONS HAVE GROUND ENTIRE TOWNS TO DUST, AND THOUSANDS HEED THE MERCILESS ORDERS OF HIS UNDYING GENERALS.**

REFLECTIONS ON THE OUTER REACHES OF WESTERN IMMOREN

When we speak of the "Iron Kingdoms" it is understood by scholars to refer to those kingdoms created by the Corvis Treaties, expanded in the aftermath of the Cygnaran Civil War to include the Protectorate of Menoth. In common use the term has grown to refer to all the adjoining lands as well, including those of our neighbors, both hostile and friendly, that are populated and led by species other than humanity.

The elven land of Ios lies nestled in a vast forest valley between barrier mountains that prevent the encroachment of the Bloodstone Marches. Even in friendlier times Ios was a nation we could never have claimed to know. The Iosans seldom accepted visitors and conducted only a trickle of trade with outsiders. Sadly, Ios has kept its borders completely sealed for the entirety of my adult life, and I have never had the opportunity to walk its fog-shrouded paths. Trespassing is unthinkable; those who violate their borders never return.

I would like nothing more than to chronicle the history of that mysterious people, but I must admit my ignorance. Rumor holds that the Iosans have powerful magic and their own mechanika, quite dissimilar to that created by either mankind or the Rhulfolk who are their neighbors. At one time Ios dispatched ambassadors to human lands, but even then they wore veils to obscure their faces and kept their own counsel, listening more than speaking. The Rhulfolk, who have maintained written records far longer than our own ancestors, say that in ancient times the region called Ios stood uninhabited. By their account, the Iosans traveled to their present home from farther in the east after a catastrophic upheaval the Rhulfolk witnessed only as fire and smoke covering the entire eastern horizon.

Regardless of past tribulations, Ios' role in the future of our region remains to be seen, and I am wary of any sign of activity from that quarter. There has been bloodshed in recent months all too close to their border, during both the invasion of Llael and subsequent battles. It could be this unfriendly nation hopes to remind its neighbors of why even the Orgoth steered clear of them.

> **INEXPLICABLY THE FORMER KING RETURNED IN 603 AR, BRINGING TERRIFYING ALLIES NEVER BEFORE SEEN IN THE WEST: THE SKORNE.**

Rhul, on the other hand, is a mountain nation governed by a council of clan lords. In addition to the dwarven people, Rhul is populated by a large number of the towering ogrun with whom Rhulfolk have long had strong ties. The dwarves of Rhul are honorable and stoic people boasting a culture that has changed little in thousands of years. They pride themselves on their mastery of stonecraft but do not believe the stories that they live only below the soil. They have erected tremendous castles, vaulted halls, and towers that scrape the sky, and their industrious nature is one we could emulate. Rhulfolk trace their heritage back to the original thirteen clans who founded their nation and appear to revere the clan fathers as gods. Just as Menite priests once ruled the land by the dictates of the True Law, the Rhulfolk obey their Codex, which serves as both a holy text and a summary of their convoluted laws.

Rhulfolk, unlike Iosans, enjoy the company of mankind. While they defend their borders from intrusion just as tenaciously, they also trade large quantities of manufactured goods and mined materials to Khador and Cygnar in exchange for food, timber, and other materials difficult to find in their rocky homeland. With every passing generation they pay greater attention to happenings abroad, and many venture south to make their fortunes. While the Iosans are rare in human lands, Rhulfolk are widely accepted and have earned their places as valued members of various communities from Khador to Cygnar.

With the onset of recent wars a large number of armed and trained Rhulic warriors have turned to the life of the sell-sword, earning a living as mercenaries. They seem to enjoy battle in a way unique to their people. Mankind seems destined to endless turmoil, and we often fight wars over abstract ideals or when pushed to violence by hatred, but the Rhulfolk seem to derive genuine satisfaction from a good battle. Perhaps it is simply that the long-enduring stability of their nation makes war seem an entertaining diversion. This attitude puzzles me; I have been in wars enough and seen sorrow enough for many lifetimes.

REFLECTIONS ON PERILS FROM THE WASTES AND THE WILDERNESS

I have looked out over the storm-blown sands of the Bloodstone Marches and wondered that any would willingly traverse its fierce expanse. The region is a sun-scorched and windswept wasteland. Beyond the perils of howling winds, mirages, and indigenous beasts lies a blasted expanse called the Stormlands. It is a withered realm plagued by constant lightning strikes and deafening thunder. Other than the Protectorate capital of Imer, the only human settlement abutting the Marches is a series of shacks and hovels called Ternon Crag where miners pry gold and coal from the reluctant mountains and mercenary companies often camp between contracts. These men face peril daily without hesitation, but both make a point to stay out of that void to the east.

Following the Lion's Coup of 594 AR, Vinter Raelthorne IV was hurled into the east in an imperfect balloon intended to soar far above the ground. This unlikely flight was thought to have killed the man, since no one had ever made it across those wastes alive. Inexplicably the former king returned in 603 AR, bringing terrifying allies never before seen in the west: the skorne.

I know little about these skorne except that they are powerful warriors with a cruel temperament. They march to battle alongside great beasts and wield strange firearms of their own invention. I wonder what the appearance of these new invaders heralds, whether it presages another dark era to test man's strength. Thus far the skorne have yet to penetrate Cygnar's border, but not for lack of trying. Determined to the end, they have constructed fortresses and holds just east of the Black River. Those are lands mankind gave up as inhospitable, but it seems the skorne find them suitable enough.

Nor are the skorne the only dangers arising unexpectedly out of the wilderness in recent years. Strange horrors have emerged from Khador's northern mountains, creatures we have yet to explain. Serpentine horrors fly and march alongside savage and deformed warriors, all intent on

slaughter and destruction. In recent months I have heard of these creatures seen farther afield, and this troubles me greatly. This seems destined to be an age noted for the rise of monsters.

Whether as a consequence or a reflection of the chaos created by recent warfare, violence has erupted elsewhere. Trollkin kriels that once peacefully inhabited the untamed regions have taken up arms and begun harassing trade routes and train lines in Cygnar, Khador, and even Ord. There have been accusations that Cygnar put the trollkin kriels in the path of the skorne to brunt their invasion. Whether this claim is true seems immaterial, as the kriels and soldiers of Cygnar's 4th Army have recently engaged in bloody skirmishes, with horrendous casualties on both sides. As if this were not enough to show the wilds are stirring, an ominous group of mystics we call the Blackclads have been on the move with well-armed bands engaged in similar clashes. They walk with wild beasts from the deeper forests, gathering in number for reasons only they can comprehend.

I am sure others have said the same in every age filled with war, yet I cannot escape the feeling that we are on the cusp of disaster. I hope it is just age catching up with an old mercenary too long on the march. Mankind is a destructive lot, and war is always around us. Our finest hours have often come in the tumult of battle. I have found that Immoren's heartfire—and perhaps even Caen's as a whole—is stoked by the wars and skirmishes around and within it.

Each of us must choose a side, raise a weapon, and lift our banner to join in the strife to come. Better to fall in heroic charge than to waste away nursing sullen regrets. We who fight will sign our names on the pages of eternity with our own blood.

For better or worse, war has become my meat and drink, my bane and muse. As long as I can I will keep accounts just as I have always done, for surely within events to come will be countless tales of glories and triumphs that will endure even past the shroud of death.

THE GAME

GAME OVERVIEW

In WARMACHINE, the very earth shakes during fierce confrontations as six-ton constructs of iron and steel slam into each other with cataclysmic force, lead-spewing cannons chew through armor plating as easily as flesh, and bold heroes set the battlefield ablaze with a tempest of arcane might to forge the fates of their unyielding nations in the fires of destruction.

WARMACHINE is a fast-paced and aggressive 30 mm tabletop miniatures battle game for two or more players set in the steam-powered fantasy world of the Iron Kingdoms. Players take on the role of elite soldier-sorcerers known as warcasters. Though warcasters are formidable combatants on their own, their true strength lies in their magical ability to control and coordinate mighty warjacks—massive combat automatons that are the pinnacle of military might in the Iron Kingdoms. Players collect, assemble, and paint fantastically detailed models representing the varied men, machines, and creatures in their army. This book provides rules for using those models in swift and brutal conflict. This is steam-powered miniatures combat, and your tabletop will never be the same!

In addition, WARMACHINE is also fully compatible with the monstrous miniatures combat of HORDES, which is set in the wilds of the Iron Kingdoms and features powerful beings who harness the strength and fury of the savage warbeasts that stalk the dark places of the realm. This allows players to pit their forces against each other in a battle of machines versus beasts.

A WARMACHINE army is built around a warcaster and his battlegroup of warjacks. Squads of soldiers and support teams can further bolster a battlegroup's combat capability. Sometimes huge armies with multiple battlegroups and legions of soldiers take the field to crush their enemies with the combined might of muscle and iron.

Warjacks, called 'jacks for short, are specialized fighting machines. They are hulking iron giants powered by a fusion of steam technology and arcane science and are controlled with deadly precision by a warcaster. Warjacks can be outfitted with a plethora of wicked melee or ranged weaponry and equipment. Specialized 'jacks known as channelers are equipped with a device called an arc node that lets the warcaster project spells through the warjack itself.

A warcaster is in constant telepathic contact with the 'jacks in his battlegroup. During the course of a confrontation, warcasters continually draw on a magical energy called focus. A warcaster's focus points can be used to boost his own combat abilities, boost those of his warjacks in his control area, or cast powerful spells.

The warcaster is the tie binding the battlegroup together but is also its weakest link. If the warcaster falls, his 'jacks become little more than iron shells.

The outcome of a battle depends on your ability to think quickly, use sound tactics, and decisively employ your forces. A crucial component of your strategy will be the management of your warcaster's focus points and how you use them to boost your warjacks' abilities. Focus points can be used to enhance a 'jack's already impressive combat power significantly. Properly allocated, they can make an entire battlegroup a nigh-unstoppable instrument of destruction.

Victory favors the bold! So bring it on, if you've got the metal.

SUMMARY OF PLAY

Before a battle begins, players agree on an encounter level and a scenario, and then they create their armies based on those guidelines. Next, determine the turn order. It will not change throughout the game. Players then deploy their forces and prepare for battle to begin.

Battles are conducted in a series of game rounds. During a game round, each player receives one turn to command his army. During his turn, a player activates all the models in his army, one after the other. When activated, a model can move and then make one of a variety of actions such

WHAT YOU NEED

In addition to this book and your army of WARMACHINE models, you will also need a few basic items to play:

- A table or playing surface where you can conduct your battles (typically 4´ x 4´).

- A tape measure or ruler marked in inches and fractions thereof to measure movement and attack distances.

- A few six-sided dice. Six will be plenty.

- A handful of tokens to indicate focus points, spell effects, etc.

- The appropriate stat cards included with each model. We suggest you put them in card sleeves and use a dry erase marker to mark damage.

- The markers and templates on pp. 255-256 of this book. You may photocopy them for personal use.

as attacking, repairing a 'jack, or casting spells. Once both players have taken their turns, the current game round ends and a new one begins starting again with the first player. Game rounds continue until one player wins by destroying the opposing warcaster or warcasters, meeting scenario objectives, or accepting the surrender of his opponent or opponents.

DICE AND ROUNDING

WARMACHINE uses six-sided dice, abbreviated d6, to determine the success of attacks and other actions. Most events, such as attacks, require rolling two dice (abbreviated 2d6). Other events typically require rolling from one to four dice. Die rolls often have modifiers, which are expressed as + or – some quantity after the die roll notation. For example, melee attack rolls are described as "2d6 + MAT." This means "roll two six-sided dice and add the attacking model's MAT stat to the result."

Some events call for rolling a d3. To do so, roll a d6, divide the result by 2, and round up.

Some instances call for a model's stat or a die roll to be divided in half. For distance measurements, use the actual result after dividing the number in question. For everything else, always round a fractional result to the next highest whole number.

DICE SHORTHAND

A six-sided die is referred to as a d6. When you need two or more of these, a numeral before the small *d* indicates the number of dice to roll. Two six-sided dice are abbreviated as 2d6, three dice as 3d6, and so on.

The term d3 is a shortcut for "roll a d6, divide by 2, and round up." Quite a mouthful! Here's how to read the results of a d3 roll quickly:

1 or 2 = 1

3 or 4 = 2

5 or 6 = 3

ADDITIONAL DICE AND BOOSTED ROLLS

Sometimes a special ability or circumstance will allow a model to roll an **additional die**. An additional die is a die added to the number of dice a model would ordinarily roll. For example, when a model makes a ranged attack roll, it generally rolls 2d6 and adds its RAT stat. If the model gains an additional die on this attack, it would roll 3d6 and add its RAT stat.

A die roll can include multiple additional dice as long as each additional die comes from a different rule or ability.

Some effects grant models boosted attack or damage rolls. Add one extra die to a boosted roll. Boosting must be declared before rolling any dice for the roll. Each attack or damage roll can be boosted only once, but a model can boost multiple rolls during its activation. When an attack affects several models, the attack and damage rolls against each individual model must be boosted separately.

EXAMPLE: *A model that hits a target with a charge attack gains a boosted damage roll, meaning it adds an extra die to its damage roll. Because this roll is boosted, the model cannot spend focus to boost the damage roll again for a total of two extra dice on the roll.*

GENERAL GUIDELINES

This section covers how WARMACHINE handles game terms, the relationship between standard and special rules, sportsmanship between players, and the procedures for resolving rules disputes.

GAME TERMS

When these rules define a game term, it appears in bold.

For the sake of brevity, the phrase "model with the ability" is sometimes replaced with the ability's name. For example, a model with the 'Jack Marshal ✪ advantage is a 'jack marshal, and a model with the Spellcaster ability is a spellcaster. Similarly, the phrases "attack with the weapon" and "attack granted by the _____ ability" can be replaced by the expression "_____ attack." For instance, Caine's feat, Maelstrom, allows him to make several attacks with his Spellstorm Pistols. These attacks are referred to as "Spellstorm Pistol attacks" in the Maelstrom text. In the same way, the extra attacks granted by the Strafe ability of a Cygnar Sentinel's Chain Gun are referred to as "Strafe attacks" and the attacks a trampling warjack makes against models it moved over are called "trample attacks."

All models in your army are **friendly models**. Models controlled by your opponent are **enemy models**. If your opponent takes control of one of your models or units during play, it becomes an enemy model or unit for as long as it is under your opponent's control. If you take control of one of your opponent's models or units, it is friendly for as long as it is under your control.

The abilities of models are written as if speaking to the current controller of the model. When a model's rule references "you" or "yours," it refers to the player currently controlling the model.

In a model's rules, "this model" always refers to the model carrying the rule.

The various nations and forces within the Iron Kingdoms are represented by the different factions; this rulebook includes information on some, but not all, of those factions. Armies are made up of a single faction and may include mercenaries that will work for that faction. When a rule references "Faction" it refers to the faction of the model carrying the rule. On a Mercenary model, for instance, "friendly Faction warjack" means "friendly Mercenary warjack"; the same text on a Cygnar model means "friendly Cygnar warjack."

A model or unit may be referenced by either line of its name, in whole or in part. The Knights Exemplar unit, for example, has the name "Knights Exemplar" and is a "Protectorate Unit." This unit could be referenced specifically by its unit name Knights Exemplar, as a Protectorate unit, as a unit, or as Exemplars.

Unless specified otherwise, when a model's rules reference another model by name, the model referenced is assumed to be a friendly model. For example, the Cryx helljack called Nightmare has an Affinity rule that grants it Stealth  while it is in Deneghra's control area. Nightmare gains Stealth only if its controlling player also controls Deneghra. An enemy Deneghra model does not grant Stealth to Nightmare.

RULE PRIORITY

WARMACHINE is a complex game providing a multitude of play options, but its rules are intuitive and easy to learn. The standard rules lay the foundation upon which the game is built and provide all the typical mechanics used in play. Additional special rules apply to specific models and modify the standard rules in certain circumstances. When they apply, special rules take precedence.

Unless otherwise specified, multiple instances of the same effect (that is, effects with the same name) on a model are not cumulative. If a model would be affected by a second instance of an effect, the second instance is not applied and does not change anything about the first instance, including its expiration. If the effect has a duration, this means it expires when the first applied effect expires. Multiple instances of the same effect are not cumulative even when the effect comes from different sources. For example, a spell that grants Dark Shroud would not be cumulative with the Dark Shroud ability of Bane Thralls.

Different effects are cumulative with each other, however, even if they happen to apply the same modifier to a model.

For example, being in a Burning Ash cloud reduces your attack rolls by 2. Choking Veil does the same thing but is a different effect, and so a model in both effects would have its attack rolls reduced by 4.

Situations can occur where two special rules conflict. Use the following guidelines, in order, to resolve special rules interactions.

- If one rule specifically states its interaction with another rule, follow it.

- Special rules stating that something "cannot" happen override rules stating that the same thing "can" or "must" occur. (Rules directing or describing actions or circumstances are treated as if they used "must." Examples include "Gain an additional die," "Knocked down models stand up," and "This model gains cover.")

EXAMPLE: *A model has a rule stating it cannot be knocked down, and it is affected by something that states it is knocked down. Since the rules make no specific mention of each other, follow the second guideline, and the model is not knocked down.*

SPORTSMANSHIP AND SHARING INFORMATION

Although WARMACHINE simulates violent battles between mammoth forces, you should still strive to be a good sportsman in all aspects of the game. Remember, this is a game meant to provide entertainment and friendly competition. Whether winning or losing, you should still be having lots of fun.

From time to time, your opponent may wish to see your records to verify a model's stats or see how much damage a particular warjack has taken. Always represent this information honestly and share your records and information without hesitation.

During the game, when a player makes a measurement for any reason he must share the information with his opponent.

RESOLVING RULES ISSUES

These rules have been carefully designed to provide as much guidance as possible in all aspects of play. That said, you still might encounter situations where the proper course of action is not immediately obvious. For instance, players might disagree on whether a model has line of sight to its intended target.

During a game, try to resolve the issue quickly in the interest of keeping the game flowing. There will be plenty of time after the game to determine the best answer, which you can then incorporate into future games.

If a situation arises in which all players cannot agree on a solution, briefly discuss the matter and check this rulebook for an answer, but do not spend so much time doing so that you slow the game. In striving to resolve an issue, common sense and the precedents set by related rules should be your guides.

If you cannot solve the dispute quickly, roll for a resolution. Each player rolls a d6, and the person with the highest roll decides the outcome. Reroll any ties. In the interest of fairness, once a ruling has been made for a specific issue, it applies for all similar circumstances for the rest of the game. After the game ends, you can take the time to reference the rules and thoroughly discuss the issue to decide how best to handle that same situation in the future.

MEASURING DISTANCES

When making any measurement, you cannot measure past the maximum range of the attack, ability, spell, or effect for which you are measuring.

When measuring the distance from a model, measure from the edge of the model's base. Similarly, when measuring the distance to a model, measure up to, but not past, the edge of that model's base. Thus, a model is **within** a given distance when the nearest edge of its base is within that distance, or equivalently, when any part of its base is within the given distance. If two models are exactly a certain distance apart, they are within that distance of each other.

A model is **completely within** a given distance when its entire base is within that distance. Equivalently, a model is completely within a given distance when the farthest edge of its base is within that distance.

If models' bases overlap, they are within 0″ of each other.

When determining the effects of a spell or ability that affects models within a specified distance of a model, the effect is a circular area extending out from the model's base and including the area under the model's base. Unless the spell or ability says otherwise, however, that model is not considered to be within the distance itself. For example, when an Ironclad uses its Tremor special attack, it affects all models within 2″ of itself, but Tremor does not affect the Ironclad.

WITHIN VS. COMPLETELY WITHIN

Bile Thrall A does not have any portion of its base in the shaded area, so it is not within the shaded area. Bile Thralls B and E do have a portion of their bases in the shaded area, so they are within it. Bile Thralls C and D are completely within the shaded area because each of their bases is entirely within the shaded area.

Each WARMACHINE combatant is represented on the tabletop by a highly detailed and dramatically posed miniature figurine referred to as a model. There are several basic **model types**: warcasters, warjacks, troopers, and solos. Warcasters, troopers, and solos are collectively referred to as **warriors**. Non-warjack models are **living models** unless otherwise noted.

INDEPENDENT MODELS

Independent models are those that activate individually. Warcasters, warjacks, and solos are independent models.

WARCASTERS

A **warcaster** is a tremendously powerful sorcerer, warpriest, or battlemage with the ability to control a group of warjacks telepathically. A warcaster is a deadly opponent highly skilled in both physical combat and arcane spell casting. A **battlegroup** includes a warcaster and the warjacks he controls. A warcaster can allocate focus points to or channel spells through only the warjacks in his battlegroup.

During battle, a warcaster commands his battlegroup of warjacks in an effort to complete his objectives. A warcaster can use his focus points to enhance his combat abilities and cast spells, or he can assign them to individual warjacks to increase their fighting abilities. A warcaster can also channel spells through 'jacks equipped with arc nodes, effectively extending the range of his magical powers.

Warcasters are independent models. A model with the model type Warcaster has many rules that are common to all warcasters and are not listed on the model's stat card (see "Warcaster Special Rules," p. 74). All warcasters are characters.

In the game of HORDES, the parallel of the warcaster is called a **warlock** and is a commander of raging beasts and feral troops.

WARJACKS

A **steamjack** is a mechanikal **construct** given the ability to reason by a magical brain, known as a **cortex**, housed within its hull. A steamjack does not possess high cognitive powers, but it can execute simple commands and make logical decisions to complete its assigned tasks. Throughout the Iron Kingdoms steamjacks perform a variety of heavy or dangerous tasks that would be impossible for a human.

A **warjack** is a steamjack built expressly to wage war. Armed with the most fearsome ranged and close-combat weaponry yet devised, a warjack is more than a match for a dozen men. Though able to think and operate independently, a warjack reaches its full destructive potential only when controlled by a warcaster. The warcaster forms a telepathic link to each of the warjacks in his battlegroup. This link lets the warcaster give his warjacks commands and use focus to boost their abilities with just a thought. Through focus, a warcaster can make his warjacks' attacks more accurate and powerful. A well-controlled warjack can even make amazing power attacks, such as slamming its opponents into buildings, grappling their weapons, or even throwing them.

The telepathic link binding a warcaster to his warjacks is fragile. A warjack whose cortex is crippled cannot be allocated focus points. Even worse, should a warcaster become incapacitated, the telepathic link to his 'jacks will be severed. The accompanying feedback of uncontrolled magical energies overloads and shorts out his warjacks' cortexes and causes the 'jacks to cease functioning and become inert.

Warjacks are classified according to base size: a **light warjack** has a **medium base** (40 mm), and a **heavy warjack** has a **large base** (50 mm). Even though it is assigned to a specific battlegroup, each warjack is an independent model.

A model with the model type Warjack has many rules that are common to all warjacks and are not listed on the model's stat card (see "Warjack Special Rules," p. 73).

SO, YOU GOTTA BE DIFFERENT

Cryx light warjacks are called "bonejacks," and Cryx heavy warjacks are known as "helljacks." Retribution warjacks are sometimes referred to as "myrmidons." Bonejacks, helljacks, and myrmidons are all warjacks.

SOLOS

Solos are individuals who operate alone, such as assassins and snipers. Solos are independent models.

UNITS

A unit is a group of similarly trained and equipped troopers operating together as a single force. A unit usually contains one Leader and one or more additional troopers. Models in units do not activate individually; instead all members of the unit activate at the same time and progress through the steps of an activation together. See "Anatomy of a Unit," p. 70, for more detailed rules on units.

TROOPERS

Troopers are individuals such as swordsmen, riflemen, and mechaniks who operate together in groups called units. A unit always operates as a single coherent force. All models in a unit are troopers. Trooper models in a unit generally share identical attributes and carry the same weapons.

Iron Lich Asphyxious:
WARCASTER

Ironclad:
HEAVY WARJACK

Paladin of the Order
of the Wall:
SOLO

Iron Fang Pikemen
Officer &
Standard Bearer:
UNIT ATTACHMENT

Iron Fang
Pikemen:
UNIT

GRUNTS

Grunts are the basic troopers in a unit.

UNIT COMMANDERS, LEADERS, AND OFFICERS

Each unit is led by a unit commander. A unit commander sometimes has different weaponry than the other models in its unit and has the ability to give his unit orders that allow the unit to perform specialized battlefield maneuvers.

In most cases, the Leader of a unit is its unit commander. Some units are led by Officers ⊗. While an Officer is in play, it is the unit commander of its unit.

ATTACHMENTS

Attachments are troopers that can be added to some units. They include unit attachments and weapon attachments. A unit can have only one of each type of attachment. Models in an attachment are not Grunts. Attachments are easily identified by their "Attachment" rule, which specifies the unit or units to which they can be attached.

MODEL PROFILES

Every model and unit has a unique profile called a **model entry** or **army list entry** that translates its combat abilities into game terms. WARMACHINE uses a set of stats to quantify and scale the attributes fundamental to gameplay. In addition, a model can have special rules that further enhance its performance. The faction section provides all the game information required for your army to battle across the tabletop. For even more models and information for the factions, check out the *Forces of WARMACHINE* books.

A model or unit's **stat card** provides a quick in-game reference of its profile and special rules. The card's front lists the model's name and model type, its model and weapon stats, field allowance, point cost, and a graphic for tracking damage if the model can suffer more than 1 damage point. The text for special rules appears on the card's back. A warcaster has an additional stat card that explains his spells and feat. Refer to this and other WARMACHINE books for the complete text of special rules and spells.

MODEL STATISTICS

Model **statistics**, or **stats**, provide a numerical representation of a model's basic combat qualities—the higher the number, the better the stat. These stats are used for various die rolls throughout the game. A **stat bar** presents model statistics in an easy-to-reference format. The abbreviation for each stat shows how it is referenced in the rules.

STRYKER						
SPD	STR	MAT	RAT	DEF	ARM	CMD
6	6	7	6	16	15	9

Commander Coleman Stryker

SPD, Speed – A model's movement rate. A model moves up to its SPD in inches when making a full advance.

STR, Strength – A model's physical strength. STR is used to calculate melee damage, grab onto or break free from a model, or determine how far a model is thrown.

MAT, Melee Attack – A model's skill with melee weapons such as swords and hammers or natural weapons like fists and teeth. A model uses its MAT when making melee attack rolls.

RAT, Ranged Attack – A model's accuracy with ranged weapons such as guns and crossbows or thrown items like spears and knives. A model uses its RAT when making ranged attack rolls.

DEF, Defense – A model's ability to avoid being hit by an attack. A model's size, quickness, skill, and even magical protection all contribute to its DEF. An attack roll must be equal to or greater than the target model's DEF to score a hit against it.

ARM, Armor – A model's ability to resist being damaged. This resistance can come from natural resilience, worn armor, or even magical benefits. A model takes 1 damage point for every point that a damage roll exceeds its ARM.

CMD, Command – A model's willpower, leadership, and self-discipline. To pass a command check, a model must roll equal to or less than its CMD on 2d6. Command also determines a model's command range.

FOCUS, Focus – A model's arcane power. Only models with the Focus Manipulation ability, such as warcasters, have a FOCUS stat. Focus determines a model's control area and beginning focus points. A model uses its FOCUS when making magic attack rolls.

BASE STATS, CURRENT STATS, AND MODIFIERS

Rules in WARMACHINE can refer to a model's base stats or its current stats. A model's **base stats** are typically those printed in its stat bar. Some special rules can change a model's base stat to a specific value, however. Apply this change before applying any other modifiers to the stat. If a model is affected by multiple rules that change a base stat, the base stat becomes the lowest value. For example, a model that is both stationary (base DEF 5) and suffering Stall (base DEF 7) would have a base DEF of 5.

A model's modified stats are referred to as its **current stats**, differentiating them from the model's base stats. Unless a rule specifies otherwise, always use a model's current stats.

To determine a model's current stat, start with the base stat and then apply modifiers in the following order.

1. Apply modifiers that double the model's stat.
2. Apply modifiers that halve the stat.
3. Apply bonuses that add to the stat.
4. Apply penalties that reduce the stat.

The result is the model's current stat. Except for DEF, a model's base and current stats can never be reduced to less than 1; its base and current DEF can never be reduced to less than 5.

EXAMPLE: *Stationary models have a base DEF of 5, and cover grants +4 DEF. Therefore, a stationary model behind cover has a current DEF of 9 (base DEF 5 + 4 DEF for cover). A stationary model (base DEF 5) affected by Deneghra's feat The Withering (–2 DEF) would still have a current DEF of 5.*

Note that these limitations apply only to the stats themselves and not to attack rolls. A Deliverer's Skyhammer with RAT 5 affected by Deneghra's feat The Withering (–2 RAT) has a current RAT of 3. The Deliverer suffers –4 to his attack roll from his weapon's Inaccurate rule; what would have been 2d6 + 3 becomes 2d6 – 1 even though the stat itself is not less than 1.

ADVANTAGES

Advantages are common model abilities, described below. A model's advantages are represented by symbols beneath its stat bar; the text of the abilities does not appear in the model entries or on the cards. Advantages are always in effect and apply every time a game situation warrants their use.

EIRYSS						
SPD	STR	MAT	RAT	DEF	ARM	CMD
7	4	6	9	16	12	9

These symbols show that Eiryss, Mage Hunter of Ios has Advanced Deployment, Fearless, Pathfinder, and Stealth.

Abomination – This model is a terrifying entity (p. 84). Models and units—friendly and enemy—within 3" of this model must pass a command check or flee.

Advance Deployment – Place this model after normal deployment, up to 6" beyond the established deployment zone.

Arc Node – This model is a channeler (p. 79).

Combined Melee Attack – This model can participate in combined melee attacks with other models in its unit (p. 62).

Combined Ranged Attack – This model can participate in combined ranged attacks with other models in its unit (p. 62).

Commander – A friendly Faction model or unit in this model's command range can replace its current CMD with the current CMD of the commander when making command checks (p. 84). Models with the Commander advantage should not be confused with unit commanders that lead individual units (p. 71). All warcaster models have this advantage.

Construct – This model is not a living model, never flees, and automatically passes command checks. All warjack models have this advantage.

Eyeless Sight – This model ignores cloud effects (p. 69) and forests (p. 87) when determining line of sight. This model ignores concealment (p. 57) and Stealth when making attacks.

Fearless – This model never flees (p. 85). All warcaster models have this advantage.

Gunfighter – This model is a gunfighter (p. 63). The gunfighter has a melee range of 0.5″ and can make ranged attacks targeting models in its melee range.

Incorporeal – This model can move through rough terrain and obstacles without penalty. It can move through obstructions and other models if it has enough movement to move completely past them. Other models, including slammed, pushed, or thrown models, can move through this model without effect if they have enough movement

to move completely past it. This model does not count as an intervening model. This model suffers damage and effects only from magical weapons, magic attacks, animi, spells, and feats and is immune to continuous effects. This model cannot be moved by a slam. When this model makes a melee or ranged attack, before the attack roll is made it loses Incorporeal for one round.

'Jack Marshal – This model is a 'jack marshal (p. 80). If this advantage is on a unit, only the unit commander is a 'jack marshal.

Officer – This model is an Officer (p. 70). The Officer is the unit commander of its unit.

Pathfinder – This model can advance through rough terrain (p. 86) without penalty and can charge and make slam and trample power attacks across obstacles (p. 87).

Standard Bearer – This model is a standard bearer (p. 70).

Stealth – Ranged and magic attacks declared against this model when the point of origin of the attack is greater than 5″ away automatically miss. This model is not an intervening model (p. 43) when determining line of sight from a model greater than 5″ away.

Terror – This model is a terrifying entity (p. 84). Enemy models/units in the melee range of this model or with this model in their melee range must pass a command check or flee.

Tough – When this model is disabled, roll a d6. On a 5 or 6, this model heals 1 damage point, is no longer disabled, and is knocked down.

Undead – This model is not a living model and never flees.

IMMUNITIES

Immunities are advantages that protect models from some types of damage and effects. A model never suffers damage from a damage type to which it is immune. If the damage has multiple damage types, a model that is immune to any of the types will not suffer the damage.

Immunity: Cold – This model does not suffer cold damage (p. 68).

Immunity: Corrosion – This model does not suffer corrosion damage and is immune to the Corrosion continuous effect (p. 68).

Immunity: Electricity – This model does not suffer electrical damage (p. 68).

Immunity: Fire – This model does not suffer fire damage and is immune to the Fire continuous effect (p. 68).

IMMUNITY TO CONTINUOUS EFFECTS

Some immunities and special rules also grant immunities to some or all continuous effects (p. 69). A model that is immune to a continuous effect never suffers the effect to which it is immune. The continuous effect is never applied to that model. If a model gains immunity to a continuous effect while the model is suffering that continuous effect, the continuous effect immediately expires.

WEAPON STATISTICS

On a model's weapon stat bar a sword icon denotes a melee weapon, a pistol icon denotes a ranged weapon, and a horseshoe icon denotes a Mount. The entry for a model with two identical weapons has a single weapon stat bar with "x2" on the icon. A weapon's stat bar lists only the stats that apply to its use. Those that are not applicable are marked with "—".

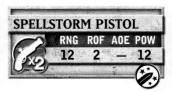

Sample Ranged Weapon Stat Bar for a Pair of Identical Weapons

Sample Melee Weapon Stat Bar

Sample Mount Weapon Stat Bar

RNG, Range – The maximum distance in inches between the attack's point of origin and the target before the attack will automatically miss. Measure range from the edge of the point of origin's base nearest to the target up to the maximum range of the attack. Spray attacks use special range descriptors including "SP" (p. 60). A RNG of "*" indicates the model's special rules contain information about determining the RNG.

ROF, Rate of Fire – The maximum number of times a model can make attacks with this ranged weapon during its activation. Reloading time limits most ranged weapons to only one attack per activation.

AOE, Area of Effect – The diameter in inches of the template an area-of-effect (AOE) weapon uses for determining which models are hit by the attack. When using an AOE weapon, center the template on the determined point of impact. All models within the template are affected and potentially suffer the attack's damage and effects. See pp. 58–60 for detailed rules on AOE attacks. Templates for AOEs can be found on p. 255.

POW, Power – The value used when making damage rolls. A weapon or attack marked with a POW of "—" does not cause damage.

P+S, Power plus Strength – The stat used for a melee weapon when making its damage rolls. The P+S value provides the sum of the model's Power and Strength stats for quick reference.

L/R/H, Location – A warjack's weapon stat bars indicate where its weapons are located: left arm (L), right arm (R), or head (H). When all the system boxes for a location have been damaged, the system is crippled (see "Crippling Systems," p. 66). These weapon locations are also used when resolving headlocks and weapon locks (p. 51). A weapon that is not in one of these locations is marked with "—".

WEAPON QUALITIES

Weapon qualities are special effects that are marked as a symbol on a weapon's stat block. Weapon qualities include damage types, magical weapons, and specific continuous effects.

These symbols show that the High Reclaimer's melee weapon Cremator has Continuous Effect: Fire, Magical Weapon, and Reach.

Buckler – This weapon has an integral buckler that gives the model a cumulative +1 ARM bonus; for example, a model with two of them gains a bonus of +2 ARM. A model does not gain this bonus while the weapon system with the buckler is crippled or being held in a weapon lock or when resolving damage that originates in its back arc.

Continuous Effect: Corrosion – A model hit by this attack suffers the Corrosion continuous effect (p. 69).

Continuous Effect: Fire – A model hit by this attack suffers the Fire continuous effect (p. 69).

Critical Corrosion – On a critical hit, the model hit by this attack suffers the Corrosion continuous effect (p. 69).

Critical Fire – On a critical hit, the model hit by this attack suffers the Fire continuous effect (p. 69).

Damage Type: Cold – This weapon causes cold damage (p. 68).

Damage Type: Corrosion – This weapon causes corrosion damage (p. 68).

Damage Type: Electricity – This weapon causes electrical damage (p. 68).

⚜ **Damage Type: Fire** – This weapon causes fire damage (p. 68).

⚜ **Magical Weapon** – This weapon is a magical weapon (p. 68).

⚜ **Open Fist** – This weapon is an **Open Fist**. A warjack's Open Fist enables it to make certain power attacks. A warjack with an Open Fist can make arm lock, headlock, and throw power attacks; a warjack with two Open Fists can also make double-hand throw power attacks. A warjack cannot use a crippled Open Fist to make power attacks.

⚜ **Reach** – This weapon has a 2″ melee range (p. 50).

⚜ **Shield** – This weapon is a shield that gives the model a cumulative +2 ARM bonus; for example, a model with two of them gains a bonus of +4 ARM. A model does not gain this bonus while the weapon system with the shield is crippled or being held in a weapon lock or when resolving damage that originates in its back arc.

⚜ **Weapon Master** – When attacking with this weapon, add an additional die to its damage rolls.

SPECIAL RULES

Most WARMACHINE combatants are highly specialized and trained to fill unique roles on the battlefield. To represent this, most models have **special rules** that take precedence over the standard rules. Depending on their use, special rules are categorized as abilities, feats, special actions, special attacks, or orders.

In addition, "Warjacks" (p. 73) and "Warcasters and Focus" (p. 74) detail many special rules common to all warcasters and warjacks that do not appear on their stat cards or in their army list entries.

ABILITIES

An ability typically gives a benefit or capability that modifies how the standard rules apply to the model. Abilities are always in effect and apply every time a game situation warrants their use.

Some abilities have a range (RNG). An ability's range is the maximum distance in inches it can be used to affect another model or unit. Measure range from the edge of the base of the model using the ability nearest to the target up to the maximum range of the ability. If the nearest edge of the target model's base is within the maximum range of the ability, the target is in range. A RNG of "CMD" indicates the ability has a range equal to the model's CMD.

When a model uses an ability with a RNG, it must target a model in its line of sight. Determine if the target is in the range of the ability. If the target model is within range, it is affected by the ability. If the target model is outside the range of the ability, it is not affected but the ability has still been used.

FEATS

Each warcaster has a unique feat that can be used once per game. A warcaster can use this feat freely at any time during his activation in addition to moving and making an action. A warcaster cannot interrupt his movement or attack to use his feat. He can use his feat before moving, after moving, before making an attack, or after making an attack, but not while moving or attacking.

SPECIAL ACTIONS (★ACTIONS)

A special action lets a model make an action normally unavailable to other models. A model can make a special action instead of attacking as its action if it meets the requirements for the special action's use.

SPECIAL ATTACKS (★ATTACKS)

A special attack gives a model an attack option normally unavailable to other models. Warjacks can also make a variety of punishing special attacks called power attacks, described on pp. 51–56. A model can make one special attack by choosing that option during its combat action if it meets the specific requirements of the attack. Special attacks can be made only during a model's activation.

ORDERS

An order lets a unit perform a specialized combat maneuver. A unit can be given an order by its unit commander at the beginning of its activation (see "Issuing Orders," p. 72).

DAMAGE CAPACITY AND DAMAGE GRIDS

A model's **damage capacity** determines how many damage points it can suffer before being destroyed. Most troopers do not have a damage capacity; they are destroyed and removed from the table when they suffer 1 damage point. The army list entry for a more resilient model gives the total amount of damage it can suffer before being destroyed. Its stat card provides a row of **damage boxes** for tracking the damage it receives. Unmarked damage boxes are sometimes called **wounds**. Some models, such as warjacks, have their damage boxes arranged in a **damage grid**.

Every time a model with multiple damage boxes suffers damage, mark one damage box for each damage point taken. A model with damage capacity is **destroyed** once all its damage boxes are marked. However, a warjack can suffer from crippled systems before its damage grid is completely filled. Some of a warjack's damage boxes are **system boxes**. These are labeled with a letter denoting the component of the model they represent. When all system boxes for a specific system have been marked, that system is crippled. See "Recording Damage" (p. 65) for more information.

Sample damage grid from a warjack stat card

BASE SIZE AND FACING

The physical models themselves have some properties important to gameplay, namely base size and facing.

BASE SIZE

The physical size and mass of a model are reflected by its **base size**. There are three base sizes: **small bases** (30 mm), **medium bases** (40 mm), and **large bases** (50 mm). Generally speaking, most human-sized warrior models have small bases, larger creatures and light warjacks have medium bases, and very large creatures and heavy warjacks have large bases. A model's army list entry states its base size.

FACING

A model's **facing** is determined by its shoulder orientation. The 180° arc in the direction its shoulders face defines the model's **front arc**; the opposite 180° defines its **back arc**. You may also make two small marks on either side of each of your models' bases to indicate where the front arc ends and the back arc begins instead of relying on the positioning of its shoulder. If a model lacks shoulders and does not have a 360° front arc, you must mark its base or discuss its facing with your opponent before the game starts.

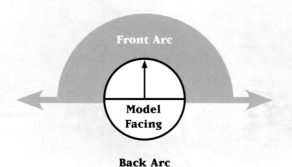

A model's front arc determines its perspective of the battlefield. A model typically directs its actions, determines line of sight, and makes attacks through this arc. Likewise, a model is usually more vulnerable to attacks from its back arc due to a lack of awareness in that direction.

A model is facing another model when the second model is within the first model's front arc. A model is **directly facing** another model when the center of its front arc aligns with the center of the second model's base.

A model with a 360° front arc has no back arc and is both facing and directly facing all models.

FACING AND DIRECTLY FACING

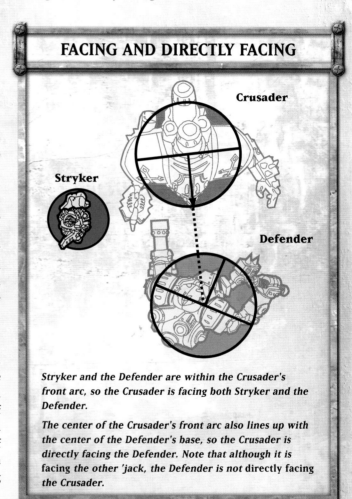

Stryker and the Defender are within the Crusader's front arc, so the Crusader is facing both Stryker and the Defender.

The center of the Crusader's front arc also lines up with the center of the Defender's base, so the Crusader is directly facing the Defender. Note that although it is facing the other 'jack, the Defender is not directly facing the Crusader.

MARKING YOUR MODEL'S FACING

We recommend players paint lines on their models' bases to define their facing clearly.

BUILDING YOUR ARMY

A warcaster and his warjacks form the central fighting group of every WARMACHINE force. Units and solos with a variety of abilities further support the warcaster and his warjacks. In larger battles, you can even field multiple warcasters for greater might.

To create an army, first choose a faction and decide on an encounter level, and then spend the allotted army points to add models and units from your chosen faction and the mercenaries who will work for that faction. You can even field an army made up entirely of Mercenary models, using the mercenary contract rules found in *Forces of WARMACHINE: Mercenaries*.

Every army list entry provides the model's or unit's point cost and field allowance values to use when designing your force. Specific scenarios can modify the standard army creation rules.

ENCOUNTER LEVELS

WARMACHINE battles are played at different encounter levels to allow for a diversity of army sizes, strategies, and game experiences. Each **encounter level** gives the maximum number of **army points** each player can spend on an army. You need not spend every point available, but your army cannot exceed the maximum number of points allowed by the chosen level.

Each encounter level also dictates the number of warcasters available to each player. Warcasters do not cost army points to include in your army but instead grant you some number of **warjack points** that can be spent only on warjacks for your warcaster's battlegroup. These bonus points are in addition to the army points determined by the encounter level. Each warcaster's warjack points that are not spent on warjacks for his battlegroup are lost.

EXAMPLE: *Kris and Rob are playing a 25-point skirmish. Kris chooses Captain Victoria Haley as his warcaster, and Rob chooses Warwitch Deneghra. Because Kris chose Haley, he has 5 warjack points to spend on warjacks in her battlegroup. Based on the encounter level, he also has 25 points that he can spend on whatever models he chooses.*

Warjack points can be divided among warjacks in the warcaster's battlegroup; they do not have to be spent on a single warjack. They can also be combined with army points to pay for an eligible warjack.

EXAMPLE: *Rob has 25 army points from the encounter level and 5 warjack points from Deneghra. He wants to add a pair of 4-point Deathrippers to Deneghra's battlegroup. He spends his 5 warjack points toward the point total of 8 for the two 'jacks and pays for the remaining 3 points with army points.*

DUEL

Max. Warcasters: 1   Army Points: 15
Est. Play Time: 20–45 Minutes

A duel occurs when two warcasters cross paths. Sometimes they are on special assignments, but other times they are out to settle vicious rivalries. A duel is the perfect match for playing with the contents of a battlegroup box.

SKIRMISH

Max. Warcasters: 1   Army Points: 25, 35, or 50
Est. Play Time: 45–90 Minutes

A skirmish is an encounter that includes a single warcaster and his warjacks supported by a small retinue of units and solos. Skirmishes can occur over such things as routine border patrols or elite surgical missions.

GRAND MELEE

Max. Warcasters: 1   Army Points: 75 or 100
Est. Play Time: 90–120 Minutes

As warfare rages across the land, escalating hostilities rage unchecked. Each faction races to bring its most devastating engines of war to the battlefield to ensure total victory. Everywhere warcasters command armies to march to battle.

BATTLE ROYALE

Max. Warcasters: 2   Army Points: 100, 125, or 150
Est. Play Time: 2–3 hours

Battles decide the pivotal events in the course of a campaign. With two warcasters in an army, you can fully realize the opportunities for army customization and heavy firepower.

WAR

Max. Warcasters: 3   Army Points: 150, 175, or 200
Est. Play Time: 3–4 hours

When objectives can no longer be achieved by deploying small forces and both sides refuse to yield, nothing less than full-out war can decide the differences. This huge game, in which each side fields up to three warcasters, allows your forces enough breadth and depth to inflict and recover from staggering blows as the fight swings back and forth.

APOCALYPSE

Max. Warcasters: 4+   Army Points: 200+
Est. Play Time: 4+ hours

When a conflict rages so bitterly that war itself cannot resolve it, the final reckoning has arrived. You have summoned the apocalypse. An apocalypse is a massive game employing four or more warcasters in each force. Although this vast endeavor should never be undertaken lightly, it yields game experiences found in no other arena. One warcaster can be added to an army for each additional increment of 50 points.

BATTLEGROUPS

Each warcaster in an army controls a group of warjacks. A warcaster and his assigned warjacks are collectively referred to as a **battlegroup**. There is no limit to the number of warjacks that can be fielded in each warcaster's battlegroup. Warjacks must begin the game assigned to a battlegroup or controlled by a 'jack marshal (p. 80).

A warcaster can allocate focus points only to warjacks in his battlegroup. If an army has multiple battlegroups, it is important to distinguish which warjacks are controlled by each warcaster. See "Warcasters and Focus" (p. 74) for more information on battlegroups.

CHARACTERS

Some models represent unique individuals from the Iron Kingdoms. These personalities carry proper names and are identified as **characters**. Characters follow the rules for their basic model type.

Unique units and units that include named characters are designated as **character units**. They remain character units even after the named characters in them are no longer part of the unit or in play at all.

An army can include only one model of each named character and only one of each character unit. For instance, you can never have two Commander Coleman Strykers in the same army. However, two battling Cygnar players could each field Stryker. How can this be?

In the chaos and tumult that engulfs war-torn Immoren, pretenders and imposters abound. Thus, a warcaster might find himself impossibly facing his apparent double across the field of battle. Which is the *real* Commander Coleman Stryker or Butcher of Khardov? Victory alone can determine the answer.

POINT COSTS

A model's point cost indicates how many army points you must spend to include one of these models (or in the case of units, one basic unit) in your army. Some models and units have different costs associated with different play options. For example, many units have one cost listed for the minimum-strength unit and a separate cost for the maximum-strength unit.

A model or unit's entry in your army list must specify which point cost option you took. Remember, a warcaster adds warjack points that can be spent only on warjacks in his battlegroup.

FIELD ALLOWANCE

Field allowance (FA) is the maximum number of models or units of a given type that can be included for each warcaster in an army. For example, Cygnar Trencher Infantry units have FA 2, indicating an army can have up to two Trencher Infantry units for each warcaster. An army with two warcasters could have up to four Trencher Infantry units.

A field allowance of "U" means an unlimited number of these models or units can be fielded in an army. A field allowance of "C" means the model or unit is a character; only one model of each named character and only one of each character unit is allowed per army regardless of the number of warcasters.

SAMPLE ARMY

The following army illustrates the force creation rules of WARMACHINE. This army is designed for a 100-point battle royale encounter, so each player can field up to two warcasters.

WARCASTER: COMMANDER STRYKER (+6 warjack points)

Stryker's Battlegroup	Army Point Cost
1 Defender Heavy Warjack	9
1 Ironclad Heavy Warjack	7
2 Lancer Light Warjacks	12 (6 ea.)

WARCASTER: CAPTAIN HALEY (+5 warjack points)

Haley's Battlegroup	Army Point Cost
3 Defender Heavy Warjacks	27 (9 ea.)
1 Charger Light Warjack	4
1 Lancer Light Warjack	6

Units	Army Point Cost
2 Arcane Tempest Gun Mage Units (FA 2)	12 (6 ea.)
1 Long Gunner Infantry Unit (FA 2) with 6 troopers	6
3 Stormblade Infantry Units (FA 2) with 6 troopers	15 (5 ea.)
1 Trencher Infantry Unit (FA 2) with 6 troopers	7
2 Field Mechanik Units (FA 3) with 6 troopers	6 (3 ea.)

TOTAL	111 Points
	(100 army points +11 warjack points)

The chosen warcasters are Commander Stryker and Captain Haley, avoiding duplication since they are named characters. Stryker adds 6 warjack points and Haley adds 5, so the army can include up to 111 points of models in addition to the warcasters. The NINE warjacks in the army are assigned to specific battlegroups.

The unit of Long Gunners and Trenchers are minimum-strength units with only six troopers each, as allowed by the unit options. There are two units of Field Mechaniks, each with six troopers as allowed by their unit option. We also included two Gun Mage units that always include six troopers each. There are three units of Stormblades, which also always include six troopers each. With the unit's FA 2 and two warcasters, this army could have a total of four such units. The total of army points spent is 111, so no points are left unused.

Field allowance is not faction-specific. If an army includes both faction and mercenary warcasters, count all the warcasters in the army when determining field allowance limits for both faction and mercenary models and units. For example, if a Cygnar army contains both a Cygnar warcaster and a mercenary warcaster, that army can include up to four Trencher units just as if it had two Cygnar warcasters.

Some solos, like Scrap Thralls, are purchased in small groups for a single point. In these cases, Field Allowance determines the number of groups of these models a player can include in his army rather than the number of individual models. For example, Scrap Thralls are FA 3 and cost 1 point for three Thralls. That means a player can add three groups of Scrap Thralls, a total of nine models, to his army for each warcaster in his army.

SETUP, DEPLOYMENT, & VICTORY CONDITIONS

WARMACHINE games can be played in a variety of ways. The primary influences on a game's setup are its encounter level, number of players, and victory conditions. Players can also agree to play a specific scenario or even design one of their own.

TWO-PLAYER GAMES

In a typical WARMACHINE game, two players match forces across a 4′ × 4′ **battlefield**, a playing surface sometimes referred to as "the table". After setting up the battlefield according to the rules in "Terrain" (p. 86), players roll a d6 to make a **starting roll**. The player who rolls the highest number chooses which player will be the **first player**.

Players then deploy their armies. The first player chooses any edge of the battlefield and deploys all his forces completely within 10″ of that edge. This area is the player's **deployment zone**. Deploy units so that all their troopers are in formation. The second player then deploys his forces on the opposite side of the battlefield following the same guidelines.

After both players have deployed their forces, the first player takes the first turn of the game. Players then alternate taking turns for the rest of the game. This is the **turn order**. Once established, the turn order remains the same for the rest of the game.

MULTIPLAYER GAMES

When playing multiplayer games of WARMACHINE, players can choose to play either a team game or a free-for-all game. Agree on the type of game to be played, then set up the battlefield and use the following guidelines to determine the game's turn order.

TEAM GAMES

Before beginning a **team game**, players split into two opposing sides. Each side decides the composition of its teams. Teams should be made up exclusively of models from the same faction and the mercenaries that will work for that faction. If a team wishes to field an all-mercenary force, all the members of the team must use the same mercenary contract. Each team can include only one of any character model. To begin, have one player from each team roll a d6 to establish the turn order. The team that rolls highest gets to choose which team goes first, and the first team chooses which of its players will be the first player. Once the first player is determined, the opposing team chooses which of its players will go next. The first team then names one of its players to be third, followed again by the opposing team. This continues until all players have a place in the turn order and ensures the turn order will alternate between players of opposing teams.

Force deployment should be done in turn order following the above guidelines, with teammates sharing the same deployment zone across the battlefield from their opponents' deployment zone.

FREE-FOR-ALL GAMES

You can also choose to play a multiplayer game in which each player fights independently in a **free-for-all game**. To establish turn order, each player rolls a d6. Starting with the highest roller and working to the lowest, each player chooses any available position in the turn order. Reroll ties as they occur with the highest reroller winning his choice of position, followed by the next highest reroller, and so on.

EXAMPLE: *Matt, Jason, Mike, and Steve roll 6, 5, 5, and 3 respectively for turn order. Matt chooses his position first. Then Jason and Mike reroll their tie, getting a 4 and a 2, respectively. Jason chooses next, followed by Mike. As the lowest roller, Steve gets the remaining position in the turn order.*

Use your best judgment to establish deployment zones based on the number of players and the size and shape of your playing surface. Deployment zones should be spaced such that no player gets a significant advantage or disadvantage—unless mutually agreed upon. As a starting point, for games with three or four players on a 4′ × 4′ playing surface, deploying forces completely within 10″ of any corner of the playing area should ensure adequate separation.

SCENARIOS

If all players agree, you can set up the game according to a specific **scenario**. Scenarios add an extra layer of excitement by incorporating special circumstances and unique rules. A player wins a scenario by achieving its objectives, not necessarily by eliminating his opponent's forces. Certain scenarios have specific guidelines for battlefield size, terrain setup, deployment zones, and turn order. See "Scenarios" (pp. 90–93) for the scenario descriptions. If you feel particularly daring, you can randomly determine which scenario to play.

As long as all players agree, you can even design your own scenarios to create a unique battle experience. Just be sure to allow a minimum of 28″ between rival deployment zones. Feel free to be creative when setting up your games. For instance, if you have three players, one player could set up in the middle of the table as a defender and the other two could attack from opposite edges. Furthermore, you could have a four-player team game with teammates deploying across from each other on opposite edges of the battlefield so everyone will have enemies on either side. Your imagination is the only limit.

VICTORY CONDITIONS

Establish **victory conditions** before deploying forces. Typically victory goes to the player who accepts his opponent's surrender or who has the last warcaster(s) remaining in play. A scenario can define other specific objectives. The objectives can even be customized for each side.

STARTING THE GAME

After establishing victory conditions and deploying forces, the first game round begins. Every warcaster and other model with the Focus Manipulation ability begins the game with a number of focus points equal to its FOCUS stat. Starting with the first player, each player takes a turn in turn order. Game rounds continue until one side achieves its victory conditions and wins the game.

A WARMACHINE battlefield as two armies prepare to clash

THE GAME ROUND

WARMACHINE battles are fought in a series of **game rounds**. Each game round, every player takes a turn in the order established during setup. Once the last player in the turn order completes his turn, the current game round ends. A new game round then begins starting again with the first player. Game rounds continue until one side wins the game.

For game effects, a **round** is measured from the current player's turn to the beginning of his next turn regardless of his location in the turn order. A game effect with a duration of one round expires at the beginning of the current player's next turn. This means every player will take one turn while the effect is in play.

THE PLAYER TURN

A player's turn has three **phases**: Maintenance, Control, and Activation.

Some effects are resolved at the beginning of a player's turn. These effects are resolved before the start of the Maintenance Phase. Remember to remove any effects that expire at the beginning of your turn.

MAINTENANCE PHASE

During the Maintenance Phase, perform the following steps in order:

1. Remove all focus points from your models.

2. Check for expiration of continuous effects on any models you control. After removing all expired continuous effects, resolve the effects of those that remain in play. All damage dealt by continuous effects is resolved simultaneously (see p. 244).

3. Resolve all other effects that occur during the Maintenance Phase.

CONTROL PHASE

During the Control Phase, perform the following steps in order:

1. Each of your models with the Focus Manipulation ability, like warcasters, replenishes its focus and receives a number of focus points equal to its current FOCUS.

2. Each model with the Focus Manipulation ability can allocate focus points to warjacks in its battlegroup that are in its control area.

3. Each model with the Focus Manipulation ability can spend focus points to maintain its upkeep spells in play. If a model does not spend focus points to maintain a spell requiring upkeep, the spell expires and its effects end immediately.

4. Resolve all other effects that occur during the Control Phase.

ACTIVATION PHASE

The Activation Phase is the major portion of a player's turn. All models you control must be activated once per turn. This is usually done during the Activation Phase, but some effects allow a model to activate earlier in the turn. Units and independent models are activated one at a time in the order you choose. A model cannot forfeit its activation unless allowed to do so by a special rule. A model must be on the table to activate.

ACTIVATING MODELS

When a model activates, it is granted its normal movement and its action. The normal movement must be resolved before the action is made.

WHAT A MODEL DOES WHEN ACTIVATED

Generally an active model moves before going on to its action. Depending on the movement option chosen, the model might be able to make either a combat action or a special action. A combat action lets a model make attacks. A special action lets a model perform a unique battlefield function such as digging in or creating Scrap Thralls.

ACTIVATING INDEPENDENT MODELS

Independent models activate individually. Only one independent model can activate at a time. The active model must end its activation before another model or unit can be activated. The model then makes its normal movement if it was not forfeited. After resolving its normal movement, if the model did not forfeit its action, then it uses its action to make either a combat action or special action. After resolving its action, the model then ends its activation.

ACTIVATING UNITS

Troopers do not activate individually. Instead, the entire unit activates at once. When a unit begins its activation, every trooper in it activates. First determine if any models in the unit are out of formation. A trooper that is out of formation at the start of its unit's activation must spend its normal movement making a full advance toward or directly toward its unit commander. If it makes a full advance, it must forfeit its action.

After resolving the normal movement of each activated trooper, each trooper can then make its action, one trooper at a time. Completely resolve the movement of one trooper before moving on to the next. After one trooper resolves its action, another can begin its action.

Units require strong leadership and guidance to be effective on the battlefield. Since a unit operates as one body, it functions best when all members are in formation. A unit must receive an order from its unit commander in order to run or charge. Some unit commanders can have other special orders that allow the unit to perform a specialized combat maneuver.

LINE OF SIGHT

Many game situations such as charging, ranged attacks, and magic attacks require a model to have **line of sight (LOS)** to its intended target. Simply put, having line of sight means a model can see another model.

There are several steps to determining whether one model has LOS to another. If any step results in a model's potential LOS being blocked, return to the first step and try a different line. If no line can be found to pass all steps, then the model does not have LOS to the desired model.

Each model occupies a **volume** of space above the bottom of its base determined by its base size. A model's volume is used for determining if terrain blocks LOS to a model.

In the following descriptions, Model A is determining LOS to Model B:

1. Draw a straight line from any part of Model A's volume to any part of Model B's volume that is within Model A's front arc.

2. The line must not pass through terrain.

3. The line must not pass over the base of an intervening model that has a base size equal to or larger than Model B.

4. The line must not pass over an effect that blocks LOS, like a cloud effect.

INTERVENING MODEL

If you can draw any straight line between the bases of two models that crosses over any part of the base of a third model, the third model is an **intervening model**.

HOW ELEVATION AFFECTS LOS

When determining if Model A has line of sight to Model B, ignore intervening models on terrain more than 1″ lower than Model A except for those within 1″ of Model B. Additionally, ignore those models within 1″ of Model B that have equal or smaller-sized bases than Model A.

When Model A is on terrain at least 1″ lower than Model B, Model A ignores intervening models on terrain more than 1″ lower than Model B.

USING REFERENCE OBJECTS

If you cannot easily determine LOS between your model and another model due to the position of terrain on the table, use reference objects for drawing the line. First confirm the other model is in your model's front arc; if it is not, your model cannot have LOS to it. Otherwise, choose an edge of your model's base and an edge of the other model's base. For each model, hold an object next to the chosen edge that is the height used to determine its volume (1.75″, 2.25″, or 2.75″). If you can draw a line from the inside edge of the object next to your model to the inside edge of the other object that does not pass through a terrain feature, your model's LOS to the other model is not blocked by terrain.

DETERMINING MODEL VOLUME

A small-based model occupies the space from the bottom of its base to a height of 1.75″.

A medium-based model occupies the space from the bottom of its base to a height of 2.25″.

A large-based model occupies the space from the bottom of its base to a height of 2.75″.

A model is considered to occupy a standard volume regardless of its pose or the size of the sculpt itself.

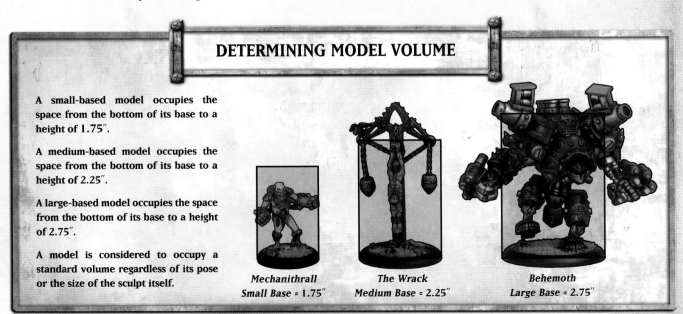

Mechanithrall
Small Base = 1.75″

The Wrack
Medium Base = 2.25″

Behemoth
Large Base = 2.75″

LOS AND TARGETING

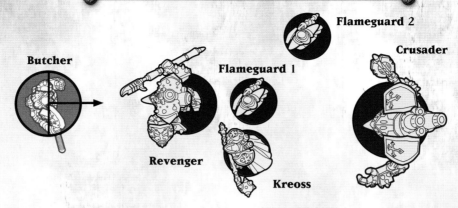

The Butcher obviously has LOS to the Revenger. Since the Revenger has a medium base, it blocks LOS to other models with medium and small bases. The Butcher has LOS to Flameguard 2 because you can draw an unobstructed line from the Butcher's front arc to the edge of Flameguard 2's base that does not cross the Revenger's base. On the other hand, the Butcher does not have LOS to Flameguard 1 because you cannot draw a line between their bases that does not cross the Revenger's base. Because they have smaller bases than the Crusader, the Revenger and the two Flameguard do not block LOS to it. The Butcher can draw LOS to the Crusader as if those models were not there.

The Butcher has LOS to Kreoss because Kreoss' base is not completely obscured.

If the Butcher were on terrain more than 1″ higher than the other models, the Butcher would have LOS to Flameguard 1. The Revenger does not block this LOS because its base is the same size as the Butcher's and it is within 1″ of Flameguard 1.

LOS AND ELEVATION

The Charger is on a hill 1″ higher than the other models.

The Charger has LOS to the Manhunter because the Manhunter is on a lower elevation and there are no intervening models that would block line of sight within 1″ of it.

The Charger has LOS to the Battle Mechanik because none of the intervening models has a base larger than the Charger's.

The Charger does not have LOS to Sorscha because the Berserker is an intervening model that is within 1″ of Sorscha and has a larger base than the Charger.

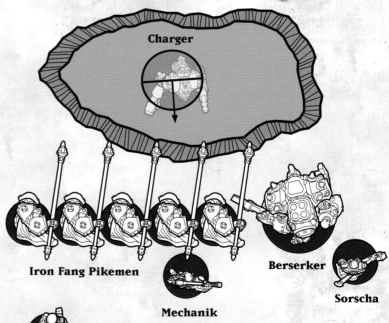

LOS AND TERRAIN

 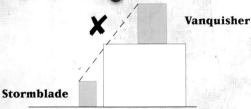

Stormblade

Here, the Vanquisher has line of sight to the Stormblade because an unobstructed line can be drawn from its volume to the Stormblade's volume.

Stormblade

Here, the Vanquisher does not have line of sight to the Stormblade because there is no unobstructed line between their volumes.

This wall is shorter than 1.75˝. It will not block line of sight to any of the models behind it.

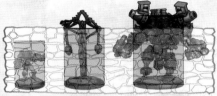

This wall is taller than 2.25˝ but shorter than 2.75˝. It will block line of sight to small- and medium-based models behind it.

This wall is taller than 1.75˝ but shorter than 2.25˝. It will block line of sight to small-based models behind it.

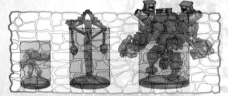

This wall is taller than 2.75˝. It will block line of sight to all models behind it.

Although the Trencher Sharpshooter's pose has it hidden below the stone wall, its defined height is greater than the wall's height. The Trencher Sharpshooter can see over the wall to the Repenter, and the Repenter can also see the Sharpshooter.

Similarly, although the top of the Guardian's banners can be seen over the wall, its defined height is lower than the wall's height. The Trenchers do not have line of sight to the Guardian.

BASE TO BASE AND CONTACT

Models whose bases are touching are in **base-to-base (B2B) contact**. If a model has an ability that allows it to move through another model, while it is moving through the other model they are considered to be in base-to-base contact.

One model contacts another when it changes from not being base to base with it to being base to base with it. Additionally, when a model is already base to base with another and would move toward it, it is considered to contact that model again.

MOVEMENT

Normally the first part of a model's activation is its normal movement. Special rules can also permit it to move at other times.

A moving model's base cannot pass over another model's base.

The term **normal movement** refers to the movement a model makes during the movement portion of its activation. **Advancing** refers to any movement a model intentionally makes, not to any movement caused by other effects such as being pushed or being slammed. A model can change its facing at anytime during its advance, but when it moves it must always move in the direction it is facing. Make all measurements from the front of an advancing model's base. Determine the distance a model advances by measuring how far the front of its base travels. The distance moved is absolute; we suggest using a flexible measuring device to keep accurate track of a model's movement. Changing facing by rotating in place does not cost any movement.

Terrain, spells, and other effects can increase or reduce a model's movement and/or its SPD. Modifiers to movement apply only to the model's normal movement, while modifiers to SPD apply whenever the model's SPD is used to determine the distance. See "Terrain" (pp. 86–89) for full details on terrain features and how they affect movement.

See "Terrain" (pp. 86–89)

MEASURING MOVEMENT

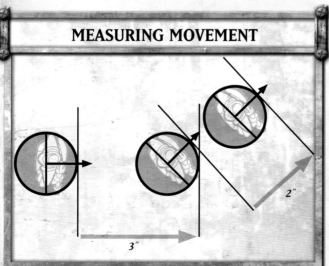

3"

2"

Remember that all intentional movement, whether full advancing, running, or charging, is considered advancing whether or not it takes place during the movement portion of a model's activation.

EXAMPLE: *A model running as its normal movement would move at twice its SPD plus any movement modifiers. If that same model then runs outside its normal movement, it would move at twice its SPD.*

There are three basic types of advancing: full advance, run, and charge.

Models can also move without advancing, typically due to being pushed or slammed or from other effects. Determine the distance a model moves in this way by measuring the distance traveled by the edge of the model's base in the direction of the movement. Unless otherwise specified, a model's facing does not change when it moves without advancing.

FULL ADVANCE

A model making a **full advance** advances up to its current speed (SPD) in inches.

RUN

A model that **runs** advances up to twice its current SPD in inches. A model that uses its normal movement to run cannot make an action, cast spells, or use feats that activation, and its activation ends immediately after it ends its movement. A model that forfeits its action cannot run during its normal movement that activation.

If a model cannot run due to some effect and is required to run, instead of running it makes a full advance, then its activation immediately ends.

Some models must meet special requirements to run:

- A warjack must spend 1 focus point to run during its normal movement.

- A trooper must receive a run or charge order to run during its normal movement, or it must be compelled to run as a result of a game effect (like fleeing or being out of formation, for example).

CHARGE

A **charging** model rushes into melee range with a target and takes advantage of its momentum to make a more powerful strike. A model suffering a penalty to its SPD or movement for any reason other than for being in rough terrain cannot charge, regardless of offsetting bonuses. A model can charge through rough terrain. A model must have both its normal movement and action in order to use its normal movement to charge. A model without a melee range cannot charge.

Declare a charge and its target before moving the model. The charging model must have LOS to a model to declare it as a charge target. After declaring a charge, the charging model turns to face any direction that will bring it to within melee range of its target, ignoring terrain, the distance to the charge target, and other models. The charging model then advances its current SPD plus 3″ in that direction, in a straight line. The charging model cannot voluntarily stop its movement until its target is in its melee range, then it can end this movement at any point. Once the charge target is in the charging model's melee range, it must stay in the charging model's melee range for the entire charge or the charge fails. The charging model stops if it contacts a model, an obstacle, or an obstruction. At the end of the charge movement, the charging model turns to face its target directly.

Some effects require a model to charge. A model required to charge must charge a model to which it can draw line of sight. If there are no models in its line of sight, or if it cannot charge, the model activates but must forfeit its movement and action.

A charging model that ends its charge movement with its charge target in its melee range has made a **successful charge**. It must use its action to make a combat action, choosing to make either initial melee attacks or (if it can make a special attack with a melee weapon) a melee special attack.

CHARGE DIRECTION

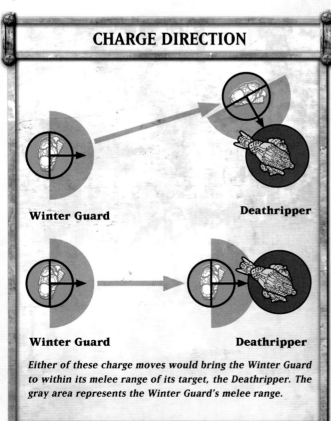

Winter Guard

Deathripper

Winter Guard

Deathripper

Either of these charge moves would bring the Winter Guard to within its melee range of its target, the Deathripper. The gray area represents the Winter Guard's melee range.

The charging model's first attack after ending its charge movement must target the model it charged. If the charging model advanced at least 3″, this attack is a **charge attack**. A charge attack is not in addition to the regular attacks a model would get for its combat action. Rather, it modifies the model's first attack after its charge movement. The attack roll is made normally and can be boosted. If the charge attack was made with a melee weapon and the attack hits, the damage roll is automatically boosted. After making a charge attack during its activation, the charging model completes its combat action normally.

If a charging model moved less than 3″, its first attack is not a charge attack because the model did not move far or fast enough to add sufficient momentum to its strike. Its first attack must still be made against the charge target, however. The charging model completes its combat action normally.

If a charging model ends its charge movement without its charge target in its melee range, then it has made a **failed charge**. If a model makes a failed charge during its activation, its activation immediately ends.

Some models must meet special requirements to charge:

- A warjack must spend 1 focus point to charge during its normal movement.

- A trooper must receive a charge order to charge during its normal movement. A trooper that receives a charge order must either run or charge during its normal movement. Troopers in the same unit can charge the same target or multiple targets.

Cavalry models have additional rules governing charges. (See "Cavalry," p. 81.)

If the charging model cannot make its first melee attack against the charge target, the charging model can make its first melee attack against another eligible target, but this is not a charge attack. It does not lose its first attack.

CHARGES OUTSIDE OF ACTIVATION

When a model charges without using its normal movement/ combat action, such as with the Counter Charge ability, follow the rules above but ignore any references to the model's action or combat action. When a model makes this type of charge, it makes only one attack. If it made a successful charge and moved at least 3″, that attack is the charge attack. If it made a successful charge but did not move at least 3″, that attack is a single normal melee attack subject to the targeting restrictions above. Counter charging cavalry models still make their impact attacks. A model that charges outside its activation cannot make a special attack when resolving that charge. If the model fails its charge it does not make any attack.

MOVEMENT RESTRICTIONS

Some effects place restrictions on how a model moves or advances. There are four types of these restrictions. In the following descriptions, Model A is moving with some restriction relative to Model B.

- *Model A Must Move **Toward** Model B*: Model A can move along any path such that the distance between Model A and Model B is always decreasing during the movement.

- *Model A Must Move **Directly Toward** Model B*: Model A moves along the straight line that connects the center points of Model A and Model B such that the distance between them decreases during the movement. A model that moves directly toward a point cannot change its facing after moving.

- *Model A Must Move **Away From** Model B*: Model A can move along any path such that the distance between Model A and Model B is always increasing during the movement.

- *Model A Must Move **Directly Away From** Model B*: Model A moves along the straight line that connects the center points of Model A and Model B such that the distance between them increases during the movement. A model that moves directly away from a point cannot change its facing after moving.

Movement restrictions are cumulative. For example, a model required to advance toward one model and away from another would need to move in a manner to satisfy both requirements. If a moving model cannot satisfy all restrictions on the movement, it cannot move at all.

MOVEMENT PENALTIES

Some rules reference **movement penalties**. A movement penalty is any effect applied to a model that reduces its SPD or movement. Effects that cause a model to move at half rate are also movement penalties.

PLACED

Sometimes models are **placed** in a new location as a result of an ability or spell. When a model is placed it is not considered to have moved or advanced. Because the model is not considered to have advanced it cannot be targeted by free strikes. There must be room for the model's base in the location the model is placed. A model cannot be placed in impassable terrain or with its base overlapping an obstacle, an obstruction, or another model's base. The player placing the model chooses its facing.

When an effect causes a friendly trooper model other than the unit commander to be placed and that model is in formation, it cannot be placed out of formation. When an effect causes a unit commander to be placed, it can be placed without restriction.

ACTIONS

An activated model might be entitled to make one action depending on the type of movement it made. There are two broad **action types**: combat and special. A combat action lets a model make one or more attacks. A special action lets a model perform a specialized function. A model cannot move after making any action unless a special rule specifically allows it to do so.

COMBAT ACTIONS

A model can use its action to make a combat action if it did not use its normal movement to run. A combat action lets a model make attacks. A **normal attack** is an attack with a weapon that is not a special attack. A model making a **combat action** chooses one of the following options:

- A model can make one normal melee attack with each of its melee weapons. These attacks are called **initial melee attacks**. A model making more than one attack can divide them among any eligible targets.

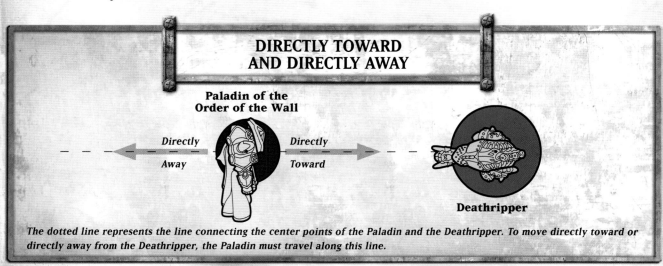

DIRECTLY TOWARD
AND DIRECTLY AWAY

Paladin of the Order of the Wall

Directly Away ← → *Directly Toward*

Deathripper

The dotted line represents the line connecting the center points of the Paladin and the Deathripper. To move directly toward or directly away from the Deathripper, the Paladin must travel along this line.

- A model can make one normal ranged attack with each of its ranged weapons. These attacks are called **initial ranged attacks**. A model making more than one attack can divide them among any eligible targets. Each ranged weapon makes only one initial attack regardless of its ROF.

- A model can make one special attack (★Attack) allowed by its special rules.

- A model that did not use its normal movement to charge can make one power attack allowed by its special rules. A power attack is considered both a melee attack and a special attack.

After resolving these attacks, a model might be able to make **additional attacks**. A model can make additional attacks only during its combat action. Each additional attack is a normal attack that can be made with any appropriate weapons the model possesses, including multiple attacks with the same weapon. A ranged weapon cannot make more attacks than its rate of fire (ROF) during a model's activation, however. Completely resolve each attack before making another attack.

Warcasters and warjacks can spend focus points to make additional attacks (see "Focus: Additional Attack," p. 75).

Unless noted otherwise, a model cannot make both melee and ranged attacks in the same combat action. A model can make additional attacks after a special attack or power attack.

Special attacks listed as a rule of a melee weapon are melee special attacks. Special attacks listed as a rule of a ranged weapon are ranged special attacks. A special attack made with a ranged weapon counts toward the ROF of the weapon. For example, if the Thunderhead makes an Energy Pulse special attack with its Lightning Coil ranged weapon, it can spend focus to make up to only two additional Lightning Coil attacks because the weapon has ROF 3. Special attacks listed as a rule of the model itself are neither melee attacks nor ranged attacks. The rules for these special attacks indicate the nature of any additional attacks that can be made afterward, if any. A model cannot make a special attack or a power attack as an additional attack.

See "Combat" (p. 50) for detailed rules on making attacks and determining their results.

SPECIAL ACTIONS

Some models can make a **special action** (★Action) as their action. A model cannot make a special action if it uses its normal movement to run or charge. A special action's description details its requirements and results.

SKILL CHECKS

Some special actions appear with a **skill value** following their names. When a model makes one of these special actions, make a **skill check** to determine its success. Roll 2d6. If the result is equal to or less than the skill value listed, the model passes its skill check and its results are applied immediately. If the result is greater than the model's skill value, the special action fails. Typically nothing happens if a model fails a skill check, but some special actions impose negative consequences for failing a skill check.

EXAMPLE: *The Cygnar Field Mechanik Crew Chief has the special action Repair [9]. The Mechanik's Repair special action will succeed on a 2d6 roll of 9 or less.*

COMBAT OVERVIEW

A model's combat action allows it to make attacks. Special rules might also permit models to make attacks at other times. An attack roll determines if an attack hits its target. A damage roll determines how much damage, if any, an attack deals.

Unless stated otherwise, an attack can be made against any model, whether friendly or enemy, and against certain terrain features.

There are three main types of attacks: melee attacks, ranged attacks, and magic attacks. A model cannot make both melee and ranged attacks during its combat action. In other words, a model cannot make a ranged attack after making a melee attack, and it cannot make a melee attack after making a ranged attack. Magic attacks have no such restrictions. Some models, such as warcasters, can make magic attacks and melee or ranged attacks during the same activation.

Certain rules and effects create situations that specifically prevent a model from being targeted. A model that cannot be targeted by an attack still suffers its effects if inside the attack's area of effect. Other rules and effects, such as Stealth, only cause an attack to miss automatically; they do not prevent the model from being targeted by the attack.

MELEE COMBAT

A model using its combat action for **melee attacks** can make one initial attack with each of its melee weapons. Some models have special rules that allow **additional melee attacks** during their activations. Warcasters and warjacks can spend focus points to make additional melee attacks during their activations, for example. Each additional melee attack can be made with any melee weapon the model possesses with no limit to the number of attacks made per weapon.

A melee attack can be made against any target in the melee range of the weapon being used and in the attacker's line of sight. A model making more than one melee attack can divide its attacks among any eligible targets.

MELEE WEAPONS

Melee weapons include such implements as spears, swords, hammers, flails, saws, and axes. Some models, such as warjacks, have attack options allowing them to make attacks without their weapons (power attacks, for example).

Melee Damage Roll = 2d6 + POW + STR

MELEE RANGE AND ENGAGING

A model can make melee attacks against any target in its melee range that is in its line of sight. A player can measure his model's melee range at anytime.

A weapon's **melee range** extends 0.5″ beyond the model's front arc for any type of melee attack. A weapon with Reach ⊘ has a melee range of 2″. Some effects and special rules increase a weapon's melee range beyond this. A model's melee range is the longest melee range of its

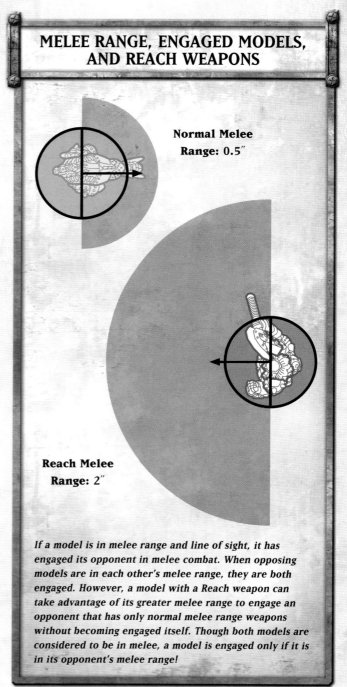

MELEE RANGE, ENGAGED MODELS, AND REACH WEAPONS

Normal Melee Range: 0.5″

Reach Melee Range: 2″

If a model is in melee range and line of sight, it has engaged its opponent in melee combat. When opposing models are in each other's melee range, they are both engaged. However, a model with a Reach weapon can take advantage of its greater melee range to engage an opponent that has only normal melee range weapons without becoming engaged itself. Though both models are considered to be in melee, a model is engaged only if it is in its opponent's melee range!

usable melee weapons. A model that has a Reach weapon and another melee weapon can attack an opponent up to 2" away with its Reach weapon, but its other weapons can only be used to attack models within their normal 0.5" melee range. Non-warjack models with no melee weapons have no melee range. Warjacks always have at least a 0.5" melee range.

When a model is within an enemy model's melee range and in that model's line of sight, it is **engaged** in combat and primarily concerned with fighting its nearest threat. When a model has an enemy model in its melee range and line of sight, it is **engaging** that model. When a model is either engaged or engaging, it is **in melee**, which prevents it from making ranged attacks.

MELEE RANGE AND ELEVATION

When a model makes a melee attack against a model 1" or less higher or lower, ignore the vertical distance between the two models when determining melee range.

FREE STRIKES

When an engaged model advances out of the enemy's melee range or line of sight, the enemy model can immediately make a **free strike** against it just before it leaves. The model makes one normal melee attack with any melee weapon that has sufficient melee range to reach the moving model and gains a +2 bonus to its melee attack roll. If the attack hits, the damage roll is boosted. Always treat the free striking model as being in the advancing model's back arc, if it has one, when the free strike is made. Free strikes do not benefit from back strike bonuses.

MELEE ATTACK ROLLS

Determine a melee attack's success by making a melee attack roll. Roll 2d6 and add the attacking model's melee attack stat (MAT). Roll an additional die if the attack roll is boosted. Special rules and certain circumstances might modify the attack roll as well.

Melee Attack Roll = 2d6 + MAT

A target is **directly hit** by an attack if the attack roll equals or exceeds the target's defense (DEF). If the attack roll is less than the target's DEF, the attack misses. A roll of all 1s on the dice is a miss. A roll of all 6s is a direct hit unless you are rolling only one die, regardless of the attacker's MAT or the target's DEF. Sometimes a special rule causes an attack to hit automatically. Such automatic hits are also direct hits.

MELEE ATTACK MODIFIERS

The most common modifiers affecting a model's melee attack roll are summarized here for easy reference. Where necessary, additional detail can be found on the pages listed.

- *Back Strike* (p. 61): A back strike gains +2 to the attack roll.

- *Free Strike* (above): A free strike gains +2 to the attack roll and a boosted damage roll.

- *Intervening Terrain* (p. 45): A model with any portion of its volume obscured from its attacker by an obstacle or an obstruction gains +2 DEF against melee attack rolls.

- *Knocked Down Target* (p. 63): A melee attack against a knocked down model hits automatically.

- *Stationary Target* (p. 64): A melee attack against a stationary model hits automatically.

POWER ATTACKS

Power attacks are special attacks that can be made by some models. The power attacks available to non-warjack models are described in their special rules. Warjacks can make power attacks as indicated by the following list.

- All warjacks: head-butt, push, and slam

- Heavy warjacks: trample

- Warjacks with at least one non-crippled Open Fist 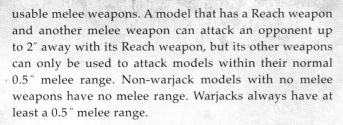: headlock/weapon lock and throw

- Warjacks with two non-crippled Open Fists 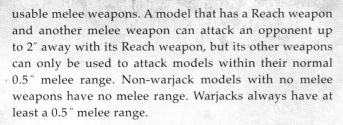: double-hand throw

A warjack must spend 1 focus point to make a power attack.

A model cannot make a power attack as its charge attack. Power attacks are melee attacks with a 0.5" melee range.

When a model makes a power attack, do not apply the special abilities on its weapons unless they specifically reference power attacks.

HEADLOCK/WEAPON LOCK

A model making a headlock/weapon lock can **lock** a warjack or warbeast's weapon or head and prevent its use. A warjack must have at least one non-crippled Open Fist to make a headlock/weapon lock power attack. Declare what the attacking model is attempting to lock before making the attack roll.

When a warjack makes a headlock/weapon lock, also declare which weapon with Open Fist it is using to make the attack before making a melee attack roll. A knocked down model cannot be locked. If the attack hits then the specified head/weapon is locked. Headlock/weapon lock attacks do not cause damage.

Maintaining Locks and Being Locked

When a weapon is locked the target model cannot make attacks with the locked weapon along with all other weapons in the same location. Locking a weapon with a location of "—" has no effect on other weapons. A model held in a headlock cannot make attacks with any weapons located in its head (H). A model held in a headlock / weapon lock cannot make special attacks.

While involved in a lock, the attacker cannot make special attacks or attack with the weapon with which it made the lock attempt, nor can it use any other weapon in the same location. The attacker and the defender are free to attack with any of their other melee weapons.

EXAMPLE: *Rob's Juggernaut successfully locks the head of Erik's Slayer with its Open Fist. The Slayer cannot make Tusk attacks or special attacks (including Combo Strikes or power attacks), and the Juggernaut cannot make attacks with its Open Fist until the headlock is broken or released.*

At the beginning of its combat action, a model suffering a headlock / weapon lock must attempt to break the lock. For each weapon lock and headlock, both models involved in the lock roll a d6 and add their STR. If the locked model's total exceeds that of the model holding the lock, the lock is broken. The locked warjack can make its initial attacks with any melee weapons not located in a locked system as normal. After resolving these attacks and attempts to break free, a warjack can spend focus points to make more attempts to break a lock or to make additional attacks with usable weapons, at 1 focus point per break attempt or additional attack. Once a lock is broken, the model can use the weapon that was locked. A model can voluntarily release a lock it is maintaining at any time during its activation.

Neither model can advance or be pushed while involved in a lock. A lock is broken automatically if:

- An effect causes either model to move or be placed;
- An effect knocks down either model;
- An effect causes either model to become incorporeal;
- An effect causes the attacker to become stationary;
- The weapon system maintaining the lock is crippled; or
- Either model is destroyed or removed from play.

HEAD-BUTT

A model making a **head-butt** power attack smashes its head into a model to drive it to the ground. The attacking model makes a melee attack roll against its target. If the attack hits, the target is knocked down and suffers a damage roll with a POW equal to the attacker's current STR.

A model cannot head-butt while held in a headlock. A model cannot head-butt a model with a larger base.

PUSH

A model making a **push** power attack uses its bulk and strength to shove another model. A push power attack automatically hits and deals no damage. Both models roll a d6 and add their STR. If the defender's total is greater, it resists being pushed. If the attacker's total equals or exceeds the defender's, the defending model is pushed 1″ directly away from the attacker.

After a model is pushed by a push power attack, the attacker can immediately advance directly toward the pushed model up to the distance the pushed model was moved.

Being Pushed

A pushed model moves at half rate through rough terrain, suffers the effects of any hazards it moves through, and stops if it contacts an obstacle, obstruction, or another model.

Remember that a pushed model is not advancing and therefore cannot be targeted by free strikes during this movement.

A pushed model falls off elevated terrain if it ends its push movement with less than 1″ of ground under its base. See "Falling" (p. 63) for detailed rules on determining damage from a fall.

SLAM

A model making a **slam** power attack rams a model with the full force of its body to send the target model flying backward and knock it to the ground. Any effects that prevent a model from charging, such as a penalty to its SPD or movement for any reason other than for being in rough terrain, also prevent the model from making a slam power attack. A slamming model can advance through rough terrain. A model must have both its normal movement and action available in order to use its normal movement to make a slam power attack.

During its activation, a model can attempt to slam any model that is in its line of sight at the beginning of its normal movement. A knocked down model cannot be moved by a slam.

Declare the slam attempt and its target before moving the model.

Declare the slam attempt and its target, then turn the slamming model to face the slam target directly. The slamming model then advances its full SPD plus 3″ directly toward its target. The slamming model cannot voluntarily stop its movement unless its target is in its melee range, but it can end this movement at any point with its slam target in its 0.5″ melee range. It must stop if it contacts a model, an obstacle, or an obstruction. The slamming model cannot change its facing during or after this movement.

A slamming model that ends its slam movement with its slam target in its 0.5″ melee range has made a **successful slam**. If it advanced at least 3″ it makes a melee attack roll against its target. A model that power attack slams a model with a larger base suffers –2 on its attack roll. If the attack hits, the target is slammed directly away from the attacker (see "Being Slammed," next).

If a slamming model makes a successful slam but moved less than 3″, it has not moved fast enough to get its full weight and power into the blow. The model makes an attack roll against its target. If the target is hit, it suffers a damage roll with a POW equal to the attacker's current STR but is not slammed. These are still slam attack rolls and slam damage rolls.

A model that does not end its slam movement within 0.5″ of the target has failed its slam power attack. If a model fails its slam power attack during its activation, its activation ends.

Being Slammed

A **slammed** model is moved d6″ directly away from its attacker and is then knocked down. If the slamming model has a smaller base than the slam target, the model is slammed half the distance rolled. It then suffers slam damage as described below. A slammed model moves at half rate through rough terrain, suffers any damaging effects through which it passes, and stops if it contacts an obstacle, an obstruction, or a model with an equal or larger-sized base. If a slammed model cannot be knocked down, it must still forfeit its action or movement if it activates later in a turn in which it was slammed.

A slammed model moves through models with smaller bases than its own. If it would end up on top of a model, follow the **rule of least disturbance** (p. 64) to move the models into legal positions.

A slammed model falls off elevated terrain if it ends its slam movement with less than 1″ of ground under its base.

See "Falling" (p. 63) for rules on determining damage from a fall. Resolve any falling damage simultaneously with slam damage.

Slam Damage

Apply **slam damage** after movement and knockdown effects, regardless of whether the model actually moves or is knocked down. The model hit suffers a damage roll with a POW equal to the attacker's current STR. Add an additional die to the damage roll if the slammed model contacts an obstacle, an obstruction, or a model with an equal or larger-sized base. Slam damage can be boosted.

Collateral Damage

If a slammed model contacts a model with an equal-sized base or moves through a model with a smaller base, that model is knocked down and suffers collateral damage. A model suffering **collateral damage** suffers a damage roll with a POW equal to the attacker's current STR. Collateral damage cannot be boosted. A contacted model with a larger base than the slammed model does not suffer collateral damage and is not knocked down. Resolve any collateral damage simultaneously with slam damage. Collateral damage is not considered to be damage from an attack or model. For example, an effect triggered by being "damaged by an enemy attack" would not trigger due to collateral damage.

THROW

A model making a **throw** power attack picks up and throws another model. A model cannot throw a model with a larger base. A warjack must have at least one non-crippled Open Fist to make a throw power attack.

SLAM MOVEMENT AND COLLATERAL DAMAGE

A Juggernaut declares a slam attack against a Crusader. Because it moved more than 3″ to make contact with the Crusader, the Juggernaut will be able to slam its target. The attack succeeds, and the Crusader is knocked back d6″. The roll comes up a 6, but the Crusader stops when it hits the wall 4″ behind it. During the slam, the Crusader passes over a Temple Flameguard, and the Flameguard suffers collateral damage. In addition, because the Crusader was slammed into a wall, it suffers a damage roll of 3d6 plus the STR of the Juggernaut (2d6 plus an extra die for colliding with a solid terrain feature). This damage roll can still be boosted on top of the additional die.

Juggernaut

Crusader

Flameguard

Wall

POWER ATTACK EFFECTS FROM OTHER SOURCES

A model can be pushed, slammed, or thrown as a result of a spell or an ability rather than from a power attack. The resolution of a push, slam, or throw caused by an effect might differ slightly from the resolution of one caused by a power attack. For example, a model slammed as a result of Lieutenant Caine's Thunder Strike spell suffers a POW 14 damage roll instead of suffering damage based on Caine's STR. When the Marauder Combo Smites a model, the POW of both of its weapons is added to the damage roll in addition to its STR.

The attacking model makes a melee attack roll against its target. If the attack hits, both models roll a d6 and add their current STR. If the target's total is greater, it breaks free without taking any damage and avoids being thrown. If the attacker's total equals or exceeds the target's, the target model is thrown.

Being Thrown

When your model throws another, choose a direction for the thrown model to be moved. This direction must be away from the attacker. Measure a distance from the target equal to half the attacker's current STR in inches along the chosen direction to a point on the table. This point is the thrown model's intended point of impact. A large-based model throwing a small-based model adds 1″ to this distance.

From this point, determine the thrown model's actual point of impact by rolling for deviation. Referencing the deviation rules (pp. 59-60), roll a d6 for direction and a d3 for distance in inches. The deviation distance cannot exceed half the distance between the thrown model and the intended point of impact.

The **thrown** model is moved directly from its current location in a straight line to the determined point of impact. A thrown model moves through models with smaller bases during this movement without contacting them. Unlike when a model is slammed, rough terrain and obstacles do not affect this movement, but the thrown model still stops if it contacts an obstruction or a model with an equal or larger-sized base. The thrown model is then knocked down and suffers throw damage. If a thrown model cannot be knocked down it must still forfeit its action or movement if it activates later in a turn in which it was thrown.

If a thrown model would end on top of another model, that model is contacted. Follow the rule of least disturbance (p. 64) to move the models into legal positions.

A thrown model falls off elevated terrain if it ends its throw movement with less than 1″ of ground under its base. See "Falling" (p. 63) for rules on determining damage from a fall. Resolve any falling damage simultaneously with throw damage.

Throw Damage

Apply throw damage after movement and knockdown effects, regardless of whether the model actually moves or is knocked down. The thrown model suffers a damage roll with a POW equal to the attacker's current STR. Add an additional die to the damage roll if the thrown model

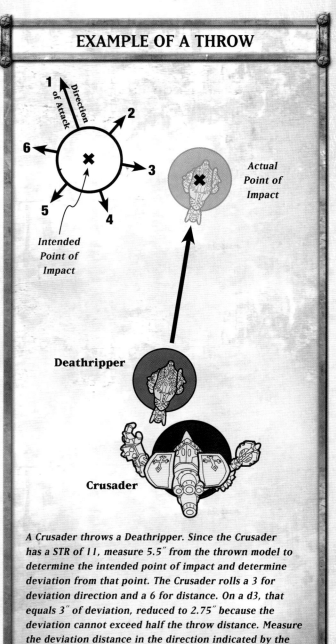

EXAMPLE OF A THROW

Direction of Attack

1
2
6
3
5
4

Intended Point of Impact

Actual Point of Impact

Deathripper

Crusader

A Crusader throws a Deathripper. Since the Crusader has a STR of 11, measure 5.5″ from the thrown model to determine the intended point of impact and determine deviation from that point. The Crusader rolls a 3 for deviation direction and a 6 for distance. On a d3, that equals 3″ of deviation, reduced to 2.75″ because the deviation cannot exceed half the throw distance. Measure the deviation distance in the direction indicated by the deviation diagram to determine the actual point of impact. The Deathripper moves from its current position directly toward the point of impact.

contacts an obstruction or a model with an equal or larger-sized base. Throw damage can be boosted.

Collateral Damage

If a thrown model contacts a model with an equal or smaller-sized base, that model is knocked down and suffers collateral damage. A model suffering collateral damage suffers a damage roll with a POW equal to the attacker's current STR. Collateral damage cannot be boosted. A contacted model with a larger base than the thrown model does not suffer collateral damage. Resolve any collateral damage simultaneously with throw damage. Collateral damage is not considered to be damage from an attack or model. For example, an effect triggered by being "damaged by an enemy attack" would not trigger due to collateral damage.

DOUBLE-HAND THROW

A model making a **double-hand throw** power attack uses both its arms to pick up and throw another model. A model cannot throw a model with a larger base. A warjack must have two non-crippled Open Fists to make a double-hand throw power attack.

The attacking model makes a melee attack roll against its target. If the attack hits, the target rolls a d6 and adds its current STR. The attacker rolls 2d6 and adds its current STR. If the target's total is greater, it breaks free without taking any damage and avoids being thrown. If the attacker's total equals or exceeds the target's, the target model gets thrown.

To determine the direction of the double-hand throw, the attacker can either follow the steps for determining the direction of a regular throw (see "Being Thrown," previous) or simply throw the model at another model within the attacker's line of sight. Ignore the model being thrown when determining line of sight to the other model. The throw distance is equal to half the attacker's current STR in inches. A large-based model throwing a small-based model adds 1" to this distance. If the other model is within range, the attacker makes a melee attack roll against it. If it is outside this range, resolve the throw using the rules in "Being Thrown" as if the thrown model were thrown directly toward the other model. On a hit, move the thrown model from its current location directly toward the other model's base until it contacts the target. This throw does not deviate. A double-hand throw at another model is not an attack against that model.

If the attack roll misses, determine the thrown model's point of impact by rolling deviation from the center of the other model's base. Referencing the deviation rules (pp. 59–60), roll a d6 for direction and a d3 for distance in inches.

If the other model is beyond the throw distance, determine deviation from a point on the line to it equal to the throw distance. The thrown model moves directly from its current location in a straight line to the determined point of impact.

A thrown model moves over models with smaller bases during this movement without contacting them. Unlike when a model is slammed, rough terrain and obstacles do not affect this movement, but the thrown model still stops if it contacts an obstruction or a model with an equal or larger-sized base. The thrown model is then knocked down. If a thrown model cannot be knocked down it must still forfeit its action or movement if it activates later in a turn in which it was thrown.

If a thrown model would end on top of a model, that model is contacted. Follow the rule of least disturbance (p. 64) to move the models into legal positions.

A thrown model falls off elevated terrain if it ends its throw movement with less than 1" of ground under its base. See "Falling" (p. 63) for rules on determining damage from a fall. Resolve any falling damage simultaneously with throw damage.

Resolve damage resulting from a double-hand throw using the "Throw Power Attack," "Throw Damage," and "Collateral Damage" rules above.

TRAMPLE

A model making a **trample** power attack crashes its way through small-based models in its path. Any effects that prevent a model from charging, such as a penalty to its SPD or movement for any reason other than for being in rough terrain, also prevent the model from making a trample power attack. A trampling model can advance through rough terrain. A model must have both its normal movement and action available in order to use its normal movement to make a trample power attack. Light warjacks cannot make trample power attacks.

Declare a trample power attack at the beginning of the model's normal movement. Choose a direction in which you wish to trample, and turn the model to face that direction. The model then advances up to its current SPD plus 3˝ in a straight line in that direction. It moves through any small-based model in its path, but there must be room for the trampling model's base at the end of the movement. It stops if it contacts a model with a medium or larger base, an obstacle, or an obstruction. The trampling model cannot change its facing during or after this movement. Do not resolve free strikes against the trampling model during this movement.

After the model has finished its trample movement, it makes a melee attack roll against each small-based model it contacted. Models hit by a trample attack roll suffer a damage roll with a POW equal to the current STR of the trampling model. Trample damage can be boosted.

Resolve free strikes against the trampling model after resolving all trample attacks. Models contacted cannot make free strikes against the trampling model. Ignore the distance between models when resolving free strikes against the trampling model; if a model was eligible to make a free strike against the trampling model during the trampling model's movement it can do so whether or not the trampling model ended its movement in the eligible model's melee range.

RANGED COMBAT

Some would argue there is no honor in defeating an enemy without being close enough to look him in the eyes. When a soul-burning helljack with two fists full of iron-shredding claws bears down on you faster than a charging destrier, however, it is a good plan to keep your distance and consider your ranged attack options.

A model using its combat action for **ranged attacks** makes one initial attack with each of its ranged weapons. Some models have special rules that allow additional ranged attacks during their activations. For example, warcasters and warjacks can spend focus points to make additional ranged attacks during their activations. Each additional attack can be made with any ranged weapon the model possesses, but a ranged weapon can never make more attacks in a single activation than its rate of fire (ROF).

A ranged attack can be declared against any target in its line of sight, subject to the targeting rules. A model making more than one ranged attack can divide its attacks among any eligible targets. A model in melee cannot make ranged attacks.

Some spells and special rules allow certain models to make magic attacks. Magic attacks are similar to ranged attacks and follow most of the same rules, but they are not affected by rules that affect only ranged attacks. See "Offensive Spells and Magic Attacks" (p. 77) for details on magic attacks.

RANGED WEAPONS

Ranged weapons include bows, rifles, flamethrowers, crossbows, harpoon guns, and mortars.

Ranged Weapon Damage Roll = 2d6 + POW

DECLARING A TARGET

A ranged attack can target any model in the attacker's line of sight (see "Line of Sight," p. 43), subject to the targeting rules. A ranged attack cannot target open ground or a permanent terrain feature. Some terrain features and objects can be targeted, but they will say so in their individual rules. A ranged attack need not target the nearest enemy model, but intervening models can prevent a model farther away from being targeted.

The attack must be declared before measuring the range to the intended target. Unless a model's special rules say otherwise, it can make ranged attacks only against models in its front arc.

MEASURING RANGE

A ranged attack must be declared against a legal target before measuring range. After declaring the attack, measure to see if the target is within the Range (RNG) of the attack. Measure range from the edge of the point of origin's base to the target up to the maximum range of the attack. If the nearest edge of the target model's base is within the maximum range of the attack, the target is in range. If the target is in range, make a ranged attack roll. If the target is beyond range, the attack automatically misses. If a ranged attack has an area of effect (AOE) and the target is out of range, the attack automatically misses, and its point of impact will deviate from the point on the line to its declared target at a distance equal to its RNG. See "Area-of-Effect (AOE) Attacks" (pp. 58–59) for details on these attacks and deviation.

RATE OF FIRE

A weapon's **rate of fire (ROF)** indicates the maximum number of ranged attacks it can make in an activation. Reloading time prevents most ranged weapons from being used more than once per activation. Some ranged weapons reload faster and can make multiple attacks if a model is able to make additional attacks. A ranged weapon cannot make more attacks per activation than its ROF, though, regardless of the number of additional attacks a model is entitled to make. Ranged attacks made outside of a model's activation are not limited by ROF.

RANGED ATTACK ROLLS

Determine a ranged attack's success by making a ranged attack roll. Roll 2d6 and add the attacking model's Ranged Attack (RAT). A boosted attack roll adds an additional die to this roll. Special rules and certain circumstances might modify the attack roll as well.

Ranged Attack Roll = 2d6 + RAT

A target is directly hit by an attack if the attack roll equals or exceeds the target's Defense (DEF). If the attack roll is less than the target's DEF, the attack misses. A roll of all 1s on the dice is a miss. A roll of all 6s is a direct hit unless you are rolling only one die, regardless of the attacker's RAT or its target's DEF.

Sometimes a special rule causes an attack to hit automatically. Such automatic hits are also direct hits.

RANGED ATTACK ROLL MODIFIERS

The most common modifiers affecting a model's ranged attack roll are summarized here for easy reference. Where necessary, additional detail can be found on the pages listed.

- *Aiming Bonus:* A model can forfeit its movement to gain an aiming bonus. The aiming bonus adds +2 to every ranged attack roll the model makes that activation. This bonus does not apply to magic attack rolls.

- *Back Strike* (p. 61): A back strike gains +2 to the attack roll.

- *Cloud Effect* (p. 69): A model inside a cloud effect gains concealment.

- *Concealment* (below): A model with concealment in relation to its attacker gains +2 DEF against ranged and magic attack rolls.

- *Cover* (next page): A model with cover in relation to its attacker gains +4 DEF against ranged and magic attack rolls.

- *Elevated Target:* If the target is on terrain at least 1″ higher than the attacker, it is an elevated target. When drawing line of sight to an elevated target, ignore intervening models on terrain at least 1″ lower than the target. An elevated target gains +2 DEF against ranged and magic attack rolls.

- *Elevated Attacker:* If the attacker is on terrain at least 1″ higher than the target, it is an elevated attacker. When drawing line of sight from an elevated attacker, ignore intervening models on terrain at least 1″ lower than the attacker unless they are within 1″ of the target. Additionally, ignore intervening models within 1″ of the target that are on terrain at least 1″ lower than the attacker and have equal or smaller-sized bases than the attacker.

- *Knocked Down Target* (p. 63): While knocked down, a model has its base DEF reduced to 5.

- *Stationary Target* (p. 64): While stationary, a model has its base DEF reduced to 5.

- *Target in Melee* (p. 58): A ranged or magic attack roll against a target in melee suffers a –4 penalty.

CONCEALMENT AND COVER

Terrain features, spells, and other effects can make it more difficult to hit a model with a ranged or magic attack. A model within 1″ of a terrain feature that obscures any portion of its base from an attacker can gain either a concealment or cover bonus, depending on the type of terrain, to its DEF against ranged and magic attacks. Concealment and cover bonuses are not cumulative with themselves or each other, but they are cumulative with other effects that modify a model's DEF. See "Terrain" (pp. 86–89) for details on terrain features and how they provide concealment or cover.

Some terrain features and special effects grant a model **concealment** by making it more difficult to be seen, but they are not actually dense enough to block an attack. Examples include low hedges or bushes. A model within 1″ of a concealing terrain feature that obscures any portion of its volume (p. 43) from an attacker gains +2 DEF against ranged and magic attack rolls. Concealment provides no benefit against spray attacks.

Cover: +4 DEF

Cover: +4 DEF

Cover: +4 DEF

Concealment: +2 DEF

Examples of Concealment and Cover

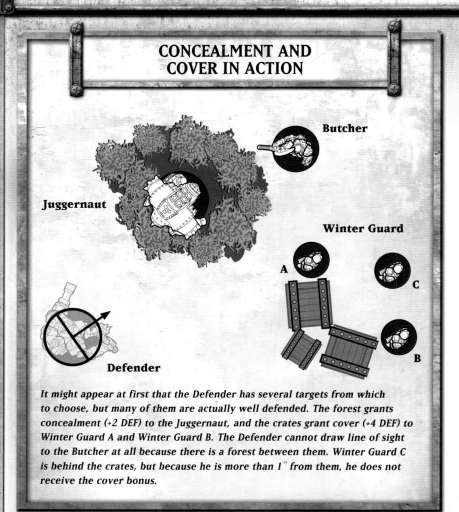

CONCEALMENT AND COVER IN ACTION

Butcher

Juggernaut

Winter Guard

A

C

B

Defender

It might appear at first that the Defender has several targets from which to choose, but many of them are actually well defended. The forest grants concealment (+2 DEF) to the Juggernaut, and the crates grant cover (+4 DEF) to Winter Guard A and Winter Guard B. The Defender cannot draw line of sight to the Butcher at all because there is a forest between them. Winter Guard C is behind the crates, but because he is more than 1″ from them, he does not receive the cover bonus.

When determining the attack's new target, the only models considered to be in the same combat are those in melee with the attack's original target and any models in melee with them. Any model meeting these criteria can become the new target. However, a model cannot become the new target if a special rule or effect prohibits it from being targeted by the attack or if the attacker's line of sight is completely blocked by obstructing terrain. Ignore intervening models when determining a new target. If multiple models in the combat are eligible targets, randomly determine which model becomes the new target (excluding the original target).

EXAMPLE: *Using a d6, if there are three other models in the combat, the first model will become the new target on a 1 or 2, the second on a 3 or 4, and the third on a 5 or 6. If the attacker cannot draw line of sight to one of those models due to an obstruction (e.g., it's around the corner of a building), ignore that model and randomize the attack between the other two: it targets the first on a 1, 2, or 3 or the second on a 4, 5, or 6. If one of those two models cannot be targeted for some reason, only one model is an eligible target and thus a random roll is not necessary.*

Other terrain features and special effects grant a model **cover** by being physically solid enough to block an attack against it. Examples include stone walls, giant boulders, and buildings. A model within 1″ of a covering terrain feature that obscures any portion of its base from an attacker gains +4 DEF against ranged and magic attack rolls. Cover provides no benefit against spray attacks.

TARGETING A MODEL IN MELEE

A model making a ranged or magic attack roll against a target in melee risks hitting another model participating in the combat, including friendly models. The standard targeting rules, including line of sight, still apply when targeting a model that is in melee.

In addition to any other attack modifiers, a ranged attack roll against a target in melee suffers a –4 penalty.

If the attack against the intended target misses and the target was in range, it might hit another combatant. If the target was not in range, the attack misses automatically and will not potentially hit another combatant.

If the target was in range, the attacker must immediately reroll his attack against another model in that combat.

If the attack against the new target misses, it misses completely without targeting any more models.

EXAMPLE: *Stryker is in melee with a Revenger affected by the Protection of Menoth spell. A Charger forfeits its movement, aims, targets the Revenger with its dual cannon, and spends 1 focus point to boost its attack roll. The Charger's attack roll gains an additional die for boosting the attack roll, gets +2 to the roll for the aiming bonus, and suffers the –4 penalty for targeting a model in melee. In addition, the Revenger's DEF against this attack is enhanced due to the spell affecting it.*

If the attack misses, the Charger rerolls the attack, this time targeting Stryker. It still includes the additional die for boosting the attack roll, the +2 aiming bonus, and the –4 penalty for targeting a model in melee. If Stryker is behind cover in relation to the Charger, he gains +4 DEF against this attack.

An area-of-effect attack that misses a target in melee deviates normally instead of following these rules. Spray attack rolls that miss a model in melee do not follow these rules; they simply miss.

AREA-OF-EFFECT (AOE) ATTACKS

An attack with an area of effect is sometimes referred to as an **AOE attack**. A ranged attack with an AOE is a ranged attack. A magic attack with an AOE is a magic attack. A

TARGETING INTO MELEE EXAMPLE

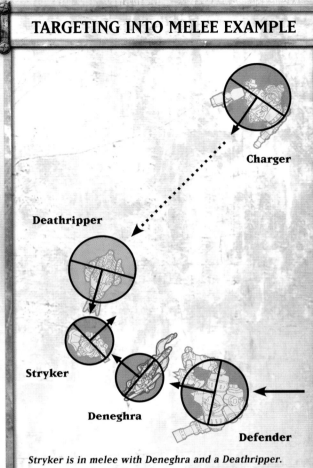

Charger

Deathripper

Stryker

Deneghra

Defender

Stryker is in melee with Deneghra and a Deathripper. A Defender enters the fight from the side to engage Deneghra but not the Deathripper. A Charger makes a ranged attack against the Deathripper and misses. Since Stryker is in melee with the Deathripper and Deneghra is in melee with Stryker, they are both in the same combat as the intended target. The Defender is not included because it is not in melee with the intended target (the Deathripper) or with another model in melee with the intended target (Stryker). It is far enough from the intended target not to be attacked accidentally.

A random die roll determines Deneghra is the new target. Unfortunately, since the Charger is more than 5″ away from Deneghra, her Stealth ⊕ ability makes the attack automatically miss without even rolling. Even though Stealth prevents Deneghra from being hit, she can still be targeted. Since the attack missed both its intended target and the new target, it misses completely with no further chance of hitting Stryker or the Defender.

melee attack with an AOE is a melee attack. An area-of-effect attack, such as from an explosive spell or a gas cloud, hits every model in an area centered on its point of impact. The attack covers an area with a diameter equal to its area of effect (AOE). Templates for AOEs appear on p. 255.

An AOE attack follows all normal targeting rules. A successful attack roll indicates a **direct hit** on the intended

target, which suffers a direct hit damage roll of 2d6 + POW. Center the AOE template over the point of impact—in the case of a direct hit, the center of the targeted model's base. Every other model with any part of its base covered by the AOE template is hit, but not directly hit, by the attack and suffers a **blast damage** roll of 2d6 + 1/2 POW. Make separate damage rolls against each model in the AOE; each roll must be boosted individually.

Blast Damage Roll = 2d6 + 1/2 POW

AOE attacks are simultaneous attacks (p. 244).

An AOE attack that misses its target deviates a random direction and distance. An AOE attack declared against a target beyond its range (RNG) automatically misses, and its point of impact deviates from the point on the line from the attack's point of origin to its declared target at a distance equal to its RNG away from the attack's point of origin. An AOE attack that misses a target in range deviates from the center of its intended target.

DAMAGE POINT OF ORIGIN

An AOE attack's point of impact determines the origin of damage and effects for models not directly hit by the attack. For instance, suppose an AOE ranged attack targets a trooper in a unit that has used the Shield Wall order. If the attack hits, the target trooper will benefit from the Shield Wall if the attacker is in the trooper's front arc, as will other troopers that have the target trooper in their front arc; troopers that do not have the target trooper in their front arc will not benefit from Shield Wall, though, as the damage is originating in their back arc. Should the attack miss and deviate long, into the target trooper's back arc, the target trooper would not benefit from being in the shield wall either. See p. 64 for more information on point of origin and origin of damage.

DEVIATION

When an AOE attack misses its target, determine its actual point of impact by rolling **deviation**. Referencing the deviation template (p. 255), roll a d6 to determine the direction the attack deviates. For example, a roll of 1 means the attack goes long and a roll of 4 means the attack lands short. Then roll another d6 to determine the deviation distance in inches. Determine the missed attack's actual point of impact by measuring the rolled distance from the original point of impact in the direction determined by the deviation roll. If the deviated point of impact would be off the table, reduce the deviation distance so the point of impact is on the edge of the table instead. If the intended target is beyond the weapon's RNG, determine deviation from the point on the line from the attack's point of origin to its declared target at a distance equal to its RNG.

DEVIATION EXAMPLE

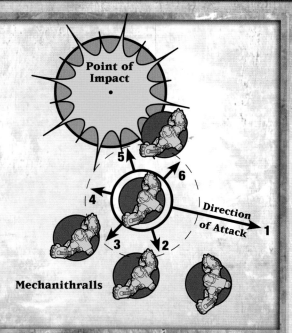

Redeemer

Point of Impact

Direction of Attack

Mechanithralls

A Redeemer makes a ranged attack with its Skyhammer rocket targeting the Mechanithrall in the middle of the unit 11˝ away. If the target is hit, the Skyhammer will catch four Mechanithralls under the template! The Redeemer's ranged attack roll misses, however, and since the attack is an AOE attack, the Redeemer's controller must roll deviation to determine the attack's point of impact. The roll is a 5 for direction and a 4 for 4˝ of deviation. Measure this distance in the deviation direction from the center of its original target to locate the point of impact. Models under the template suffer blast damage and are subject to the attack's special effects. The Redeemer does not hit as many Mechanithralls as it wanted, but it still catches one under the template.

If the target is within range of the attack, the point of impact will not deviate more than half the distance from the attack's point of origin to its intended target. If the target is not within range of the attack, the point of impact will not deviate more than half the RNG of the attack. Use the exact value for this maximum; do not round it. For instance, an attack made at a target 5˝ away from the attack's point of origin will deviate a maximum of 2.5˝ even if the attacker rolls a 3, 4, 5, or 6 for deviation distance.

Terrain features, models, or other effects do not block deviating AOE attacks. They always take effect at the determined point of impact.

Center the AOE template over the point of impact. Every model with any part of its base covered by the AOE template is hit, but not directly hit, by the attack and takes a blast damage roll. Deviating AOE attacks never cause direct hits even if the point of impact is on top of a model.

SPRAY ATTACKS

An attack using the spray template is sometimes referred to as a **spray attack**. Some weapons and spells, such as flamethrowers and Deneghra's Venom spell, make spray attacks. This devastating short-ranged attack can potentially hit several models. A spray uses the spray template and will have a RNG of "SP 6," "SP 8," or "SP 10." Effects that modify RNG do not affect spray attacks. The spray template appears on p. 256.

When making a spray attack, center the spray template laterally over an eligible target with the narrow end of the template touching the nearest edge of the point of origin's base. The target itself need not be under the template. The targeting rules apply when choosing the attack's primary target. Every model with any part of its base covered by the appropriate section of the spray template can be hit by the attack.

Make separate attack rolls against each model under the template. Remember that each roll must be boosted individually. Spray attacks ignore concealment, cover, Stealth, and intervening models because the attack comes over, around, or in some cases through its protection.

A spray ranged or magic attack roll against a model in melee does not suffer a –4 penalty and a spray attack roll against a model in melee that misses is not rerolled against another model. It misses completely.

A model under the spray template cannot be hit by the attack if the attacker's line of sight to it is completely blocked by terrain.

Every model hit by a spray attack suffers a direct hit. Make separate damage rolls against each model hit. A spray attack is a simultaneous attack.

SPECIAL COMBAT SITUATIONS

The chaos of a battlefield is constantly producing the unexpected. Although situations can arise as a result of unique circumstances or a model's special rules, the rules in this section should enable a smooth resolution. Savvy players will use these rules to their best advantage.

ATTACK-GENERATING ABILITIES

When a model is granted more attacks as a result of an attack it made, it gains only one. If two or more abilities

EXAMPLES OF SPRAY ATTACKS

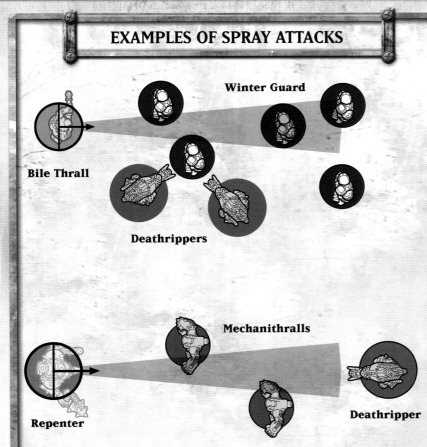

A Bile Thrall makes a spray attack against a group of Winter Guard. The Cryx player centers the SP 8 spray template laterally over an eligible target, choosing the centermost Winter Guard. Targeting that trooper also lets the player cover the greatest number of Winter Guard without covering his own nearby Deathrippers. He makes a ranged attack roll against each of the four Winter Guard in the spray. If an attack roll against the Winter Guard in melee with the Deathrippers misses, it will not hit one of the Deathrippers.

A pair of Mechanithralls has advanced to within range of a Repenter's Flame Thrower. The Cryx player has been careful to place them far enough apart so a spray attack targeted against either one of them will not catch the other under the template. Unfortunately he has not taken the Deathripper behind them into account. The Repenter has line of sight to the Deathripper and therefore can target it with its Flame Thrower even though it is out of range. Doing this will cover both Mechanithralls with the spray template.

would grant the model another attack as a result of making an attack, its controlling player chooses which ability to apply. The attack is then resolved using the rules for that ability. These attacks can, in turn, earn more attacks of their own.

For example, Terminus casts Ravager on a Slayer in his battlegroup. The Slayer then destroys a model in a unit affected by Epic Skarre's Black Spot spell with a melee attack. Both Ravager and Black Spot grant the Slayer an additional attack, but the Slayer can gain only one of the two. The Slayer's controller chooses to make the attack granted by Ravager and resolves the attack according to Ravager's rules. If that granted attack destroys another model in the same unit, the Slayer's controller will again choose which ability will grant another attack.

ATTACKS THAT HIT OR MISS AUTOMATICALLY

Some special rules cause attacks to hit automatically or miss automatically. If a special rule causes an attack to **hit automatically**, you do not have to make an attack roll. If you do make a roll (because you want to try for a critical hit,

for example), the attack no longer hits automatically. If the attack roll fails, the attack misses.

If a special rule will cause an attack to **miss automatically**, do not make an attack roll. The attack just misses.

If one rule causes an attack to hit automatically and one causes it to miss automatically, the automatic hit takes precedence over the automatic miss. For instance, an effect that allows attacks to hit automatically would override special rules such as Stealth that would otherwise cause an attack to miss automatically.

BACK STRIKES

A **back strike** grants a +2 bonus to the attack roll of any melee, ranged, or magic attack made against a model from its back arc. For a model to receive the back strike bonus, the point of origin of the attack must have been in the target's back arc for the attacker's entire activation up to the moment of the attack. If the attack's point of origin was in the target's front arc at any time during the attacking model's activation, the attacker does not receive this bonus. A model receives a back strike bonus only during its activation.

MAKING A BACK STRIKE

Cannot Make a Back Strike

Can Make a Back Strike

Back Arc   Front Arc

COMBINED MELEE ATTACKS

During their unit's activation, two or more troopers with this ability with the same target in their melee range can combine their melee attacks against that target. In order to participate in a combined melee attack, a trooper must be able to declare a melee attack against the intended target. Choose one model in the attacking group to be the primary attacker and make one melee attack roll for the group. Add +1 to the attack and damage rolls for each model participating in the attack, including the primary attacker. All other bonuses and penalties to the attack and damage rolls, such as the bonus for intervening terrain, are based on the primary attacker.

**Each model in a combined melee attack =
+1 to the attack and damage rolls**

In a combined melee attack, only the primary attacker actually makes an attack. The other participants lose their attacks, contributing them to create the combined attack. A model that charged during its activation can participate in a combined melee attack, but the combined attack cannot be a charge attack unless all contributed attacks are charge attacks. If any non-charge attack is contributed, the combined attack is not a charge attack.

A unit's melee attacks can be grouped in any manner, including multiple combined melee attacks. Troopers capable of multiple melee attacks can divide them among eligible targets and participate in multiple combined melee attacks. Units with Combined Melee Attack ignore the rule that one trooper's combat action cannot begin until the previous model's combat action ends.

EXAMPLE: *Four members of a Protectorate Temple Flameguard unit make a combined melee attack against a Cygnar Defender. One model is chosen to make the melee attack for the group, adding +4 to his attack and damage rolls since there are four models participating in the attack. Two other troopers in the same Flameguard unit make a combined melee attack against a nearby Sentinel. The trooper declared as the primary attacker makes one melee attack and adds +2 to his attack and damage rolls.*

COMBINED RANGED ATTACKS

During their unit's activation, two or more troopers with this ability can combine their ranged attacks against the same target. In order to participate in a **combined ranged attack**, a trooper must be able to declare a ranged attack against the intended target and be in formation. Choose one model in the attacking group to be the primary attacker and make one ranged attack roll for the group. Add +1 to the attack and damage rolls for each model participating in the attack, including the primary attacker. All bonuses and penalties for the attack are based on the primary attacker.

**Each model in a combined ranged attack =
+1 to the attack and damage rolls**

Combined ranged attacks cannot target a model in melee.

In a combined ranged attack, only the primary attacker actually makes an attack. The other participants lose their attacks, contributing them to create the combined attack. After declaring all participants, check each one to see if a ranged attack made on its own would have automatically missed due to lack of range or a special rule. Models that would have automatically missed do not contribute to the attack and damage roll bonus but still forfeit their attacks. If the primary attacker would have automatically missed, the combined attack automatically misses. For example, models found to be more than 5″ away from a target with the Stealth ability do not contribute to the combined attack, and the entire combined attack automatically misses if the primary attacker is more than 5″ away from the target.

A unit's ranged attacks can be grouped in any manner, including as multiple combined ranged attacks. Troopers capable of multiple ranged attacks can divide them among eligible targets and participate in multiple combined ranged attacks. Units with Combined Ranged Attack ignore the rule that one trooper's combat action cannot begin until the previous model's combat action ends.

EXAMPLE: *Four members of a Cygnar Long Gunner unit that are in formation declare a combined ranged attack against a Khador Juggernaut. When measuring range, the player discovers one trooper is out of range. That model's participation in the attack will not add to the attack or damage roll, though it still forfeits its attack. The model chosen to make the ranged attack for the group gains only +3 to its attack and damage rolls since only three of the four models participating in the attack contribute to it.*

GUNFIGHTER ⏣

A model with the Gunfighter advantage has a melee range of 0.5″ and can make ranged attacks targeting models in its melee range. This model does not get an aiming bonus when targeting a model in its melee range but can forfeit its movement to use other special abilities. A ranged attack roll does not suffer the target in melee attack roll penalty when the attacker is in melee with the target. However, if such an attack misses and there are multiple models in the combat, the attack can still hit another random model in the combat, excluding the attacker and the original target. Resolve these situations following the rules in "Targeting a Model in Melee" on p. 58.

A model with the Gunfighter advantage can make charges. If it makes a charge, the model can make its initial attacks with its ranged weapons; if its first attack is made with a ranged weapon, however, that attack is not a charge attack. A model with Gunfighter can make free strikes with its ranged weapons.

Remember that Gunfighter does not allow this model to make melee and ranged attacks during the same activation.

MODEL DESTRUCTION AND TOKENS

Special rules cause some models to gain certain types of tokens when a model is destroyed. A model generates only one of each type of token when destroyed. If multiple models are eligible to gain a specific token, the nearest eligible model gets the token. If a model has a limit on how many of a specific token it can have and is at that limit, it is not considered an eligible model.

FALLING

A model that is slammed, thrown, pushed, or that otherwise moves off of an elevated surface to another surface at least 1 full inch lower falls. A **falling** model is knocked down and suffers a damage roll. A fall of up to 3″ causes a POW 10 damage roll. Add an additional die to the damage roll for every additional increment of 3″ the model falls, rounded up.

Fall Damage Roll = 2d6 + 10 + d6 for every 3″ of the fall after the first

EXAMPLE: *A model falling 3″ suffers a damage roll of 2d6 + 10. One falling 5″ suffers a damage roll of 3d6 + 10, and one falling 7″ suffers a damage roll of 4d6 + 10!*

If a falling model lands on top of another model, follow the rule of least disturbance (p. 64) to move the non-falling model into a legal position.

If a falling model contacts a model with an equal or smaller-sized base, the contacted model is knocked down and suffers the same damage roll as the falling model. A contacted model with a larger base than the falling model, however, does not suffer damage and is not knocked down. All damage resulting from the fall is simultaneous.

KNOCKDOWN

Some attacks and special rules cause a model to be **knocked down**. While knocked down a model cannot move, make actions, make attacks, cast spells, use animi, use feats, be used to channel a spell, or give orders and does not have a melee range. A knocked down model does not engage other models and cannot be engaged by them. As a consequence, a model is never in melee with a knocked down model. A melee attack roll against a knocked down model automatically hits. A knocked down model has a base DEF of 5. A knocked down model does not block line of sight and is never an intervening model. A knocked down model cannot be locked or moved by a slam.

A knocked down model can stand up at the start of its next activation unless it was knocked down during its controller's turn; in that case it cannot stand up until its controller's *next* turn even if it has not yet activated this turn. A model cannot become knocked down while it is knocked down. For example, if a model is knocked down during your opponent's turn and before it gets a chance to stand up is affected by an effect that would ordinarily cause it to be knocked down on your turn, it is not affected by the second instance of knockdown and can still stand up on your turn.

To stand up, a model must forfeit either its movement or its action for that activation. A model that forfeits its movement to stand can make an action, but it cannot make attacks involving movement such as a slam. A model that forfeits its action to stand can use its normal movement to make a full advance but not to run or charge. When a model stands, it ceases to be knocked down. Some special rules allow a model to stand up. In that case, the model may stand up even if it was knocked down during the current player's turn

BEYOND THE PLAY AREA

If an effect would cause a model to move or be placed beyond the table edge (such as being thrown or slammed), the model stops at the table edge and remains in play. The table edge does not count as an obstacle; models do not take additional damage for stopping there.

POINT OF ORIGIN

The **point of origin** of an effect or attack is the location or model from which the attack or effect originates. Typically this is the model causing the effect or making the attack, but not always. For example, when a warcaster channels a spell through an arc node, the arc node is the point of origin of the spell even though the warcaster is the model casting the spell. For attacks or effects that require line of sight to the target model, both line of sight and any attack roll modifiers that depend on line of sight (such as concealment) are checked from the point of origin of the attack. Range is also checked from the point of origin, including the placement of spray templates. Ignore the target in melee attack roll penalty when the point of origin of the magic attack is in melee with the model against which the attack roll is being made.

For most attacks, the **origin of damage** will be the same as the point of origin of the attack. The origin of damage for a *direct hit* with an AOE attack is the attack's point of origin, but the origin of damage for *any other* damage caused by an AOE attack is the point of impact.

Finally, some non-AOE attacks, such as Ashes to Ashes and Chain Lightning, have special rules that allow them to damage models besides the attack's target. The origin of

damage in those cases is the model or point from which you measure the range to other affected models. For example, the origin of damage for the target of Ashes to Ashes is the spell's origin, but the origin of damage for the other models affected by the spell is the target model. Similarly, when the lightning generated by Chain Lightning arcs to another model, the immediately previous model struck by the lightning is the origin of that damage.

REPLACING MODELS

When **replacing** one model with another, place the new model so the area covered by the smaller of their bases is completely within the area covered by the larger. If the two bases are the same size, place the new model in the same location as the one being replaced. There must be room for the model's base in the location the model is placed. The player choosing the placed model's new location chooses its facing.

ENTERING

A model **enters** an area when its position in play changes such that its previous position was not within the area and its new position is within the area, or when it is put into play in the area. A model can suffer the effects of entering any particular area only once each time it advances.

STATIONARY MODELS

A **stationary model** cannot activate. A stationary model does not have a melee range. A stationary model does not engage other models nor can other models engage a stationary model. A model is never in melee with a stationary model. A stationary model cannot advance, make actions, make attacks, cast spells, use animi, use feats, or give orders.

A melee attack roll against a stationary model automatically hits. A stationary model has a base DEF of 5.

LEAST DISTURBANCE

Some rules can cause moving models to overlap the bases of other models temporarily, such as when a model is thrown or slammed. Once the model has stopped moving, models must be repositioned so that there are no longer any overlapping bases. The model that was moving stays in its final position; other models are moved out of the way to make room.

To determine which models to move and where to move them, first identify the fewest models that would need to be moved to make room. Then find the locations to move them that create the least *total* distance moved. If there are multiple options that yield the least distance—if one model is centered over another, for example—randomly determine the option to use. A model's facing does not change if it moved as a result of this rule.

FORFEITING

Some rules require a model to forfeit its activation, movement, or action, or allow it to do so voluntarily for some benefit.

A model cannot voluntarily forfeit something if it is also required to forfeit it. A model cannot forfeit the same thing to multiple effects. For example, a model that is knocked down cannot forfeit its movement to stand up and also gain an aiming bonus for forfeiting that movement.

A model can forfeit its activation only before it activates in a turn. If it does so, resolve the effect to which the activation is being forfeited, then the model ends its activation, triggering any relevant effects. A model cannot forfeit its activation if it cannot activate. A model cannot forfeit its activation unless it is required to do so or has a rule that allows it to do so. Forfeiting a model's activation does not trigger effects that take place at the end of movement and those that take place at the end of an action.

A model can forfeit its movement anytime before it moves. When a model forfeits its movement, resolve the effect to which the movement is being forfeited, then the model ends its movement, triggering any relevant effects. A model cannot forfeit its movement if it cannot move or does not have a movement available.

A model can forfeit its action anytime before it takes an action. When a model forfeits its action, resolve the effect to which the action is being forfeited, then the model ends its action, triggering any relevant effects. A model cannot forfeit its action if it cannot take an action or does not have an action.

REROLLS

Some models have special abilities that enable them to reroll attack or damage rolls or that cause another model to reroll its attack or damage rolls. These rerolls occur before applying effects that are triggered by hitting/missing for attack rolls or by damaging/not damaging for damage rolls. The results of a reroll completely replace the results of the roll that was rerolled. For example, if a reroll causes a hit model to be missed, it is missed. If a reroll causes a missed model to be hit, it is hit. Multiple reroll effects can come into play on the same roll. Resolve them all before resolving any other effects dependent on hitting/missing or damaging/not damaging.

SWITCHING TARGETS

Some models have the ability to cause another model to be directly hit by an attack in their place. Others can cause themselves to be directly hit by an attack in place of another model. Switching targets occurs immediately after a hit or a miss has been determined, including the resolution of all rerolls.

DAMAGE

Warcasters, warjacks, and some other models can take a tremendous amount of damage before they fall in combat. What might be an incapacitating or mortal wound to a regular trooper will just dent a warjack's hull or be deflected by a warcaster's arcane protections.

DAMAGE ROLLS

Determine how much damage is dealt to a model by making a **damage roll**. In the case of ranged, magic, and most other damaging effects roll 2d6 and add the Power (POW) of the attack. In the case of melee attacks, roll 2d6 and add the POW + Strength (STR), or P+S, of the attack. A boosted damage roll adds an additional die to this roll. Special rules for certain circumstances might modify the damage roll as well.

Damage Roll = 2d6 + POW (+ STR if melee)

Compare this total against the Armor (ARM) of the model suffering the damage. That model takes 1 **damage point** for every point that the damage roll exceeds its ARM.

A weapon or attack with POW "—" does not cause damage.

Attacks that generate multiple attack and/or damage rolls do so simultaneously. See "Simultaneous and Sequential" (p. 244) for details on simultaneous damage.

RECORDING DAMAGE

A model's army list entry gives the total amount of damage it can suffer before being **disabled** (p. 66). For models without damage boxes, this is 1 damage point. A model resilient enough to take more than 1 point of damage will have a row of **damage boxes** on its stat card for tracking damage it receives. Record its damage left to right by marking one damage box for each damage point taken. A model is disabled once all its damage boxes are marked. Unmarked damage boxes are sometimes called **wounds**.

Some models, such as warjacks, have **damage grids** consisting of six columns of damage boxes labeled with the numbers 1 through 6. Different damage grids might be slightly different in shape and number of damage boxes, but they function the same way. When a model with a damage grid suffers damage, roll a d6 to determine which column takes the damage. Starting with the uppermost unmarked box in that column and working down, mark one damage box per damage point taken. Once a column is full, continue recording damage in the next column to the right that contains an unmarked damage box. If all the damage boxes in column 6 are marked, continue recording damage in column 1 or the next column that contains an unmarked damage box. Continue filling columns as required until every damage point taken has been recorded.

When a rule specifically states a model suffers damage to the "first" box of a given type, find the lowest numbered column on the model's card that has an unmarked damage box of that type. Within that column, mark the topmost unmarked damage box of that type.

FORCE FIELDS

Some warjacks, notably Retribution myrmidons, have two damage tracks: a set of boxes representing their **force fields** and another representing their damage grids. Mark the field boxes before marking the damage grids.

EXAMPLE: *When damage is dealt to column 2, mark damage first in the force field boxes and then in column 2 if the force field is filled (even if the column was chosen by the attacker as a result of a special rule such as Eiryss' Death Bolt).*

When damage must be dealt simultaneously to each column, mark damage to the force field boxes first (damage from the first column, damage from the second column, and so on). If all of the field's boxes are filled, mark remaining damage to the last columns.

EXAMPLE: *Gorton Grundback hits a warjack with a force field with his Molten Metal spell. That spell deals 1 point of damage to each column on the warjack's damage grid; the damage grid has six columns, so the spell deals 6 damage points. If the warjack has three unmarked force field boxes remaining, the damage points that would otherwise be marked in the first three columns are marked in the force field instead. The remaining 3 damage points are assigned to columns 4, 5, and 6.*

Damage to a specific system is marked in that system; in this case, the force field is ignored.

EXAMPLE: *If a warjack with a force field is hit by a Lancer's Shock Shield attack, the warjack hit suffers 1 damage point to its first available Cortex system box. This damage is applied to an unmarked Cortex system box, not to the warjack's force field.*

WARJACK DAMAGE KEY

On a warjack's damage grid, the following letters represent the warjack's systems:

C: Cortex

L: Left Arm weapon system

R: Right Arm weapon system

H: Head weapon system

M: Movement

A: Arc Node

G: Field Generator

CRIPPLING SYSTEMS

When a model with systems suffers damage, individual systems critical to its combat performance can be damaged and **crippled**. Blank damage boxes represent a warjack's hull. The hull is not a system. Beneath the hull are the model's vital systems, represented by system boxes. Each of these boxes is labeled with a letter designating the system it supports. System boxes are still damage boxes; when recording damage, mark both blank boxes and those containing system labels to record the correct amount of damage. While all its system boxes are marked, a system is crippled. Mark the appropriate system status box below the damage boxes to show this. The effects of crippled systems are as follows:

- **Crippled Arc Node:** The model loses the Arc Node ⊕ advantage.

- **Crippled Cortex:** The model loses any focus points on it and cannot be allocated focus points. It cannot spend focus points for any reason.

- **Crippled Movement:** The model has its base DEF changed to 7. It cannot run or charge. A model that has its Movement system crippled while advancing as part of a charge, slam, or trample immediately stops advancing, and its activation ends.

- **Crippled Arm or Head Weapon System:** The model rolls one fewer die on the attack and damage rolls with weapons in the crippled location. Additionally, a model cannot use weapons in a crippled location to make special attacks, including power attacks. A model cannot make a chain attack or combo special attack, such as Combo Smite or Combo Strike, while either of the weapon systems with the ability is crippled. If a weapon in the crippled location has the Buckler or Shield weapon quality, the model loses the ARM bonus for that quality while the location is crippled.

- **Crippled Field Generator:** A model with a crippled field generator cannot spend focus to remove damage from its field damage track.

If 1 or more damage points are removed from a crippled system, the system is no longer crippled.

DISABLED AND DESTROYED

A model is **disabled** when all of its damage boxes are marked, or when it suffers 1 damage point if it does not have damage boxes. When a model is disabled, immediately resolve any effects triggered by being disabled. A model cannot suffer more damage than it has damage boxes. If 1 or more damage points are healed or removed from a model, it is no longer disabled.

After resolving any effects triggered by being disabled, if it is still disabled it is considered to be **boxed**. When a model is boxed, after resolving any effects triggered by being boxed it is **destroyed**, triggering any relevant effects. Remove the destroyed model from the table.

If an effect causes a model to leave play or cease being disabled, such as when damage is removed on a successful Tough roll, do not resolve any more effects triggered by the model being disabled. The model does not become boxed or destroyed, thus effects triggered by the model becoming boxed or destroyed do not occur.

Likewise, if an effect causes a boxed model to leave play or no longer be boxed, do not resolve any additional effects triggered by the model being boxed. For example, if an effect causes a boxed model to be removed from play, no additional effects triggered by the model being boxed take place, and the model is not destroyed. In this case, the removed model does not provide a soul token because it was not destroyed.

In most cases, a model simply takes damage and is destroyed. Some abilities and effects can interrupt or modify the process of taking damage, though, and that's when these steps come into play.

DESTROYED WARJACK

When a destroyed warjack is removed from the table, replace it with a wreck marker corresponding to its base size. A wreck marker is not a model and cannot be repaired. A wreck marker is rough terrain and provides cover to models within 1" whose bases are partially obscured from the attacker by the wreck. Models at least partially within the area of the wreck also gain cover. Any effects on a warjack expire when it is destroyed.

REMOVED FROM THE TABLE AND REMOVED FROM PLAY

Some rules cause a model to be **removed from the table**, such as when it is destroyed or does something like burrowing into the ground. The model is removed from the playing field and set aside.

Destroyed models can be returned to the table by many means, but other effects that remove a model from the table list specific rules on how and when it can return to play.

Some rules cause a model to be **removed from play**; sometimes this is instead of being destroyed, and at other times it is in addition to being destroyed. A model removed from play is removed from the table and set aside for the rest of the game; it cannot return to the table for any reason.

WARCASTER DESTRUCTION

Should a warcaster be unfortunate enough to fall in combat, his entire army suffers from the harsh blow. When a warcaster is destroyed or removed from the table, all upkeep spells cast by the warcaster immediately expire. Every warjack in the warcaster's battlegroup immediately becomes **inert**. While it is inert, a warjack is stationary, has no facing, loses all special abilities, and does not gain an ARM bonus for shields or bucklers.

In many cases, the loss of a warcaster heralds the end of the battle. If the game does not end with the warcaster's loss, though, other warcasters or 'jack marshals can reactivate the inert warjacks.

REACTIVATING WARJACKS

An inert warjack can be reactivated by a friendly Faction model with the Battlegroup Commander special ability, such as a warcaster, or by a friendly Faction 'jack marshal that ends its movement in base-to-base contact with it. To reactivate the warjack, the model must forfeit its action this turn but can still cast spells, use its feat, and use special abilities. The reactivated warjack is no longer inert, but it must forfeit its activation and cannot be used to channel spells the turn it is reactivated.

HEALING, REPAIRS, AND REMOVING DAMAGE

Some abilities, spells, and other effects remove damage points from a model. When a model with a damage grid is **healed**, **repaired**, or has **damage removed**, remove the damage points from anywhere on the model's damage grid. Remember, if a model heals damage while disabled, it is no longer disabled.

RETURN TO PLAY

Some special rules can cause a model to **return to play** after it is removed from the table. Unless otherwise specified, a model that is returned to play can activate that same turn and has all damage removed. Returned models cause their units to lose benefits or effects received from the original destruction of the models returned. Models removed from play cannot be returned to play.

If a model has an ability it can use once per game that it has already used this game, it cannot use that ability again even if it returns to play.

DAMAGE TYPES

Some weapons inflict a specific **damage type** that might affect some models differently than others. When a damage type is referenced in text, it is described as an "X damage roll." For example, a damage roll that causes electrical damage is described as an "electrical damage roll."

A model with immunity to a certain damage type does not take damage of that type. A single attack can inflict damage of several types. If a model is immune to any of those types, it does not suffer damage from the attack. A model that is immune to damage from an attack can still suffer other effects from the attack.

Example: *The Stormclad is a warjack with Immunity: Electricity. If it were hit by an attack that caused electrical damage and Disruption, the warjack would not suffer a damage roll from the attack but would still suffer Disruption.*

Some damage types are identified by their attack type. For example, damage caused by a ranged attack might be referred to as "ranged attack damage."

Damage types and immunity to those types include:

Cold	**Corrosion**	**Electricity**	**Fire**
Immunity: Cold	**Immunity: Corrosion**	**Immunity: Electricity**	**Immunity: Fire**

MAGICAL WEAPONS

A magical weapon can damage and affect models with the Incorporeal ability. Attacks made with magical weapons are not magic attacks. Magical ranged weapons make ranged attacks. Magical melee weapons make melee attacks.

SPECIAL EFFECTS

Many attacks cause special effects in addition to causing damage. Each special effect is unique in its application. There are three categories of special effects: automatic effects, critical effects, and continuous effects. A special effect can belong to more than one category, and its category can change depending on the weapon. For instance, one weapon might cause the Fire continuous effect automatically on a successful hit, but another might require a critical hit to cause the Fire continuous effect.

Pay close attention to the exact wording for each model's special effects. Even if the effect is the same for different models with the same weapon or ability, it might require different conditions to function. Some models' special effects function if the target is hit, and others require the target to take damage. Critical effects require a critical hit on the attack roll.

AUTOMATIC EFFECTS

Apply an automatic effect every time it meets the conditions required to function.

Example: *The Repenter's Flame Thrower has the Continuous Effect: Fire weapon quality. Any model hit by the Flamethrower automatically suffers the Fire continuous effect.*

CRITICAL EFFECTS

Apply a critical effect if any two dice in the attack roll show the same number and the attack hits; this is a **critical hit**. The target model suffers the special effect even if it takes no damage from the damage roll. An AOE attack's critical effect functions only with a direct hit, but every model under the template suffers the critical effect.

CONTINUOUS EFFECTS

Continuous effects remain on a model and have the potential to damage or affect it some other way on subsequent turns. A model can have multiple continuous effects on it at once, but it can have only one of each continuous effect type on it at a time.

Resolve continuous effects on models you control during your Maintenance Phase. First roll a d6 for each continuous effect; if the result is a 1 or 2 the continuous effect immediately expires without further effect. On a 3, 4, 5, or 6 the continuous effect remains in play. After rolling for expiration for all continuous effects, apply the effects of all continuous effects that remain in play simultaneously.

Continuous effects do not require focus points for upkeep and cannot be removed voluntarily. Remove a continuous effect only when it expires, a special situation causes it to end, or the affected model is removed from the table.

EXAMPLE: *A Crusader attacks a Defender with its Inferno Mace and rolls a critical hit. The Inferno Mace has Critical Fire ⊛, so the Defender now suffers the Fire continuous effect. It takes no damage from the fire at this point. During its controller's next Maintenance Phase, the Defender's controller rolls a d6. The result is a 5, so the Defender suffers a POW 12 damage roll from the fire. The Crusader attacks it again on its turn and rolls another critical hit, but since the Defender is already on fire, there is no further effect from the critical hit. When the Defender's controller's Maintenance Phase comes around again, he rolls another d6 for the fire. This time the result is a 1, so the fire goes out without causing the Defender to suffer another damage roll.*

Some common continuous effects are represented on a weapon's stat bar as weapon qualities.

⊛ **Corrosion** – A model hit by this attack suffers the Corrosion continuous effect, which slowly erodes its target. Corrosion does **1 damage point each turn** to the affected model during its controller's Maintenance Phase until it expires. Models with Immunity: Corrosion ⊛ (p. 34) never suffer this continuous effect.

⊛ **Fire** – A model hit by this attack suffers the Fire continuous effect, which sets it on fire. A model on fire suffers a **POW 12 damage roll each turn** during its controller's Maintenance Phase until the continuous effect expires. Models with Immunity: Fire ⊛ (p. 34) never suffer this continuous effect.

⊛ **Critical Corrosion** – On a critical hit, the model hit suffers the Corrosion continuous effect.

⊛ **Critical Fire** – On a critical hit, the model hit suffers the Fire continuous effect.

CLOUD EFFECTS

A **cloud effect** produces an area of dense smoke, magical darkness, thick mists, or the like that remains in play for a specified length of time. Use an AOE template of the appropriate diameter to represent the cloud. Every model with any part of its base covered by the cloud's template is within the cloud and susceptible to its effects.

In addition to being affected by a cloud's special rules, a model inside a cloud effect gains concealment (see p. 57). The cloud effect does not block line of sight from models within it to those outside of it, but it completely obstructs line of sight from models outside of it to anything beyond it. Thus, a model can see into or out of a cloud effect but not through one. A cloud effect provides no protection from melee attacks.

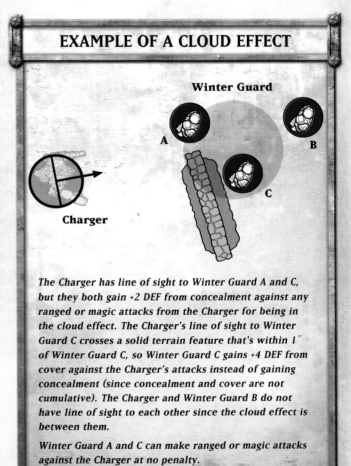

EXAMPLE OF A CLOUD EFFECT

The Charger has line of sight to Winter Guard A and C, but they both gain +2 DEF from concealment against any ranged or magic attacks from the Charger for being in the cloud effect. The Charger's line of sight to Winter Guard C crosses a solid terrain feature that's within 1″ of Winter Guard C, so Winter Guard C gains +4 DEF from cover against the Charger's attacks instead of gaining concealment (since concealment and cover are not cumulative). The Charger and Winter Guard B do not have line of sight to each other since the cloud effect is between them.

Winter Guard A and C can make ranged or magic attacks against the Charger at no penalty.

ANATOMY OF A UNIT
COMPONENTS, FORMATION, AND MOVEMENT

An army's soldiers and support personnel are organized into **units**. Every member of a unit is similarly equipped and trained to fill a certain battlefield role. Some units specialize in melee combat, others excel with ranged weapons, and some provide critical or highly specialized capabilities.

UNIT COMPONENTS

Most units are made up of a single Leader model and one or more Grunts that all share the same stat profile. Some units are led by an Officer with a different stat profile than the models it leads. All models in a unit are troopers in addition to their types explained below.

GRUNTS

Grunts are the basic troopers in a unit. The number of Grunts in a unit is noted on the unit's card.

LEADER

In most units, the **Leader** is the unit commander.

When the Leader model in a unit is destroyed or removed from play, immediately promote a Grunt model in the unit to become the new Leader by replacing the Grunt with the Leader model. See "Field Promotion" (p. 72) for details on this. The new Leader cannot make an attack during the turn it was promoted.

OFFICERS

An **Officer** is a special type of unit commander. Unlike with a Leader, if an Officer is destroyed or removed from play, do not promote a Grunt in the unit to be the new Officer.

OTHER TROOPER MODELS

Some units contain models that are not Leaders or Grunts. These models might have different stats and weapons than the other models in the unit.

STANDARD BEARER

While the **standard bearer** is in formation, models in its unit that are also in formation can reroll failed command checks. Additionally, the unit can reroll failed unit-wide command checks while the standard bearer is in formation. Each failed roll can be rerolled once as a result of the presence of a standard bearer.

When the standard bearer is destroyed or removed from play, you can choose a Grunt in its unit that is within 1″ of it to take its place and become the new standard bearer. If you choose to replace the standard bearer, replace the Grunt model with the standard bearer model. Effects on the destroyed or removed standard bearer expire. Effects on the replaced Grunt are applied to the new standard bearer. The new standard bearer has the same number of unmarked

damage boxes remaining as the Grunt it replaced. The new standard bearer cannot make an attack during the turn it replaced the Grunt.

UNIT COMMANDER

The **unit commander** is the focal point of a unit. In most cases, the unit commander is the Leader of the unit. If a unit is led by an Officer ⊛, the Officer is the unit commander. If a unit has neither an Officer or a Leader, designate another model in the unit to be the unit commander. That model remains the unit commander as long as it is part of the unit.

A trooper's proximity to its unit commander determines whether it is in unit formation. The unit commander issues orders to its unit and can attempt to rally its unit when the unit flees.

ATTACHMENTS

Attachments are made up of one or more models that can be added to a unit of the same type as the attachment. They can be fielded only as part of a unit, not as individual models. Attachments cannot be added to weapon crews. There are two different types of attachments: **unit attachments** and **weapon attachments**. A unit can have only one of each type of attachment added to it. Models in an attachment are not Grunts.

Each attachment's rules list the unit types to which it can be added.

An Officer ⊛ can be added to a unit with a normal unit Leader as part of a unit attachment. If the unit contains both an Officer and a normal unit Leader, the Officer is the unit commander.

TACTICS

Tactics are abilities granted to units by some unit attachments. The unit retains these abilities even if the model that granted them is destroyed or removed from play.

WEAPON CREWS

Weapon crews are small units that operate light artillery. Weapon crews cannot have attachments.

The unit Leader is on the same base as the light artillery and is treated as having the same base size as the Grunts in its unit.

Unlike with other units, if the Leader of a weapon crew leaves play it replaces a Grunt in the unit only if the Grunt is within 1″. Otherwise the Leader model leaves play and the player controlling the weapon crew chooses another model in the unit to become the unit commander. See "Field Promotion" on p. 72.

UNIT FORMATION

Regardless of a unit's role on the battlefield, one thing is certain: a unit is most effective when all its members are **in formation**. The unit commander is always in formation. A model is in formation if it is within its unit commander's command range. A unit's controller can measure the distance between the unit commander and a model in its unit anytime during that unit's activation.

All models in a unit must begin the game in formation.

OUT OF FORMATION

While **out of formation**, a trooper cannot make actions, advance outside of its normal movement, receive orders, cast spells, or make attacks, including attacks that do not take place during the model's or unit's activation, such as a free strike. The trooper also suffers –2 CMD.

At the beginning of a unit's activation, determine if any troopers are out of formation. Those who are will not receive any order given to their unit. A trooper that is out of formation at the start of its unit's activation must use its normal movement to make a full advance toward or run directly toward its unit commander. If it makes a full advance, it must forfeit its action.

At the end of a unit's activation, every out-of-formation trooper must pass a command check or flee. Unlike most

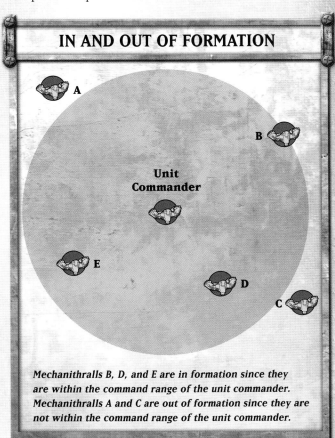

IN AND OUT OF FORMATION

Mechanithralls B, D, and E are in formation since they are within the command range of the unit commander. Mechanithralls A and C are out of formation since they are not within the command range of the unit commander.

other command checks made by troopers, an out-of-formation trooper makes this command check individually. If he fails the check, he does not cause the entire unit to flee. See "Command" (p. 84) for detailed rules on command checks and fleeing.

MOVING UNITS

When a unit makes its normal movement, troopers can move in any order. Remember, a trooper that is out of formation at the start of its unit's activation must advance toward or run directly toward its unit commander. If it makes a full advance, it must forfeit its action.

A unit required to make a command check as a result of its proximity to a terrifying entity during its normal movement does not do so until after every trooper in the unit has completed its movement.

ISSUING ORDERS

Orders let models make specialized combat maneuvers during their activation. Unlike other warrior models, troopers cannot automatically choose to run or charge during their normal movement; they must receive an order to do so. Similarly, a cavalry trooper must receive an order to make a ride-by attack (see "Cavalry," p. 81). A unit can receive an order from its unit commander at the beginning of its activation. The unit commander is the only model in a unit that can issue its unit orders.

Some units have orders described in their special rules that can be issued by their unit commanders, such as the Trencher Infantry's Assault order. A unit commander can issue any order to its unit that is specified in the unit's special rules.

Orders that appear in the special rules of an Officer ⬨ can be issued only by that Officer. If the Officer leaves play, those orders cannot be issued by the new unit commander.

A unit can receive only one order per activation. Every trooper in formation receives the order and is affected by it. Out-of-formation troopers are not affected by orders received by their units. Models in a unit that do not receive an order can make a full advance and make their actions normally. Orders do not carry over from one activation to another.

FIELD PROMOTION

When a unit's Leader is destroyed, removed from play, or otherwise no longer part of its unit, choose a Grunt in that model's unit to take its place and become the new Leader. Replace the Grunt model with the Leader model. Effects on the destroyed Leader expire. Effects on the replaced Grunt are applied to the new Leader. The new Leader has the same number of unmarked damage boxes remaining as the Grunt it replaced. Leader models are replaced even if there is an Officer model in the unit. The new Leader cannot make an attack during a turn it was promoted.

If the Officer leading a unit leaves play and there is a Leader model in its unit, the Leader model becomes the unit commander.

If the unit's Leader is the unit commander and it leaves play and there is no Grunt to replace it, or if an Officer is destroyed and there is not a Leader model in the unit, choose another model in the unit to become the unit commander. That model remains the unit commander as long as it is part of the unit. If that unit commander is destroyed, choose another model to become the unit commander.

EXAMPLE: *The Kapitan of a Man-O-War unit is destroyed. The unit's controlling player decides to make a Grunt with four unmarked damage boxes remaining the new unit commander. He replaces the Grunt model with the Kapitan model. The new Kapitan model has the same number of unmarked damage boxes remaining as the Grunt it replaced. If the Grunt was also suffering from the Fire continuous effect when it was replaced, the new Kapitan would continue to suffer from the continuous effect.*

EXAMPLE: *The Officer in charge of a Temple Flameguard unit is destroyed. Instead of replacing a Grunt in the unit with the Officer model, the Officer leaves play and the Leader of the unit becomes the new unit commander.*

EXAMPLE: *Because he is an Officer and not a Leader, if Boomhowler is destroyed during play he does not replace another model in his unit. Instead, the player controlling Boomhowler's unit chooses a Grunt in the unit to become the new unit commander.*

EXAMPLE: *If a Trencher Infantry unit currently consists of a Leader, a Sniper, a Grenade Porter, and a Grunt, and an AOE attack destroys both the Leader and the Grunt, the controlling player must make the Sniper or the Grenade Porter the unit commander. In either case, the model is not replaced by the Leader because neither is a Grunt.*

SPELLS AND EFFECTS

Some special rules and spells affect entire units. Those special rules and spells are noted in their descriptions. If a special rule or spell specifies "target unit," it must target a trooper in a unit but will affect all models in the unit. Effects that specify "target model/unit" can target any model, including non-troopers, but if the target model is a trooper the effect will apply to the entire unit.

Warjacks represent the pinnacle of military technology in the Iron Kingdoms and are the greatest assets in a warcaster's arsenal. They are equipped with a broad variety of melee and ranged weaponry and embody the strengths of their respective factions. A single warjack can annihilate dozens of men, and side by side, several warjacks together comprise a threat no enemy can ignore.

WARJACK SPECIAL RULES

All warjacks have the following special rules in common.

DAMAGE GRID

Warjacks have damage grids. A warjack is not destroyed until all the boxes in its damage grid are marked. See "Destroyed Warjack" (p. 67) for details.

CONSTRUCT ⊘

Although the icon does not appear on their stat lines, all warjacks have the Construct advantage (see p. 34).

FOCUS: ADDITIONAL ATTACK

This model can spend focus to make additional melee or ranged attacks as part of its combat action (see "Combat Actions," p. 48). It can make one additional attack for each focus point spent.

FOCUS: BOOST

This model can spend 1 focus point to boost any of its attack rolls or damage rolls during its activation. Add an extra die to the boosted roll. Boosting must be declared before rolling any dice for the roll.

Remember, a single roll can be boosted only once, but a warjack can boost as many different rolls as you can afford.

FOCUS: SHAKE EFFECT

During your Control Phase after allocating focus, if this model is knocked down it can spend 1 focus point to stand up.

During your Control Phase after allocating focus, if this model is stationary it can spend 1 focus point to cause the stationary status to expire.

WARJACK MELEE RANGE

Warjacks always have at least a 0.5″ melee range.

WARJACK POWER ATTACKS

This model can make power attacks. To choose the power attack option for its combat action, it must spend 1 focus point. All warjacks can make the slam, head-butt, and push power attacks. Heavy warjacks can make the trample power attack. Warjacks with at least one non-crippled weapon with the Open Fist weapon quality can make headlock/weapon lock and throw power attacks. Warjacks with two non-crippled weapons with the Open Fist weapon quality can make double-hand throw power attacks.

CORTEX

This model can be allocated focus. This model can have no more than 3 focus points at any time as a result of allocation. This limit does not apply to focus gained by means other than allocation.

Unless otherwise stated, this model can spend focus only during its activation.

Warcasters are the most powerful models in WARMACHINE. They are highly trained combat wizards as effective in martial combat as when wielding arcane forces. A warcaster's greatest function on the battlefield, however, is controlling his warjacks, whether he's ordering them to attack or defend, head for an objective, or channel a spell.

Battles can be won or lost purely by how well a player manages his warcasters' focus, the magical energy that lets him control warjacks and cast spells. Often a player must decide between casting a spell and allocating focus to the warjacks in its battlegroup—and that choice can easily make the difference between victory and defeat.

WARCASTER SPECIAL RULES

All warcasters have the following special rules in common.

BATTLEGROUP COMMANDER

This model can control a group of warjacks. This model and its assigned 'jacks are collectively referred to as a **battlegroup**. This model can allocate focus points to warjacks in its battlegroup and can channel spells through warjacks in its battlegroup with the Arc Node ⊕ advantage.

Since warcasters and warjacks are independent models, each model in a battlegroup can move freely about the battlefield separate from the rest of the group. Although warjacks usually benefit from remaining within their warcaster's control area, they are not required to do so.

Only friendly models can be part of a battlegroup. If a rule causes a 'jack to become an enemy model, it is not part of its original battlegroup while that rule is in effect.

If an effect causes a battlegroup commander to fall under your opponent's control, while he is controlled by your opponent the warjacks in his battlegroup remain under your control and become autonomous. If you regain control of the battlegroup commander, he resumes control of the warjacks in his battlegroup unless some other model has already taken control of them.

ALLOCATING FOCUS POINTS

A battlegroup commander can keep his focus points himself or allocate them to as many of his warjacks as desired during your Control Phase as long as they meet the following criteria. The warjack must be in the battlegroup commander's own battlegroup and in his control area (see "Control Area," next page), though it need not be in his line of sight. Take care to remember which warjacks

belong to which battlegroup; a battlegroup commander cannot allocate focus points to warjacks in another model's battlegroup even if they are both part of the same army. A warjack can be allocated up to 3 focus points but can have no more than 3 focus points at any given time as a result of allocation. It can gain focus by means other than allocation without this limit, however.

COMMANDER ✪

Though the icon does not appear on their stat lines, all warcasters have the Commander advantage (see p. 33).

FEARLESS ✠

Though the icon does not appear on their stat lines, all warcasters have the Fearless advantage (see p. 34).

FEAT

Each warcaster has a unique **feat** that can turn the tide of battle if used at the right time. A warcaster can use his feat at any time during his activation. A warcaster cannot use his feat if he runs and cannot interrupt his movement or attack to use it. He can use his feat before moving, after moving, before an attack, or after an attack, but not while moving or attacking.

A warcaster can use his feat only once per game.

FOCUS MANIPULATION

This model has a Focus (FOCUS) stat. During your Control Phase, this model **replenishes** its focus points, receiving a number of them equal to its current FOCUS. This model begins the game with a number of focus points equal to its FOCUS. Unless otherwise stated, this model can spend focus points only during its activation.

POWER FIELD

Warcaster armor is perhaps the most sophisticated blend of magic and mechanics to be found anywhere. Besides its seemingly impossible strength, this armor creates a magical field to surround and protect the warcaster from damage that would rend a normal man to pieces.

This model's damage capacity is largely a result of its power field's protection. At any time during its activation, this model can spend focus points to heal damage it has suffered. For each focus point spent this way, this model heals 1 damage point.

This model's unspent focus points **overboost** its power field and give it increased protection. This model gains +1 ARM for each focus point remaining on it.

SPELLCASTER

This model can **cast spells** at any time during its activation by paying the COST of the spell. This model cannot cast spells during an activation it runs. (See "Casting a Spell" on p. 77 for details.)

THE POINT OF FOCUS

Players should use coins, colored beads, or tokens to represent focus points. During a player's control phase, place a number of tokens equal to the warcaster's current FOC next to the model. These tokens can be allocated to eligible warjacks in that warcaster's battlegroup by moving them next to those models. Remove focus point tokens from the table as they are used. Each of a warcaster's unspent focus points next to the warcaster gives him a +1 ARM bonus.

CONTROL AREA

This model has a **control area**, a circular area centered on this model with a radius that extends out from the edge of its base a number of inches equal to twice its current FOCUS. A model is always considered to be in its own control area. When a special rule changes a model's FOCUS, its control area changes accordingly. Some spells and feats use the control area, noted as "CTRL," as their range or area of effect.

A warjack must be in its warcaster's control area to receive focus points from the warcaster or to channel spells.

MEASURING CONTROL AREAS

You can measure the control area of your models at any time for any reason. Specifically, you can measure the distance from a model to any point within its control area at any time.

For control area effects against opposing models, you do not have to measure the control area until after the enemy model commits to its movement or action.

EXAMPLE: *A warcaster casts a spell that turns his control area into rough terrain. That warcaster's controller does not have to measure his control area prior to an enemy model entering it. The opposing player will have to adjust his model's position after completing its movement if it entered the warcaster's control area and had its movement reduced by the spell's effect.*

FOCUS: ADDITIONAL ATTACK

This model can **spend focus** to make additional melee or ranged attacks as part of its combat action (see "Combat Actions," p. 48). It can make one additional attack for each focus point it spends.

FOR THE MATHEMATICALLY INCLINED

Some effects use terminology like "increases control area by 2″." Inches are a unit of length, not area, and so the phrase may seem a bit odd. Likewise, some effects "double the control area." The correct interpretation is that the length of the line extending out from the model's base is the value being modified, not the area enclosed by sweeping that line around the model.

FOCUS: BOOST

This model can spend 1 focus to boost any of its attack rolls or damage rolls during its activation. Add an extra die to the boosted roll. Boosting must be declared before rolling any dice for the roll.

Remember, a single roll can be boosted only once, but a warcaster can boost as many different rolls as you can afford.

FOCUS: SHAKE EFFECT

During your Control Phase after allocating focus, if this model is knocked down it can spend 1 focus point to stand up.

During your Control Phase after allocating focus, if this model is stationary it can spend 1 focus point to cause the stationary status to expire.

PERFORMANCE POWER

Remember that a warjack must spend focus to run, charge, or make a power attack. Warcasters can also spend their focus points to cast spells or heal damage.

SPELLS

Some models have the ability to cast spells during their activations. Models with the FOCUS stat, like warcasters, cast spells by paying the spell's COST in focus points. A model can cast any number of spells during its activation for which it can pay the COST. A spell can be cast multiple times per activation if the COST can be paid.

When a model casts a spell, resolve the spell's effects immediately.

A spell's point of origin is the model casting the spell or the model through which the spell is channeled (see

"Channeling," p. 79). Unless noted otherwise, spells that target a model other than the casting model or the model channeling the spell require line of sight to their targets. Unlike ranged attacks, being in melee does not prevent a model from casting a spell.

A model can cast spells at any time during its activation but cannot interrupt its movement or attack to cast a spell. It can cast a spell before moving, after moving, before an attack, or after an attack, but not while moving or attacking. A model cannot cast spells during an activation it ran.

EXAMPLE: *A warcaster could cast a spell, move, use his combat action to make a melee attack, cast two more spells, and then spend another focus point to make an additional melee attack.*

SPELL STATISTICS

A spell is defined by the following six statistics:

COST – The number of focus points that must be spent to cast the spell.

RNG, Range – The maximum distance in inches from the spell's point of origin to its target. Measure range from the edge of the point of origin's base to the target up to the maximum range of the spell. If the nearest edge of the target model's base is within the maximum range of the spell, the target is in range. A RNG of "SELF" indicates the spell can be cast only on the model casting it. A RNG of "CTRL" indicates the spell uses the spellcaster's control area as its range.

POW, Power – The base amount of damage a spell inflicts. The POW forms the basis of the spell's damage roll. A spell with POW "—" does not cause damage.

AOE, Area of Effect – The diameter in inches of the template an AOE spell uses for damage effects. When casting an AOE spell, center the template on the determined point of impact. A model with any part of its base covered by the template potentially suffer the spell's effects. See pp. 58–60 for details on AOE attacks. Templates for AOEs appear on p. 255. A spell with an AOE of "CTRL" is centered on the warcaster and affects models in his control area.

UP, Upkeep (Yes/No) – Whether the spell can be upkept. An upkeep spell remains in play if the model that cast it spends 1 focus point to maintain it during its controller's Control Phase.

OFF, Offensive (Yes/No) – Whether the spell is offensive. An offensive spell requires a successful magic attack roll in order to take effect. If the attack roll fails, the attack misses and the spell has no effect. A failed attack roll for an offensive spell with an area of effect deviates.

If a stat is listed as "*" the spell does not use the stat in a normal way and contains special rules relating to that aspect of the spell.

EXAMPLE: *A spell that has an AOE but does not use one of the standard 3", 4", or 5" templates would have "*" as its AOE stat and include rules explaining how its AOE is measured.*

OFFENSIVE SPELLS AND MAGIC ATTACKS

An **offensive spell** is a magic attack that requires that the model casting the spell succeed in a magic attack roll to put its effects in play. Magic attacks are similar to ranged attacks and follow most of the same rules but are not affected by a rule that affects only ranged attacks.

An offensive spell cannot target its point of origin.

Some spells have "*" in the OFF column rather than "YES" or "NO." Treat these spells as non-offensive when targeting friendly models and offensive when targeting enemy models.

CASTING A SPELL

To cast a spell, a model must first pay its COST. If the spell is an upkeep spell, any other copies of that spell cast by the spellcaster immediately expire. Next, declare the target. A spell can target any model in the caster's line of sight (see "Line of Sight," p. 43) subject to the targeting rules. Non-offensive spells with a numeric RNG can also target the point of origin of the spell. A spell cannot target open ground or a permanent terrain feature.

Certain rules and effects create situations that specifically prevent a model from being targeted. A model that cannot be targeted by an attack still suffers its effects if inside the attack's AOE. Other rules and effects, such as Stealth, only cause an attack to miss automatically. They do not prevent the model from being targeted by the attack.

MEASURING RANGE

After declaring the target, **measure** to see if the target is within the Range (RNG) of the spell. Measure range from the edge of the point of origin's base to the target up to the maximum range of the spell. If the nearest edge of the target model's base is within the maximum range of the spell, the target is in range. If the target is in range and the spell is non-offensive, apply the spell's effects. If the target is in range and the spell is offensive, make a magic attack roll to see if it hits. If the target is beyond maximum range, a non-offensive spell does not take effect and an offensive spell automatically misses. If a magic attack has an area of effect (AOE) and the attack's target is out of range, it automatically misses, and its point of impact will deviate from the point on the line to its declared target at a distance equal to its RNG. See "Area-of-Effect (AOE) Attacks" on pp. 58–60 for details on these attacks and deviation.

MAGIC ATTACK ROLLS

Determine a magic attack's success by making a **magic attack roll**. Roll 2d6 and add the attacking model's current FOCUS. Roll an additional die if the roll is boosted. Special rules and certain circumstances might modify the attack roll as well.

$$\text{Magic Attack Roll} = 2d6 + \text{FOCUS}$$

A target is directly hit if the attack roll equals or exceeds the target's DEF. If the attack roll is less than the target's DEF, it misses. A roll of all 1s on the dice causes an automatic miss. A roll of all 6s is a direct hit unless you are rolling only one die, regardless of the attacker's FOCUS or its target's DEF.

Sometimes a special rule causes an attack to hit automatically. Such automatic hits are also direct hits.

A magic attack roll does not suffer the target in melee attack roll penalty when the attacker is in melee with the target. If such an attack misses and there are multiple models in the combat, however, the attack can still hit another random model in the combat, excluding the attacker and the original target. Resolve these situations following the rules in "Targeting a Model in Melee" on p. 58 and "Spell Targeting" on the next page. An AOE spell that misses in this situation will deviate normally.

MAGIC ATTACK ROLL MODIFIERS

The most common modifiers affecting a model's magic attack roll are summarized here for easy reference. Where necessary, additional detail can be found on the pages listed.

- *Back Strike* (p. 61): A back strike gains +2 bonus to the attack roll.

- *Cloud Effect* (p. 69): A model inside a cloud effect gains concealment.

- *Concealment* (p. 57): A model with concealment in relation to its attacker gains +2 DEF against ranged and magic attacks.

- *Cover* (pp. 57–58): A model with cover in relation to its attacker gains +4 DEF against ranged and magic attacks.

- *Elevated Attacker:* If the attacker is on terrain at least 1" higher than the target, it is an elevated attacker. When drawing line of sight from an elevated attacker, ignore intervening models on terrain at least 1" lower than the attacker unless they are within 1" of the target. Additionally, ignore intervening models within 1" of the target that are on terrain at least 1" lower than the attacker and have equal or smaller-sized bases than the attacker.

- *Elevated Target:* If the target is on terrain at least 1" higher than the attacker, it is an elevated target. When drawing line of sight to an elevated target, ignore intervening models on terrain at least 1" lower than the target. An elevated target gains +2 DEF against ranged and magic attack rolls.

- *Knocked Down Target* (p. 63): While knocked down, a model has its base DEF reduced to 5.

- *Stationary Target* (p. 64): While stationary, a model has its base DEF reduced to 5.

- *Target in Melee* (p. 58): A ranged or magic attack roll against a target in melee suffers a –4 penalty. Remember that a model making a magic attack while in melee with its target does not suffer this penalty. If the attack misses, it will deviate and might hit a nearby model instead.

SPELL TARGETING

Many spells can be cast only on certain types of models, such as warjacks or enemy troopers. Such restrictions are noted in a spell's description. To abbreviate these targeting restrictions, when a spell's description mentions an effect against a "target something," the spell can be cast only on that type of model.

EXAMPLE: *The Witch Coven of Garlghast's spell Infernal Machine states "target warjack in this model's battlegroup gains +2 MAT, +2 SPD, and Terror ☾." Therefore when a witch casts this spell it can target only a warjack in the Coven's battlegroup.*

When using an offensive spell to attack a structure, ignore its targeting restrictions.

When an offensive spell targeting a model in melee misses, ignore its targeting restrictions when determining which

model in the combat might be hit instead. If the new target is an invalid one for the spell, the spell has no further effect. (See "Targeting a Model in Melee" on p. 58 and "Offensive Spells and Magic Attacks" above for details on resolving a magic attack against a model in melee.) An AOE spell that misses will deviate normally instead.

EXAMPLE: *Warwitch Deneghra attempts to cast Crippling Grasp on a Protectorate Temple Flameguard trooper in melee with one of her Deathrippers, which is itself in melee with two other Flameguard troopers. Thus, there are four models in the combat. If she misses, determine which of the other three models might be hit by the spell instead as usual.*

UPKEEP SPELLS

Upkeep spells can be maintained for more than one round. During your Control Phase, your models can spend focus to keep their upkeep spells in play. Each upkeep spell requires 1 focus point for its upkeep every time. A model can maintain an upkeep spell even if the spell's effects are outside that model's control area. If focus is not spent to maintain one of your upkeep spells during your Control Phase, the spell immediately expires.

A model can have only one instance of each specific upkeep spell in play at a time, but it can maintain any number of different upkeep spells simultaneously if it spends enough focus points to do so. A model or unit can have only one friendly and one enemy upkeep spell in play on it at a time. If another upkeep spell is cast on a model or unit that already has one from the same side—friendly or enemy— the older upkeep spell expires and is replaced by the newly cast one when the affected model is hit by the spell. The older upkeep spell expires even if only a single model in the unit is affected by the new upkeep spell. Likewise, an upkeep spell on one model expires if its unit is affected by a new upkeep spell from the same side.

A model can recast any of its upkeep spells already in play. If this happens, the spell's previous casting immediately expires when the COST of the new casting is paid.

If an upkeep spell affecting a unit expires on one model in the unit, it expires on all models in the unit.

EXAMPLE: *A unit of Khador Iron Fang Pikemen currently has the Iron Flesh spell in play on it. The Khador player decides it would be more beneficial to have the Fury spell cast on the unit instead and casts it, which immediately removes the Iron Flesh spell when he pays Fury's COST. During the Cryx player's turn, Deneghra casts Crippling Grasp on the unit. This does not remove the Fury spell because an enemy upkeep spell does not replace a friendly one.*

Pay particular attention to this restriction when casting upkeep spells with a target of "SELF." If Severius has Eye of Menoth active, casting Vision on himself would cause Eye of Menoth to expire.

MULTIPLE SPELL EFFECTS

Although it is not possible to have more than one friendly upkeep spell and one enemy upkeep spell on a model or unit at a time, it *is* possible for a model or unit to be affected by more than one spell or animus at a time. As long as a model or unit is under the effects of no more than one friendly and one enemy upkeep spell, it can be affected by any number of non-upkeep spells and up to one friendly animus effect at the same time.

EXAMPLE: *Haley casts Deadeye on a unit of Arcane Tempest Gun Mages already under the effects of Arcane Shield. Arcane Shield does not expire when Deadeye is cast because Deadeye is not an upkeep spell.*

CHANNELING

Models with the Arc Node advantage, known as **channelers**, are equipped with devices called arc nodes that act as passive relays for spells and extend their effective range. A spellcaster can cast spells through any channeler in its battlegroup that is also within its control area. The spellcaster is still the attacker and the model casting the spell, but the channeler becomes the spell's point of origin. This means that eligible targets and the spell's range are measured from the channeling warjack and that the channeling warjack must have line of sight to the spell's target. Channeling a spell does not require the spellcaster to have line of sight to either the channeler or the spell's target. There is no additional focus cost for channeling a spell.

A channeler engaged by an enemy model cannot channel spells. A stationary channeler can channel spells, but one that is knocked down cannot. A channeler can be the target of a non-offensive spell it channels, but a spell with a RNG of "SELF" cannot be channeled. A channeler cannot be the target of an offensive spell channeled through it.

Make a magic attack for a channeled offensive spell normally. The warcaster can spend focus to boost die rolls or otherwise enhance the spell normally.

Remember, the channeler is just a relay. Being used to channel a spell is a passive effect that occurs during a spellcaster's activation and has no impact on the channeler's own activation. Focus points allocated to a channeler cannot be used to pay the spell's COST or boost its rolls, for example.

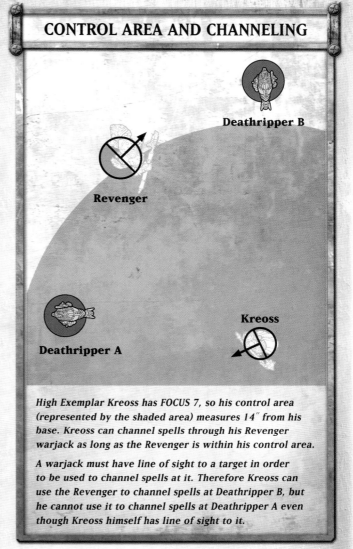

CONTROL AREA AND CHANNELING

High Exemplar Kreoss has FOCUS 7, so his control area (represented by the shaded area) measures 14″ from his base. Kreoss can channel spells through his Revenger warjack as long as the Revenger is within his control area.

A warjack must have line of sight to a target in order to be used to channel spells at it. Therefore Kreoss can use the Revenger to channel spells at Deathripper B, but he cannot use it to channel spells at Deathripper A even though Kreoss himself has line of sight to it.

CHANNELING 101

Channeling a spell does not require the spellcaster to have line of sight to either the channeler or the spell's target. The channeler must have line of sight to the spell's target, though.

A warcaster can channel a spell through only a single channeler at a time. Spells cannot be relayed from one channeler to another.

The warcaster casts the spell, but the channeler is the spell's point of origin. A warjack cannot be the target of an offensive spell channeled through it.

'JACK MARSHALS ✪

Warcasters are elite military leaders representing a combination of mage and warrior rare in the Iron Kingdoms. Supporting their armies are capable soldiers specially trained to command warjacks without the benefit of magical skills. These specialists, called **'jack marshals**, can control warjacks using both gestures and commands shouted across the battlefield. Though not as efficient as using focus, the 'jack marshal's skills can guide a warjack to perform maneuvers it normally would not be able to manage on its own.

Although they are not warcasters, 'jack marshals can begin the game controlling warjacks. These warjacks are not part of any warcaster's battlegroup. A 'jack marshal can control up to two Faction warjacks. Mercenary 'jack marshals can control only mercenary warjacks.

Once during each of its activations while in its controller's command range, a warjack controlled by a 'jack marshal can gain one of the following benefits:

- The warjack can use its normal movement to run or charge.

- The warjack can make one additional attack during its combat action.

- The warjack can boost one attack or damage roll.

A warjack cannot gain one of these benefits while its controlling 'jack marshal is fleeing, knocked down, or stationary.

If a 'jack marshal is removed from the table, his warjacks become autonomous but do not become inert. Autonomous warjacks remain active but do not have a controller. An autonomous warjack acts normally but cannot be marshaled or have focus allocated to it, though it can receive focus from other sources. A warjack must have a controller at the start of the game. It cannot begin the game autonomous.

A 'jack marshal can reactivate one inert friendly Faction warjack per turn in the same manner as a warcaster (p. 68). The reactivated warjack comes under the 'jack marshal's control unless he already controls two warjacks; in that case, the reactivated warjack becomes autonomous.

If an effect causes your 'jack marshal to fall under your opponent's control, while your 'jack marshal is controlled by your opponent, the warjacks under its control remain under your control and become autonomous. If you regain control of your 'jack marshal, the 'jack marshal resumes control of the warjacks unless some other model has already taken control of them.

A warcaster, or a 'jack marshal who does not already control his limit of warjacks, can take control of an autonomous friendly Faction warjack. To do this, he must end his movement in base-to-base contact with the autonomous warjack and forfeit his action, though he can still cast spells, use his feat, and use special abilities. The warjack must forfeit its activation and cannot channel spells on the turn it becomes controlled. Beginning with the next turn, it can be marshaled or allocated focus.

UNITS

If a unit has the 'Jack Marshal advantage, the unit commander of the unit is the 'jack marshal.

If the unit commander leaves play, the new unit commander of that unit gains the 'Jack Marshal advantage and automatically becomes the controller of any warjacks previously controlled by the unit commander that left play.

EXAMPLE: *The Arcane Tempest Gun Mage Officer unit attachment has the 'Jack Marshal advantage. If the Officer leaves play, the Leader of the Arcane Tempest Gun Mage unit becomes the new unit commander and gains the 'Jack Marshal advantage.*

DRIVES

Drives are special commands that some 'jack marshals can issue to the warjacks they control. A 'jack marshal's drives are described in its special rules. A 'jack marshal can attempt to drive each warjack under its control that is in its command range once during its activation. A 'jack marshal can attempt to drive a warjack at any time during its activation. When the 'jack marshal attempts to drive a warjack, he must make a command check. If the 'jack marshal passes the check, the warjack is affected by the drive. If the 'jack marshal fails the check, the warjack cannot benefit from 'Jack Marshal for the rest of the turn.

Drives that appear in the special rules on an Officer ⚜ can be used only by that Officer. If the Officer leaves play, its drives cannot be used by the new unit commander.

ALLIES

Allies are Faction models that will work for mercenary contracts that specify they can include models that will work for the ally's faction. Allies are Mercenary models when included in a Mercenary army. (Rules for fielding contract armies can be found in *Forces of WARMACHINE: Mercenaries*.)

EXAMPLE: *The Highborn Covenant mercenary contract says it can include mercenaries that will work for Cygnar, so Precursor Knights (Cygnar allies) can be included in a Highborn Covenant contract army.*

CAVALRY

Mounted forces are renowned for their terrifying charges, which couple tremendous speed with great weight. Even troops who can avoid being cut down by lances and sabers are still vulnerable to being crushed underfoot. It is little wonder the cavalry charge has remained a valid military tactic since its inception thousands of years before the arrival of the Orgoth.

Certain WARMACHINE models and units are designated as **cavalry**. In addition to all the standard rules for models of their types, cavalry models have the following additional rules in common.

TALL IN THE SADDLE

Cavalry models ignore intervening models with bases smaller than their own when making melee attacks.

RIDE-BY ATTACK

A cavalry model can combine its normal movement and action in a **ride-by attack**. Declare that the model is doing so at the beginning of its normal movement. The model makes a full advance and can halt its movement at any point to make its combat action. Do not resolve abilities that trigger when the model ends its normal movement at this time. After it ends its combat action, the model resumes its movement. Therefore, a model making a ride-by attack triggers end-of-action effects before end-of-normal-movement effects. A cavalry trooper making a ride-by attack must complete both its movement and its combat action before the next model begins its normal movement.

Models in a cavalry unit must receive an order to make a ride-by attack. A cavalry model that received a ride-by attack order can make its attacks that activation even while out of formation.

MOUNT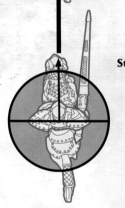

A cavalry model's **Mount** not only provides transportation but also is a weapon in its own right. Mounts are indicated by a horseshoe icon in their stat bars. A Mount weapon has a 0.5″ melee range. Attacks made with a Mount are melee attacks and are resolved normally except that the damage roll is only 2d6 plus the POW of the Mount. Do not add the cavalry model's STR to Mount damage rolls. Mount attack and damage rolls cannot be boosted.

> **Mount Melee Attack Roll = 2d6 + POW of Mount**

Normally a model can use its Mount only to make impact attacks (see "Cavalry Charge," next).

CAVALRY CHARGE

A charge made by a cavalry model differs in several ways from a standard charge. When declaring a charge target, cavalry models ignore intervening models with bases smaller than their own.

CAVALRY CHARGE EXAMPLE

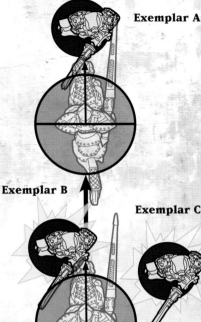

The Storm Lance declares a charge targeting Exemplar A. The Storm Lance then moves in a straight line toward his target. After moving 4″, he stops short when he moves into base-to-base contact with Exemplar B. He then makes impact attacks targeting Exemplars B and C since both models are in his Mount's melee range.

After hitting and destroying Exemplars B and C, the Storm Lance continues his charge movement to Exemplar A.

If Exemplar C had not been destroyed, the Storm Lance could have continued the charge anyway, although he would have suffered a free strike. If Exemplar B had not been destroyed, the Storm Lance's charge would have been unable to continue, and the charge would have failed.

If a charging cavalry model contacts another model during its movement and has moved at least 3″, it stops and makes **impact attacks** with its Mount (see "Mount," previous) against all models in the Mount's melee range. The model makes these attacks even if it is out of formation. Impact attacks are simultaneous. After resolving the impact attacks, the charging model resumes its charge movement. It cannot make further impact attacks during this charge. If the charging cavalry model did not move at least 3″ before contacting the other model, it does not make any impact attacks and must stop its movement at that point. If the cavalry model's target is not in melee at the end of the charge movement, the charge fails. If the charge target is the first model contacted by the charging cavalry model, the charging model can still make an impact attack against it.

A cavalry model gains +2 to charge attack rolls. Impact attacks do not receive this bonus.

DRAGOONS

Dragoons are cavalry models that begin the game mounted but can become dismounted during play. For some dragoons the ability to be dismounted is optional. Adding this ability to the dragoon increases its point cost and total damage capacity.

While mounted, a dragoon is subject to all the normal cavalry rules. Once the dragoon has become dismounted, it is no longer a cavalry model and loses all cavalry abilities, including its Mount weapon. A model's Dragoon rule might list abilities and weapons that the model loses when it becomes dismounted. Dragoons have stats with two different base values. Use the first value while the dragoon is mounted and the second once the dragoon has become dismounted.

When a mounted dragoon suffers damage, apply the damage to its mounted dragoon damage boxes. When all these damage boxes are marked, the dragoon becomes disabled unless it has the ability to become dismounted. If the dragoon does have that ability, it becomes dismounted instead. Damage points in excess of the mounted dragoon's remaining unmarked damage boxes are not applied to its dismounted damage boxes. If this occurs while the dragoon is advancing, it cannot continue to advance; if it occurs during the dragoon's activation, the activation ends immediately. Remove the mounted dragoon and replace it with the dismounted dragoon model (see "Replacing Models," p. 64). Apply effects that were on the mounted dragoon to the dismounted dragoon. Once this replacement is complete, any further damage the dragoon suffers will be applied to its dismounted dragoon damage boxes. The model is disabled when all its dismounted dragoon damage boxes have been marked.

LIGHT CAVALRY

Some cavalry models are designated as **light cavalry**. They follow all the normal cavalry rules with the following alterations.

Immediately after an independent light cavalry model or all models in a light cavalry unit complete their activation, the model/unit can advance up to 5″. A light cavalry model cannot make ride-by attacks or impact attacks. A light cavalry model can make initial attacks with its Mount. When making additional attacks, a light cavalry model can use its Mount.

CHARACTER WARJACKS

Character warjacks represent the pinnacle of each faction's mechanikal development. Due to their experimental or unpredictable nature, character warjacks cannot typically bond unless a special rule specifically allows them to do so. (For details see Appendix B: Warjack Bonding on p. 246 and "Affinities," below.) In addition, character warjacks cannot begin a game under the control of a 'jack marshal. If a 'jack marshal reactivates a character warjack, the warjack becomes autonomous instead of coming under the 'jack marshal's control.

AFFINITIES

Affinities are special abilities conveyed to some character warjacks when the warjack is part of a specific warcaster's battlegroup. The warjack gains the affinity when controlled by any version of the warcaster listed in the name of the ability. A character warjack with an affinity can be bonded to that warcaster (see Appendix B: Warjack Bonding, p. 246). The "warcaster" referenced in the text of an affinity always refers to the warjack's controller.

IMPRINTS

Some character warjacks have **imprints** representing a partial awakening of the warjack's cortex. A warjack with an imprint can use the imprint at any time during its activation by spending 1 focus point but cannot interrupt its movement or attack to use an imprint. It can use its imprint before moving, after moving, before an attack, or after an attack, but not while moving or attacking.

ELITE CADRES

Some models confer abilities to other models of a certain type in an army. Models that gain abilities from an **Elite Cadre** rule retain them even if the model that granted those abilities is destroyed or removed from play.

EPIC MODELS

Constant exposure to the carnage of the battlefield and the tumultuous nature of combat takes its toll. The warriors of western Immoren are locked in world-shaping conflict and must continually push themselves to the limits of their capabilities. The rigors of war affect the most stalwart men, and not even the mightiest of warcasters can weather them unchanged.

Epic models are variations of character models with fresh abilities, strengths, and weaknesses. Epic models are not more powerful versions of the original characters but instead reflect character growth and changes described in major story arcs. If these models were simply improvements on older versions, the older models would quickly become obsolete. Epic models do not replace the original models on which they are based but instead offer players the opportunity to play whichever version they prefer. There may be several epic versions of a model from which to choose.

In story terms, these characters have not lost their original abilities but have instead adapted to the demands of war by adopting new tactics, equipment, and spells as necessary.

Because all versions of a model are considered the same character, an army or team can include only one of those versions. Just as a player cannot field two Reinholdt, Gobber Speculator models in the same army, he cannot field both Commander Coleman Stryker and epic warcaster Lord Commander Stryker at the same time.

EPIC WARCASTER BONDING

Some epic warcasters have the **Warjack Bond** ability, representing an exceptionally powerful connection between the warcaster and some of his warjacks. This ability allows the epic warcaster to start a game bonded to a warjack in his battlegroup. These bonds follow the rules given in Appendix B: Warjack Bonding (p. 246) except as noted here. Do not roll on the bond effect tables for these bonds. Their effects are described in the epic warcaster's special rules.

Designate which warjack is bonded to the epic warcaster before the start of the game.

Campaign Play

In **campaign play**, the warcaster need not bond with the same warjacks from battle to battle. These bonds are in addition to any other bonds the warcaster forms during play (see Appendix B: Warjack Bonding, p. 246). A warjack can be bonded to only one warcaster at any time, however. If an epic warcaster's Warjack Bond ability is applied to a warjack that is already bonded to a warcaster, including himself, the previous bond is broken and its effects are lost. After the battle, do not make a bonding check for a warjack affected by the Warjack Bond ability; it is already bonded to the warcaster.

MAGIC ABILITY

Some models have the ability to cast spells as a special action or attack without spending focus. The spells a model can cast are listed in its entry under its **Magic Ability** special rules. Magic Ability special attacks are magic attacks but are resolved using the model's Magic Ability score instead of the FOCUS stat. A model's Magic Ability score appears in brackets next to "Magic Ability"; for example, a Greylord Ternion model has "Magic Ability [7]."

Determine a Magic Ability attack's success by making a magic attack roll. Roll 2d6 and add the attacking model's Magic Ability score.

Magic Ability Attack Roll = 2d6 + Magic Ability Score

Casting a Magic Ability spell does not require a skill check.

MERCENARY WARCASTERS AND WARJACKS

A **mercenary warcaster** counts toward the maximum number of warcasters allowed in an army. Field allowance is not faction-specific. If an army includes both faction and mercenary warcasters, count all the warcasters in the army when determining field allowance limits for both faction and mercenary models and units. If the only warcasters in an army are mercenaries, only mercenary models can be included in that army.

Mercenary warjacks can be controlled and reactivated only by mercenary warcasters and 'jack marshals. By the same token, a mercenary warcaster or 'jack marshal can control and reactivate only mercenary warjacks.

THEME FORCES

Theme Forces are themed armies for specific warcasters. A Theme Force can include only the warcaster named in its title. If you are playing a game with two or more warcasters in each army, you cannot use these rules.

Theme Forces are broken into tiers. Each tier has a set of requirements that restricts your army composition. If your army meets the requirements of a tier and the tiers before it, you gain the benefits listed. These benefits are cumulative: you gain the benefits of every tier for which your army meets the requirements.

If a Theme Force can include a given unit, you can add any attachments to the unit that are available to it.

Theme Forces and their requirements and benefits can be found in each faction's *Forces of WARMACHINE* book.

Regardless of a soldier's skill at arms, his real worth to an army is measured by his will to fight. Warriors might break and flee after suffering massive casualties or when confronted by terrifying entities, while manipulative spells can warp the minds of the weak-willed and cause them to attack their allies. The inspiring presence of a nearby warcaster or unit commander can steel the nerves of warriors faced with these mental assaults and even rally them before their panic becomes a full-blown rout. Command checks determine the outcome of these game situations that test a combatant's discipline or mental resolve.

COMMAND RANGE

Every model has a **command range** equal to its CMD in inches. A model is always in its own command range.

Models in a unit that are in their unit commander's command range are in formation. A unit commander can rally and give orders to models in its unit that are in formation. A trooper that is out of formation cannot rally and will not receive orders (see p. 72). A trooper making an individual command check can use its unit commander's CMD if it is in formation.

Some models have the **Commander ⊕ advantage**, which allows friendly Faction models or units in the model's command range to use its current CMD in place of their own when making a command check if they prefer. When making a command check for a unit, only one model in the unit must be in the command range of the model with the Commander advantage in order for the unit to use that model's CMD for the command check. A model with the Commander advantage can rally any friendly Faction model or unit that is in its command range (see "Rallying," next page).

COMMAND CHECKS

Several different circumstances require a model or unit to make a command check: massive casualties, terrifying entities, and a spell or other attack's special rules.

When a model or unit is required to make a **command check**, roll 2d6. If the result is equal to or less than its Command (CMD) stat, it passes the check.

Passed Command Check: 2d6 ≤ CMD

Failed Command Check: 2d6 > CMD

In most cases, this means the model or unit continues to function normally or rallies if it was fleeing. If the roll is greater than the CMD, the check fails and the model or unit suffers the consequences. When a unit fails a command check, every trooper in that unit suffers the effects, including out-of-formation troopers.

EXAMPLE: *A Khadoran Manhunter has a CMD of 9. The Manhunter passes a command check on a 2d6 roll of 9 or less.*

An independent model makes a command check on an individual basis using its own CMD. It can use the CMD of a friendly Faction model with the Commander ⊕ advantage instead of its own if it is in that model's command range, but it is not required to do so.

In most cases, troopers make command checks at the unit level. Some exceptions include troopers that end their activations out of formation and spells that specifically target single models. When you make unit-level command checks, use the unit commander's CMD, and apply its results to every trooper in that unit unless stated otherwise. Just as with an individual model, a unit making a command check within command range of a friendly Faction model with the Commander advantage can use that model's CMD instead. Only one model in a unit must be in the commander's command range for a unit-level check to be able to use the commander's CMD.

A trooper making an individual command check can use its unit commander's CMD if it is in formation. Alternatively, it can use the CMD of a friendly Faction model with the Commander advantage if it is within that model's command range, but it is not required to do so.

MASSIVE CASUALTIES

A unit suffers **massive casualties** when it loses 50% or more of the models that were in it at the beginning of the current turn. The unit must immediately pass a command check or flee. A unit makes only one command check per turn due to massive casualties. After you make a massive casualty roll during a turn, pass or fail, you will not make another one for that unit that turn for any reason. If you pass, the unit will not flee as a result of massive casualties that turn.

TERRIFYING ENTITY

A **terrifying entity** is one with the **Abomination ⊕** or **Terror ⊕ advantage**.

A model or unit within 3″ of a model with Abomination—friendly or enemy—must pass a command check or flee.

A model or unit in melee range of an enemy model with Terror, or a model or unit with an enemy model with Terror in its melee range, must pass a command check or flee.

Make command checks due to proximity with terrifying entities during a model's or unit's normal movement when the model or unit ends its normal movement. If a model

or unit encounters a terrifying entity at some other time, such as when an enemy model gains the Terror ability or a terrifying entity is placed near the model or unit, make the command check immediately after resolving the attack or effect that caused the encounter.

EXAMPLE: *If Iron Lich Asphyxious moves into melee with a Temple Flameguard, the Flameguard's unit makes a command check as soon as Asphyxious ends his movement. If a Flameguard moves into melee with Asphyxious, however, make a command check for his unit after all the troopers in the unit finish moving. In either case, make the command check before any model makes an action. If Asphyxious used Teleport to place himself into the melee range of a Flameguard, make the command check after the placement is resolved.*

A single terrifying entity can cause a model or unit to make only one command check per turn due to proximity. Additionally, a model or unit that passes a command check caused by its proximity to a terrifying entity does not make further command checks as a result of proximity to the entity if it remains inside the range that triggered the effect. If these models become separated and encounter each other during a later turn, another command check will be required.

A unit that consists of terrifying entities counts as a single terrifying entity for the purpose of these rules. A model or unit need only make a single command check for encountering the unit regardless of how many of its troopers it actually encounters.

FLEEING

A model or unit that fails a command check against fleeing **flees**. Some special rules can even cause a model to flee without making a command check at all. If this occurs during the model's or unit's activation, the activation immediately ends. Fleeing does not cause the model to move until its next activation; a model that is already fleeing cannot flee again and does not make command checks against fleeing.

EXAMPLE: *If the terrifying entity the Butcher of Khardov moves within melee range of a fleeing model, the fleeing model does not make a command check against fleeing.*

A fleeing model must run during its activation. It is not required to move the full distance of its run, however, and it can even run 0″ if desired. If a fleeing model cannot run, it makes a full advance and must forfeit its action. A fleeing model cannot advance toward any enemy models. While fleeing, a model cannot make actions, advance outside of its normal movement, give orders, cast spells, or make attacks, including attacks that do not take place during the model's or unit's activation, such as a free strike.

At the end of its activation, a fleeing model or unit might have an opportunity to rally.

RALLYING

A fleeing model or unit can make a command check to **rally** at the end of its activation. If a trooper is fleeing but its unit is not, it can make a command check to rally only if it is in formation with its unit commander or if it is within the command range of a friendly Faction model with the Commander advantage. If a fleeing unit makes a command check to rally, every trooper in the unit is affected by the result regardless of its formation status.

If the model or unit passes the command check, it rallies. When a model or unit rallies, it is no longer fleeing. If the fleeing model or unit fails the command check, it is still fleeing.

FEARLESS MODELS

A model with the **Fearless** ✠ advantage never flees and automatically passes command checks against fleeing. It still makes other command checks as normal. Fleeing models that become Fearless immediately rally.

TERRAIN—YOUR BEST FRIEND
THE BATTLEFIELD, HAZARDS, AND STRUCTURES

The lay of the land has a tremendous impact on an army's ability to maneuver. The most cunning commanders use terrain conditions to their best advantage. These terrain rules provide guidelines for establishing the effects and restrictions a battlefield's objects and environment can have on a game. Covering the rules for every possible terrain type would be an endless task, so players themselves must determine the exact nature of each terrain feature on the battlefield before the game begins.

BEFORE PLAY

Players must discuss the terrain setup and agree on the characteristics for different terrain features prior to deploying their armies. Decide which terrain features grant cover or concealment, which provide elevation and at what level, which are impassable, and so on. It is vital to understand the rules for all terrain features in play before the start of the game; developing the habit of discussing terrain before the game will help you avoid unnecessary disagreements and misunderstandings during play.

SETTING TERRAIN DETAILS

When discussing the specifics of terrain features, it may be handy to keep the following questions in mind:

- Does it provide cover or concealment?

- Is it rough terrain? Impassable?

- Does it provide elevation? If so, does it have a gradual or sloped surface? Are some parts of the elevated terrain feature gradual while others are sheer?

- Does it have any special rules? Is it forest, shallow water, a trench, a structure, or so on?

- What characteristics of terrain are likely to become important during the game due to the abilities and spells of the models in my army?

BATTLEFIELD SETUP

When placing terrain, strive for a visually appealing and tactically challenging battlefield. These qualities provide the most exciting and memorable games. Battlefield setup and terrain placement is not a competitive portion of the game—players should not strategically place terrain features in a manner that unfairly aids or penalizes a specific army. However, a scenario might dictate doing so to represent an overmatched force defending a village or mountain pass,

for example. In such a scenario, giving the defending army a strong defensive position would be one way to make up for being outclassed by its opponent.

Use the amount of terrain that suits the type of game you wish to play. A table with few terrain features favors ranged attacks and swift movement, while using more terrain features shifts the emphasis toward melee combat.

Consider model base sizes when placing terrain features close together, since a model can move between obstructions or impassable terrain only if its base will fit between them. With careful placement, you can create narrow passages that can be accessed only by models with smaller bases.

TERRAIN TYPES

A model's movement can be affected by the type of ground it covers. In WARMACHINE, terrain falls into one of three categories: open, rough, and impassable.

OPEN TERRAIN

Open terrain is mostly smooth, even ground. A model in open terrain moves 1″ for every 1″ of its movement. Examples include grassy plains, barren fields, flat rooftops, dirt roads, sloped hillsides, elevated walkways, and paved surfaces.

ROUGH TERRAIN

Rough terrain can be traversed but at a significantly slower pace than open terrain. As long as any part of its base is in rough terrain, a model suffers a movement penalty that causes it to move only 0.5″ for every 1″ of its movement. Examples include thick brush, rocky areas, murky bogs, shallow water, and deep snow.

IMPASSABLE TERRAIN

Impassable terrain is terrain that completely prohibits movement. Examples include cliff faces, oceans, and lava. A model cannot move across or be placed within impassable terrain.

TERRAIN FEATURES

Natural and man-made objects on the battlefield are terrain features. Each terrain feature is unique, so you must decide its specific qualities before staring the game. Terrain features are virtually limitless in their variety, but you can quantify each by how it affects movement, the type of protection it affords, and any adverse effects it causes.

In addition to hindering movement, terrain features can also provide protection against attacks. A terrain feature such as a hedge grants a model concealment by making

it more difficult to be seen even though the feature is not dense enough to block the attack itself. A terrain feature such as a stone wall or a building grants a model cover by being solid enough to block an attack physically.

OBSTACLES

An **obstacle** is any terrain feature less than 1″ tall. These affect a model's movement, provide protection from attacks, and serve as intervening terrain during melee combat.

A model with any portion of its volume obscured from its attacker by an obstacle gains +2 DEF against melee attack rolls.

MOVING OVER OBSTACLES

Obstacles are low enough that they can be climbed upon or, in some cases, easily crossed. An obstacle must be at least 1″ thick, such as a raised platform or the sides of a ziggurat, in order for a model to climb atop and stand on it.

An advancing model suffers a movement penalty when it climbs atop an obstacle. Once the model has contacted the obstacle, it needs to spend 2″ of its movement to climb up. A model cannot climb an obstacle if it does not have at least 2″ of movement remaining. Place a model that climbs an obstacle atop it with the front of the model's base making only 1″ of forward progress. Once atop an obstacle, the model can continue with the remainder of its movement. Remember that a charging model cannot pay this movement penalty, cannot climb an obstacle and ends its movement upon contact.

A medium- or large-based model might have trouble balancing atop an obstacle if it does not continue moving after initially climbing it. With only 1″ of forward progress, the back of the model's base will overhang the back of the

obstacle. This is fine—just prop up the model with some extra dice or replace it with an empty base until it can move again.

A moving model can descend an obstacle without penalty.

LINEAR OBSTACLES

An obstacle up to 1″ tall but less than 1″ thick, such as a wall or hedge, is a **linear obstacle**. A non-charging advancing model can cross a linear obstacle at no penalty as long as the model can move completely past it. Otherwise the model must stop short of the linear obstacle. A model cannot partially cross, climb atop, or stand atop a linear obstacle.

OBSTRUCTIONS

An **obstruction** is a terrain feature 1″ tall or greater, such as a high wall or a gigantic boulder. A model cannot move through or climb an obstruction. Like an obstacle, obstructions provide protection from attacks and serve as intervening terrain during melee combat. A model with any portion of its volume obscured from its attacker by an obstruction gains +2 DEF against melee attack rolls.

VARIABLY SIZED TERRAIN FEATURES

Terrain features can have some parts that are greater than 1″ tall and some parts that are less, such as a crumbling wall. In such cases players should decide before the start of the game whether they are treating the terrain feature as an obstacle, an obstruction, or both. If they are treating it as both, the portions less than 1″ tall are obstacles and the parts over 1″ tall are obstructions.

FORESTS

A typical **forest** has many trees and dense underbrush, but any terrain feature that hinders movement and makes a model inside it difficult to see can also be designated a forest. A forest is rough terrain and provides concealment to a model with any part of its base inside its perimeter.

When drawing line of sight to or from a point within a forest, the line of sight can pass through up to 3″ of forest without being blocked, but anything more blocks it. When a model outside of a forest attempts to draw line of sight to another point outside of a forest, the forest blocks line of sight to anything beyond it. Thus, a model can see 3″ into or out of a forest but not completely through one regardless of how thick it is.

HILLS

A **hill** is a terrain feature with a gentle rise or drop in elevation. Since many terrain pieces use stepped sides instead of gradual slopes to represent a hill's elevations, be sure to declare whether the terrain feature is a hill or an obstacle.

A hill might be open or rough terrain depending on the ground's nature. Unlike obstacles, hills do not impose any additional movement penalties, nor do they provide cover or concealment. They simply provide elevation to models on them. A model can charge up or down a hill in open terrain at no penalty.

WATER

Depending on its nature, water can be hazardous to both warriors and warjacks. When placing a water terrain feature, declare whether it is deep or shallow.

DEEP WATER

A warjack in **deep water** is removed from play.

A model cannot begin a charge or run while in deep water. As long as any part of its base is in deep water a model moves only 0.5″ for every 1″ of its movement and cannot make actions, cast spells, use feats, or give orders. A model in deep water cannot engage other models or make attacks. A warcaster in deep water can still allocate focus points and use them to maintain upkeep spells.

A model in deep water has base DEF 7. A warrior model ending its activation in deep water automatically suffers 1 damage point.

SHALLOW WATER

Shallow water is rough terrain.

A warjack that is knocked down in shallow water has its furnace extinguished and is stationary until its furnace is restarted. A friendly warrior model in base-to-base contact with the warjack can restart it by forfeiting its action. The warjack must forfeit its activation and cannot channel spells the turn it is restarted, but it functions normally next turn.

Even if a warcaster other than its controller restarts it, the warjack remains part of its original battlegroup. When a warjack's furnace is restarted, the warjack automatically stands up.

TRENCHES

Trenches are earthwork fortifications represented by 3″ × 5″ templates (included on p. 256). Trench templates are designed to be placed in contact with each other to create networks of trenches on the table.

A model completely within the area of one or more trench templates has cover from attacks made by models not touching at least one of the trench templates the model is in. Models completely within the area of a trench template do not suffer blast damage unless the origin of damage is in a trench template they are touching. When drawing line of sight to a model not completely within one or more trench templates, ignore models completely within one or more trench templates.

TRENCHES

Assault Kommandos A, B, and C are completely within the area of one or more trench templates, so they have cover and do not suffer blast damage unless the origin of the damage is in a trench template they are touching.

Assault Kommandos D and E are not completely within the area of one or more trench templates, so they do not gain the benefits of being within the trench.

STRUCTURES

Structures present unique opportunities for terrain arrangement and tactical play. A **structure** is any terrain feature that can be damaged and destroyed. The most common structures are buildings, but you can use these guidelines for fortress walls, bridges, and similar constructions as well. Keep in mind that these rules are guidelines and might need to be adapted to the actual terrain pieces you are using.

EXAMPLE: *A burned-out building that has only its exterior walls remaining might be large enough that models deep*

Structure Material	ARM	Damage Capacity (points per inch)
Wood	12	5
Reinforced Wood	14	5
Brick	16	10
Stone	18	10
Iron	20	20
Steel	22	20

within its interior are far enough away from those walls not to suffer damage when the structure collapses.

EXAMPLE: *A house might have attached fences and field walls. Those walls and fences are best treated as separate structures from the house itself even though they are part of the single terrain piece. After all, shooting at a fence should not cause the house to collapse!*

Before the start of the game, players must agree which, if any, terrain features can be damaged during play.

DAMAGING AND DESTROYING STRUCTURES

An attack against a structure must target a section of the structure. An attack against a structure in range automatically hits. A structure is also automatically hit by a spray attack if any part of the structure is within the spray template. Not all weapons are effective against structures, however, so a model must have a weapon that will do the job if it intends to punch through. Ranged weapons such as handguns, rifles, and crossbows are all but useless. A ranged attack must have a POW of at least 14 to damage a structure. Melee attacks, magic attacks, and AOE attacks do full damage against structures, as do ranged attacks that cause fire or corrosion damage. Structures suffer blast damage and collateral damage. A magic attack does only its normal damage to a structure; except for its stats and damage type, ignore a spell's rules when it targets a structure. A structure cannot be charged or slammed.

A structure can suffer only so much damage before being destroyed. Every structure has an Armor (ARM) stat and damage capacity corresponding to its composition, size, and nature. Before the start of the game, the players must agree on each damageable structure's ARM and damage capacity. A structure's damage capacity is determined by its composition and size. A wooden structure typically has a capacity of 5 damage points per inch of perimeter. The damage capacity of stone structures is typically 10 per inch. A reinforced stone or metal structure has a capacity of 20 or more damage points per inch. See the table below for typical ARM and damage capacity values. For mixed-composition structures, ARM values might vary from location to location. Assign damage capacity of mixed-composition structures proportionally.

EXAMPLE: *A 1"-wide or so wooden door in an otherwise stone building would contribute only 5 points to the structure's damage capacity. The door has ARM 12 while the surrounding stone has ARM 18.*

Undamaged portions of walls or other freestanding structures remain intact as the structure suffers damage, so the total damage capacity of such structures is determined by their total perimeter (or length, for linear structures such as walls or small structures such as obelisks). Complex structures such as buildings and bridges, however, rely on the support of all portions to remain standing. Such a structure's damage capacity is only half the value determined by its composition and perimeter or length.

EXAMPLE: *A 3"-wide stone wall is destroyed once it suffers a total of 30 damage points (3" length × 10 points per inch), but a 3" × 6" stone building collapses when it suffers 90 points of damage (18" perimeter × 10 points per inch ÷ 2).*

When a structure is destroyed it **collapses**. Remove the collapsed structure from the table and replace it with an equal-sized ruin. A ruin is rough terrain and provides cover to a model with any part of its base inside the ruin's perimeter. In addition, the destroyed structure can damage models that are inside it when it collapses.

A model inside the structure when it collapses suffers a damage roll with Power (POW) equal to the structure's ARM times the number of levels in the structure, after which the model is knocked down.

EXAMPLE: *A warjack inside a three-story brick building when it collapses suffers a POW 48 (brick structure ARM 16 × 3 levels) damage roll. Whatever is left of the warjack is then knocked down.*

ENTRYWAYS

Some terrain features such as buildings and walls have **entryways** that allow models to pass through or enter them. A model cannot enter a terrain feature if the interior is not physically accessible to the players.

EXAMPLE: *A model can enter a ruined building that is missing its roof or one that has a removable roof. It cannot enter a building with a fixed roof that cannot be opened in some other way to allow access to the models inside of it.*

Before the start of the game, players must agree on which terrain features can be entered and the locations of any entryways into those terrain features. Player should also determine which base sizes those entryways accommodate.

EXAMPLE: *Players might decide that a heavy warjack is unable to pass through a doorway much smaller than its base size or that warrior models of any size can move through ground floor windows.*

SCENARIOS–WHY WE CAN'T ALL BE FRIENDS
VARIATIONS OF GAMEPLAY

There are as many reasons for war as there are wars themselves. Sides seldom clash with only the intent to eliminate one another. It could be a skirmish over boundaries, a fight over resources, or an attempt to hold important strategic ground. Conceiving a reason for your conflicts can greatly enhance your WARMACHINE gaming experiences.

Here you will find six scenarios ready to play. Each occurs on a balanced playing field conveying no specific advantage to any one army. You can agree with your opponent on which scenario to play or roll a d6 prior to building your army and play the scenario indicated on the table included here.

Each scenario provides special rules that describe how to handle the unique circumstances of the scenario. Certain scenarios will also have restrictions on army composition as well as how the game table should be set up. Most scenarios can be played at any encounter level you choose. Experiment with different combinations, and feel free to create variations or unique scenarios of your own!

Unless otherwise noted in the rules of a scenario, all scenarios are intended to be played on a 4′ × 4′ table with a fair amount of terrain. Players decide how much terrain to use and then take turns placing terrain.

Determine deployment and turn order with a standard starting roll (detailed on p. 40). Players are allowed to place their forces completely within 10″ of the table edge.

OBJECTIVE MARKERS

Some scenarios use **objective markers** to denote key strategic points on the table. Objective markers are circular areas 50 mm in diameter placed as directed by the scenario.

A player holds an objective marker when the only models with bases overlapping the marker are his. Inert warjacks, wild warbeasts, and incorporeal models 👻 cannot hold an objective.

RANDOM SCENARIO DETERMINATION

If both players agree, instead of choosing a scenario for battle, you can roll a d6 and consult this table to determine the scenario you will play.

Roll	Result
1	Break the Line
2	Killing Field
3	Mangled Metal
4	Mosh Pit
5	No Man's Land
6	Throw Down

BASIC BATTLE

A mortal man is never so close to divinity as when he commands an army in battle. The tides of war rise and fall by the will of generals.
— Kommandant Gurvaldt Irusk

DESCRIPTION

The loss of a warcaster will deal a crippling blow to any force and may shatter the morale of an entire army. In this battle, two armies clash with the goal of destroying the opposing commander.

SPECIAL RULES

There are no special rules for this scenario.

VICTORY CONDITIONS

A player wins the game when he has the only remaining warcaster(s) in play.

MULTIPLAYER GAME

In a multiplayer Basic Game scenario, all players should have the same size deployment zones, equidistant from each other.

BREAK THE LINE

There is a method to exploiting the chaos of war. If your orchestration of battle deafens them with its cacophony, so much the better.

—Grand Scrutator Severius

DESCRIPTION

Bold advances are required on this battlefield as each army drives forward to break the enemy line and claim enemy territories without losing regions under its own control.

SPECIAL RULES

Divide the table between the deployment zones into six 14″ × 16″ **territories**.

A player controls a territory if he has one or more models completely within it and his opponent does not. For a unit to control a territory, all models in the unit still in play must be completely within it. A warrior model must have a CMD greater than 1 to control a territory. Ignore inert warjacks, wild warbeasts, and fleeing models when checking for control.

VICTORY CONDITIONS

A player wins the game when he has the only remaining warcaster(s) in play. Starting at the end of the first player's third turn, a player will also win if he holds two territories on his half of the table and one territory on his opponent's half of the table at the end of his opponent's turn.

MULTIPLAYER GAME

Break the Line is not suited to multiplayer play.

KILLING FIELD

Victory can be measured in terms of both ground gained and casualties inflicted.

—Major Markus "Siege" Brisbane

DESCRIPTION

Killing Field is a desperate struggle between two armies to seize control of the battlefield either by entrenching themselves on the centerline or by inflicting crippling losses on the opposition.

SPECIAL RULES

Before the start of the game, place three objective markers in the middle of the table, one at the center and one 8″ from each side of the table. Any terrain features preventing a model from standing on one of these markers should be moved.

A player scores **control points** by holding objective markers at the end of his turn. A player scores 1 control point for each marker held. Control points cannot be scored during the first round of the game.

VICTORY CONDITIONS

A player wins the game when he has the only remaining warcaster in play or when he has scored 7 or more control points.

MULTIPLAYER GAME

Killing Field is not suited to multiplayer play.

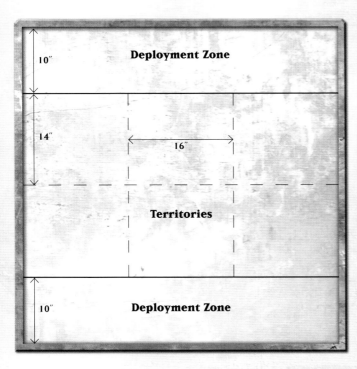

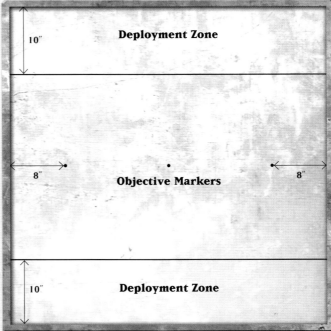

MANGLED METAL

There's nothing like the glorious clamor of warjacks crashing together, hulls ringing and furnaces spewing ash with gouts of sparks and flame, and the deafening screech of metal as one rends the other apart.

—Casner Feist, leader of the Daggermoor Rovers

DESCRIPTION

Mangled Metal is a brutal clash between warjacks in which the only goal is survival. Such a battle proves a warcaster and his 'jacks are the equal of an entire army.

SPECIAL RULES

Each player is allowed only a single warcaster. Besides its one warcaster, each army can include only warjacks; units and solos have no place in Mangled Metal.

VICTORY CONDITIONS

A player wins the game when he has the only remaining warcaster in play or when all his opponents' warjacks have been wrecked or removed from play.

MULTIPLAYER GAME

In multiplayer Mangled Metal, all players should have equal deployment zones, equidistant from each other.

MOSH PIT

Their sacrifice is meaningless. With each death we gain ground.

—Lich Lord Terminus

DESCRIPTION

The rhythm of warfare often leads to decisive moments as enemy lines are crossed or territories lost. Mosh Pit is a bitter, disorganized brawl in the center of the battlefield in which the only rule is to seize the initiative and never back down.

SPECIAL RULES

Mark a 14″-diameter circle centered on the table. This is the **mosh pit**.

A player controls the mosh pit if he has one or more models completely within the mosh pit and his opponent does not. For a unit to control the mosh pit, all models in the unit in play must be completely within it. A warrior model must have a CMD greater than 1 to control the mosh pit. Ignore wrecked or inert warjacks, wild warbeasts, and fleeing models when checking for control.

VICTORY CONDITIONS

A player wins the game when he has the only remaining warcaster(s) in play. Starting on the first player's third turn, a player will also win if he ends his turn in control of the mosh pit.

MULTIPLAYER GAME

In multiplayer Mosh Pit, all players should have equal deployment zones, equidistant from each other.

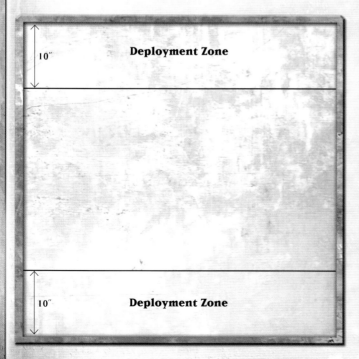

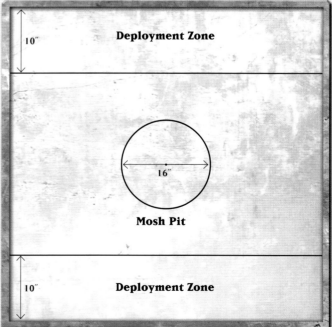

NO MAN'S LAND

In Menoth's name, we shall consecrate this land with the blood of their fallen!

—Grand Scrutator Severius

DESCRIPTION

With battle lines drawn, two great armies converge on the no man's land between them.

SPECIAL RULES

Mark an 8"-wide area, running east to west, centered on the centerline of the table. This is the **no man's land**.

A player controls the no man's land if he has one or more models completely within it and his opponent does not. For a unit to control the no man's land, all models in the unit still in play must be completely within it. A warrior model must have a CMD greater than 1 to control the no man's land. Ignore wrecked or inert warjacks, wild warbeasts, and fleeing models when checking for control.

VICTORY CONDITIONS

A player wins the game when he has the only remaining warcaster(s) in play. Starting on the first player's third turn, a player wins when he ends his turn in control of the no man's land.

MULTIPLAYER GAME

No Man's Land is not suited to multiplayer play.

THROW DOWN

Striking the killing blow is meaningless if you open yourself to a fatal retaliation. This is as true for an army as when fighting blade to blade.

—Vladimir Tzepesci, the Dark Champion

DESCRIPTION

Armies desperately clash across the muddy, blood-drenched field to secure two points of vital strategic importance. Each side strives to gain supremacy while trying to manage their divided forces.

SPECIAL RULES

Mark two points on the centerline of the table, one 8" from the left table edge and one 8" from the right table edge. Each **control zone** is a 10"-diameter circle centered on one of the points.

A player controls a control zone if he has one or more models completely within it and his opponent does not. For a unit to control a control zone, all models in the unit still in play must be completely within it. A warrior model must have a CMD greater than 1 to control a control zone. Ignore wrecked or inert warjacks, wild warbeasts, and fleeing models when checking for control.

VICTORY CONDITIONS

A player wins the game when he has the only remaining warcaster(s) in play. Starting on the first player's third turn, a player will also win if he ends his turn controlling both control zones.

MULTIPLAYER GAME

Throw Down is not suited to multiplayer play.

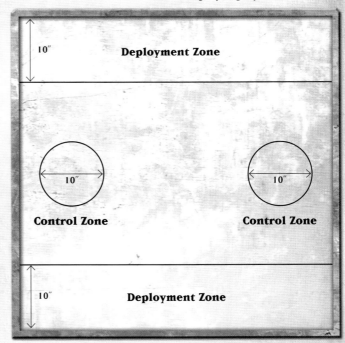

THE FACTIONS OF WARMACHINE

Immoren is a continent fraught with danger and adventure. It is a land steeped in a history of brutal struggles between proud peoples, and the current era has been swept up by the turmoil of war. Whether clashing over land, religion, or more nefarious agendas, each of the peoples of the region is convinced its faction deserves ultimate supremacy.

The warcasters, warjacks, and soldiers depicted in *Prime* serve merely as an introduction to the forces each faction can bring to bear on its enemies. Full rules for many more models for each WARMACHINE faction can be found in its corresponding *Forces of WARMACHINE* book.

CYGNAR
|SIG-nahr|

Cygnar is the crown jewel of the Iron Kingdoms, rich in both resources and manpower. This great nation originally developed warjack technology and is the most technologically advanced of the human factions. Cygnar prides itself on waging war for honorable reasons—though its enemies may dispute that claim.

Cygnar's greatest strength in battle is its ability to deliver unsurpassed damage at a distance with its plentiful supply of cannons, rifles, and pistols. It is well suited to a combined-arms approach to the battlefield and has many abilities that augment ranged attacks. This army contains a strong electrical storm theme.

THE PROTECTORATE OF MENOTH
|MEN-awth|

The devoted masses of the Protectorate of Menoth march forth from the gates of their cathedral fortresses to enlighten the surrounding heathen nations for Menoth's greater glory. They worship the Creator of Man fervently and believe all others should  follow suit. What they lack in technological sophistication they more than make up for with devotion and strength of numbers. Virtually the entire population of the Protectorate can be called to war in times of need.

The Protectorate thrives on protective spells and abilities that use its enemy's actions to make its own forces stronger. Its army contains a strong theme of magic nullification and fire.

KHADOR
|KAY-dohr|

Khador is home to a proud tradition of strength and endurance. Building on this, its empress seeks to expand her empire to reclaim ancient glories and spread the influence of her winter-hardened people. Though Cygnar may have invented the warjack, Khador invented  the first steam engine, and its engineers pride themselves on the rugged reliability of their battle-tested machines. This nation has modernized its military in the last few decades to create a crushingly effective and varied force.

Khador foregoes speed and mobility for sheer brute force and armor. Its warjacks are among the toughest in the game and are supported by powerful artillery. Khador carries a strong theme of ice and wind.

CRYX
|kriks|

The Nightmare Empire of Cryx is a terrifying legion of undying creatures. These worshipers of the Dragonlord Toruk are led into battle by horrible necromantic warcasters who seek to spread his blight of malevolence and life-devouring savagery over the land. The forces of Cryx specialize  in speed and exploiting weaknesses, however small. They have no problem sacrificing their soldiers to set up the perfect assassination strike.

Cryx can field large numbers of troops to overwhelm the enemy and can sometimes create additional troops even in the middle of battle. They also excel at weakening the enemy, giving even their less powerful models a chance to inflict heavy damage. Cryx maintains a strong theme of corrosion and corruption.

OTHER NATIONS OF THE IRON KINGDOMS

The four main kingdoms are central to the conflict in the Iron Kingdoms, but there are other nations and factions as well.

IOS AND THE RETRIBUTION OF SCYRAH

|EYE-ohss| and |SIGH-rah|

The elven nation of Ios has long secluded itself from the kingdoms of man, but recent turmoil among the Iosans has seen the once-outlawed Retribution of Scyrah sect rise to power. The Retribution believes it can save their dying god Scyrah by eliminating the spread of mankind's magic. They are emerging from the shadows with their mighty myrmidons and an army bent on victory at all costs.

Retribution warjacks, called myrmidons, have regenerating force fields that protect them from harm. Within the Retribution exists a duality between the professional soldiers of the Dawnguard and the shadowy assassins of the Mage Hunters. Together these elements join to create forces that can combine speed and stealth with resilience.

RHUL

|rule|

The dwarven nation of Rhul lies in the cold mountains of the north, where they generally keep themselves from the wars of men. Their skilled clansmen and powerful warjacks can often be hired as mercenary support, and though they do not seek to dominate other nations their warriors are among the fiercest fighters in the Iron Kingdoms. The dwarves of Rhul live closely alongside the towering and heavily muscled ogrun, oath-bound warriors who gladly fight as bodyguards for their smaller neighbors.

Rhul's slow-moving but incredibly powerful machines were originally built for industrial use but serve well in warfare. Rhulic soldiers are disciplined and benefit from heavy armor. Explosives and firearms are both aspects of war the Rhulfolk have embraced with undeniable enthusiasm.

ORD

|ohrd|

Squeezed between the rival nations of Cygnar and Khador, Ord struggles to maintain a level of neutrality. Ord's potent navy guards its bustling port cities as its king continually positions himself as a potential trade partner to both larger nations. The Ordic people are known to be brave and stubborn, and their tenacious army has long stood firm against incursions by their northern neighbors. Not all its sailors and fighters serve the crown, however; Ord has become a haven for mercenaries and privateers.

LLAEL

|layl|

Once an ally and trading partner to Cygnar, Llael has been a victim of the ongoing wars and a prize in the battles between other nations. Most of Llael has been occupied by Khador and is counted part of the northern nation's empire while the Protectorate of Menoth managed to seize one of its major cities in the east. The Llaelese people do not know what the future brings, but some among them fight for their freedom, calling on whatever allies they can muster.

Llael was once famous for its skilled alchemists, some of whom have submitted to serve Khador while others have taken their skills abroad. A number of mercenaries have also arisen from this war-torn land, whether driven by patriotism or by the simple lure of coin.

MERCENARIES

As the nations of the Iron Kingdoms war on each other, there are great profits to be made by those willing to risk life and limb in pursuit of coin. The mercenaries of Immoren are as diverse in appearance and approach to combat as they are in motivation. Many of them operate almost as businesses and utilize official charters detailing their conduct and under what circumstances they will sell their bloody services. Other sell-swords have more dubious reputations as bandits, assassins, traitors, and pirates. All find their services in demand by the commanders of Immoren. Not every mercenary is solely motivated by wealth or adventure; some sell their services to fund their own private agendas or personal wars.

Although mercenary forces are not as well supplied as the standing armies of the Iron Kingdoms, their inherent diversity is their strength. Groups of highly trained specialists form armies of incredible flexibility.

BEYOND THE IRON KINGDOMS

Lurking in the shadows of the wilderness are still more threats to the kingdoms of man. The displaced kriels of trollkind maintain a presence in the forests between Cygnar and Khador. An enigmatic organization of druids known as the Circle Orboros inhabit the forests and patiently monitor the machinations of Immoren's dragons. In the east a massive army of warrior tyrants from the Skorne Empire establishes a foothold and prepares for another invasion. Meanwhile, the disembodied dragon Everblight gathers his army of blighted minions to stage his return and eventual challenge to Lord Toruk himself. Explore these factions in greater detail in HORDES, the fully compatible game to WARMACHINE.

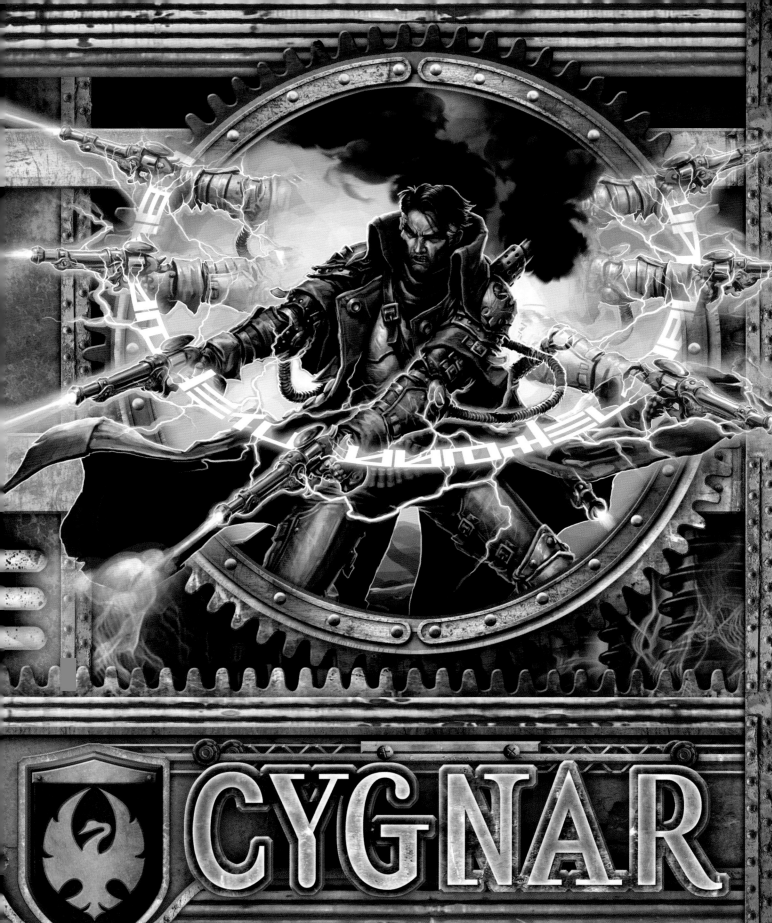

CYGNAR

THE HEAVY CROWN
AN OVERVIEW OF CYGNAR'S HISTORY

The history of Cygnar is as rich as its diverse citizenry. May no mortal man forget the heroic sacrifices of those who have brought us here today.

—King Leto Raelthorne speaking at the expansion of the Royal Cygnaran University

The following is a transcription of a lecture by Professor Gertrude Wickens, professor of Cygnaran history at Corvis University, delivered at the end of the year in 607 AR.

The history of the people of these lands stretches back much further beyond our founding as a single nation. We are the inheritors of ancient and mighty kingdoms whose peoples settled this region long before the landing of the Orgoth invaders.

Our capital Caspia, the City of Walls, was once Calacia and stood thousands of years ago as the center of civilization against the Molgur barbarians. The Midlunds, from whom we here in Corvis trace our roots, brought stability and commerce to a region otherwise fractured by constant warfare and bloodshed. The western Thurians reached intellectual heights and created architectural wonders in an age otherwise dominated by barbarism and fear. Cygnar is a bastion of higher thought, reason, morality, and civilization. This is as true now that we stand united under the Cygnus as when our separate peoples first tamed these lands. We must hold fast to these values even in the face of enemies who would tear down everything our ancestors have built.

In 202 AR the Corvis Treaties brought with them a brief pause in hostilities and ushered in a short golden era. These treaties established our borders and gave birth to the kingdom of Cygnar stretching from the Thornwood and the Dragon's Tongue River in the north to the Broken Coast and the Gulf of Caspia in the south. This new kingdom encompassed an expansive territory boasting fertile farmlands in the northwest and east but also hundreds of miles of trackless wilderness, including the Wyrmwall Mountains, the Gnarls, and the Thornwood Forest. Cygnar is known for its wealth, but those riches have been gained only through the determination and back-breaking toil of its people.

The brief respite following the Corvis Treaties was not to last, as old grudges and ancient feuds were not forgotten. While Khador and Cygnar were "new" nations after the Corvis Treaties, the peoples of these regions had been bitter enemies since the long-gone days of the expansion wars of the old Khardic Empire. Even during the rebellion period against the Orgoth, the generals of the north and the south were distrustful of one another and frequently at odds.

Since the founding of Cygnar our kings have oft been both warriors and sages, and one of the most notable to occupy the throne was the legendary King Woldred the Diligent. Woldred was Cygnar's fourth king and came to power at a time when the royal bloodline had yet to be firmly established and remained bitterly contested. He was our first great king, a man who laid a solid foundation for his successors.

King Woldred was immediately hurled into the chaos of war upon the death of his father, King Benewic II, in the Colossal War. The Colossal War was a truly horrific clash that presaged the nature of modern war. The same colossals by which we had overthrown the Orgoth were now our most formidable weapons.

Woldred set the tone for his reign when, during the first year of his rule, he led a coalition including Ord and Llael to crush Khador's thirst for conquest. Khador was so soundly defeated in the war that its sovereign was forced to accept the harsh terms of the Disarmament Conferences of 257 AR, which included the dismantling of the north's mighty constructs and the establishment of the Colossal Guard. This significantly hindered Khador's capabilities to wage war and allowed for four decades of peace. In 286 AR Woldred would voluntarily give up Cygnar's colossals as well. A series of bloody skirmishes with unruly trollkin populations in the interior demonstrated the inherent vulnerabilities of these hulking machines. With the extreme costs of maintaining the great machines, the Colossal Guard proved unsustainable. This gave rise to the modern warjacks, smaller yet equally formidable constructs that could better negotiate the hazards of the battlefield.

Woldred's last act was the establishment of "Woldred's Covenant," by which he reformed Cygnar's laws of succession. This stated that each king could abdicate the throne on his own terms and choose his successor, thereby avoiding "kin of bad quality." Primogeniture would apply only if other terms were not provided. The Temple of Menoth—which had clung tenaciously to its standing as the state religion despite dwindling numbers—supported the contract only under the condition that their priesthood retained the exclusive right to witness and notarize each king's terms. Though the Morrowan faith was already dominant among the wider population, Menites remained a political, spiritual, and moral force in Cygnar's capital.

When Woldred died unexpectedly in 289 AR, his terms of succession could not be found, though Menite priests insisted they had been drafted. Within a fortnight his nephew Malagant the Grim seized the palace with a force of five hundred soldiers and claimed the throne. The Temple of Menoth refuted Malagant's right to rule and called him a usurper. As a result of this interference, Malagant ordered over two hundred Menite priests arrested and hung over the next several years.

> **PREVIOUS CLASHES WERE NOTHING COMPARED TO THE RIFT THAT WOULD TEAR CASPIA IN HALF STARTING IN 483 AR.**

In 293 AR Malagant proclaimed the Church of Morrow as Cygnar's official religion and dissolved all Menite authority within the government. Public sentiment was strongly in favor of this declaration of a change in state religion; remember, the Morrowan faith had suffered considerable oppression in earlier eras when the Menites had dominated the halls of power. Malagant was seen as a beloved champion of the faith. The Menite minority seethed and protested, prompting some to fear civil war.

The growing strife had consequences abroad. Like a wolf on a blood-scent, Khador's Queen Cherize initiated a border war with Cygnar in 293 AR that lasted until 295, when Queen Cherize suddenly disappeared. King Malagant died shortly thereafter. Ill omens and superstitious rumors surrounded the loss of both sovereigns. They suggested Queen Cherize had relied on dubious allies, such as barbaric cultists twisted into the service of dark and forbidden gods. While Queen Cherize's hostilities were cut short, Khador had not seen its thirst for conquest diminished.

Queen Ayn Vanar V, a mere girl of five winters, was crowned in Khador. Because she was too young to rule, she was represented by Lord Regent Velibor. This charismatic noble exploited his position to initiate an aggressive campaign to expand Khador's borders. Lord Velibor was a warmonger, it is true, but he was also a cunning and shrewd governor.

He proved his ingenuity by turning what could have been a troublesome internal conflict to his benefit.

Just as the trollkin inside Cygnar undermined Woldred's peace, Khador struggled with its own tribal peoples, remnants of a forgotten age. A large number of barbarian tribes persisted on the periphery of that nation, particularly dwelling in its frozen northern mountains and forests and its untamed eastern hills. The last great alliance of these tribes assembled during Velibor's rule, intent on pillaging the fertile farmlands of Khador's interior. Velibor met with tribal leaders and convinced this horde that greater gain could be found to the south. He enticed them with promises of the riches they could garner off the soft southerners, starting with those dwelling in Ord. He intended to dispatch his own forces to follow in the wake of the barbarians and fall upon the weakened armies that stood against them, after which he could conquer new lands. Velibor hoped such tactics would allow him to reclaim territories once held by the Khardic Empire, including swaths of northern Cygnar.

This plan might have succeeded if not for the Siege of Midfast at Ord's northern border in 305 AR. Captain Markus Graza, an Ordic champion of Morrow, single-handedly turned the tide and humbled the northern barbarian chieftains. Ordic reinforcements arrived and swept the barbarians from the field. The cost in blood fell most heavily on the savage tribes, which never again recovered. The Khadoran Army was left unscathed and pursued their border wars for another decade. As a result, Khador seized lands from both Ord and Llael, including the Ordic city once known as Radahvo that is now Port Vladovar. In time this city would become vital to the Khadoran Navy, perfectly situated as it was to harbor mighty war vessels and stage assaults on southern shipping.

Unfortunately nations can be proud, and even these losses did not serve to unite the enemies of Khador. While a formal alliance was sealed between Llael and Cygnar after the border wars, Ord remained neutral and aloof. It is likely they believed Khador had seized enough to satisfy. History has proven the gluttony of that nation knows no bounds.

Other troubles festered. For the next hundred and fifty years, Cygnar simmered with an ever-rising tide of religious animosity. The Menites sowed constant unrest. They vilified the Church of Morrow and denounced its adherents as heretics against the True Law, despite Morrowan attempts to appease them. Many innocents on both sides lost their lives.

Previous clashes were nothing compared to the rift that would tear Caspia in half starting in 483 AR. The eastern city—that portion across the Black River—had always been a haven for the Menite minority. Their charismatic and vocal leader, Visgoth Sulon, called for a pilgrimage of all

Cygnaran Menites to rally to him. Word spread quickly, and tens of thousands of Menites made the trek, coming from all corners of the kingdom. As the masses gathered, Sulon proclaimed himself hierarch of the faith and seized control of Caspia east of the river, pushing out any non-Menites who lingered. Thinking a riot was looming but unaware of the organized and incensed nature of the Menite throngs, the Caspian city watch tried to disperse the crowds. The Menite leaders had violence on their minds, though: thousands of pilgrims rose against the Cygnaran militia and slew over three hundred guards in a frenzied revolt.

This incident ignited the Cygnaran Civil War, which raged from 482–484 AR. Zealous Menites nearly razed the river districts on the west bank of the City of Walls in the extensive fighting that followed. Fueled by a clash of faiths and opportunistic looting, the battles were so fierce and disruptive of the general peace that even the normally restrained priests and defenders of the Church of Morrow joined the fight.

The fate of our capital might have been sealed but for the timely fall of Sulon. His death in battle dealt a great blow to the morale of the Menites and opened the door for peace. High Prelate Shevann, head of the Morrowan Church treasury and a woman of spotless reputation and honesty, stepped forward. Serving as spokeswoman for King Bolton Grey V, she entreated Sulon's successor, Visgoth Ozeall, for an end to the violence. After protracted discussions that elicited concessions on both sides, the Protectorate of Menoth was created in the hopes of ending the religious strife. For a time this succeeded.

The Menites were ceded an expanse of land east of the Black River and the entirety of eastern Caspia, which they immediately named Sul in honor of Hierarch Sulon. The Protectorate had leave to govern their people as they saw fit without interference by the Cygnaran throne. It was understood that the Protectorate was nominally part of Cygnar and subject to disarmament and taxation.

Crowned in 589 AR, five years after the end of the civil war, King Grigor Malfast led the nation into an era of growth not seen since the days of Woldred the Diligent. Steamjacks became more common, and the once-depleted Cygnaran coffers filled with coin. At Malfast's side was his most trusted vassal, Archduke Vinter Raelthorne II. Raelthorne was instrumental in transforming King Malfast's grand schemes into pragmatic reality. The Raelthorne bloodline was already inextricably woven into the fabric of the Cygnaran courts, the first Vinter Raelthorne having been a king decades before and their blood claims tracing back to ancient kings of Caspia and Calacia. Without Vinter II to manage the details of the kingdom, King Malfast would have wasted much of his treasury and this era may have been remembered quite differently.

The Khadoran king of the day, Ruslan Vygor, was a misanthrope with a dark heart, and Cygnar's prosperity stoked his jealous rage. He gathered the largest war host yet seen in the north and executed a wild scheme. In late 510 AR, he sent a portion of this force, including the bulk of the renowned Khadoran cavalry, to the borders of Llael. He knew this would force Malfast to respond. Cygnar's king sent warjacks and riflemen led by Vinter II north to beat back the impending invasion. No one suspected this was only a ruse. Vygor personally led an even larger force of warjacks and the full might of Khador's heavy infantry straight into the forest hoping to drive south and take key Cygnaran territories all but unopposed. They chopped straight

month Thornwood War, which ended with Vygor's demise on the blade of Vinter Raelthorne II.

A few short years later, King Malfast fell ill. He drafted terms from his deathbed according to Woldred's Covenant and handed his crown to then-titled Archduke Vinter Raelthorne II, who accepted the burden. In 515 AR, Vinter Raelthorne II was crowned king, and Cygnar entered the Raelthorne Era.

Vinter II ruled with the same prudent approach he had adopted managing Malfast's kingdom, priding the utilitarian over the frivolous. Typically found deep in thought

through the Thornwood itself, razing a path two hundred miles long that later came to be called the "Warjack Road."

If not for the work of scouts from Fellig who discovered this secondary force, Cygnar would have felt the full brunt of an unexpected Khadoran army deep behind its borders. Hastily gathered soldiers from Corvis, Point Bourne, and Rivercleft met the Khadorans at the Dragon's Tongue even as the main army previously rushing to aid Llael turned back in a desperate forced march to intercept the Khadoran advance.

The Battle of the Tongue, in early 511 AR, remains one of the bloodiest clashes in Cygnaran history. It took all our superior training and leadership to hold the river. The confrontation saw the loss of more warjacks in a single battle than any in the history of western Immoren, only recently exceeded at the Fall of Northguard. It took decades to replace and repair the warjacks destroyed in the comparatively short four-

over matters of state, he was called the Stone-Faced King. He survived two assassination attempts and developed a reputation as both an opponent of unregulated sorcery and a man suspicious of leaders who relied on religious sentiment over common sense.

In 539 AR the crown passed to his son, Vinter Raelthorne III. Vinter III filled the kingdom's coffers through burdensome taxes in order to bolster the navy and fund privateers to secure the western sea-lanes rife with pirate vessels. Many people hated him for his rigid demands despite his successes against raiders along the Broken Coast. He earned a name that played off his father's: the Stoneheart.

The Stoneheart was stern and brooked no nonsense. He claimed to be surrounded by self-interested bureaucrats and sycophants and concluded he could trust no one. He had no use for priests, be they Menite or Morrowan. He dismissed his courtly advisors and looked to "the counsel of his own mind" for making the kingdom's decisions. He may not have been widely praised, but Vinter III moved Cygnar toward greatness. His taxes were harsh, but he was a pragmatist, and his collected monies went to strengthen the kingdom. He did not allow debtors to waste away in prison; citizens who could not pay were instead put on board ships or into quarries to work off what they owed. Many died, but by their toil the kingdom prospered.

Vinter III had two sons: his heir, also named Vinter, and Leto, our good king. When Vinter III died suddenly—some say suspiciously—in 576 AR, the kingdom fell to his eldest son Vinter IV, as no other instructions were found. If the Stoneheart was stern, it is fair to call Vinter IV both paranoid and tyrannical. He was a king of dark demeanor and a violent temper. His father and grandfather had been suspicious of religion, but Vinter IV nursed a hatred of the benevolent Church of Morrow that defied all reason. Woe for us that the Stoneheart had taken no time for Woldred's Covenant.

Vinter IV suspected enemies everywhere. Perceived rivals and dissidents were silenced or forced into obedience. His paranoia gave rise to the Inquisition, when he transformed his father's discreet network of spies into a merciless system of judges and executioners. With their assistance Vinter ruled by terror and murder. Those who opposed him disappeared in the night never to be seen or heard from again.

It was a dark time, and the people grew increasingly eager for reassurance that the government was protecting them from dangers both known and unknown. The targets of the Inquisition were alleged witches and sorcerers, those accused of practicing fell magic and consorting with dark powers. Most people did not realize how often those targeted and invariably convicted were innocent of any crime.

Adding to this fear of supernatural horrors was the sudden rise of Cryxian activity in the midst of Vinter's reign as Cygnar was battered by a series of coastal assaults known as the Scharde Invasions. From 584–588 AR, blackships emerged from the mists and rain to send rapacious raiders into unsuspecting villages and towns, bent on slaughter, arson, and pillage. Graves were despoiled and slain soldiers were dragged away to feed the industries of the Nightmare Empire. Counterstrikes against the Scharde Islands resulted in the loss of a great number of ships and their crews.

For years after these battles, survivors related the tales of the merciless but uncompromising King Vinter "the Elder" Raelthorne IV and his willingness to personally lead Cygnaran forces in battle, while his younger brother Leto "the Younger" was praised for his own valor along the coast. Both the royal brothers led armies in this war, and eventually the Cryxians were driven from our shores. Such heroics made the people far more ready to accept the extreme measures by which King Vinter enforced the peace

on the mainland, at least for a time. Over the years of brutal treatment and harsh taxation, otherwise loyal citizens who had once sung Vinter's praise fell silent. As rumors of torture and barbarity at the hands of the Inquisition persisted, many began to doubt their king's sanity.

Prince Leto watched his brother, appalled at what had become of Cygnaran law and justice. He served his kingdom as best he could, attempting to mitigate the king's tyranny by good works. Unlike his father and brother, Leto had long been a pious Morrowan. Primarch Arius, the current leader of the Church of Morrow, stood as his mentor and spiritual advisor, and in his youth Leto had nearly entered the clergy. Certainly his convictions played a role in the eventual Lion's Coup, a revolt led by Leto in the winter of 594 AR, a decade after the brothers joined together to battle Cryx.

> **VINTER RULED BY TERROR AND MURDER. THOSE WHO OPPOSED HIM DISAPPEARED IN THE NIGHT NEVER TO BE SEEN OR HEARD FROM AGAIN.**

After the Scharde Invasions, Vinter named Leto his Warmaster General. Such a decision proved prophetic, as Leto fostered the most pious officers along with nobles close to his own thinking and weary of their tyrant. These officers would be instrumental in his coup, which was led by prominent officers and royal guard who could no longer endure their sovereign's profane orders. These included: the Magus Arland Calster now head of Caspia's Fraternal Order; Kielon Ebonhart IV, heir to the Northern Midlunds; Alain Runewood, heir to the Eastern Midlunds; and the Scharde Invasion war hero Commander Adept Sebastian Nemo; among others.

This force waged battle through Castle Raelthorne, consuming the east wing of the palace. Whatever his failings as a king, Vinter was a man with no equal with the blade. His blood thirst and practiced skill made him practically invincible. All reports of the battle confirm that Vinter himself cut down scores of Leto's men. Bearing his grandfather's sword Kingslayer, he waded through plate and flesh like an armored galleon cutting through a sea of Cygnaran blood. In the end he stood alone, his own allies defeated, surrounded by the corpses of those who had come against him. He refused all entreaties to surrender. Leto was a veteran of battle and an accomplished bladesman, but he could not match the peerless skill of his older brother. After a short and brutal duel, Vinter dealt Leto what seemed to be a fatal wound.

One moment Leto seemed defeated, but in the next the elder brother was disarmed and laid low and the younger brother's own injury miraculously vanished. Most who have examined the events agree they show signs of Morrow's intervention, likely through Primarch Arius. If anyone short of Morrow could conjure such a miracle, it would be that wise and resolute priest.

Leto declared himself king and cast Vinter into the royal dungeons. Sadly the Elder had many secret allies, who moved immediately. Operatives of the Inquisition took hostage Lady Danae Cresswell, Leto's beloved wife and now queen, and demanded Vinter's release. Leto felt he had little choice and gave the command. It was a ruse; the queen was never seen again. Vinter escaped in an experimental airship at the top of the palace. He rose out of reach of his pursuers but fell mercy to the whims of the wind and drifted east over the arid and desolate Bloodstone Marches.

The grief-stricken King Leto Raelthorne was crowned in a solemn ceremony while noblemen still whispered of the grim circumstances leading to his coronation. The Royal Assembly conducted a trial for the Elder in absentia whereby they stripped him of all Cygnaran rights for his proven crimes and dark alliances. He was convicted of high treason, and his life was declared forfeit.

> ## WE ARE LIVING IN DIFFICULT TIMES. OUR WAY OF LIFE IS THREATENED.

Leto Raelthorne proved true to his word in the years after the coup by abolishing the Inquisition and restoring our nation. We experienced a decade of unprecedented growth, mechanikal inventions and advancements, flourishing trade, and the harmony and efficiency that is the hallmark of a fair and just government.

Still, enemies began to stir around our great kingdom while we remained entranced by our good fortune. Cryx demonstrated it had recovered from what losses it had suffered during the Scharde Invasions, with new strikes along Cygnaran shores. Skirmishes with Protectorate of Menoth zealots along our eastern border began to escalate into organized assaults backed by formidable weaponry as well as blind faith. This gave rise to considerable religious tension in eastern Cygnar as Morrowans became wary of all Menites, even their neighbors. To the north our great ancient enemy, Khador, renewed its dreams of empire.

The first foreshadowing of the state of war in which we now find ourselves began in 603 AR with an attack from an unexpected direction. This was the assault on this very

city by the inhuman skorne. These cruel invaders from across the Bloodstone Marches were a new threat that caught us entirely by surprise. Witnesses identified Vinter Raelthorne IV leading them. It became clear that the tyrant had done the impossible: he had led an army across the desert to strike at Cygnar. He planned to use our city as a stronghold and from here move south to attack Caspia.

Fortunately the resolve of the city was more than he had expected. Those were strange days filled with inexplicable events, and some say Morrow had a hand in our preservation, sending the spirits of soldiers slain in the time of King Malagant to our aid. By force of arms and the help of these unexpected allies, Corvis was rescued and Vinter and the skorne withdrew back across the desert dunes for a time. We should count our blessings; the skorne have a predilection for slavery that nearly matches the Orgoth's.

It is easy to second-guess those entrusted to shoulder the crushing weight of responsibility. Recent accounts suggest King Leto considered a preemptive strike against one of our many enemies as early as 604 AR, not long after the liberation of Corvis. His military advisors analyzed the merits of a costly attack on Cryx or a punitive campaign against the Protectorate of Menoth for its countless treaty violations. Both plans anticipated very high casualty rates for Cygnar and could not guarantee success. I side with those who believe these hypothetical campaigns would have emboldened whichever enemies we ignored and cost too much for too little gain. Striking in one direction would have weakened our defenses in another.

Yet even as King Leto's war council debated their options, Khador hatched new plans of conquest. With little warning they massed their full might against the small nation of Llael. Likely they hoped Cygnar would be too preoccupied to aid its longtime ally. Llael's own prime minister may have collaborated in its betrayal, which would explain why the country's defenses folded rapidly under the merciless Khadoran assault. The western border was penetrated in mere days during the winter season, and later attempts to shore up interior garrisons proved futile.

Cygnar rushed to its ally's defense and was quickly caught up in a series of increasingly desperate battles. Our soldiers bolstered the garrisons at Redwall Fortress and died by the hundreds when it fell. More of our men and machines rushed to the defense of the Llaelese capital, Merywyn, when it was besieged. The Cygnaran Army fought on every front to preserve their freedom, but Khador had strong momentum. Swift and merciless, their invasion swept through Llael like a flood. Khador proved their lack of human decency with the slaughter of the citizens of Riversmet. They razed the entire city to the ground. The entire war lasted less than six months before Llael's corrupt nobles surrendered and capitulated. The fighting fell entirely to Cygnar as our armies withdrew to protect our own borders.

The timing of this invasion could not have been worse. While many of our soldiers were diverted away to die on foreign soil, to the east the Protectorate of Menoth rose up in full defiance. They openly brought siege engines against the very gates of Caspia and infiltrated our land with saboteurs who destroyed our train lines and burned our fields. Hierarch Garrick Voyle called for a crusade against our people and sent his forces abroad, striking wherever we were most vulnerable. So too did Cryx reveal they had been burrowing into the mainland to prey on the living. The Thornwood—our greatest natural barrier against Khador— became riddled with the walking dead and foul necrotite-burning machines led by the tireless lords of the Nightmare Empire. Cryxian forces kept our army and navy occupied by assaulting Highgate, sending ships to intercept trade from Mercir to Ceryl, and otherwise continually harassing our coastal defenses.

The events of recent months within Sul and Caspia are particularly chilling, as we can see in them echoes of the old Cygnaran Civil War. After numerous acts of Menite sabotage, the authorities felt compelled to isolate Cygnaran citizens of that faith lest they commit treachery. These fears were justified by the recent rise of a holy figure called the Harbinger, a young woman they say speaks Menoth's will. She has united their faith as never before. Allegedly the mere glimpse of this woman can turn a rational Cygnaran Menite into a zealot for the Protectorate cause. I do not know if such tales are exaggerated, but events of recent years have proven the truth of many supernatural wonders and horrors previously thought to be mere superstition or rumor.

In response to the Protectorate's failed siege on Caspia, the army launched its own invasion of Sul, an unprecedented and historical feat. Cygnaran warjack cannons breached the supposedly invulnerable walls of Sul and allowed the army to sweep into what was once eastern Caspia, there to disabuse its people of their intended violence. Religious fervor gave the enemy desperate strength and led to an exhausting year of bitter street-to-street fighting. With Cygnar's army unable to seize a quick victory, the Menites regrouped and repelled our forces.

Caspia itself was invaded as Hierarch Voyle led a massive crusade to annihilate our capital. Our good and brave king marched forth with sword in hand to confront the enemy directly, rallying the defenders, but was grievously injured. It was not until the Menites were nearly at the gates of Castle Raelthorne that the tide turned at last. Like Sulon in the Civil War, Hierarch Voyle was struck down and killed by the righteous defenders of the City of Walls. But this victory arrived only after Voyle had carved a tremendous path of

destruction through the ancient capital, annihilating every gate and defender that stood before his fearsome wrath. It will be long before Caspia recovers from this campaign.

This has been the darkest year in Cygnar's history. Despite the slim victory in Caspia, our shores have been raided and our navy occupied battling an endless supply of Cryxian vessels. After years of fighting trench-to-trench along the northern border, Khador managed to reverse the course of the first Thornwood War by toppling Northguard, a previously impregnable bastion. Despite brave deeds and sacrifice, Khador consumed the Thornwood and pushed their soldiers to the Dragon's Tongue River, to the very gates of Corvis. Even as I deliver this lecture, we stand not far from those who would seize this city. Nor is this the end of our troubles. The Skorne Empire returned to test our eastern border, and trollkin tribes in our interior have risen up from the wilderness to harass our trains and beset our roadways.

Here in the streets of Corvis we have seen the army arrive in great strength to preserve the city. I have no doubts regarding the courage of these soldiers, yet there is no one in Cygnar who does not fear for the future of our nation. For a short while the cannons have been silent. After the death of Hierarch Voyle, the Protectorate pulled back to tend its wounds. Khador has slowed its advance, perhaps sated for the time being. History has proven, though, that the only way to convince them to return to their cold northern soil is to break the resolve of their leaders. Our defenses must hold.

We are living in difficult times. Our way of life is threatened. Kingdoms come and go; there is no longer any Morrdh, Tordor, Thuria, Umbrea, or Ryn. One day Cygnar also could be relegated to a historical footnote like these vanished nations.

Our future lies in the hands of our military and the young, men and women such as you who listen to me today. It may be that some of you will decide to put aside the quill and book and take up the rifle instead. Some professors would scoff at this choice, but not I. Morrow preserve us all in these troubling times, and in particular may he shield those who stand watch and protect us from the wolves at the gate.

LIEUTENANT ALLISTER CAINE
CYGNAR WARCASTER

Some men do not wear the uniform comfortably yet are such prodigious killers a nation must put them to use or risk them turned against it.

—*Warmaster General Olson Turpin*

CAINE						
SPD	STR	MAT	RAT	DEF	ARM	CMD
7	5	4	8	17	13	8

SPELLSTORM PISTOL			
RNG	ROF	AOE	POW
12	2	–	12

x2

SWORD	
POW	P+S
3	8

FOCUS	6
DAMAGE	15
FIELD ALLOWANCE	C
WARJACK POINTS	+6
SMALL BASE	

CAINE

Range Amplifier – When this model casts a spell and is the point of origin for the spell, the spell gains +5 RNG.

SPELLSTORM PISTOL

⊘ **Magical Weapon**

FEAT: MAELSTROM

In an awesome display of speed and skill, Allister Caine launches himself into the air and spins about, firing his brace of Spellstorm pistols in rapid succession to rain death upon his enemies.

Caine makes a normal Spellstorm Pistol attack against every enemy model currently in his control area, ignoring intervening models. Caine cannot use Maelstrom while he is in melee. When resolving Maelstrom, Caine has no back arc and his front arc extends to 360°.

SPELLS	COST	RNG	AOE	POW	UP	OFF
BLUR	2	6	–	–	YES	NO
Target friendly model/unit gains +3 DEF against ranged and magic attack rolls.						
DEADEYE	2	6	–	–	NO	NO
Target friendly model/unit gains an additional die on each model's first ranged attack roll this turn.						
SNIPE	2	6	–	–	YES	NO
Target friendly model's/unit's ranged weapons gain +4 RNG.						
TELEPORT	2	SELF	–	–	NO	NO
Place this model anywhere completely within 8″ of its current location, then its activation ends.						
THUNDER STRIKE	4	8	–	14	NO	YES
Instead of suffering a normal damage roll, a non-incorporeal model hit by Thunder Strike is slammed d6″ directly away from the spell's point of origin regardless of its base size and suffers a POW 14 damage roll. Collateral damage from this slam is POW 14.						

TACTICAL TIPS

MAELSTROM – Remember, if Caine forfeited his movement to gain an aiming bonus this activation, he gains +2 on all Maelstrom attack rolls. These attacks are simultaneous.

RANGE AMPLIFIER – Channeled spells do not benefit from Range Amplifier.

TELEPORT – This model cannot be placed in an obstruction or in impassable terrain as a result of this spell.

THUNDER STRIKE – Incorporeal models are not slammed; they just suffer a damage roll.

The Militant Order of the Arcane Tempest requires a great degree of control over its students, for each is expected to graduate as an elite soldier. When it inducted an intense and troubled former hoodlum by the name of Allister Caine, the order had no idea what it had on its hands. He would soon become a warcaster who would single-handedly pioneer gunplay into an art of war.

Caine's warcaster capability was revealed by accident during his gun mage training. His Arcane Tempest instructors were relieved, for the discovery allowed them to speed the brash and defiant young man through their regimen and pass him to other hands. Even after being urged to enlist as a warcaster by King Leto—based on a demonstration of his impressive talents—Caine chafed under instruction and thirsted to put his skills to use in battle.

Shortly after Caine graduated from the Tempest Academy, he made an unfortunate visit back to his hometown of Bainsmarket. There he was incarcerated for the murder of a gangster of no small status. The brash new officer made no attempt to deny his guilt. Rumors suggest invisible hands were involved in extricating the up-and-coming warcaster and officer from his legal troubles. This started his career with a black mark that has never entirely faded.

Despite his significant skill, Caine's ego and irreverent attitude made him a difficult man to befriend. He quickly gained a reputation as a loner, drifter, and scoundrel. He frequented seedy dives along the borders of Cygnar and Ord. He enjoyed slumming in the guise of a common drunk to show off his unmatched skills for a handful of crowns. He spent many nights sleeping in jail cells. His drinking, improprieties with countless women, unrelenting swagger, and insubordination all precluded him from advancement. In fact he is the only warcaster in recent memory to lose his captain's rank just weeks after his initial promotion for "conduct not befitting an officer."

Despite his reputation, those who have fought alongside Caine view him differently. For any who have seen the determination in his eyes when he is outnumbered by an enemy before he unleashes a blazing storm through his pistols, there is no question why he has kept his commission and the right to lead men to war. Observant soldiers who have survived these bloody engagements note Caine's uncanny knack for finding trouble. The frequency with which threats to Cygnar have been neutralized in the ensuing chaos of these supposedly chance encounters suggests some more deliberate providence.

CAPTAIN VICTORIA HALEY
CYGNAR WARCASTER

Burn the dead, consecrate the bones, and render them to ashes lest they return to haunt us.

—Captain Haley, after a decisive victory over a Cryxian invasion force

HALEY						
SPD	STR	MAT	RAT	DEF	ARM	CMD
6	5	6	5	16	14	8

HAND CANNON			
RNG	ROF	AOE	POW
12	1	–	12

VORTEX SPEAR	
POW	P+S
6	11

FOCUS	7
DAMAGE	15
FIELD ALLOWANCE	C
WARJACK POINTS	+5
SMALL BASE	

FEAT: BLITZ

Though she generally prefers a regimented and conservative approach to battle, Captain Haley is capable of launching a massive unified assault with a single command. Carefully managing the energy and resources of her forces, Haley will trigger a deadly offense at precisely the right moment.

Friendly Faction models beginning their activations in Haley's control area can make one additional attack during their activations this turn regardless of a weapon's ROF.

HALEY

Arcane Vortex – This model can immediately negate any spell that targets it or a model within 3" of it by spending 1 focus point before the RNG of the spell is measured. The negated spell does not take effect, but its COST remains spent.

VORTEX SPEAR

⚡ **Magical Weapon**

⟳ **Reach**

Set Defense – A model in this model's front arc suffers –2 on charge, slam power attack, and impact attack rolls against this model.

SPELLS	COST	RNG	AOE	POW	UP	OFF
ARCANE BOLT	2	12	–	11	NO	YES

Magical bolts of energy streak toward the target model.

SPELLS	COST	RNG	AOE	POW	UP	OFF
ARCANE SHIELD	2	6	–	–	YES	NO

Target friendly model/unit gains +3 ARM.

CHAIN LIGHTNING	3	10	–	10	NO	YES

A model hit by Chain Lightning suffers a POW 10 electrical damage roll ⚡, and lightning arcs from that model to d6 consecutive additional models. The lightning arcs to the nearest model it has not already arced to within 4" of the last model it arced to, ignoring this model. Each model the lightning arcs to suffers a POW 10 electrical damage roll ⚡.

DEADEYE	2	6	–	–	NO	NO

Target friendly model/unit gains an additional die on each model's first ranged attack roll this turn.

SCRAMBLE	3	10	–	–	NO	YES

Target enemy warjack immediately advances its current SPD in inches in a direction determined by the deviation template. During this movement, it moves through models with smaller bases if it has enough movement to move completely past their bases. Models it moves through are knocked down. The warjack is knocked down if it contacts an obstacle, an obstruction, or a model with a base equal to or larger than its own. A warjack can be affected by Scramble only once per turn.

TEMPORAL BARRIER	4	SELF	CTRL	–	NO	NO

While in this model's control area, enemy models suffer –2 DEF. Enemy models beginning their activation in this model's control area cannot run or charge. Temporal Barrier lasts for one round.

TACTICAL TIPS

BLITZ – You do not have to spend focus for the additional attacks.

CHAIN LIGHTNING – The lightning can arc to models with Immunity: Electricity; it just cannot damage them. Damage from Chain Lightning strikes is magic damage and is not considered to have been caused by a hit.

SCRAMBLE – Position the deviation template normally, with 1 pointing directly away from the origin of the attack.

TEMPORAL BARRIER – If a model cannot charge, it cannot make a slam or trample power attack either.

A strong-willed woman capable of both grim resolve and singular heroism, Victoria Haley has risen from meager origins to become one of the greatest assets of the Cygnaran Army. She was born in Ingrane, a small but once-thriving fishing village on the western coast of Cygnar, north of Frog's Bight. Her parents were humble folk who endured a hard existence to provide for Victoria and her twin sister. Their lives were simple but happy, and it would have stayed that way were it not for the horrifying intervention of Cryxian raiders.

The girls were just five summers old in late spring of 584 AR when raiders from the Scharde Islands landed on the wooden docks. They charged into the peaceful village and met little resistance. Their mother barely had enough time to push Victoria and her sister Gloria through the cellar trapdoor before the Cryxian forces battered their way inside. Through cracks in the floorboards, Victoria watched in horror as her mother was murdered. She sat frozen in the dark corner as the trapdoor was wrenched open from above, but Gloria was spotted and dragged whimpering from the cellar. Victoria never saw her sister again.

Nothing but dark memories and restless spirits dwell in the ruins of Ingrane. Now the village is a place of shadowy things, and icy winds howl down from the high bluffs to scrape across the necks of travelers and sailors who venture too near. The few survivors of that night gathered what they could of their old lives and made the voyage through moors and woods to the larger nearby town of Ramarck.

Victoria Haley was fostered at a nearby Morrowan abbey. There she was not treated unkindly, but the sisters of the order tried to curb her budding arcane power, believing it was unhealthy. At thirteen summers Victoria fled the school, made her way to New Larkholm, and found employ as a fishmonger's assistant. It was while in the proximity of a laboring steamjack on the docks that her warcaster talents manifested and she caught the eye of military recruiters. In

the army her latent power was ultimately fostered and unleashed, like water rushing through a broken dam. Two years later in 599 AR at the age of 20, she finished her arcane training and joined the ranks of the Cygnaran Army as a powerful warrior and a determined warcaster.

Captain Victoria Haley has a furious loathing for anything Cryxian. Where the armies of the Nightmare Empire assemble she is soon found throwing everything she can muster toward the undead hordes. She has attracted the attention of a particular warwitch, and the two seem hell-bent on mutual destruction. Where Haley moves, Deneghra maneuvers to counter, and more than once their forces have collided in bloody conflict. Captain Haley's motive is clear: there will never be enough bloodshed to balance what the minions of Lord Toruk took from her on the bluffs of Ingrane years ago.

COMMANDER COLEMAN STRYKER
CYGNAR WARCASTER

Coleman in a word? Patriot.

—Captain Victoria Haley

STRYKER						
SPD	STR	MAT	RAT	DEF	ARM	CMD
6	6	7	7	16	15	9

DISRUPTOR PISTOL			
RNG	ROF	AOE	POW
10	1	—	10

QUICKSILVER	
POW	P+S
7	13

FOCUS	6
DAMAGE	17
FIELD ALLOWANCE	C
WARJACK POINTS	+6
SMALL BASE	

FEAT: INVINCIBILITY

Commander Stryker is renowned for his strategic prowess and his protective regard for the soldiers under his command. With powerful arcane energies he shields those around him in a warding that deflects powerful explosions and disperses torrents of incoming fire.

While in Stryker's control area, friendly Faction models gain +5 ARM for one round.

DISRUPTOR PISTOL

Magical Weapon

Disruption – A warjack hit loses its focus points and cannot be allocated focus or channel spells for one round.

QUICKSILVER

Magical Weapon

Disruption – A warjack hit loses its focus points and cannot be allocated focus or channel spells for one round.

SPELLS	COST	RNG	AOE	POW	UP	OFF
ARCANE BLAST	3	10	3	13	NO	YES
A magical energy blast radiates from a single point to strike all models in the AOE.						
ARCANE BOLT	2	12	–	11	NO	YES
Magical bolts of energy streak toward the target model.						
ARCANE SHIELD	2	6	–	–	YES	NO
Target friendly model/unit gains +3 ARM.						
BLUR	2	6	–	–	YES	NO
Target friendly model/unit gains +3 DEF against ranged and magic attack rolls.						
EARTHQUAKE	3	10	5	–	NO	YES
Models hit by Earthquake are knocked down.						
SNIPE	2	6	–	–	YES	NO
Target friendly model's/unit's ranged weapons gain +4 RNG.						

TACTICAL TIPS

EARTHQUAKE – This means every model in the AOE is knocked down, friendly and enemy alike.

Coleman Stryker was only nineteen years old when King Leto took the throne in 594 AR. He fought during the Lion's Coup palace revolt, and though he started the day on the side of Vinter's loyalists, in the end he was instrumental in Leto's success—forever changing the course of history as well as his own destiny.

Born with sorcerous ability, Stryker was a hotheaded youth who wanted nothing more than to become a celebrated hero. Time and experience would temper his passion, and eventually a senior warcaster named Sebastian Nemo would forge him into a great leader.

Under the direct tutelage of Commander Adept Nemo, Stryker mastered the art of martial spellcraft and honed his natural abilities to control the Cygnaran warjacks. They obeyed him with uncanny precision, and he demonstrated none of the usual fumbling and uncertainties of other fresh warcasters. One notable early demonstration of this talent was his ability to tame and control a particularly ornery Ironclad, a battle-seasoned 'jack nicknamed Ol' Rowdy that continues to fight alongside him today.

It was with no small measure of pride that Stryker accepted his mentor's pronouncement that he was ready to hold his own as a full warcaster. He had come a long way, inducted into military life by a less-than-scrupulous benefactor who had set the naive youth on an initially darker path. Had

things gone differently during the Lion's Coup, Coleman Stryker would surely be a different man. But under the often heavy-handed guidance of Nemo, Stryker's course was realigned, and he stalwartly pursued his role as a champion of Cygnar even before earning his first commission.

Not content to idly await the call to battle, Stryker committed to proactive patrols along the border regions, spending time in every significant post where hostile enemies threatened Cygnaran soil. He has had to kill many enemy soldiers and seen close friends die ugly deaths, and at times their faces haunt his thoughts. Still, he knows sacrifice is necessary to preserve the nation he loves.

His dedication to Cygnar's defense allowed him to advance rapidly through the ranks to the coveted position of commander—a distinction he achieved at a remarkably young age. King Leto himself was present for Stryker's promotion ceremony, publicly affirming that this warcaster was the nation's finest young battlefield leader.

Though Commander Stryker sees himself as just another soldier fighting for the crown and his young age may deceive some into believing he has not earned his rank compared to the aged generals leading the king's army, battlefield experience has made him wise beyond his years. He goes to great lengths to preserve the lives of his men.

A fine leader, a better soldier, and one of the most accomplished warcasters in the Iron Kingdoms, Coleman Stryker was born to be a hero of Cygnar and expects to die defending her.

CHARGER
CYGNAR LIGHT WARJACK

If the first shot doesn't get them, the second one will.

—Commander Coleman Stryker

CHARGER						
SPD	STR	MAT	RAT	DEF	ARM	CMD
6	8	6	6	13	16	—

DUAL CANNON			
RNG	ROF	AOE	POW
12	2	—	12

BATTLE HAMMER	
POW	P+S
4	12

DAMAGE

1	2	3	4	5	6
	L			R	
L	L	M	C	R	R
	M	M	C	C	

FIELD ALLOWANCE	U
POINT COST	**4**
MEDIUM BASE	

DUAL CANNON

Powerful Attack – When attacking with this weapon, this model can spend 1 focus point to boost all attack and damage rolls for the attack.

HEIGHT/WEIGHT:	8'7" / 2.6 TONS
ARMAMENT:	DUAL CANNON (LEFT ARM), BATTLE HAMMER (RIGHT ARM)
FUEL LOAD/BURN USAGE:	297 LBS / 6.5 HRS GENERAL, 75 MIN COMBAT
INITIAL SERVICE DATE:	567 AR
CORTEX MANUFACTURER:	FRATERNAL ORDER OF WIZARDRY
ORIG. CHASSIS DESIGN:	CYGNARAN ARMORY

More Chargers have rolled off Cygnaran factory assembly lines and been hammered together in far-flung steamjack shops than any other light warjack in history. Commanders continue to rely on the Charger to bring versatility to the modern battlefield. This mainstay remains a dependable element stationed at nearly every forward post of the army.

The combination of a powerful and reasonably accurate light dual cannon and a heavy battle hammer allows this 'jack to operate with equal ease at range or in close melee. Many journeyman warcasters have cut their teeth with Chargers, sending them forward to blast shells into oncoming infantry and support the advance of heavier warjacks.

The Charger is an improvement on the old reliable Talon, its immediate predecessor. The newer 'jack retains the Talon's powerful pistons and compact steam engine capable of driving it forward at surprising speeds. In addition, a number of subtle upgrades to the leg and hip components afford the Charger greater articulation, which enables it to react more quickly to threats in combat. Its cannon utilizes the reloading assembly originally developed for the Defender's heavy barrel but adds a recoil-based mechanism that helps reload the second cannon barrel for another shot.

LANCER
CYGNAR LIGHT WARJACK

*The Lancer is the most perfect tool of war at our disposal. Give me half a dozen,
and keep the factories cranking.*
—Captain Victoria Haley

Height/Weight:	9´1˝ / 3.15 tons
Armament:	War Spear (right arm), Shock Shield (left arm), Arc Node
Fuel Load/Burn Usage:	363 lbs / 7 hrs general, 70 min combat
Initial Service Date:	601 AR
Cortex Manufacturer:	Cygnaran Armory
Orig. Chassis Design:	Cygnaran Mechaniks Coalition at the Royal Cygnaran University

The development of the arc node and its precursor, the arcantrik relay, is among the most significant advances in modern warfare. A device of unquestionable utility, the arc node allows a warcaster to extend his arcane reach across the battlefield.

For years before the creation of the Lancer, Cygnaran warcasters complained about lacking a proper chassis to support this arcane relay. Cygnaran mechaniks had pioneered the field with such 'jack designs as the Javelin used in the Thornwood War and the Arcane of later years, but neither of these predecessors performed adequately. After several decisive Cryxian victories along Cygnar's western coast, King Leto pressured Warmaster General Turpin to heed the warcasters' assessment and challenged the Royal Cygnaran University to provide a better platform for the costly arc node.

Adapted from the reliable Charger chassis, the Lancer is a rugged yet agile masterpiece. The Lancer was

LANCER
🔷 Arc Node

SHOCK SHIELD
+2 Shield

Cortex Damage – When a warjack is hit by this weapon, it suffers 1 damage point to its first available Cortex system box.

Shock Field – If a warjack in this model's front arc hits it with a melee attack, immediately after the attack is resolved the attacker suffers 1 damage point to its first available Cortex system box. This model loses Shock Field while this weapon system is crippled or locked.

WAR SPEAR
⟳ Reach

Set Defense – A model in this model's front arc suffers –2 on charge, slam power attack, and impact attack rolls against this model.

LANCER						
SPD	STR	MAT	RAT	DEF	ARM	CMD
6	8	6	6	13	16	—

SHOCK SHIELD		
L	POW	P+S
	1	9

WAR SPEAR		
R	POW	P+S
	4	12

DAMAGE

1	2	3	4	5	6
	□	□			
	□	□	□		
□	□	□	□	□	
	L	A	A	R	
L	L	M	C	R	R
	M	M	C	C	

FIELD ALLOWANCE	U
POINT COST	6
MEDIUM BASE	

TACTICAL TIPS

Cortex Damage – Because this damage is caused by the effect when the model is hit, mark it before making the damage roll.

developed with an emphasis on defense and survivability. The machine's main weapon is a heavy spear designed to keep adversaries at bay, and its sturdy shield generates a shock field capable of burning out a warjack cortex on contact. These innovations are the basis for arguably the most valued light warjack in the Cygnaran arsenal.

SENTINEL
CYGNAR LIGHT WARJACK

I'd give my left jewel for a pair of those.

—Lieutenant Allister Caine

SENTINEL						
SPD	STR	MAT	RAT	DEF	ARM	CMD
6	8	6	6	13	16	—

CHAIN GUN

RNG	ROF	AOE	POW
10	1	—	10

ASSAULT SHIELD

POW	P+S
2	10

DAMAGE

1	2	3	4	5	6

	L		R	
L	L	M	C	R	R
	M	M	C	C	

FIELD ALLOWANCE	U
POINT COST	4
MEDIUM BASE	

ASSAULT SHIELD
+2 Shield

SENTINEL

Shield Guard - Once per round, when a friendly model is directly hit by a ranged attack during your opponent's turn while within 2″ of this model, this model can become the target of the attack and be automatically hit instead. This model cannot use Shield Guard if it is incorporeal, knocked down, or stationary.

CHAIN GUN

Strafe [d6] (★Attack) – Make d6 ranged attacks targeting a primary target and any number of secondary targets within 2″ of the first target. Ignore intervening models when declaring secondary targets. A secondary target cannot be targeted by more attacks than the primary target. Strafe counts as one attack for ROF.

HEIGHT/WEIGHT: 8′6″ / 3.25 TONS

ARMAMENT: ASSAULT SHIELD (LEFT ARM), CHAIN GUN (RIGHT ARM)

FUEL LOAD/BURN USAGE: 300 LBS / 6 HRS GENERAL, 65 MIN COMBAT

INITIAL SERVICE DATE: 573 AR

CORTEX MANUFACTURER: CYGNARAN ARMORY

ORIG. CHASSIS DESIGN: ALBERE GUNGRIA, ARCANE MECHANIK AT ROYAL CYGNARAN UNIVERSITY

TACTICAL TIPS

STRAFE – These attacks are simultaneous. Attacks against targets beyond this weapon's range will automatically miss.

The first Cygnaran warjack outfitted with the infantry-shredding chain gun, the Sentinel fills an essential role on the battlefield. Its rapid-fire weapon enables it to cut down swathes of infantry, making it invaluable against charging platoons of Winter Guard, tides of Menite zealots, or waves of Cryxian mechanithralls.

Closing with the Sentinel costs enemies dearly. Once within striking range of the machine, they encounter the crushing power of its assault shield. The warjack has few rivals when deployed in the hands of cunning warcasters who know how to exploit its firepower.

CYCLONE
CYGNAR HEAVY WARJACK

A single Metal Storm cannon can rotate through its barrels nearly once per second, giving it a maximum fire rate in excess of two hundred rounds per minute. The Cyclone has two of them.
—Senior Crew Chief Davlin Rodgers

HEIGHT/WEIGHT:	12´3˝ / 6.5 TONS
ARMAMENT:	DUAL CYCLONE CHAIN GUNS
FUEL LOAD/BURN USAGE:	638 LBS / 5 HRS GENERAL, 50 MINUTES COMBAT
INITIAL SERVICE DATE:	599 AR
CORTEX MANUFACTURER:	FRATERNAL ORDER OF WIZARDRY/CYGNARAN ARMORY
ORIG. CHASSIS DESIGN:	ENGINES EAST

TACTICAL TIPS

RAPID FIRE – Roll for each Metal Storm.

The Cygnaran Armory prides itself on its innovation and technological superiority. This tradition of excellence has been maintained with the recent introduction of the Cyclone, a singularly deadly warjack capable of terrifying displays of rapid firepower.

The Cyclone's chain guns are a refined evolution of their older counterparts on the smaller Sentinel, with smoother cycling of ammunition and a reduced likelihood of jamming after protracted fire. With two sets of spinning barrels at its disposal, this hulking 'jack is a nightmare to Cygnar's enemies. Those unfortunate enough to find themselves caught in its field of fire are literally ripped apart in a hail of smoke and lead.

METAL STORM

Dual Covering Fire (★Action) – Place two 3˝ AOEs anywhere completely within this weapon's RNG, centered on points in this model's LOS, ignoring intervening models. Place one less AOE for each crippled arm system on this model. A model entering or ending its activation in the AOEs suffers a damage roll with POW equal to the POW of this weapon. The AOEs remain in play for one round. If this model is destroyed or removed from play, immediately remove the AOEs from play.

Rapid Fire [d3] – When you decide to make initial attacks with this weapon at the beginning of this model's combat action, roll a d3. The total rolled is the number of initial attacks this model can make with this weapon during the combat action, ignoring ROF.

OPEN FISTS

✊ Open Fist

CYCLONE						
SPD	STR	MAT	RAT	DEF	ARM	CMD
5	11	7	6	12	18	—

METAL STORM				
	RNG	ROF	AOE	POW
L	10	1	—	12

METAL STORM				
	RNG	ROF	AOE	POW
R	10	1	—	12

OPEN FIST		
	POW	P+S
L	3	14

OPEN FIST		
	POW	P+S
R	3	14

DAMAGE

1	2	3	4	5	6
		☐	☐		
	☐	☐	☐	☐	
	☐	☐	☐	☐	
	☐	L		R	☐
L	L	M	C	R	R
	M	M	C	C	

FIELD ALLOWANCE	U
POINT COST	9
LARGE BASE	

Thanks to the warjack's furious suppressive fire, in the Cyclone Cygnaran commanders have a tool capable of supporting sweeping advances across the battlefield, affording them greater ability to engage the enemy where and when they choose.

DEFENDER
CYGNAR HEAVY WARJACK

Today we have revolutionized warfare. With the Defender there is no need to wait to see the whites of their eyes. We will engage the enemy before he realizes the battle has begun.

—Lord General Everett Cathmore upon observing field trials, 563 AR

DEFENDER						
SPD	STR	MAT	RAT	DEF	ARM	CMD
5	11	7	6	12	18	—

HEAVY BARREL			
RNG	ROF	AOE	POW
16	1	—	15

L

SHOCK HAMMER	
POW	P+S
5	16

R

DAMAGE

1	2	3	4	5	6
		□	□		
□	□	□	□	□	□
□	□	□	□	□	□
	L			R	
L	L	M	C	R	R
	M	M	C	C	

FIELD ALLOWANCE	U
POINT COST	9
LARGE BASE	

SHOCK HAMMER

Cortex Damage – When a warjack is hit by this weapon, it suffers 1 damage point to its first available Cortex system box.

The Defender is a stout heavy warjack boasting unprecedented long-range and accurate firepower without sacrificing effectiveness in melee. It is a deadly machine no enemy can ignore, as dangerous at a distance as when it closes.

The primary weapon of this impressive warjack is the enormous heavy barrel, a dec-

HEIGHT/WEIGHT: 12´2˝ / 6.5 TONS
ARMAMENT: HEAVY BARREL (LEFT ARM), SHOCK HAMMER (RIGHT ARM)
FUEL LOAD/BURN USAGE: 655 LBS / 5 HRS GENERAL, 45 MIN COMBAT
INITIAL SERVICE DATE: 564 AR
CORTEX MANUFACTURER: FRATERNAL ORDER OF WIZARDRY
ORIG. CHASSIS DESIGN: CYGNARAN ARMORY

TACTICAL TIPS

CORTEX DAMAGE – Because this damage is caused by the effect when the model is hit, mark it before making the damage roll.

eptively simple-looking cannon. In addition to a rapid reloading mechanism, the cannon has mechanikal stability enhancements that provide accurate fire at tremendous ranges, aided by custom-designed targeting protocols in the machine's advanced cortex. The armory also provided the 'jack with a shock hammer whose electrical jolt causes immediate damage to an enemy cortex.

The design of the Defender marks a significant evolution in Cygnaran military tactics. After bloody clashes with Khador along the northern border during the reign of Vinter III, Cygnaran generals demanded more accurate and longer-ranged firepower. The Cygnaran armory delivered by modifying the chassis of the Ironclad to create a uniquely powerful warjack that has yet to be surpassed in its performance on the battlefield.

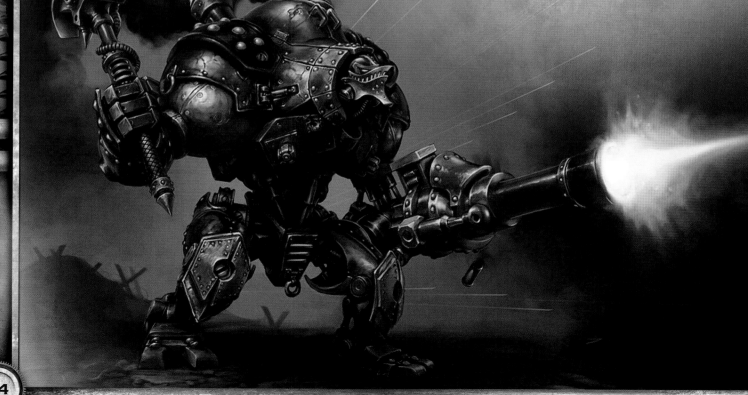

IRONCLAD
CYGNAR HEAVY WARJACK

Six tons of tempered iron and a hammer that can split the earth to knock a 'jack on its exhaust pipes? Pure perfection.
—Gamack Redhammer, Engines East, Corvis

HEIGHT/WEIGHT:	12´3˝ / 6 TONS
ARMAMENT:	QUAKE HAMMER (LEFT ARM)
FUEL LOAD/BURN USAGE:	582 LBS / 5.5 HRS GENERAL, 60 MIN COMBAT
INITIAL SERVICE DATE:	556 AR
CORTEX MANUFACTURER:	FRATERNAL ORDER OF WIZARDRY/CYGNARAN ARMORY
ORIG. CHASSIS DESIGN:	ENGINES EAST

The Ironclad is a walking behemoth of metal twice the height of a man. Gigantic smokestacks blow sooty "breath" from its heartfire's furnace, and the bright orange glow emitting from its mechanikal eyes gives it a fearsome demeanor. Armed with a powerful quake hammer, the Ironclad effortlessly smashes lesser combatants to scrap.

When it came time to upgrade Cygnar's frontline heavy warjack in the 550s, the contract went to Engines East in Corvis. This independent shop had earned its fame a century earlier creating several mainstays of the Cygnaran Army. As good as those predecessors were, they were designed on old principles evolved from mundane

QUAKE HAMMER

Critical Knockdown – On a critical hit, the model hit is knocked down.

Tremor (★Attack) – Tremor affects every model within 2˝ of this model and does not require a target. Make one melee attack roll. If the roll equals or exceeds the DEF of an affected model, it is knocked down. This attack roll cannot be rerolled. This model can make a Tremor special attack if it charges.

OPEN FIST
 Open Fist

IRONCLAD						
SPD	STR	MAT	RAT	DEF	ARM	CMD
5	11	7	6	12	18	—

QUAKE HAMMER		
L	POW	P+S
	7	18

OPEN FIST		
R	POW	P+S
	3	14

DAMAGE

1	2	3	4	5	6
		L		R	
L	L	M	C	R	R
	M	M	C	C	

FIELD ALLOWANCE	U
POINT COST	7
LARGE BASE	

laborjacks. The Ironclad, by contrast, was built from the ground up to be nothing but a weapon of war.

The two most notable advances in this design are the use of a more sophisticated cortex, allowing considerably better performance in combat, and the addition of its signature quake hammer. Even when completely surrounded, the Ironclad can seize victory by smashing the earth with its hammer to send surrounding enemies tumbling to the ground. If an Ironclad cannot break something, it is safe to say that thing cannot be broken.

TACTICAL TIPS

TREMOR – This attack roll is boostable.

ARCANE TEMPEST GUN MAGES
CYGNAR UNIT

Deliver the thunder and fire of your pistols to smite the enemies of our nation.
—Warmaster General Laddermore at the founding of the Militant Order of the Arcane Tempest

LEADER & GRUNTS

SPD	STR	MAT	RAT	DEF	ARM	CMD
6	4	5	7	15	11	8

MAGELOCK PISTOL

RNG	ROF	AOE	POW
10	1	—	10

SWORD

POW	P+S
3	7

FIELD ALLOWANCE	2
LEADER & 5 GRUNTS	6
SMALL BASE	

LEADER & GRUNTS

Arcane Inferno (Order) – Models that received this order can participate in a combined ranged attack this activation. The unit commander must be the primary attacker. When resolving this attack, the AOE of the unit commander's ranged weapon is 3˝. Do not choose an attack type for this attack. A unit can make only one Arcane Inferno attack per activation.

Attack Type – Each time this model makes a normal ranged attack, choose one of the following abilities:

• **Critical Brutal Damage** – On a critical hit, gain an additional die on this weapon's damage roll against the model directly hit.

• **Snipe** – This attack gains +4 RNG.

• **Thunderbolt** – Enemy models hit are pushed d3˝ directly away from the attacking model. On a critical hit, the enemy model is knocked down after being pushed.

MAGELOCK PISTOL
Magical Weapon

Gun mages represent an elite caste of gun fighters within the Cygnaran military. For over two decades the Militant Order of the Arcane Tempest has trained pistol-attuned sorcerers to harness their unique powers. Tempest members focus arcane energy into ammunition for their magelock pistols, which are crafted from an expensive steel alloy noted to be particularly responsive to arcane forces. In the hands of members of the Arcane Tempest these pistols unleash a torrent of deadly energies to enhance their firepower with tactical versatility.

When gun mages of the Arcane Tempest march to join their comrades on the front line, the Tempest uniforms inspire immediate confidence. The mages' pistols portend pyrotechnics to come when these elite gunslingers spring into action. Working as a smoothly oiled machine, they unleash a hail of rune-carved bullets enchanted by their unique sorcery.

Since the invention of the firearm, only a select few have been born with the talent to become gun mages. Such sorcerers feel an instant affinity with pistols and an urge to extend their power through the gun's barrel. Only recently organized by the Cygnaran military, this once secret and exclusive fellowship of duelists has been absorbed into the ranks as gun mages. Arcane Tempest instructors temper talent with discipline and instill each gun mage with unwavering patriotism and utter loyalty to the crown.

Gun mages must earn the right to wield the magelock pistol and wear the uniform of their order. Gun mages are deployed as precision teams to take down adversaries by attacking with coordinated strikes that can knock back enemy warjacks or tear entire ranks of soldiers to shreds with an inferno of concentrated arcane fire.

There's nothing heavier, more expensive, or more useless than a disabled warjack a hundred miles from home.
—Commander Coleman Stryker

Armor gets mangled. Firearms misfire. Warjacks break down.

Any of these things could spell doom to a battlefield commander if it were not for the mechaniks who brave the combat zone. These staunch soldiers dive into the midst of battle wearing little in the way of armor. They shun anything that would impede their ability to move into position and make necessary repairs quickly. Their fixes can be miraculous, and many battles have been turned at the point of defeat by the reappearance of a warjack thought to have been destroyed just moments earlier.

TACTICAL TIPS

REPAIR – A wreck marker cannot be repaired.

CREW CHIEF – Note that as the unit commander, this model is a 'jack marshal. Because the Crew Chief is an Officer, it is the unit 'jack marshal while it is in play. When it is destroyed it does not replace a Gobber Bodger model. Instead a Gobber Bodger in the unit becomes the new unit commander and 'jack marshal.

CREW CHIEF
(★) 'Jack Marshal

(✦) Officer

Iron Sentinel – While B2B with a friendly Faction warjack, this model gains +2 DEF and ARM and cannot be knocked down.

Repair [9] (★Action) – This model can attempt repairs on any damaged friendly Faction warjack. To attempt repairs, this model must be B2B with the damaged warjack and make a skill check. If successful, remove d6 damage points from the warjack's damage grid.

GOBBER GRUNTS
Assist Repair (★Action) – This model can make this special action only when B2B with a friendly Faction warjack. When this model makes an Assist Repair special action, choose another model in this unit with the Repair ability also B2B with that warjack. The chosen model gains a cumulative +1 to its Repair skill on its next Repair skill check to repair that warjack this activation. If it passes the Repair check, remove 1 additional damage point from the warjack for each model that used Assist Repair on the chosen model.

Repair [6] (★Action) – This model can attempt repairs on any damaged friendly Faction warjack. To attempt repairs, this model must be B2B with the damaged warjack and make a skill check. If successful, remove d6 damage points from the warjack's damage grid.

CREW CHIEF						
SPD	STR	MAT	RAT	DEF	ARM	CMD
5	4	3	4	12	11	7

RIVET GUN			
RNG	ROF	AOE	POW
4	1	–	10

MONKEY WRENCH	
POW	P+S
2	6

GOBBER GRUNTS						
SPD	STR	MAT	RAT	DEF	ARM	CMD
6	4	2	2	14	9	4

MONKEY WRENCH	
POW	P+S
2	6

FIELD ALLOWANCE	3
CREW CHIEF & 3 GRUNTS	2
CREW CHIEF & 5 GRUNTS	3
SMALL BASE	

A mechanik's pockets, pouches, and satchels overflow with extra parts and tools. Any self-respecting field mechanik can never have enough gear, as not having a single specific piece might mean disaster for hundreds of soldiers. This is why they keep company with the ever-present and ever-willing gobber bodgers.

Gobbers love to tinker—no matter what, where, or how. They earn a pittance for the dangers they endure to carry extra parts and tools for their crew chiefs, but to them the adventure and excitement of the work is at least half its reward. Nevertheless, the buggers are known for tossing equipment and diving for cover until danger has passed.

LONG GUNNER INFANTRY
CYGNAR UNIT

"I heard they were going to start taking missed shots out of our wages."
"Well, I reckon we don't miss, then."

—Two long gunners conversing at the Falling Star tavern

LEADER & GRUNTS

SPD	STR	MAT	RAT	DEF	ARM	CMD
5	4	4	5	13	12	8

REPEATING LONG GUN

RNG	ROF	AOE	POW
14	2	—	10

SWORD

POW	P+S
3	7

FIELD ALLOWANCE	2
LEADER & 5 GRUNTS	6
LEADER & 9 GRUNTS	10
SMALL BASE	

LEADER & GRUNTS
⊘ Combined Ranged Attack

Dual Shot – When this model forfeits its movement to gain the aiming bonus it can also make one additional ranged attack this activation.

Since the advent of the long gun, Cygnar has assembled skilled riflemen to support its vast armies. Originally the guns were muzzleloaders, and gunners had to line up in pairs with one gunner shooting while the other reloaded each ball down the barrel by hand. The introduction of the breechloader eliminated the need for firing in pairs and vastly improved the rate of fire. Current long guns employ the ammo wheel, with which single gunners can cycle up to six shots by cranking a lever atop the gun. Preloaded replacement wheels are easy to substitute even in the heat of combat, allowing ranks of long gunners to deliver a constant hailstorm of crippling fire.

Long gunners make up the majority of Cygnar's rank-and-file soldiers and represent Cygnar's relatively modern focus on outfitting its army with the best weapons for war. Rifle soldiers were once seen only in small squads providing support fire to the main

TACTICAL TIPS

DUAL SHOT – This is how the model gets to take the second shot allowed by the ROF 2 of its weapon.

line, but now Cygnar relies on them to man its garrisons and defend its borders. Working together with squads of hardened trenchers, the long gunners are the face of the contemporary Cygnaran soldier. They are well trained in concentrating their fire and release barrages of withering shots that tear through even thickly armored enemies and warjacks. Fresh recruits who have just learned to handle their weapons fight alongside seasoned veterans who have earned widespread fame and notoriety for their skill.

STORMBLADE INFANTRY
CYGNAR STORM KNIGHT UNIT

Gods use lightning to wage war. Now Leto can, too!
—Chief Mechanik Garrison Grohl immediately after firing the first storm glaive

Stormblades are ready to face insurmountable odds and wield the most advanced mechanika Cygnar has to offer. Part of an initiative begun by Warmaster General Leto Raelthorne in the years before he seized the crown from his brother, these heavily armored soldiers were each handpicked to become knights of storm. They have become the finest fighting men serving the king, supplementing ancient martial tradition with state-of-the-art weaponry.

Upon selection for the Stormblades, each soldier begins intensive training in the use of the storm glaive. This ingenious weapon builds on the Caspian enthusiasm for sword warfare with powerful mechanikal storm technology. The blade itself, forged to exacting specifications, contains a lattice of conductive materials to direct and regulate the flow of powerful electrical energies from its storm chamber. In properly trained hands, a storm glaive can even send lightning forth to blast enemies at a distance.

Each Stormblade sergeant carries a modified storm glaive specifically designed to work in synergy with the glaives of his unit and capable of conducting massive electrical surges. In wielding this weapon, the sergeant becomes the heart of an electrical storm that feeds on the energy of each glaive and amplifies each weapon's electrical charge.

A Stormblade's armor insulates him against the currents of his weapon and is designed to withstand the deadly fingers of energy that arc from each member to the next. In combat Stormblades are surrounded by a nimbus of flashing lightning, a sight that represents a fearsome presage of the future of Cygnaran warfare.

LEADER & GRUNTS

⚔ **Combined Melee Attack**

⚡ **Immunity: Electricity**

Electrical Arc – The Leader and models in this unit within 5˝ of it gain +2 RNG to ranged attacks and +2 to melee and ranged attack damage rolls.

STORM GLAIVE BLAST

⚡ **Damage Type: Electricity**

LEADER & GRUNTS						
SPD	STR	MAT	RAT	DEF	ARM	CMD
5	6	7	5	12	15	9

STORM GLAIVE BLAST			
RNG	ROF	AOE	POW
4	1	—	12

STORM GLAIVE	
POW	P+S
7	13

FIELD ALLOWANCE	2
LEADER & 5 GRUNTS	5
SMALL BASE	

TRENCHER INFANTRY
CYGNAR UNIT

They endure a life hunkered down in hip-deep mud as explosions rattle the landscape. Armed against war's horrors with only a rifle and courage, it is by their sacrifice our borders stay safe.

—King Leto Raelthorne

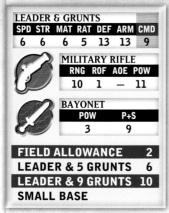

LEADER & GRUNTS						
SPD	STR	MAT	RAT	DEF	ARM	CMD
6	6	6	5	13	13	9

MILITARY RIFLE			
RNG	ROF	AOE	POW
10	1	—	11

BAYONET	
POW	P+S
3	9

FIELD ALLOWANCE	2
LEADER & 5 GRUNTS	6
LEADER & 9 GRUNTS	10
SMALL BASE	

LEADER & GRUNTS

➲ **Advance Deployment**

⊘ **Combined Ranged Attack**

Assault (Order) – Affected models must charge or run. As part of a charge, after moving but before making its charge attack, an affected model can make one ranged attack targeting the model charged unless they were in melee with each other at the start of the affected model's activation. Models that received this order cannot make combined ranged attacks this activation. When resolving an Assault ranged attack, the attacking model does not suffer the target in melee penalty. If the target is not in melee range after moving, the affected model must still make the ranged attack before its activation ends.

Dig In (★Action) – This model gains cover, does not suffer blast damage, and does not block LOS. The model remains dug in until it moves, is placed, or is engaged. The model cannot dig into solid rock or man-made constructions. This model can begin the game dug in.

Smoke Bombs (★Action) – Place a 3" AOE cloud effect in play. Its center point must be within 1" of this model. This AOE remains in play for one round.

and hold it, enduring the concussive blasts of cannon and warjack fire to buy time for the rest of the army to advance.

These steadfast soldiers embody the courage of young Cygnaran patriots, and each is aware that every day he or his friends may be returning home in a box. Trenchers are armed with heavy rifles ready to be set with trench knife bayonets, and they carry hazer smoke grenades that emit thick, gray clouds of smoke to obscure their position from the enemy. When the time is right, trenchers charge forth from their ditches to decimate the enemy with bayonets flashing and rifles roaring.

Trenchers began as an experiment by Cygnaran generals to see if hard training could shape surly or even insubordinate youths into skillful warriors. Every trencher endures a harsh regimen to be forged into a soldier capable of enduring war's horrors. Over the years many retired veterans have eagerly answered the call back to duty to train the next generation for war, teaching recruits their first lesson: "Once a trencher, always a trencher."

The trenchers have earned a reputation as being men of grit who can be found at the forefront of every battlefield. Sometimes informally called "gravediggers," they are the first onto the field and often the last to leave. It is the trenchers' duty to precede the van and prepare the battlefield. Across trench lines and hastily dug emplacements, they seize ground

TACTICAL TIPS

ASSAULT (ORDER) – The assaulting model ignores the target in melee penalty even if is not in melee range of its charge target after moving.

JOURNEYMAN WARCASTER
CYGNAR SOLO

When you can caress a flower with the same hand you use to render stone to dust,
only then are you ready.

—Ideal given to apprentice warcasters by their mentors

SPELLS	COST	RNG	AOE	POW	UP	OFF
ARCANE BOLT	2	12	–	11	NO	YES
Magical bolts of energy streak toward the target model.						
ARCANE SHIELD	2	6	–	–	YES	NO
Target friendly model/unit gains +3 ARM.						

JOURNEYMAN WARCASTER

✪ **Fearless**

Journeyman Warcaster – This model is not a warcaster but has the following warcaster special rules: Battlegroup Commander, Control Area, Focus Manipulation, Power Field, and Spellcaster.

MECHANIKA BLADE

◉ **Magical Weapon**

JOURNEYMAN WARCASTER						
SPD	STR	MAT	RAT	DEF	ARM	CMD
6	5	5	4	14	14	7

HAND CANNON			
RNG	ROF	AOE	POW
12	1	–	12

MECHANIKA BLADE	
POW	P+S
5	10

FOCUS	3
DAMAGE	5
FIELD ALLOWANCE	1
POINT COST	3
SMALL BASE	

The tales of warcaster accomplishments have brought many hopefuls to the Strategic Academy to see if they have the spark. It is difficult to predict who will manifest the ability to meld his mind with a warjack cortex. Those who prove promising begin training with veterans of the warcaster discipline in the hopes of unlocking their potential. Finding new warcasters is one of the kingdom's highest priorities.

Becoming a warcaster requires a soldier to reinvent himself. Many fresh warcasters have already served for years before realizing their ability to sense cortexes and must work hard to master these new skills. Beginning as apprentices, they control labor-exclusive steamjacks. Soon they move to disarmed warjacks and eventually earn the right to command a warjack—albeit typically an old or battered one—when reaching journeyman rank.

As part of a tradition as old as the Strategic Academy, each journeyman spends a tour of duty under the tutelage of a veteran warcaster before graduating to the title of magus. In a time of war, this means journeymen must learn vital lessons while evading death, and some will not survive the tour. New warcasters are juicy targets of opportunity, and enemies seek to kill them before they can mature into greater threats. As they develop they become great assets, fighting alongside their mentors and learning to become leaders of men and machines. Some mentors wince at allowing a rookie to command a six-ton powerhouse with lives on the line, but most know it is a crucial step in their development. Only the heat of battle burns hot enough to forge even the strongest talents into accomplished warcasters.

TACTICAL TIPS

JOURNEYMAN WARCASTER – This model is a non-warcaster model and is not affected by special rules that specifically affect warcasters. Models with the Attached rule cannot be attached to this model.

PROTECTORATE OF MENOTH

TRIALS OF FAITH
A HISTORY OF THE PROTECTORATE OF MENOTH

We are justified by faith, and faith is the heart of our salvation. The road to salvation, however, is long and narrow, and it must be paved with the skulls of heretics. Those of you with faith are the builders of this road—our road—to salvation!

—Hierarch Sulon, welcoming pilgrims to Caspia, 481 AR

The following were the words of Grand Scrutator Severius on the topic of the Protectorate's history, recorded in 604 AR for posterity.

As long as man could speak the words of prayer, he has worshipped Menoth. Mankind arose from the froth when the shadow of the Creator fell on the still-forming waters of the world. Since that creation, we have been His. Never forget that our flesh, our souls, all our works are His, and He may reclaim us whenever it suits His needs. In the dawn of our creation the Creator did not coddle us because He knew our strength must rise from travail.

Humanity gathered into tribes in the difficult and wild lands where every shadow hid a threat and every nightfall presented the uncertainty of waking. Great beasts stalked us, and we learned to hunt them in turn. Our tribes wandered for millennia, enduring the elements and toiling to survive. We became stronger and more worthy. In our ignorance we did not know, even then, that we fought the Creator's ancient foe, the Devourer Wurm. We were being forged into weapons by His hand.

We know not the extent of the tribes of ancient man, but we gathered on the fertile land by riverbanks and the coasts of the ocean seeking to learn our place in the world. In the beginning man was a trivial thing to his Shaper, but our resilience did not go unnoticed. Man ascended above the beasts. To those deemed worthy Menoth gave the gifts of fire, stonework, and agriculture. The first and greatest of these men we know of was Cinot, to whom Menoth revealed the True Law transcribed in stone as the Canon at Icthier. We made structures to glorify Menoth and walls to shield our people from the wilderness.

By the favor of Menoth the first priest-kings rose up as a caste above all lesser citizens, and each man knew his place in the order of things. Menoth's covenants ensured we led our lives in obedience to His priests, who themselves remained obedient to the True Law. We offered prayers in recognition of our Creator so that He would never be forgotten, lest we lose all and surrender our rightful dominance over beast and wilderness. This was the birth of the Temple and the Sacred Flame, an imperishable fire that would burn in every temple, uniting them as one and symbolizing our promises. Villages arose; some few survived and still stand as cities today.

Heed my attention to these ancient times. You must feel in your bones and sinew that we are part of a sacred covenant with our Creator from the dawn of mankind. The ills of this world arise from those who have forgotten or shamelessly abandoned this first and most important promise. Menoth is our Creator and Lawgiver, and He gave us everything we required to foster civilization and thrive. When He turned away to manage divine affairs He left His priests in His place.

Men are akin to children—so easily do they go astray. Even a priest may lose his path if we scrutators do not remain firm and willing to provide discipline. After millennia the first tribes broke apart, and many forgot their place. Man fell to worshipping false idols and revering his ancestors rather than the Lawgiver. Some wayward tribes entered a deeper betrayal by offering worship to the Devourer Wurm, the Beast of All Shapes, enemy of the Creator. Lesser gods arose, allowed to exist only by the sufferance of benevolent Menoth, while those they led astray forgot to praise Him without whom they would be only dust.

Time is as nothing to Menoth and at long last He turned back to survey his creation. When He saw how many had forgotten the True Law, He was much displeased, and His wrath was awakened. In spite of His anger, Menoth did not yet wish to destroy His creation. Rather, He sent a peril to test us: in 600 BR, the Orgoth arrived on our shores. Their invasion would be a lesson of what might come to us if humanity neglected its faith.

Without Menoth's favor, our bones would lie moldering in the earth, or we would be adrift in a void of lawlessness. Mankind experienced absolute despair under the grip of the Orgoth and were thereby humbled. Menoth allowed the Rebellion to succeed to afford us a second chance to rectify our follies.

After the Orgoth quit our lands, the priesthood rebuilt our temples and walls and erected monuments to His glory. We helped the peoples of Immoren recover while spreading His word. Some listened, but others chose to abide by heretical teachings, once more turning their backs on the Creator.

Our missionaries walked among them to teach the lesser faiths their place, particularly those calling themselves Morrowans—members of a dangerous faith increasing in popularity. Those who followed the creed of their deceitful god and his even more wretched sister were seduced by easy and slothful tenets and showed a devotion requiring no discipline or adherence to ancient laws. We tolerated this unworthy rabble only as long as they acknowledged Menoth as supreme. Perhaps we were too indulgent.

> ## THAT THE POPULACE TOLERATED SUCH UNFORGIVABLE ACTIONS WAS A SIGN OF HOW MANY HAD FALLEN FROM GRACE.

Man is lazy and weak, so the lesser faiths spread over time, especially among the uneducated and lowborn. Those descended from the ancient priest-kings understood better that each man must know his place, both those born to govern and those born to be governed. During the rule of Woldred the Diligent in the 280s, our right to oversee the proper passing of the Cygnaran crown was formalized in law. Woldred understood the priesthood should be entrusted to recognize and authorize a worthy king, yet those who would undermine our faith were busy seeking to overthrow divine law. When Woldred became ill and died suddenly, our priests ushered his soul back to the Creator, but heretics calling themselves Morrowans unleashed their plot. The usurper Malagant toppled the rightful order by removing our priesthood from the halls of power and replacing them with those more amenable to his designs. Malagant went so far as to order the murder of hundreds of our priesthood. His blasphemy went unchecked.

That the populace tolerated such unforgivable actions was a sign of how many had fallen from grace. Our priests could not be faulted for their efforts, except to say they sought too hard to preserve the peace when it had already been broken. They fought in the Cygnaran courts for generations attempting to reconcile ancient Menite law with the increasingly corrupted revisions created through the influence of false prophets. They did not realize those very courts had lost all legitimacy and that violence would be required to restore the divine order.

Menoth watched and was displeased with the Cygnaran kings. His wrath stirred. The Cygnarans had turned away from Him in great numbers. They were like sheep scared away from their shepherd by a howling wolf intent on devouring them, and that wolf was their heretic king.

Things could not have been bleaker for the faithful when the Creator sent us Sulon. A visionary, he proved to be the greatest mortal leader since the ancient priest-kings Khardovic and Golivant. Sulon was granted the holy sight, and he quickly rose to the station of visgoth of Caspia. Soon his words were known in every corner of Cygnar. He announced a great pilgrimage by which all servants of the Creator should join him in Caspia. In eastern Caspia, Visgoth Sulon organized those who flocked to him, initiated more scrutators, and trained the faithful as warriors, knights, and war priests. Knights Exemplar and others willing to bear arms were called from their posts and temples throughout the kingdom to join the visgoth at the new era's birthplace.

A vast number journeyed to the site of our new beginning, the City of Walls. This was the city that had once been Calacia, the birthplace of Priest-King Golivant. It was holy ground long before the heresy of the Twins and the building of their indolent Sancteum.

By 482 AR Visgoth Sulon stood atop the ancient Great Temple of the Creator. His vision had become reality. From the summit of this temple's elevated altar platform he looked out over a sea of tents and wagons filling the open spaces with faithful men and women involved in the industry of arming and preparing for what must come. Eastern Caspia had become the largest temple to Menoth in the world. Hundreds of thousands of our brothers and sisters joined in prayer. On the holy day we now call the Birth of Sulon, Sulon donned new vestments and became the first to adopt the title of hierarch since before the time of the Orgoth. Those amassed wept, overcome by rapture. Though the overly proud Khadoran visgoths refused to acknowledge Sulon's claim, among those gathered he was embraced as the uncontested leader of all the Faithful.

That same year, the hierarch banished any unbelievers lingering in eastern Caspia to west of the bridge, seeking to make room for the faithful in the crowded streets of the district. We were overly indulgent in those times, for we allowed them to depart in peace and take what possessions they could carry. Those same people to whom we offered mercy would soon take up arms against us.

The jealous heretic puppets in the Cygnaran court and their primarch master sent armed soldiers to the bridges in preparation to disrupt our holy gathering. Their excuse that they sought to enforce order was a transparent ploy for what was clearly an assassination attempt. Hierarch Sulon, knowing this would come to pass, implored the Menites to "Send them to Urcaen!" With that, the faithful fell on the Cygnarans with righteous fury and overcame them. Hierarch Sulon gave the order, and our forces flooded across the Black River into western Caspia, igniting the fires in which a new kingdom would soon be forged. Amid the battles the bridges fell, and soon all roads joining the two halves of the city were barricaded on either side. Caspia was a city besieged from within.

For two years we fought. It was a tremendous test of our faith. On the first full moon of 484 AR, reinforcements from the north entered Caspia, and Sulon fell in battle against the infidels under the shadow of the Sancteum. Sulon had done enough, and it was Menoth's will His hierarch should join Him in Urcaen. It became clear to those who fought that this would not be the day the Menites would claim Caspia. Their times of trial and testing were not over, and a different path would be required. To commemorate his valor and clarity of vision, every year on the first full moon—on Sulonsphar—our tongues remain still and our hands stay idle for the entire day.

Shortly after the hierarch's defeat, King Bolton Grey V agreed to send an emissary to meet with Visgoth Ozeall, Sulon's most trusted subordinate, and the conflict was soon declared over. A long stretch of land on the southeastern corner of Cygnar became ours to rule as we would. The crown feigned agreement that the Cygnarans would not impose their political will upon us. We were ceded eastern Caspia, for they knew they could never root us out from this sacred land. No longer wishing to be tied to the Cygnaran title, we declared this a new city named

Sul in honor of the first hierarch of the new age. We were Caspians no longer; through our faith we became Sulese.

We knew the land so close to the Bloodstone Marches was bitter and hot, but as Hierarch Sulon once said, "Hardship is the coin of Urcaen." Menoth would be proud of His children should they survive in such a place. Within the borders of this new protectorate, we could mold the vision for which Sulon had sacrificed himself: a Sulese theocracy living life by the True Law and utterly dedicated to Menoth the Creator! So pure a theocracy had not been seen in western Immoren since ancient times. Unhindered by secular distractions we were able to recreate the proper castes of our faith and a society driven solely by worship of the Lawgiver.

There were, of course, terms. This new protectorate would remain part of Cygnar in title and taxes, if not in law or religion. A percentage of coin, Ozeall stated, was a small cost to pay for control over our own destiny. Another term disallowed us from maintaining a standing army, but Ozeall's foresight ensured we would be allowed to raise what defenders were required to preserve our borders from the hostile tribes to the east and to defend our temples. This became the seed from which the true military of our new nation would grow by slow but inexorable measures. A stream of humanity ventured out from the walls of Sul to claim farmland from the difficult soils east of the Black River. It was the new land of the Protectorate of Menoth,

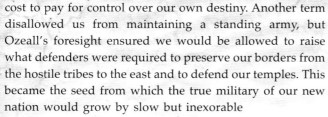

land won by the blood of the faithful.

The land was not easily worked, but increasingly the people realized the fruits of providence. Here had once stood Icthier, one of the most ancient cities of mankind where Cinot had discovered the True Law. Other holy and forgotten temples of those ancient and primal days of our faith awaited our discovery. They would be well worth the looming dangers of the Bloodstone Marches. It is an environment reflective of Menoth and His ancient battles with His first foe. The early years were difficult, and thousands perished trying to civilize these forgotten regions.

Something far better than unearthed relics also presented itself—the Idrian people. At first they seemed a curse rather than a blessing. While we erected our temples amidst brambles and dust and worked to carve our homes from the red sandstone from which the Marches takes its name, the

howling Idrian tribes descended upon us time and again. Sulese and Idrian blood watered the desert from repeated raids, but we remained unwavering. Emboldened by our visgoths and scrutators, we retaliated in kind, putting them to the sword wherever we could find them. If they did not know the name of our Creator or could not accept our holy mandate, they would perish into the earth.

The greatest clash came in 504 AR well to the east of Sul as we moved on the collection of crude huts and hovels of their largest city, called Imer. Suddenly the hand of Menoth struck the earth as a sign, shaking the ground in a tremendous earthquake that sent the Idrians prostrate but left the faithful standing. This was His sign that the slaughter would not serve us nearly as well as converting the savages to His faith. The Idrians had been ignorant, but they were not easily seduced by false gods. They recognized the hand of the divine. Immediately the majority of those tribes, particularly the masses native to Imer, converted to the True Faith and joined us.

Our battles against the Idrians did not end on that day. It would take decades of strife and bloodshed to bring the southern tribes into our faith, but this was the great beginning of the unity of our people. The Idrians brought much-needed numbers to our young nation and showed themselves to be capable warriors and zealous citizens. Imer experienced the fruit of our knowledge and became a modern city with true walls and temples. The converted

Idrians soon proved their loyalty and usefulness to the Temple and later the armies of the Faith.

It was the Idrians who led us to the diamonds beneath the Marches. We have no lust for wealth, but the heretics of the west crave such jewels, and trade was necessary for us to prosper. Harvested gems trickled into the hands of the Cygnaran tax collectors to blind them to our activities and to allow us to retain our more important resources. As long as the shining stones fell into their pockets, they paid no attention as the hierarchs who followed after Sulon began to build the strength of our nation.

Idrians also aided in discovering the pure and blessed oil abundant under the cracked soil, first refined into the weapon known as Menoth's Fury under the rule of Hierarch Turgis. The unrefined fluid is useful to fuel forge fires and keep hearths blazing in temples, but through refinement it becomes truly potent. The oil becomes so volatile it can ignite the instant it is exposed to air, roaring like the manifest wrath of Menoth. Praise Him for revealing this weapon to us, and let its fire consume the heretics who seek to defy His word.

Fifty years after the foundation of the Protectorate, King Vinter Raelthorne III was crowned in Cygnar. He was a man who would tax and harass us mercilessly. The stonehearted reprobate drained our coffers even with the bounty of our diamonds. Tensions rose as our people starved. Vinter III died in 576 AR, and the crown passed to his eldest son. Vinter IV embodied Cygnar's corrupt ways in his treatment of his subjects. He found solace in darkness and put much of his efforts into strangling the life from his people. He was a richly deserved plague on them for having given themselves over to false faiths. The paranoia through which he saw his own followers was a boon to us, for we were able to gather our strength without interference. By Menoth's will, Cygnar was further distracted as horrors from the western islands beset their coasts. As they bled, our strength grew.

We are a people who thrive on strong leadership. Sadly not all leaders of the faith have the same uncompromising strength of character. Hierarch is a title that must be earned and is not given. The founding of the Protectorate saw this from the earliest days when Visgoth Ozeall refused to take the title. He knew his limits and recognized he was not the same caliber of man as Hierarch Sulon. The death of each hierarch has brought a time of turmoil and transition as the Temple adjusted to a new voice, a new manifestation of Menoth's will in the form of man.

Sometimes there is contention among the visgoths; this strife is natural, since we must ensure Menoth's will above petty aspirations. After the death of Hierarch Luctine it was thirteen years before the ascension of Hierarch Turgis,

during which the Synod of Visgoths underwent many changes. It was nineteen years after the death of Turgis before Hierarch Ravonal took the mantle. We were relatively blessed that Ravonal's death presaged only eight years of uncertainty among the ruling Synod. A number of visgoths and senior scrutators sought to elevate themselves at this time, and from the records it seems many forgot their first duty was to Menoth. Visgoth Garrick Voyle rose from this storm of bickering voices, silenced all opposition, and took absolute control over our destinies. Here at last was a man worthy of Ravonal's legacy who would carry us forward into a new age.

It was in 588 AR, at the height of Vinter Raelthorne IV's rule, when Voyle seized power and proclaimed himself hierarch. The divided visgoths and their followers were forced either to recognize his claim or oppose him. Most realized his invincibility and chose the wise course, but for some it would require an abject lesson and punishment. Aside from those few malcontents who soon received their discipline at Tower Judgment, the Temple bowed to him. His strong voice was just what the faithful needed to stand united and more powerful than ever before.

> **PRAISE HIM FOR REVEALING THIS WEAPON TO US, AND LET ITS FIRE CONSUME THE HERETICS WHO SEEK TO DEFY HIS WORD.**

The hierarchy of Garrick Voyle was also accompanied by a miraculous manifestation. He stood before the subjugated visgoths and showed where the True Law had emerged of its own accord upon his skin. Every word of the holy text was divinely scribed on his flesh as the sign of a new dawn. Here was a leader who would fulfill the dream spoken by Hierarch Ravonal, to sever all ties with Cygnar and see our rise as a truly independent nation.

Hierarch Voyle brought our nation to its greatest height since its inception. It was he who relocated the capital from Sul to Imer. It was he who made arrangements with our brothers and sisters across Immoren to ensure warjack cortexes could be crafted in number within our borders rather than relying on the spoils of war or the charity of the faithful in other nations. The Vassals of Menoth were instituted at his insistence. They captured and subdued foreign arcanists and bent their unholy skills to a sacred purpose with our powers of persuasion and torment. The Creator has allowed us to adapt to the challenges of the battles ahead without losing sight of our divine purpose.

Our gaze has turned to Cygnar again. The perfidy of their monarchy has been made clear even to their citizens. In 594 AR Cygnar's prince overthrew the king and gave us King Leto, a man of false faith who could not even heed the laws of his own nation, having usurped the throne from his brother. Cygnar is surrounded by enemies, and we will be the righteous flame that engulfs their capital and returns it to the True Faith. Tempers flare on other borders, and the corruption of the west is about to erupt in a war that will decide the fate of humanity.

> **WE SHALL FINISH WHAT HIERARCH SULON BEGAN SO MANY GENERATIONS BEFORE. WE WILL CONVERT OR CONQUER THE LESSER FAITHS, BEGINNING WITH THAT OF MORROW THE BETRAYER.**

In the last year we received the greatest sign that our rise to triumph is imminent—the emergence of a prophetess and oracle long presaged in our holy texts. She is the Harbinger of Menoth, a miraculous young woman whose sacred flesh refuses to touch the unclean soil. She is the embodiment of Menoth's will and speaks with His voice, arriving unto our capital of Imer for the Synod of the Visgoths to receive her and witness her affirmation of the hierarch's crusade. The great labors our people have endured in the last few years to create hidden factories, stockpile caches of arms and supplies, and build weapons enough to arm every citizen— young or old—will soon come to fruition.

We shall finish what Hierarch Sulon began so many generations before. We will convert or conquer the lesser faiths, beginning with that of Morrow the Betrayer. Every one of our faithful, and even some of our estranged brothers in Khador, will answer the call and recognize the miracle of the Harbinger. Never before have we come together so quickly and with such great purpose.

The following was appended to the preceding historical account by Visgoth Juviah Rhoven of Sul and was widely distributed among the faithful by 607 AR.

It is my honor to record the continuing history of our righteous people. We stand in a time of transformation, and I am struck by Grand Scrutator Severius' foresight. He understood that the sound of our actions today would echo down the ages for eternity. Nothing great is gained without sacrifice.

Shortly after penning the preceding history, Grand Scrutator Severius embarked on his greatest campaign, leading an army that would in time become the Northern Crusade. The impetus for this campaign was a vision delivered by Menoth directly to the Harbinger. She revealed to Hierarch Voyle an imminent threat arising in Cygnar's Thornwood Forest that required her personal intervention. As this was the first time the Harbinger had gone to war, Hierarch Voyle entrusted the leadership of her army to the grand scrutator and decreed that many of our greatest and most holy warriors should accompany them. In addition to confronting the enemies of the Harbinger's vision, the crusade would fight to establish a new bastion of the faith in the north, one that could reach out to the countless wayward Menites living in Khador and elsewhere.

Deep within the vile and corrupted Thornwood—long a haven of those who cleave to the Devourer Wurm—the Harbinger and her holy soldiers clashed with darkness incarnate. I am forbidden to reveal the exact details of this battle to those not of the cloth, but consider that the clash took place on the defiled remains of an Orgoth temple that had been the site of countless atrocities.

During this battle the Harbinger made the ultimate sacrifice to save the souls of thousands of Menites. In giving up her life she thwarted a plan that threatened the integrity of the afterlife itself. Her holy stewards risked terrors and countless threats to return her to Imer for burial. Menoth demonstrated she still had work left to do here on Caen when he graced Hierarch Voyle with the awesome power to restore her to life. Hundreds of thousands of the faithful witnessed her draw breath again and arise to inspire us anew.

While these miracles transpired, the Northern Crusade marched on. Even the temporary loss of the Harbinger was not enough to deter Severius in the tasks set before him. His victories in the north were beyond counting, including the razing of the faithless town of Fisherbrook, the obliteration of a heretical Morrowan monastery outside Fellig, and countless battles against those who would stand in the way of Menoth's glory as he advanced his army into occupied Llael. Accomplished while cut off from reinforcements or support and far from our holy lands, each of these victories was its own miracle and reaffirmed Hierarch Voyle's confidence in Severius. This campaign eventually resulted in the seizure of the fortified city of Leryn, which has been sanctified as the northern bastion from which the crusade could be carried forth indefinitely.

Here in the south other trials of faith awaited us. Our enemies are many, and they are cunning and dangerous. Victory is never a foregone conclusion. I learned this painful lesson in 606 AR.

At that time here in the great and holy city of Sul, we prepared for a massive attack on Caspia while our Cygnaran enemies were distracted by wars abroad. Our battles had become increasingly bitter in recent years as the heretics focused malignant hatred on the destruction of our faith. They went so far as to root out faithful among their own citizens and strip them of lands and liberty, preparing to send them to a squalid island prison for no crime other than paying respect to the Creator. Even as these prison barges steamed down the Black River toward the Gulf of Cygnar, we readied our forces.

To our surprise the Cygnarans succeeded in what we believed was impossible. For weeks they had committed to the apparently futile bombardment of Sul's walls, blessed structures that had never succumbed to force. We underestimated the enemy and paid a great price as those walls were breached and invaders poured forth to defile our sacred streets. The Knights Exemplar and Temple Flameguard gathered to face them resolutely, but the attack was fierce and proved even the faithless can inflict grievous wounds when led by those skilled in battle.

Never has my heart fallen so low as when I beheld the wound in Sul's walls, and yet never have I been so proud of our people as when they rallied to the city's defense. As we fought in the shadow of Sulon's tomb it seemed the souls of warriors from throughout the ages lent us their strength in Menoth's name. Sul was invaded, but it would not fall. We protected the Great Temple of the Creator. We proved that the sacrifices of the faithful could form a wall stronger than any built of stone.

This interminable battle was carried from street to street in Sul for over a year, a grinding stalemate that earned both sides little besides blood and grief. After several reversals we began to gain ground. Upon the fall of one of their most clever, if treacherous, commanders, we pushed Cygnar out of Sul. Our soldiers surged into Caspia, but progress soon stalled and the stalemate resumed.

While we had broken through the outer walls of Caspia, we lacked the strength to push aside its desperate defenders entirely. Hierarch Garrick Voyle paid close attention to the reports of these battles from the heart of his temple in Imer, where he eventually tired of this stalemate. Knowing there could be no victory without his personal invocation of Menoth's powers, Hierarch Voyle marched for Sul with the armies of Imer at his command.

I feel blessed indeed that my eyes have witnessed the wrath of a hierarch incited to battle backed by Menoth's own hand. With Hierarch Voyle leading the way, we charged into the midst of the Cygnarans and left them shattered and destroyed. Everything changed in that hour as we marched through the winding streets of Caspia and won victory after victory.

The Harbinger warned Hierarch Voyle that this would not be the time for our ultimate triumph, but he was not deterred. Garrick Voyle had always been a man of uncompromising principle and inviolable resolve. It was not in his nature to turn aside from an enemy once committed. He accepted the risk of death to strike a significant blow against the heart of our enemy.

After securing a long chain of divinely inspired victories through the streets of Caspia, Voyle eventually reached his limit. Like Sulon over a century before, he fell in battle. Menoth reclaimed him in his hour of glory, while his might lay undiminished. This was a reminder to us that we should be humble and remember that our wars are as nothing compared to the War of Souls in Urcaen.

Our army withdrew in grief from Caspia, and yet we had reclaimed our holy city and demonstrated the strength of our faith. Cygnar witnessed the power of the Creator and countless of their citizens have crossed to join our ranks.

In his history of our nation, Grand Scrutator Severius spoke of how we as a people are at our best when led by a strong leader. How prophetic those words seem. He described the long years of confusion that typically follow a hierarch's passing before another rises to take the reins. For the first time in our history, after Voyle's death we were immediately granted divine omens that made plain the will of Menoth. It was decreed that none other than Severius could assume the governance of our people.

The crusade continues without interruption, and we must focus on the battles at hand. The need to wage war upon the faithless is more crucial now than ever. Whether we do battle here in the lands of our ancestors or abroad with the crusades to bring new faithful to the fold, we must never shrink from the trials that Menoth sets before us.

THE HIGH RECLAIMER
PROTECTORATE WARCASTER

He is nameless and without identity or mercy. He is the High Reclaimer. Heretics flee his approach in terror, but no soul can escape his grasp.

—*High Exemplar Mikael Kreoss*

HIGH RECLAIMER						
SPD	STR	MAT	RAT	DEF	ARM	CMD
5	7	6	4	14	15	8

CREMATOR	
POW	P+S
7	14

FOCUS	5
DAMAGE	18
FIELD ALLOWANCE	C
WARJACK POINTS	+6
SMALL BASE	

FEAT: RESURRECTION

Though the High Reclaimer's primary purpose is to usher souls into the next existence, he has been given the authority to return them from death in order to carry out Menoth's will. This is among the greatest of miracles granted by the Creator of Man, only bestowed on those who will fight to preserve the faith.

Return d3 + 3 friendly destroyed Faction troopers to play. Place those models in formation in their original units completely in the High Reclaimer's control area.

HIGH RECLAIMER

⊙ **Terror**

Oath of Silence – This model does not have the Commander advantage.

Reclaim – This model gains one soul token for each friendly living Faction warrior model destroyed by a continuous effect, an enemy attack, or collateral damage from an enemy attack in its control area. During your Control Phase, after this model replenishes its focus but before it allocates focus, replace each soul token with 1 focus point.

Soulstorm – While this model has one or more soul tokens, enemy models entering or ending their activations within 2″ of it immediately suffer 1 damage point.

CREMATOR

🔥 **Continuous Effect: Fire**

⊘ **Magical Weapon**

⊙ **Reach**

Menoth creates, and He destroys. It is the job of the Reclaimant Order to assist in the latter. They are an extension of Menoth's will, and they return souls to the Shaper of Man to add strength to his wars in Urcaen.

Even other religious orders of the Protectorate balk at the unbending standards and principles to which reclaimers adhere. Their severe masks of iron are bolted shut anytime their wearers walk from the unadorned cells in which they live and eat in solitude. Their last spoken words are their oath to the order before their masks are sealed, and forever after no words escape their lips. Even their prayers are silent.

One man who took the Oath of the Reclaimer's Last Breath has risen above his peers. Through this man the divine power of Menoth flows without effort as he sends forth clouds of burning ash and causes the unworthy to burst into flame, consumed with brutal agony before their lives are snuffed out and their souls sent to Urcaen. Hierarch

SPELLS	COST	RNG	AOE	POW	UP	OFF
ASHES TO ASHES	4	8	*	10	NO	YES

If target model is hit, it and the d6 nearest enemy models within 5″ of it suffer a POW 10 fire damage roll 🔥.

BURNING ASH	1	CTRL	3	–	NO	NO

Place a 3″ cloud effect anywhere completely within this model's control area. While in the AOE, living enemy models suffer –2 to attack rolls. The AOE remains in play for one round.

IMMOLATION	2	8	–	12	NO	YES

Immolation causes fire damage 🔥. On a critical hit, the model hit suffers the Fire continuous effect 🔥.

SACRIFICIAL LAMB	1	CTRL	–	–	NO	NO

Remove one friendly living Faction model in this model's control area from play to allocate 1 focus point to each warjack in this model's battlegroup that is currently in its control area. Sacrificial Lamb can be cast only once per turn.

TACTICAL TIPS

RESURRECTION – You cannot return models to a unit that has been completely destroyed. Remove all damage from returned models. They can activate normally this activation.

SACRIFICIAL LAMB – A warjack cannot exceed normal focus allocation limits as a result of Sacrificial Lamb.

Voyle publicly recognized him as the High Reclaimer, a title denoting absolute unity with the will of the Lawgiver. Never before had a man of this order demonstrated the warcaster talent, and it was immediately obvious that he would bring tremendous strength to the upcoming crusades.

The High Reclaimer's sole weapon is a ceremonial torch called Cremator. It is kept aflame by a continuous supply of concentrated Menoth's Fury. One crushing blow from the High Reclaimer's great weapon smashes limbs and collapses torsos, rends warjack armor like mortified flesh, and ignites anything it does not immediately demolish.

Those soldiers who have marched at his side in battle attest that they know his will without being told. To prepare for each upcoming conflict, the High Reclaimer spends countless hours in meditation and tests his limits with a rigorous regimen of exercises and fasting that tempers his body into corded muscle and sinew akin to iron.

No one is safe from reclamation. It is said Menoth whispers to the High Reclaimer during his prayers, naming those who are to be returned to Him. Enemies, allies, even so-called innocent bystanders are oft reclaimed with no more foreknowledge than the sudden pressure of a crusader's grip or Cremator's hiss as it delivers a killing blow. Even lesser reclaimers know they must not be deficient in their duties, for failure means their own reclamation, perhaps by the High Reclaimer himself.

HIGH EXEMPLAR KREOSS
PROTECTORATE WARCASTER

If you didn't believe in the Creator before, you will today.
—Long Gunner Sergeant Terschel Bannock to a fresh recruit sent into battle against the Knights Exemplar

KREOSS						
SPD	STR	MAT	RAT	DEF	ARM	CMD
5	6	7	4	14	15	8

SPELLBREAKER		
	POW	P+S
	8	14

FOCUS	7
DAMAGE	18
FIELD ALLOWANCE	C
WARJACK POINTS	+5
SMALL BASE	

FEAT: MENOTH'S WRATH

High Exemplar Kreoss stands in perfect harmony with the Old God. With but a few chanted words from an ancient litany, Kreoss unleashes the anger of man's creator to smite all who oppose him to their knees.

Enemy models currently in Kreoss' control area are knocked down.

SPELLBREAKER

⊗ Magical Weapon

⊗ Reach

Chain Weapon – This attack ignores the Buckler and Shield weapon qualities and Shield Wall.

Dispel – When this weapon hits a model/unit, upkeep spells on the model/unit hit immediately expire.

SPELLS	COST	RNG	AOE	POW	UP	OFF
CLEANSING FIRE	3	8	3	14	NO	YES
DEFENDER'S WARD	2	6	–	–	YES	NO
IMMOLATION	2	8	–	12	NO	YES
LAMENTATION	3	SELF	CTRL	–	YES	NO
PURIFICATION	3	SELF	CTRL	–	NO	NO

Cleansing Fire causes fire damage 🔥. On a critical hit, models hit suffer the Fire continuous effect 🔥.

Target friendly Faction model/unit gains +2 DEF and ARM.

Immolation causes fire damage 🔥. On a critical hit, the model hit suffers the Fire continuous effect 🔥.

Enemy models pay double the focus or fury point cost to cast or upkeep spells while in this model's control area.

Continuous effects, animi, and upkeep spells in this model's control area immediately expire.

TACTICAL TIPS

DISPEL – Because they expire immediately, upkeep spells that had an effect when the model was hit or damaged will have no effect.

Though few are blessed enough to know Menoth's will directly, the god's mandates are set in stone and passed from one generation to the next by orders devoted to divine service. These have perfected the means to prepare the Lawgiver's chosen followers for the wars of Caen. Mikael Kreoss, a high exemplar of the Knights Exemplar, is a prime example of Menoth's worldly influence embodied by mortal man.

Kreoss was born into a community of the Old Faith in the rugged north of Khador. Bereft of his mother from birth, the young Mikael aspired to become a paladin of the Order of the Wall to serve as a guardian of the people after debtors conscripted his father into forced labor. The elder Kreoss was overwhelmed with the unrelenting work to reduce his debt while trying to raise his son alone. At last, in hopes of giving his child a better life, he entrusted Mikael to the care of a group of visiting Protectorate pilgrims who took him south to the Protectorate to provide him a proper upbringing surrounded by the faithful.

Mikael channeled the pain of separation from his family into a quest for perfection. So strong was his conviction that he sought to enter the priesthood. As an acolyte, he encountered a band of heathens robbing a sacred crypt. Enraged, Mikael assailed them with no more than his fists and his faith, cracking bones with his bare hands. Towering over his quaking foes, the Khadoran-born Menite seemed a wrathful, unstoppable giant. After crushing these desecrators, he prayed to Menoth for direction at the adjoining temple. While in vigil, Mikael Kreoss realized

his destiny rested with neither the clergy nor the paladins he had admired as a youth. A visiting member of the Knights Exemplar overheard the acolyte at prayer and was impressed enough to invite Kreoss to join their brotherhood. Exemplars say their initiation is their true birth, when old lives and family are put aside. Kreoss left his past behind to pursue his true calling.

Mikael Kreoss quickly rose in Menoth's grace and in the opinion of the ruling visgoths. His efforts were effective in stamping out heretics and blasphemers wherever they were rooted. Even before the Protectorate initiated its larger crusades, Kreoss dedicated himself to going where "the wayward masses spurned Menoth's laws." Kreoss believes every man and woman lives as a gift of the Creator, and those who take Menoth for granted are unworthy of their flesh. He has sent many a dissenting soul to Urcaen for judgment.

High Exemplar Kreoss' concentration is unmatched as he directs interdictions of thousands of zealous soldiers and warjacks to key points in a battle. So strong is his faith that a mere touch from his blessed weapon can revoke the unwholesome sorcery granted by lesser gods to their wayward followers.

Among the people of the Protectorate, Kreoss has become a living legend. When the decision was made to renew war with the Cygnarans, thousands gathered to listen to him stir the faithful in preparation for battle. His flowing robes and thick rune-inlaid armor enhance his impressive physique, while his unwavering faith makes him a leader upon whom the scrutators can rely with absolute confidence.

GRAND SCRUTATOR SEVERIUS
PROTECTORATE WARCASTER

This man embodies my voice on the battlefield. None shall question his authority, lest they incur my wrath.
—Hierarch Garrick Voyle to the assembled Synod of the Nine Visgoths

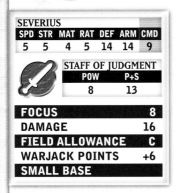

SEVERIUS						
SPD	STR	MAT	RAT	DEF	ARM	CMD
5	5	4	5	14	14	9

STAFF OF JUDGMENT		
	POW	P+S
	8	13

FOCUS	8
DAMAGE	16
FIELD ALLOWANCE	C
WARJACK POINTS	+6
SMALL BASE	

FEAT: DIVINE MIGHT

Endowed with the authority to pass judgment on his fellow man, Grand Scrutator Severius may invoke the prohibitions of Menoth to deny the use of profane magics in his presence.

For one round, enemy models cannot cast spells and lose the Arc Node advantage while in Severius' control area. While in Severius' control area, enemy models with the Focus Manipulation ability do not replenish focus points during their controller's next turn.

SEVERIUS

Convert (★Action) – RNG CMD. Target living enemy non-character trooper model. If the model is in range, it must pass a command check or it becomes a friendly Faction solo under your control for the rest of the game. The converted model cannot activate this turn.

Sacred Ward – This model cannot be targeted by enemy spells.

STAFF OF JUDGMENT

Magical Weapon

Reach

SPELLS	COST	RNG	AOE	POW	UP	OFF
ASHES TO ASHES	4	8	*	10	NO	YES

If target model is hit, it and the d6 nearest enemy models within 5″ of it suffer a POW 10 fire damage roll.

DEATH SENTENCE	2	8	–	–	YES	YES

When a friendly Faction model misses target enemy model/unit with an attack, it can reroll the attack roll. Each attack roll can be rerolled only once as a result of Death Sentence.

DEFENDER'S WARD	2	6	–	–	YES	NO

Target friendly Faction model/unit gains +2 DEF and ARM.

EYE OF MENOTH	3	SELF	CTRL	–	YES	NO

While in this model's control area, friendly Faction models gain +1 to attack and damage rolls.

IMMOLATION	2	8	–	12	NO	YES

Immolation causes fire damage. On a critical hit, the model hit suffers the Fire continuous effect.

VISION	2	6	–	–	YES	NO

The next time target friendly Faction model is directly hit by an attack, it suffers no damage roll from the attack, then Vision expires.

Scrutators require a singular strength of presence; they belong to the inner circle of priests responsible for policing the clergy itself, who in turn control the entire Protectorate of Menoth. They must be able to snap the minds of the faithless and overwhelm them with feelings of piety, servitude, and fear of a divine reckoning. Scrutators cannot show the slightest weakness or doubt. Grand Scrutator Severius is the stoutest pillar holding up the grand Temple of Menoth. Severius answered only to the hierarch and was given command over the entirety of the Protectorate's military.

Severius has single-handedly converted thousands of heathens and infidels to the True Law. In past decades he marched far afield into other nations as an unofficial ambassador of the faith—one too powerful to ignore and too dangerous to confront. After a particularly fruitful trip to Khador in the 570s, he was banned from that nation for the thousands who abandoned the Motherland and answered his call to join the Protectorate. Since the Protectorate has mounted increasingly militant and aggressive crusades, Severius has ceased these missions to focus on leading Menite forces in battle. Conversion remains a priority, but he conducts it now on subjugated villages and towns whose defenders have been slaughtered or driven away.

In a parallel to Menoth's ancient war with the Devourer, Severius lives to battle the enemies of his faith. He has a powerful thirst for the blood of blasphemers and brings a commanding presence and undeniable genius to the battlefield. His warjacks come alive with the same fervor as his converts. His plans are laid well in advance, for he has a brilliant grasp of both strategy and tactics. Indeed, Severius has a plan in motion that will not come to fruition until far past his lifetime. While he is a visionary, he is also deeply traditional and strives to return the world to a state ordained by Menoth at the dawn of civilization.

Age may have withered the warcaster and stolen his former strength, but what he lacks in bodily prowess he makes up for with divine power. As the blaze of Menoth's wrath, he is able to breach the minds of non-believers with a single word. So potent is his righteousness, he wades through otherwise deadly arcane attacks as if they were no more than illusion. Severius is the eye of the hurricane and a center of focused spiritual control willing to annihilate anything around him that threatens his faith.

Severius' divine nature is so strong that if he so chooses, he can thunder the Litany of Menoth declaring the Creator's glory. With a great boom, this divine rite reverberates to all enemy warcasters within earshot, rending their blasphemous connection to their impure mechanika. The litany proves that all things are Menoth's and neither pagan sorcery nor heathen witchcraft can stand against Him. Through Grand Scrutator Severius, Menoth's glory is unmistakable, and His voice shall be heard.

REDEEMER
PROTECTORATE LIGHT WARJACK

Never again shall you fear being outnumbered by heretics. Under a hail of blessed fire their numbers will wither to nothing, scattered by Menoth's hand.

—Senior Scrutator Vorn

REDEEMER						
SPD	STR	MAT	RAT	DEF	ARM	CMD
5	9	6	5	12	17	—

SKYHAMMER			
RNG	ROF	AOE	POW
16	3	3	12

BATTLE MACE	
POW	P+S
4	13

DAMAGE

1	2	3	4	5	6
	L		R		
L	L	M	C	R	R
	M	M	C	C	

FIELD ALLOWANCE	U
POINT COST	6
MEDIUM BASE	

SKYHAMMER

Inaccurate – This model suffers –4 to attack rolls with this weapon.

Armed with devastating long-range rockets, the Redeemer was designed to deliver judgment from afar. This warjack carries an ample supply of Menite-manufactured explosives and a mechanikal rig to launch them. Borrowing technology developed for the Repenter's ignition system, the Redeemer uses vented heartfire to light the propellants. The simple rockets are launched recklessly into enemy ranks to explode in a cascade of deadly debris that leaves enemy infantry with horrible lacerations and extensive burns that are notoriously difficult to heal. The Redeemer can deliver devastating salvos of rocket fire, though the inaccuracy of its weapon usually spreads the projectiles across a wide area, and it wields a brutal mace for close fighting.

In the earliest decades after its production, the Redeemer was instrumental in expanding the borders of the Protectorate to the east and south. It was often employed against rugged and determined bands of

HEIGHT/WEIGHT: 9´10˝ / 4.85 TONS
ARMAMENT: SKYHAMMER ROCKET POD (LEFT ARM), BATTLE MACE (RIGHT ARM)
FUEL LOAD/BURN USAGE: 154 LBS / 5.5 HRS GENERAL, 1.2 HRS COMBAT
INITIAL SERVICE DATE: 545 AR
CORTEX MANUFACTURER: VASSALS OF MENOTH
ORIG. CHASSIS DESIGN: ENGINES EAST/KHADORAN MECHANIKS ASSEMBLY (MODIFIED BY THE SUL-MENITE ARTIFICERS)

Idrian holdouts who refused to convert. Since that time the warjack has been more actively turned against Cygnar and other enemies of the Protectorate, deploying to support both border defenses and active assaults abroad. Many Cygnarans still wait hopefully for long-lost kin, not knowing their bodies lie unrecognizable in the battlefields, torn apart by Redeemer fire.

Our enemies rightly fear its fire, as the cleansing flame inflicts unimaginable pain. Such excruciation forces repentance before death claims them.
—Grand Scrutator Severius

HEIGHT/WEIGHT:	9′10″ / 4.25 TONS
ARMAMENT:	FLAME THROWER (LEFT ARM), WAR FLAIL (RIGHT ARM)
FUEL LOAD/BURN USAGE:	165 LBS / 6 HRS GENERAL, 1.5 HRS COMBAT
INITIAL SERVICE DATE:	533 AR
CORTEX MANUFACTURER:	VASSALS OF MENOTH
ORIG. CHASSIS DESIGN:	ENGINES EAST/KHADORAN MECHANIKS ASSEMBLY (MODIFIED BY THE SUL-MENITE ARTIFICERS)

The Protectorate of Menoth uses the volatile oil known as "Menoth's Fury" in great abundance, a fiery reminder of the faith's burning wrath. Older warjacks like the Repenter are outfitted with the crudest and least refined supply of Menoth's Fury, as it is readily available in quantity. The Repenter was first used to police the borders of the Protectorate, and it brought these scourging flames to bear against any who dared to trespass.

FLAME THROWER

- Continuous Effect: Fire
- Damage Type: Fire

WAR FLAIL

Chain Weapon – This attack ignores the Buckler and Shield weapon qualities and Shield Wall.

REPENTER						
SPD	STR	MAT	RAT	DEF	ARM	CMD
5	9	6	5	12	17	—

FLAME THROWER			
RNG	ROF	AOE	POW
SP 8	1	—	12

WAR FLAIL	
POW	P+S
4	13

DAMAGE					
1	2	3	4	5	6
	L		R		
L	L	M	C	R	R
M	M	C	C		

FIELD ALLOWANCE	U
POINT COST	4
MEDIUM BASE	

When they designed the Repenter decades ago, the Sul-Menite artificers armed the light warjack with a great three-headed flail. Into its other arm they integrated a rudimentary flame thrower. That first model was little more than a pipe and an ignition system attached to a reservoir with a simple pump, but newer versions utilize fanning spray nozzles and refined mechanikal systems to propel the blazing fluid a considerable distance. The latest weapon foregoes an external igniter and instead vents superheated heartfire directly into the fuel.

Arguably as important as the damage wrought by this fire is the impact of a Repenter's blaze on enemy morale. Those of weak faith who face the Protectorate in battle have no stomach or fortitude for seeing their friends burned alive, screaming in terror while allies try desperately to extinguish the hungry flames. The Repenter is a favored vehicle for delivering Menoth's wrath to any enemies who defy his will.

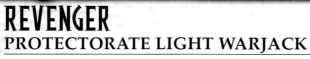

REVENGER
PROTECTORATE LIGHT WARJACK

We carry the words of the Lawgiver to the living, enact his will on Caen, and strike with his fist.

—Hierarch Caltor Turgis to his scrutators

REVENGER						
SPD	STR	MAT	RAT	DEF	ARM	CMD
5	9	6	5	12	17	—

REPULSOR SHIELD		
	POW	P+S
L	1	10

HALBERD		
	POW	P+S
R	4	13

DAMAGE

1	2	3	4	5	6
		☐			
	☐	☐	☐		
	☐	☐	☐	☐	
	L	A	A	R	
L	L	M	C	R	R
	M	M	C	C	

FIELD ALLOWANCE	U
POINT COST	**6**
MEDIUM BASE	

REVENGER
⊕ Arc Node

REPULSOR SHIELD
⊕2 Shield

Repel – When this model hits an enemy model with this weapon during its activation, the model hit is pushed 1″ directly away from this model. When this model is hit with a melee attack made by a model in its front arc, after the attack is resolved the attacking model is pushed 1″ directly away from this model. This model loses Repel while this weapon system is crippled or locked.

HALBERD
⊘ Reach

Powerful Charge – This model gains +2 to charge attack rolls with this weapon.

HEIGHT/WEIGHT:	9′8″ / 4.45 TONS

ARMAMENT: REPULSOR SHIELD (LEFT ARM), HALBERD (RIGHT ARM), ARC NODE

FUEL LOAD/BURN USAGE: 165 LBS / 5.5 HRS GENERAL, 1.2 HRS COMBAT

INITIAL SERVICE DATE: 546 AR

CORTEX MANUFACTURER: VASSALS OF MENOTH

ORIG. CHASSIS DESIGN: ENGINES EAST/KHADORAN MECHANIKS ASSEMBLY (MODIFIED BY THE SUL-MENITE ARTIFICERS)

Menite artificers crafted the powerful repulsor shield to protect this vital weapon in battle. Aided by priests, the artificers inlaid runes of protection on the warjack's shield. If the powerful runes come into contact with an enemy, the foe is immediately rebuked and hurled away. This has given the Revenger the ability to distance itself from superior combatants like heavier 'jacks so that it may retaliate from a safe distance.

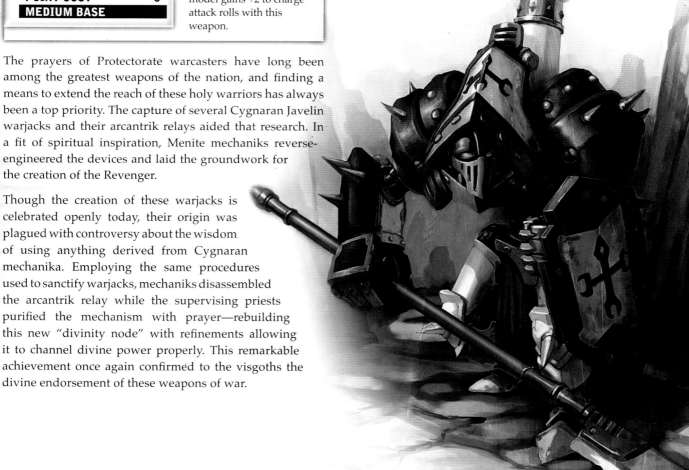

The prayers of Protectorate warcasters have long been among the greatest weapons of the nation, and finding a means to extend the reach of these holy warriors has always been a top priority. The capture of several Cygnaran Javelin warjacks and their arcantrik relays aided that research. In a fit of spiritual inspiration, Menite mechaniks reverse-engineered the devices and laid the groundwork for the creation of the Revenger.

Though the creation of these warjacks is celebrated openly today, their origin was plagued with controversy about the wisdom of using anything derived from Cygnaran mechanika. Employing the same procedures used to sanctify warjacks, mechaniks disassembled the arcantrik relay while the supervising priests purified the mechanism with prayer—rebuilding this new "divinity node" with refinements allowing it to channel divine power properly. This remarkable achievement once again confirmed to the visgoths the divine endorsement of these weapons of war.

CRUSADER
PROTECTORATE HEAVY WARJACK

Behold! We have sanctified this weapon, made by the hands of man, to march and fight at our side. By our combined strength we will wrest a nation loyal to the Creator from these forsaken sands!
—Hierarch Gerard Luctine, at the unveiling of the Crusader

HEIGHT/WEIGHT: 12′ / 8 TONS

ARMAMENT: INFERNO MACE (RIGHT ARM)

FUEL LOAD/BURN USAGE: 253 LBS / 6 HRS GENERAL, 1 HR COMBAT

INITIAL SERVICE DATE: 513 AR

CORTEX MANUFACTURER: VASSALS OF MENOTH

ORIG. CHASSIS DESIGN: ENGINES EAST/KHADORAN MECHANIKS ASSEMBLY (MODIFIED BY THE SUL-MENITE ARTIFICERS)

In its peace terms after the Civil War, Cygnar decreed the Protectorate could not keep a standing army. Visgoth Ozeall acquiesced but secretly commanded engineers to build warjacks using cortexes smuggled from Khador down the Black River and Cygnaran parts salvaged from fields of battle. Those early 'jacks were designed with open hands to pass as laborjacks in casual inspection. Meanwhile, artificers worked to forge weapons for these warjacks to wield as Menoth willed.

The greatest of the new Protectorate designs was the Crusader, a massive warjack boasting heavy armor and capable of crushing attacks. The chassis originated during the reign of Hierarch Luctine, who devoted himself to subjugating outlying Idrian tribes. Even after most converted after the earthquake of 504 AR, many tribes resisted and continued to harass the young nation. The Crusader was unleashed to provide an unstoppable force in the battles to come. It also proved its strength against Cygnar when friction between the two nations prompted clashes along the Black River.

OPEN FIST
👊 Open Fist

INFERNO MACE
🔥 Critical Fire

Already possessed of an immensely durable armored frame and powerful laborjack arms, after the development of Menoth's Fury the Crusader was enhanced by the inferno mace. This weapon, inspired by the flaming maces of the Reclaimers, can easily rend most armor into flaming scrap. When the call to arms sounds, Crusaders assemble at the front line ready to hammer and burn the foes of Menoth to dust and ash.

CRUSADER						
SPD	STR	MAT	RAT	DEF	ARM	CMD
4	11	6	5	10	19	—

OPEN FIST		
	POW	P+S
L	3	14

INFERNO MACE		
	POW	P+S
R	7	18

DAMAGE

1	2	3	4	5	6
	L			R	
L	L	M	C	R	R
	M	M	C	C	

FIELD ALLOWANCE	U
POINT COST	6
LARGE BASE	

TEMPLAR
PROTECTORATE HEAVY WARJACK

Like the Wall with which Menoth blessed us, so is the Templar unassailable. With the judgment of the righteous the Templar strikes down our enemies. These are essential virtues of war.

—Hierarch Caltor Turgis

TEMPLAR						
SPD	STR	MAT	RAT	DEF	ARM	CMD
4	11	6	5	10	19	—

SHIELD L

	POW	P+S
	1	12

FLAIL R

	POW	P+S
	6	17

DAMAGE

1	2	3	4	5	6
	L			R	
L	L	M	C	R	R
	M	M	C	C	

FIELD ALLOWANCE	U
POINT COST	8
LARGE BASE	

SHIELD
⊕2 Shield

FLAIL
⟳ Reach

Beat Back – Immediately after a normal attack with this weapon is resolved during this model's combat action, the enemy model hit can be pushed 1″ directly away from the attacking model. After the enemy model is pushed, the attacking model can advance up to 1″.

Chain Weapon – This attack ignores the Buckler and Shield weapon qualities and Shield Wall.

HEIGHT/WEIGHT: 12′2″ / 8.4 TONS
ARMAMENT: SHIELD (LEFT ARM), FLAIL (RIGHT ARM)
FUEL LOAD/BURN USAGE: 253 LBS / 4 HRS GENERAL, 50 MIN COMBAT
INITIAL SERVICE DATE: 539 AR
CORTEX MANUFACTURER: VASSALS OF MENOTH (CURRENTLY)
ORIG. CHASSIS DESIGN: ENGINES EAST/KHADORAN MECHANIKS ASSEMBLY (MODIFIED BY THE SUL-MENITE ARTIFICERS)

TACTICAL TIPS

BEAT BACK – The attacking model can advance even if the enemy model is destroyed by the attack.

The Templar embodies the Protectorate's simple philosophy of war: smash enemies with overwhelming force from an unassailable position. The strength with which this warjack wields its iron flail is such that its adversaries are hurled back, their shields smashed from their hands and their armor crushed. Even as the Templar beats down enemies of the Faith, it advances further into their midst with unstoppable wrath. Those lucky few who survive its initial onslaught are doomed to fall beneath its inexorable enforcement of the Lawgiver's will.

When former Hierarch Caltor Turgis reunited the Temple in 535 AR, he broadened the Protectorate's borders and ordered the construction of Tower Judgment, with the first Templars created to guard this edifice. The isolation of the Tower was such that the Temple dispensed with the usual practice of convincing the Cygnaran authorities that the warjacks were actually laborjacks. Freed from this pretense, the Protectorate's artificers armed the Templars with simple but impressive weaponry—forever associating the warjack with defending the Protectorate's most important fortifications. Now Templars have become a common sight marching among the crusading ranks of the faithful.

VANQUISHER
PROTECTORATE HEAVY WARJACK

The Canon of the True Law states that his children will walk as giants among men.
Perhaps this Vanquisher is the means to a Great Truth.

—High Exemplar Mikael Kreoss

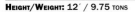

HEIGHT/WEIGHT: 12′ / 9.75 TONS

ARMAMENT: FLAME BELCHER (LEFT ARM), BLAZING STAR FLAIL (RIGHT ARM)

FUEL LOAD/BURN USAGE: 275 LBS / 5 HRS GENERAL, 1 HR COMBAT

INITIAL SERVICE DATE: 598 AR

CORTEX MANUFACTURER: VASSALS OF MENOTH

ORIG. CHASSIS DESIGN: ENGINES EAST/KHADORAN MECHANIKS ASSEMBLY (MODIFIED BY THE SUL-MENITE ARTIFICERS)

The Vanquisher is one of the more recently designed warjacks in the Protectorate's arsenal. Originally assembled in secret in the late 590s from imported parts and armed with distinctive Menite weaponry, this heavy warjack is as subtle as the faith it serves—in other words, not at all. Some say the Vanquisher was the first sign of the full crusade that would later come.

The Vanquisher is a towering behemoth, its great flail a whirling harbinger of death. One arm wields a length of chain nearly as long as a man is tall, its end capped with the "blazing star"—a viciously spiked sphere. It visits swift justice upon infidels, crunching limbs, heads, and torsos in one devastating movement.

FLAME BELCHER
🔥 **Continuous Effect:** Fire

🔥 **Damage Type:** Fire

BLAZING STAR
Chain Weapon – This attack ignores the Buckler and Shield weapon qualities and Shield Wall.

Thresher (★Attack) – This model makes one melee attack with this weapon against each model in its LOS and this weapon's melee range.

In addition to the perilous blazing star, the Vanquisher also wields a flame belcher to send destruction from afar. The flame belcher uses a more recently refined form of Menoth's Fury that requires only exposure to air to ignite. Compressed into a heavy cannonball, these shells burst on impact, spreading an oily blaze hot enough to melt metal before consuming itself.

VANQUISHER						
SPD	STR	MAT	RAT	DEF	ARM	CMD
4	11	6	5	10	19	—

FLAME BELCHER			
RNG	ROF	AOE	POW
10	1	4	14

BLAZING STAR	
POW	P+S
5	16

DAMAGE					
1	2	3	4	5	6
		L		R	
L	L	M	C	R	R
	M	M	C	C	

FIELD ALLOWANCE U
POINT COST 8
LARGE BASE

TACTICAL TIPS
THRESHER – The melee attacks are all simultaneous.

CHOIR OF MENOTH
PROTECTORATE UNIT

Let the True Law be delivered by word as well as deed. Speak Menoth's holy mandates as a shield against those who oppose us. Voiced by the faithful in our righteous cause, these words will become miracles made manifest.

—Hierarch Sulon during the Cygnaran Civil War

LEADER & GRUNTS						
SPD	STR	MAT	RAT	DEF	ARM	CMD
6	4	4	4	12	12	8

BATTLE STAFF	
POW	P+S
2	6

FIELD ALLOWANCE	3
LEADER & 3 GRUNTS	2
LEADER & 5 GRUNTS	3
SMALL BASE	

LEADER & GRUNTS

Hymn – RNG 3. Target friendly Faction warjack. When a model in this unit performs a Hymn special action, choose a hymn. Each activation, all models in this unit performing a hymn must perform the same one. If the target warjack is in range, it is affected by the hymn. While affected by a hymn, a warjack cannot be affected by another hymn.

- **Battle (★Action)** – The warjack gains +2 to attack and damage rolls for one turn.

- **Passage (★Action)** – The warjack cannot be targeted by non-magical ranged attacks. Passage lasts for one round.

- **Shielding (★Action)** – The warjack cannot be targeted by enemy spells. Shielding lasts for one round.

BATTLE STAFF
⊘ Reach

Sacred scrolls in hand, devout warpriests lead the choirs onto the field of battle. These valiant faithful are chosen from among those deemed most likely to demonstrate the rare gift of connecting to and controlling warjacks in battle. The warpriest directs a powerful, ancient canticle reinforcing the existing bonds between warjacks and their warcaster masters. The choir's prayers turn aside incoming projectiles, unravel enemy spells before they can reach their targets, and divinely guide warjack weapons to smite unbelievers. Requiring unassailable concentration and great effort to achieve, these perfect, meditative chants are the choir's sole purpose on the battlefield.

The Protectorate has long had an uncomfortable relationship with the mechanikal tools upon which its military relies. Since shortly after the Cygnaran Civil War, the Menites have seen the need to use the laborjacks and warjacks they had collected and cobbled together, armored, and modified for battle. By the strict interpretation of the tenets of their faith, however, such fabrications are inherently blasphemous.

Hierarch Luctine first derived the means to sanctify the use of these arcane machines of war, purifying profane artifices with fervent prayer and blessings. Successful accomplishments in battle are taken as a sign of Menoth's favor, for it seems the Creator smiles on their efforts. Often choirs of Menoth march alongside the iron-and-steel giants to further empower them with holy chants and prayers.

I choose to stand with the faithful and deliver Menoth's judgment upon the faithless as long as I am able.
—Arms Master Krill Mayven

Whistling through the air in long and deadly arcs, the Skyhammer rockets of deliverers rain down across the battlefield to bring the wrath of the Lawgiver in fiery, thundering explosions. Few enemies are brave or hardy enough to face a withering barrage of Deliverer fire long enough to close, knowing entire formations can be consumed in roaring blossoms of flame.

Expanding the Deliverers from a niche auxiliary unit into a mainstay of the Protectorate was one of several achievements made during Hierarch Garrick Voyle's push to reform the Protectorate military. After assessing the effective Redeemer, Voyle realized the essential role long-range explosives would have on the modern battlefield. Unlike expensive warjacks, the faithful could be easily replaced and thus could be deployed in far greater numbers.

Early deliverers launched the dangerous, self-propelled explosives by hand, holding a length of wood aloft until the fuse burned down and the rocket spiraled into the air. Most of the time the rockets landed within the enemy lines before exploding in a shower of fiery shrapnel. Sometimes, however, they detonated immediately or fell to the ground woefully short of the foe. Ranking arms masters developed reinforced cylindrical tubes that could be aimed at the enemy and provided more control. Even with these improvements, only the most devoted become deliverers: walking into battle loaded down with explosives requires deep and abiding faith and courage.

LEADER & GRUNTS

Inaccurate – This model suffers –4 to attack rolls with this weapon.

Rocket Volley – Instead of making ranged attacks separately, two or more models in this unit can make a combined ranged attack. Do not add a damage bonus for the number of models participating in the combined ranged attack. If 3–5 models participate in the attack, it has base AOE 4″ and base POW 14. If 6 or more models participate in the attack, it has base AOE 5″ and base POW 16.

LEADER & GRUNTS						
SPD	STR	MAT	RAT	DEF	ARM	CMD
5	4	4	5	12	11	7

SKYHAMMER			
RNG	ROF	AOE	POW
16	1	3	12

SWORD	
POW	P+S
3	7

FIELD ALLOWANCE	1
LEADER & 5 GRUNTS	5
LEADER & 9 GRUNTS	8
SMALL BASE	

HOLY ZEALOTS
PROTECTORATE UNIT

Conviction is more lethal than any blade, truth stronger than any shield. No one can withstand the force of so many so eager to die to preserve their faith.

—Hierarch Sulon to the faithful

LEADER & GRUNTS						
SPD	STR	MAT	RAT	DEF	ARM	CMD
6	4	4	4	12	12	8

FIRE BOMB			
RNG	ROF	AOE	POW
5	1	3	12

MACE	
POW	P+S
3	7

FIELD ALLOWANCE	3
LEADER & 5 GRUNTS	4
LEADER & 9 GRUNTS	6
SMALL BASE	

FIRE BOMB
- Damage Type: Fire
- Critical Fire

LEADER

Prayers – The Leader of this unit can recite one of the following prayers each turn anytime during its unit's activation. Each model in this unit gains the benefits listed.

- **Fervor** – Affected models gain +2 to attack and damage rolls this activation.
- **Warding** – Affected models cannot be targeted by enemy spells for one round.

to rush to one of these weapon caches and prepare to hurl themselves into the chaos of battle. Even after the need for secrecy had passed, this effective system was retained. Protectorate citizens are given the liberty to go about their normal lives, be it farming or other industry, so long as they are ready to fight when called.

To bolster the faith of their people—and to remind them of the just torments of a coward's death—Menite priests walk among the zealots in combat, sermonizing and leading them in prayer. Should a priest fall in battle, one among the zealots will invariably take up his prayers and lead the faithful. If one fanatic is a dangerous foe, a hundred thousand promise to be utterly apocalyptic.

One of its concessions in the treaties with Cygnar was that the Protectorate was not permitted to retain a standing army. Even as Visgoth Ozeall penned his name to those papers, he knew that should any leader of the Protectorate put forth the call to arms, he would not lack for enthusiastic volunteers. Many regular citizens feel the stirrings of their religion so strongly they would gladly give their lives to confront the enemies of the faith. They are willing to employ any weapon, even bare hands if need be, to serve that cause.

The Menite clergy prepared their citizens, secretly training them for combat and creating massive stockpiles of weapons with which to arm them at a moment's notice. When the zealots heard the call, they knew

May Menoth guide us to strike quickly at the hearts of his foes.
—High Exemplar Kreoss

Many scholars compare the various aspects of the Protectorate to Menoth himself: the faithful serve as the body of Menoth on Caen; the hierarch represents his head; the scrutators his mouth; the masses of the laboring faithful his bones; and the battle-ready zealots his blood. In this analogy, the Knights Exemplar are undoubtedly the weapons in his hands.

Heavily armored in blessed plate engraved with rites and wards of protection, these fanatical warriors stand undaunted as blows glance off their armor with tones akin to a hammer striking an anvil. The mere unsheathing of their relic blades in war is considered a sacrament. Though formidable in their own right, the Knights are made nearly unstoppable by the divine gifts they receive from the Creator. They will not be deterred from their cause; even seeing their brethren fall in battle and pass into Menoth's hands makes them stronger, fueling their faith and righteous anger.

The first time exemplars raised arms as a large force was within the City of Walls during the Cygnaran Civil War. At that time only a few hundred of the holy warriors served the clergy. Now their numbers surge with thousands of the faithful who feel the calling to take up the sword.

LEADER & GRUNTS

✠ **Fearless**

Bond of Brotherhood – Models in this unit gain +1 STR and ARM for each model in this unit that has been destroyed or removed from play. The bonuses for a model are lost if it returns to play.

RELIC BLADE

Ⓜ **Magical Weapon**

Ⓟ **Weapon Master**

LEADER & GRUNTS						
SPD	STR	MAT	RAT	DEF	ARM	CMD
5	6	7	4	12	15	9

RELIC BLADE	
POW	P+S
5	11

FIELD ALLOWANCE	3
LEADER & 5 GRUNTS	5
SMALL BASE	

TACTICAL TIPS

BOND OF BROTHERHOOD – Do not apply these bonuses until after the attack and its damage resolve. If several Knights are affected by a simultaneous attack, such as Strafe or an AOE attack, the bonus does not increase until after damage has been dealt to all the models.

TEMPLE FLAMEGUARD
PROTECTORATE UNIT

They have proven their dedication watching over our sacred walls and holy temples. Now let them prove their faith in battle.

—Hierarch Garrick Voyle

LEADER & GRUNTS						
SPD	STR	MAT	RAT	DEF	ARM	CMD
6	5	6	4	13	13	8

FLAME SPEAR	
POW	P+S
5	10

FIELD ALLOWANCE	3
LEADER & 5 GRUNTS	4
LEADER & 9 GRUNTS	6
SMALL BASE	

LEADER & GRUNTS
⊘ **Combined Melee Attack**

Shield Wall (Order) – For one round, each affected model gains a +4 ARM bonus while B2B with another affected model in its unit. This bonus does not apply to damage originating in the model's back arc. Models in this unit can begin the game affected by Shield Wall.

FLAME SPEAR
⊘ **Reach**

Set Defense – A model in this model's front arc suffers –2 on charge, slam power attack, and impact attack rolls against this model.

The Flameguard train ceaselessly with their seven-foot steel spears, the hafts of which are filled with reservoirs of the fiery Menoth's Fury developed under Hierarch Turgis. The liquid is piped to surface vents in the barbed tip and ignited by a mechanism triggered from the base of the spear. In battle, the spears drip oily fire and are capable of inflicting excruciating wounds.

Since the time of Sulon, the stated purpose of the Flameguard has increasingly been a justification for creating a well-trained, well-armed military. Over time, these pious soldiers have become elite infantry prized as both the first and last line of defense in battle, where they become a living wall protecting the clergy from harm.

Outside the temples of Menoth, the Flameguard stand ever vigilant. The great Hierarch Sulon created the order as it is presently known by conscripting able-bodied Menites in the days leading up to the Cygnaran Civil War. Though the temples had long gathered armed guardians from among the faithful, this Flameguard was something new, unified in instruction and discipline to become true soldiers of the faith.

Garbed in heavy, flowing white tabards and gleaming helms and trained to use spear and shield, the Flameguard protect temples and holy sites and preserve the sacred flame burning in each. In return for making themselves useful to Menoth, they are granted indulgences by order of Sulon and earn favored status and comfort for their families.

PALADIN OF THE WALL
PROTECTORATE SOLO

Among Menoth's first gifts to man was the Wall, by which we protect our people.
Atop the first wall at civilization's dawn, a paladin stood vigil.
—High Paladin Dartan Vilmon

With members who embody ideals at odds with the harsh dictates of the ruling scrutators, the Order of the Wall has experienced a turbulent past. Its enrollment has periodically dwindled to near extinction, only to surge back again in periods of turmoil to reassure the population that Menoth offers protection and not only wrath. Paladins of this order have served mankind since the first words of the Canon of the True Law, acting as bastions of stability when the wilderness threatened to overthrow civilization. The wall of their namesake stands for every barrier erected to shelter a community from external threats.

Paladins prioritize mercy and protection of the innocent, which can force them to disobey orders given by the scrutators. Priests take this as a sign that paladins lack the

PALADIN
✠ **Fearless**

Stone-and-Mortar Stance – During its activation, this model can forfeit its normal movement or action to gain +5 ARM. The affected model cannot be knocked down. Stone-and-Mortar Stance lasts for one round.

FIREBRAND
⊕ **Critical Fire**

⊗ **Magical Weapon**

ⓟ **Weapon Master**

PALADIN						
SPD	STR	MAT	RAT	DEF	ARM	CMD
6	7	8	4	13	16	9

FIREBRAND		
	POW	P+S
	7	14

DAMAGE	5
FIELD ALLOWANCE	2
POINT COST	2
SMALL BASE	

obedience that is the hallmark of the Knights Exemplar. Paladins prefer to protect the members of Menoth's flock rather than drown them in rivers of blood, and they believe even the wayward can be guided back to the path of the Creator—a philosophy for which they are beloved by the people.

Encased in the protection of tempered steel and trained to hold against any enemy, each paladin is akin to an unbreakable fortress. When a paladin strikes with his Firebrand sword, it erupts in holy fire like a sliver of the sun. Those who witness a paladin in combat cannot doubt Menoth's power flows through him.

For every soul saved by a paladin's actions, two are lost to the wracks and thumbscrews of the scrutators. Paladins cannot be deterred in their sacred obligation to protect the faithful, believing that each martial order has its function in Menoth's temple. If theirs is to be one of endless sacrifice, so be it.

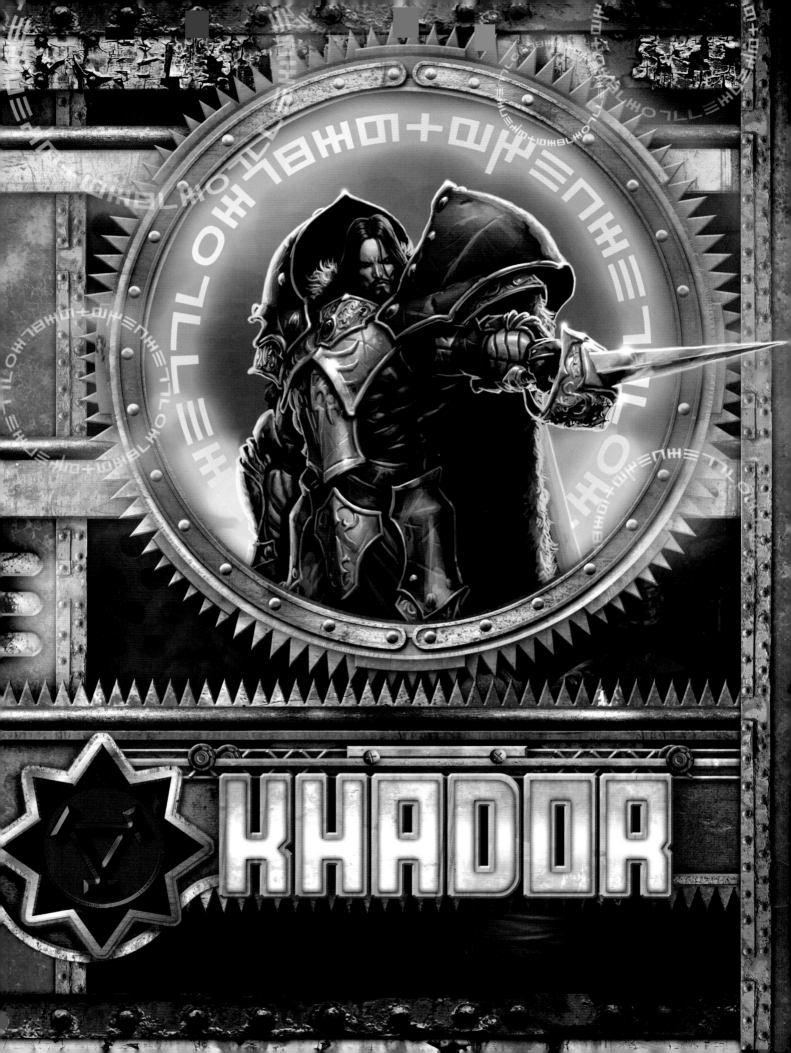

KHADOR

LEGACY OF STRENGTH
A BRIEF HISTORY OF KHADOR

No other people have as rich a history of breeding strength and courage. Our soldiers fight boldly to uphold that legacy. Never again will we suffer compromises and appeasements or give up what we have earned in blood.

—Queen Ayn Vanar XI while conducting a visit to the officers of the First Army, 604 AR

The following is a transcript from Kommandant Grezko Antonovich's "A Concise History of the Khadoran Empire and a Call to Action," printed winter 607 AR.

We must remember that our current greatness rests on the shoulders of countless generations stretching back to the Khardic Empire. A nation cannot endure without weapons wielded by strong hands, and our ancestors forged their strength in war. They united the Kossites of the Scarsfell Forest, the Skirov of the northern mountains, and the Umbreans of the eastern plains under one Khardic emperor. At the height of our glory, our hand stretched east to conquer the weak-willed Ryn and south to throttle the petty northern fiefdoms of Tordor. These once-proud men bowed to us and swore eternal fealty to the horselords of the north. Our civilization stood poised on the cusp of total dominion before the arrival of the damnable Orgoth. Our battles today serve to restore the path of our proper destiny.

Remember this when you hear the weeping indignation of those who fear us. Our cause is just. Those lands others squat upon as scavengers, scrabbling for our leavings, are ours still by right of oaths sworn in blood. I leave it to you to remind them with axe and cannon of what they have forgotten.

The Orgoth defeated us, but there was no shame in this. They unleashed accursed sorceries and weapons against which we had no defense. We fought them for every inch and took many of them with us into Urcaen. We forced them to send more ships to our shores and to overwhelm us by sheer numbers. If the southerners had been as strong as we, the Orgoth would be nothing but a forgotten speck in history. The soft underbelly of the south is where they took hold first, but here we halted their campaigns. We sank them in a quagmire of their own blood spilled by Khadoran blades.

The Orgoth ruled for generations and defaced our great and ancient cities with their grotesque fortresses, strange temples, and twisted monuments. Our forebears suffered greatest under Orgoth oppression as punishment for the ferocity with which we fought them. Your kin of times past were forced to feed the Orgoth by working the soil, enrich them by mining the earth for gems, and please them with blood sport. They offered a simple but painful choice: submit or die. They could kill our people but could never subdue our spirit, and we endured.

Each nation has taken credit for victory over the Orgoth. It is true that the first rebellion occurred in Cygnar, but their Iron Fellowship failed utterly and was quashed almost before it began. The Tordorans and Thurians put up a brave but futile fight called the Battle of the Hundred Wizards. Again the Orgoth returned in force and obliterated those who defied them. So too with the Army of Thunder our Llaelese subjects describe with misty eyes. That was their single valiant moment in an otherwise forgettable history. Khadoran horselords won the first true victory against the invaders in 147 AR. An enormous gathering of strong northmen surrounded and engulfed the first Orgoth city. They razed it, leaving only a jagged scar upon the earth, and deliberately excised its name. They then wrested the great city of Korsk from the Orgoth grasp.

The Orgoth regrouped and beset the city. They sent infernal evils such as men made of metal and flesh and fiery engines of destruction against her walls, but the city stood strong—as strong as she does to this very day. Korsk never shook and never again allowed hostile forces entry beyond her beloved walls. This was our turning point. Inspired by our success, a ragtag group of infant nations came together as the Iron Alliance in 160 AR and soon declared all-out war. The alliance organized the combined efforts that would give rise to the colossals.

Other nations do not speak much of this period and pretend that unity reigned among the Council of Ten. The Caspians revealed the depths of their treachery even in this dark hour when we fought against a common foe. The southerners feared our strength and spoke poison words in the halls of the Rhulfolk, convincing them to assist in the creation of the colossals. They isolated us from their debates and selected Caspia as the sole site of construction. The Rhulfolk agreed to this plan, for they had long feared our warriors.

When we learned of their schemes, we duplicated the colossal plans without their knowledge as a means of safeguarding our people. It was a small deception made necessary to safeguard the success of the alliance. Our secret factories in Korsk began their work.

Always they underestimate us. Cygnarans forgot it was we who invented the first steam engine. Our engineers are as innovative and capable as any in other lands—better!—for they have strength of heart and loyalty bred into their bones. They proved that their hatred exceeded all sense when in 188 AR the southerners or the Rhulfolk—we know not which—betrayed us to the Orgoth. Against all bonds of alliance they pretended to hold sacred, they used spies to learn the location of our factories and revealed them to our shared enemy. Though the Orgoth had been fighting on every front, they now turned their wrath completely against our people. They brought an immense army of inhuman warriors against our ancestors.

> ## ALWAYS THEY UNDERESTIMATE US. CYGNARANS FORGOT IT WAS WE WHO INVENTED THE FIRST STEAM ENGINE.

The Motherland itself has ever been our greatest ally. She awoke, having had enough of the pestering fleas biting her skin, and conjured a winter to meet the armies of the great enemy. Razor-sharp winds and tower-deep snows immobilized the armies. Trapped in the valleys and the plains, the Orgoth were beset by a vicious cold that stole the very breath from their lungs. Khador herself had saved us.

While the Orgoth could not obliterate us as they had hoped, they managed to destroy the factories we had erected. Who knows how many lives would have been saved had this not come to pass? We would have emerged from the rebellion against the Orgoth stronger than ever before. Instead our strength was for the moment exhausted, and our leaders were forced to be prudent. The obliteration of the Orgoth was too important, so our leaders cooperated with the other members of the Council of Ten despite their treachery. If one must sleep beside a foe to guard against a greater one, so be it.

Caspian colossals emerged and attacked the Orgoth in 191 AR. Our great generals and warriors fought alongside southerners as we pushed back the invaders. In 198 AR after many smaller gains, we combined northern and southern strength for an enormous push and risked all to seize final victory. The Orgoth turned back like a swarm of locusts, slaying innocents, ruining cities, and burning fields in a swath of destruction called the Scourge. The day came when the last of them boarded their black ships and fled, sailing across the Meredius back to whatever infernal land had spawned them. Immoren was once again ours. Never forget what our ancestors endured for our freedom!

The time came for rebuilding. In 202 AR the Council of Ten convened in Corvis, the sinking city, to establish a new age. For weeks the Council debated, outlined, and scribed plans only to burn the parchment and begin again. The Cygnarans and their Ordic pawns asserted it was easiest to maintain the lines drawn by our former captors for their provinces. They insisted the claims of the Khardic Empire and its old borders were no longer valid. Blinded by greed, ambition, or fear, the council agreed to this preposterous idea! What had become of our heritage? The southerners took advantage of our armies' tremendous losses and the fact that we had no colossals to back our demands. Subtle threats made it clear our cities might see the same fate as the Orgoth fortresses if we did not comply.

The final maps greatly reduced our territories to make room for the upstart kingdoms of Ord and Llael, built on the tattered remains of old Tordor and Ryn. Though the Tordorans had earned our respect as a tough people standing bravely in battle, the claims of the Ryn were galling. They had never been more than a tiny fiefdom at the base of the mountains. Their squabbling people were unworthy of a place in the company of their betters.

The southerners still cling to the travesties of the Corvis Treaties. We had earned what was ours by right of conquest, yet at that moment, with our strength diminished, they set upon us like jackals. The northern reaches of our land are impassable mountains so rugged and difficult they are nearly worthless to modern industry. Our mines, few and in difficult elevations, require twice the effort and investment of those in Cygnar. We are proud of our heritage, but only our southern reaches support the farmland needed to feed our people. Our empire stretched forth its mailed gauntlet because we had need of resources, and in the time of the Thousand Cities we had bled to win them. We had accepted oaths from those who surrendered to our benevolent rule. Southerners find it convenient to ignore promises when it suits them.

It became clear after the Corvis Treaties how cleverly Cygnar had manipulated border negotiations to avoid confronting us. Cygnar backed the claims of Ord and Llael to create a barrier between their soldiers and our axes. Leaders of those two nations were their puppets. The so-called kings frequently met in Caspia and fawned for favor.

Much blame has been heaped on our representatives who agreed to those treaties, but those of us who understand history know they were placed in a difficult—and perhaps impossible—situation. It was not yet the time to reclaim our birthright. We had first to rebuild our strength.

Yet after decades had passed, learned men in Korsk brought to light an interesting fact. The families of those first councilors had, for whatever reason, no surviving heirs. Clearly this was a blessing from the gods. Perhaps it was a sign of Menoth's approval of our respect for the written law, for by the wording of the Corvis Treaties, the old agreements no longer had any hold. None who had agreed to those tenets lived, nor did their descendants hold power in the halls of our sovereigns. The lands refused us by those deceitful papers could be ours again without any inherent dishonor.

In 242 AR King Lavash Tzepesci sent forth the call for all loyal Khadorans outside our borders to return home. Our kinsmen had scattered to earn wages and learn skills during the reconstruction but had not forgotten their loyalty. These far-flung and well-educated Khadorans gave up lives abroad and returned to the embrace of the Motherland. Most important were those who had learned the arcane mysteries of the Fraternal Order of Wizardry. The returning arcanists severed ties to that corrupt and foreign fellowship. In 243 AR the Greylords founded their Covenant.

These men carried magic and occult lore back to our cities in a great tide of power and brought modern arcane and mechanikal weapons with them. This included knowledge of the construction of cortexes, which at long last allowed us to build our own colossals. No longer subject to the intimidation of the Caspians, all our nation's industry bent to the task of readying our people for war. By 250 AR we had put together an army mighty enough to stand against Llael, Cygnar, and Ord together. For seven years

the massive constructs wreaked havoc upon their lands and people. These glorious battles proved to the world that Khador could not be dismissed. It required all three of these nations to defeat us, like dusty farmers struggling to restrain a mighty ox. Although in the end our colossals were dismantled, we had proven the strength of our people.

In 293 AR our new sovereign, Queen Cherize, renewed the struggle against our enemies. Queen Cherize was a strong but enigmatic leader. She brought unusual allies to fight the southerners, including tribes of savages from the Thornwood called Tharn. These tribes hurled themselves against Cygnar but proved insufficient to the fight, tainted as they were by association of their bestial god.

Queen Cherize disappeared under mysterious circumstances in 295 AR. The battle continued at the urging of Lord Regent Velibor, who ably represented the throne while the child

Queen Ayn Vanar V grew into her maturity. These so-called Border Wars were fought with steel and cannon, but, more significantly, they saw the rise of the earliest true warjacks, nimbler constructs that had replaced the formally retired colossals a decade earlier. These warjacks now played an important part in our armies, particularly in the battles at Ravensgard and then the Ironfields in 299 and 300 AR. In the years to come we pushed Llael and Ord back and reclaimed our rightful borders.

In early 305 AR a great alliance of barbarian tribes from the mountains and plains of Khador assembled. These were the last

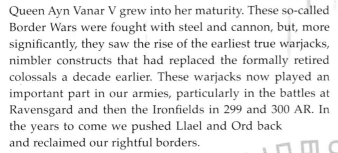

remnants of heathen tribes that had never properly joined our nation. Some were primitive and savage. Others were crude but noble, a legacy of the once-great line of horselords stretching back before Priest-King Khardovic. These men came to plunder the wealth of our civilization. Drawing on the example of Queen Cherize, Lord Velibor saw that these warriors could be turned from the Motherland to her enemies. He convinced the tribal leaders of the enormous spoils awaiting them in the fat southern lands of Ord.

Though most southerners are cowardly and weak, the men of Midfast in Ord had proven their ability to withstand siege time and time again. They had even endured an attack by our colossals in 250 AR without falling. While we had claimed a sizable piece of the lands north of Midfast and its line of rugged hills, the Ordic Army had proven tenacious when pressed against this natural wall. Velibor sent the barbarian tribes against this fortress city to see if an endless

tide of savages might succeed where more organized forces had failed. He sent our army to follow in their wake and exploit any vulnerabilities opened by their hordes. The plan nearly succeeded.

These fourteen barbarian tribes with 50,000 savages, so they say, laid siege to Midfast. There seemed little hope of the city surviving such a horde, but clearly divine will stood against Velibor's victory. Some took it as a sign that only a true king of Khador could accomplish such a deed. I do not pretend to understand the will of the gods.

Whatever the case, the Ordfolk fought well. They lack the stomach to meet us on the open field or to march forth from their border holds, but they remain resolute when cornered.

We recognize the rare occasions a great warrior arises on foreign soils. On this day a Tordoran officer named Markus—perhaps descended of Khadoran blood—stood to rally the defenders of Midfast in their hour of desperation. He endured this siege beyond all hope. He went sleepless for a week and remained an inspiration to his soldiers. To buy reinforcements time, he went out alone and challenged the chieftains of every one of the barbarian tribes to personal combat. I wish I had been alive to see those battles, two a day for an entire week. He suffered grievous wounds in the confrontations but ignored them and fought on. It was only after defeating the final champion that he succumbed to his grave injuries and death took him. Ordic reinforcements reached the field of battle just as Markus ascended to join

Morrow. I have read the account of a Khadoran officer who witnessed the event, and I believe it was a true miracle. It was not destined that those lands would be ours that day.

This was a small defeat that did not cost the army of Khador anything but pride. Had we taken our gains and bided our time it may have served us better, but one cannot fault Lord Velibor for his ambition. Perhaps it was his lack of royal blood that prevented his success. When Queen Ayn Vanar V came of age and took the throne, she decided we had accomplished enough for a time. She was a soft-hearted queen and called for peace in 313 AR to allow our soldiers rest. We had won Port Vladovar and many fine and fertile lands north of Midfast. Port Vladovar became one of our greatest port cities and the heart of our naval shipyards. Its capture is worth a dozen dry and barren fortress-holes like Midfast.

We suffered further indignities in the peace negotiations, including the loss of lands we had taken from Llael on our eastern border. At the time we considered these lands of little consequence despite their historical significance. The region had been heavily despoiled during the wars with the Orgoth, noted primarily for their littered ruins and battlefields that served now as vast graveyards. While some nobles protested we must reclaim Old Korska, once the eastern capital of the Khardic Empire, most were content to leave such ruins to the Llaelese.

It is from this time that our troubles with the Umbreans began, a topic worthy of some attention. Once the Umbreans were part of the old Khardic Empire, like the conquered peoples of Kos and Skirov. They too had been horselords in ancient times and had ridden the plains as fighters knowing few equals. We made a tactical mistake in our settlements after the Border Wars, for we let the Umbreans become a divided people. While the region claimed by Llael was strategically unimportant, it included the ancestral homes of thousands of proud Umbreans, a people as rooted in their lands as any tree in the Gallowswood.

In letting them go we gave to the otherwise meek and cowardly Ryn stalwart allies, Umbreans of real mettle and warrior spirit. Llaelese merchants may be weak of arm and reluctant to fight, but they are shrewd and can estimate worth. They took in the Umbreans and rebuilt their homes, restoring Old Korska to create a new city they named Laedry. This and other projects funded in part by Cygnaran gold won the hearts and minds of the easternmost Umbreans, confusing their loyalties. While a goodly number of Umbreans remained loyal to the Motherland, almost as many began calling themselves Llaelese. These in turn joined the Llaelese Army and rose to positions of influence, as is to be expected of our distant kinsmen. It would be centuries before we could rectify our error.

Some call the time after the Border Wars peace, but even without a declaration of war there is never rest for our soldiers. Then came the Cygnaran Civil War. In Khador, though the two religions devoted to Menoth and Morrow have their occasional tensions, they still exist side by side. The rise of the Harbinger of Menoth in the lands of the Protectorate has challenged our national resolve, but even today most of our citizens strand strong as Khadorans first, despite any religious calling. Cygnar failed to accomplish what we take for granted. The state heavily favored one religion over the other, which resulted in division and much bloodshed. By contrast, we have always given proper respect and loyalty to the Creator even while acknowledging the wisdom of Morrow and his benevolent ascendants.

> **THE CYGNARAN COWARDS REFUSED TO FACE THE STRENGTH OF OUR ARMY DIRECTLY. HATE THEM, BUT DO NOT UNDERESTIMATE THEIR CUNNING.**

Our King Ruslan Vygor was a devoted Menite who learned from an early age to loathe Cygnar. Whether mad or inspired by genuine visions, King Vygor claimed to be Priest-King Khardovic reborn. When he took the crown, he decreed he would use whatever force was required to ensure a new and more prosperous future for our people. He saw the Cygnaran Civil War as an opportunity to do this and in 511 AR gathered the combined might of Khador. Vygor's forces carved the path through the perilous Thornwood that we now know as the Warjack Road hoping to reach the site of Cygnar's first transgression at the city of Corvis. They reached the Dragon's Tongue River before Cygnar's armies met them.

The Cygnaran cowards refused to face the strength of our army directly. Hate them, but do not underestimate their cunning. Their tactics are slippery and elusive like the twisting of a snake—a lesson Vygor learned too late to avoid death. Cygnar's forces evaded his, and they bombarded our army from across the river. Thousands of soldiers died, and scores of warjacks obliterated each other in a series of fierce battles.

What sealed our fate was the betrayal of our mercenaries, the Ironbears. One can never fully trust those who fight for coin, and never was that more clear than at the Battle of the Tongue. As the vice closed on our army from both sides, the Ironbears abandoned the flank they were assigned to protect and turned on our soldiers. His forces thrown into panic and disarray, King Vygor fought on bravely but finally fell in battle against the man who would be Cygnar's next king. His surviving men endured a long and difficult retreat.

Even in defeat we were not cowed, and many of our people refused to give up the fight. The valiant Fifth Border Legion swore revenge against Cygnar. For those stalwart men and women on the southern border, the Thornwood War never truly ended; they continued to sap the resources of our enemy even in times of apparent peace. We must be thankful for their constant vigilance. Their experiences in myriad battles provided invaluable training and intelligence.

Unbeknownst to those who witnessed the event, the crowning of Queen Ayn Vanar XI would mark the coming of a new and glorious era for our people. Helping usher in this era was the peerless stewardship of her mentor and predecessor, Lord Regent Simonyev Blaustavya—today Great Vizier Blaustavya. This giant of a man did much to strengthen our nation during the long years that Ayn Vanar grew to adulthood before receiving the crown that formalized her authority. It was Lord Regent Blaustavya who pioneered the rail lines that would connect our cities like vital arteries stretching across the long miles between. Industry flourished under his capable hands as factories and ironworks proliferated, adding sinews of steel to the Khadoran military. All that Blaustavya achieved was done to lay a solid foundation for the rule of the woman who was like a granddaughter to him and who would become a sovereign of fierce spirit and iron will.

THE LOVE OF THE PEOPLE FOR OUR QUEEN DEVELOPED INTO ABSOLUTE FAITH AND DEVOTION

We cannot fault the people for being uncertain when in 587 AR, at the tender age of 18, Queen Ayn Vanar took the throne. The people were so accustomed to the wisdom of Blaustavya that it took time to trust their young queen. The nobles quickly came to understand her merits and to appreciate that in this woman's veins flowed the blood of kings and Khardic emperors. This was not a sovereign content to stay the course and meekly accept historical injustice. She chose instead the far harder path of restoring our ancient birthrights.

Like Lord Regent Blaustavya, Queen Ayn spent her early years in power strengthening the nation and overhauling the military to eliminate excesses and hone our strengths. She saw many corrupt and self-indulgent nobles, kayazy, and officers of the High Kommand purged and replaced by more faithful servants of the Motherland.

The love of the people for our queen developed into absolute faith and devotion, particularly as she bridged the divide between Morrowan and Menite. She had been raised as a pious Morrowan but nonetheless convinced the Menite visgoths of her respect and deep reverence for the Creator. She afforded the clergy of both faiths a voice in her councils. Meanwhile weapons and ammunition were produced at a prodigious rate, with a steady line of warjacks emerging from our factories. Young men and women eagerly rushed to fill the ranks of the military. The queen urged us not to take our mastery of warfare for granted but instead to prepare our sons and daughters properly for battles ahead.

All of this Queen Ayn fostered to ensure that her entire nation stood at her side as she initiated a bold plan of conquest. When we launched a massive assault on Llael's western border in the winter of 604 AR, its defenders were caught entirely off guard. The crushing power of this assault was the proof not only of our strength in matters of war but also of the genius of our military commanders. There is no better example of what our nation can accomplish when our nobles, our military, and our society are of one mind. Llael's western defenses crumbled under a simultaneous three-pronged assault against northern Laedry, Redwall Fortress, and the southern city of Elsinberg.

Many ignorant observers may try to cheapen this victory by suggesting the Llaelese Army was no worthy foe. Such a force could not hope to stand before Khadoran troops, true, but do not undervalue the valor of our soldiers or the accomplishment of conquering this nation in a handful of months. No one thought it could be done so quickly. The misguided Umbreans who bolstered the Llaelese defenders fought hard and well against us, their former kinsmen. Cygnar rushed countless thousands of soldiers and hundreds of warjacks armed with sophisticated weapons to intercept our advance. Such a battle could have ground on for years, but in just a few months we surrounded Merywyn, Llael's capital, and forced the capitulation of its Prime Minister. Those refusing to bow were executed.

Some few armed malcontents and the last remnants of defiant rebels clung to the impossible dream of recovering their nation. They fled into the eastern corners of what was once Llael and have occasionally stirred like buzzing hornets, but this is a minor inconvenience. After the fall of the capital we began the difficult process of bringing our Umbrean kinsmen back to their rightful place at our side. This process will not be quickly completed, as centuries of mistrust and Llaelese lies have infected these people, but in time they will realize how much better their fortunes stand with us. Even the Ryn will see that life in the empire is far superior to what passed for culture in corrupt and degraded Llael.

This great victory brought tremendous wealth and resources to Khador as well as proving to our enemies they had little chance of opposing our might. After our forces were in firm control of Llael, Queen Ayn made her most historic move: she announced that we existed as a kingdom no more but as an empire reborn, and she proclaimed herself Empress Ayn Vanar of the new Khadoran Empire. Yet this was not by any means a declaration that the battles had ended, as there remained far more to accomplish before we could claim to have met or exceeded the glories of our ancestors.

Even as this pronouncement was made, Cygnar was pushed back. Our army chased them from Llael and made them fear for their own borders. We beset their entrenched defenders at Fellig, Deepwood Tower, and the massive fortress of Northguard. There is nothing sweeter than the resumption of battles against old and worthy adversaries.

Made tenacious by fear, for a time Cygnar held fast against our strength. No army can resist a superior foe forever, and we bled them unrelentingly. After years of harsh warfare, their great border fortress fell to our victorious forces. The once-proud castle had been battered by the merciless onslaught of our cannons, the defending network of trenches slowly emptied as entire ranks of their soldiers were slain. Still, they clung to the belief that they could best us, and the fighting was grim for a time. Eventually we washed over them as an inexorable red tide.

That ancient forest, the Thornwood, has been a barb in our side for centuries and stood in the way of a clash on proper ground against our southern rival. Now it belongs to us. Our borders have expanded once again, and now our lands stretch from the northern Shard Spires all the way to the Dragon's Tongue River. Across those waters, defenders of the Cygnaran cities of Corvis and Point Bourne quake as they witness our might and think of the inevitable day we will besiege their walls.

Despite recent defeats, our southern enemy remains strong. They hope to drive us back and reclaim the Thornwood. There are many great battles ahead of us. Other enemies beset us at every turn, seeking to weary our resolve or distract us from our destiny. Rebels still persist in our occupied lands, and new threats have arisen, including strange terrors from the frozen mountains or the wilderness. Inexplicable horrors plague our western coast and seek to despoil our wealth.

We have in recent years clashed with the fanatical Sul-Menite sect begotten during Cygnar's civil war. The Protectorate of Menoth has proven it has grandiose ambitions and seeks to undermine the sovereign rule of all nations. During the war in Llael word spread of a Harbinger speaking Menoth's will in the south. Far be it for me to dispute or legitimize such an unlikely claim, but I can report its impact: Menites throughout Khador and other kingdoms began to flock south to view this miraculous manifestation, abandoning their loyalties and common sense. Even now a sizable force of the Sul-Menites from the Protectorate battle with our soldiers in eastern Llael, where they seek to contest our supremacy and turn our people against one another.

Our loving empress has been forced to resort to harsh measures to curtail treason, making an example of any who would forsake their vows in favor of a foreign sovereign. For make no mistake: the hierarch of the Protectorate of Menoth *is* a foreign sovereign, not simply the head of the southern branch of the Menite faith. Swearing fealty to him while asserting loyalty to Empress Ayn is a contradiction. Fortunately, while the existence of the Harbinger has increased religious tensions at home and abroad, the majority of Khador's Menites remain steadfast and loyal, looking to their local priests and not to foreign-born, self-appointed prophets or potentates for guidance.

It is the responsibility and honor of those of us in uniform to risk our lives in battle to ensure our empire prospers and grows. The work of the farmer, the laborer, the merchant—none are possible without the sacrifice of the soldier. I say this to all who hear my call: Do not falter! Take up the axe and rifle! You are Khador's children! The Motherland that defended you and kept you safe now calls upon you. It is your strength that will overcome our enemies in the battles ahead. War is our oldest and finest tradition. Trust your strength, and accept nothing less than total victory!

ORSUS ZOKTAVIR, THE BUTCHER OF KHARDOV
KHADOR WARCASTER

Zoktavir is a force of nature as wild as Khador itself. Some say his manners and methods are crude and shortsighted, but I ask you, would you deny that he is the personification of victory at any cost? Has he ever failed us?

—Queen Ayn Vanar XI

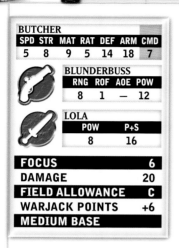

BUTCHER						
SPD	STR	MAT	RAT	DEF	ARM	CMD
5	8	9	5	14	18	7

BLUNDERBUSS			
RNG	ROF	AOE	POW
8	1	–	12

LOLA	
POW	P+S
8	16

FOCUS	6
DAMAGE	20
FIELD ALLOWANCE	C
WARJACK POINTS	+6
MEDIUM BASE	

BUTCHER
- 💀 Terror

LOLA
- Magical Weapon
- Reach
- Weapon Master

FEAT: BLOOD FRENZY

The Butcher's rage runs deep. It is the well from which he draws his power and the drive to lead his forces into battle. When the Butcher relinquishes what little control he has over this infectious fury, all who march by his side—man and machine alike—succumb to its bloodlust.

While in the Butcher's control area, friendly Faction models gain an additional die on attack damage rolls this turn.

SPELLS	COST	RNG	AOE	POW	UP	OFF
FURY	2	6	–	–	YES	NO

Target friendly model/unit gains +3 to melee damage rolls but suffers –1 DEF.

IRON FLESH	2	6	–	–	YES	NO

Target friendly warrior model/unit gains +3 DEF but suffers –1 SPD.

FULL THROTTLE	3	SELF	CTRL	–	NO	NO

Warjacks in this model's battlegroup beginning their activations in its control area can run, charge, or make slam or trample power attacks without spending focus that activation. While in this model's control area, models in its battlegroup gain boosted melee attack rolls. Full Throttle lasts for one turn.

OBLITERATION	4	10	4	15	NO	YES

The force of this attack blasts apart the earth itself.

The varied cultures of Khador's vast lands are proud of their fighting spirit, and Orsus Zoktavir embodies elements of each of these proud lines. Although his parentage is uncertain, each of the peoples of Khador have at times claimed him as their own. Seven and a half feet tall and over half as wide, he is a massive man who manifested natural arcane skills early in life.

Orsus' past is wrapped in mystery; none seem to know of his life before he appeared in Korsk with two old warjacks in tow, demanding to be enlisted in the army. He was sent to the Orgoth fortress turned industrial city named Khardov, which would become his only home. Before long he was given his first command and dispatched to patrol the southern border alongside the 5th Border Legion.

He gained notoriety during these patrols in 587 AR when a village just north of Boarsgate Keep announced its withdrawal from Khador to join with Ord. Orsus took it upon himself to crush the "traitorous rebellion." When a waiting contingent of militiamen tried to parley, Orsus howled and charged. What followed was carnage. Halfway through the slaughter the militiamen surrendered, but Orsus kept cutting them down. His accompanying soldiers tried to restrain him, but in a wild rage he turned on his own men and with his massive axe rent every living man to pieces. His fury was boundless. Moments later, a total

of eighty-eight warriors were simply dismembered parts strewn about the village square. Those who witnessed the aftermath told of blood so thick in the muddy streets that rats leapt from one body to the next to avoid drowning. The event became known as the Boarsgate Massacre.

Word spread quickly, earning Orsus the title "Butcher of Khardov." The news ultimately reached the ears of the newly crowned Queen Ayn Vanar. The pragmatic young queen absolved the warrior of blame, openly condoning his behavior as the reaction of any true patriot. Most of her kommanders guessed at the queen's true intent. In parading a new weapon against internal dissent, she instilled fear that to speak or act against her could result in a visit from the Butcher. Her maneuver had the desired effect and instantly stifled all speculation of whether the young queen would be a strong monarch.

The Butcher remains both an embodiment of Ayn Vanar's strength and a potent symbol of the consequence of treachery. Younger warcasters view him with disdain and do not comprehend the leniency he has been afforded by the High Kommand. More traditional warcasters like Vladimir Tzepesci see him as nothing more than a weapon.

Orsus Zoktavir wields his axe Lola—rumored to be named after a love whose loss fuels his rage—with singular fury. He wears a modified suit of steam-powered armor that was shaped from the hull of a warjack to suit his frame by loyal battle mechaniks once in his service. In its protective casing, the Butcher is a force of destruction, a one-man wrecking crew. Soldiers across western Immoren cannot forget the vision of the axe-wielding giant from their nightmares, a man become a living personification of warfare and bloodshed.

KOMMANDER SORSCHA
KHADOR WARCASTER

She is a perfect example of what a woman should be: pale as the ice that blankets us, beautiful but distant as the starry sky, yet deadly as a winter storm.

—Lieutenant Yurik Belavdon of the 12th Iron Fang Uhlan Kompany

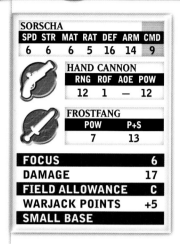

SORSCHA						
SPD	STR	MAT	RAT	DEF	ARM	CMD
6	6	6	5	16	14	9

HAND CANNON

RNG	ROF	AOE	POW
12	1	–	12

FROSTFANG

POW	P+S
7	13

FOCUS	6
DAMAGE	17
FIELD ALLOWANCE	C
WARJACK POINTS	+5
SMALL BASE	

FEAT: ICY GAZE

Wherever Kommander Sorscha treads, winter follows. The celebrated Khadoran warcaster manipulates extreme cold through sorcery, storing up her power to unleash a massive blanket of ice that freezes her enemies in their tracks.

Enemy models without Immunity: Cold 🌀 currently in Sorscha's control area and LOS become stationary for one round.

SORSCHA
🌀 Immunity: Cold

FROSTFANG
⚔️ Magical Weapon

🏹 Reach

Critical Freeze – On a critical hit, the model hit becomes stationary for one round unless it has Immunity: Cold 🌀.

SPELLS	COST	RNG	AOE	POW	UP	OFF
BOUNDLESS CHARGE	2	6	–	–	NO	NO

During its activation, target friendly model can charge without spending focus or being forced and gains +2″ movement and Pathfinder 🌀 when it charges. Boundless Charge lasts for one turn.

FOG OF WAR	3	SELF	CTRL	–	YES	NO

Models gain concealment while in this model's control area.

FREEZING GRIP	4	8	–	–	NO	YES

Target model/unit without Immunity: Cold 🌀 becomes stationary for one round.

RAZOR WIND	2	10	–	12	NO	YES

A blade of wind slices through the target model.

TEMPEST	4	8	4	12	NO	YES

Models hit by Tempest are knocked down and suffer a POW 12 damage roll.

WIND RUSH	2	SELF	–	–	NO	NO

This model can immediately make a full advance and gains +2 DEF for one round. Wind Rush can be cast only once per turn.

TACTICAL TIPS

TEMPEST – This means every model in the AOE is knocked down, friendly and enemy alike.

When a teary-eyed Sorscha Kratikoff looked into her father's face at the age of thirteen winters and asked to be a soldier like him, he just smiled, patted the black hair on her head, and strode out the door to join his unit. Later that month her mother received word of the massacre at Boarsgate. Sorscha's father lay among the dead, killed by Orsus Zoktavir, the Butcher of Khardov. Two years later, Sorscha lied about her age and joined the Winter Guard. She fought against all odds and excelled as a soldier, surviving the rigors and mayhem of war fueled by the image of her father's bloody end.

Sorscha served in three consecutive tours of duty with the prestigious border garrisons at Ravensgard and participated in frequent bloody conflicts with Llaelese mercenaries and her Cygnaran counterparts. She demonstrated considerable natural tactical prowess and was chosen for officer training at the Druzhina in Korsk before returning to her men as a lieutenant. She advanced quickly through the ranks to kapitan and kovnik. A warcaster named Torisevich valued her opinion above his other officers' and picked her to serve as an aide. Perhaps some part of her felt an affinity with armored machines even before she demonstrated her gift for warcasting. Sorscha had already shown hints of inborn sorcery but had kept them to herself, for she had been raised in a rural border area where such powers prompted superstition and dread.

Her true potential surfaced during a conflict near the Ordic border when Torisevich was slain in an ambush and his 'jacks suddenly fell dormant. In desperation, Sorscha charged unescorted into the combat. She cut men down like stalks of grain, but her troops were demolished and she found herself far outnumbered. One foe sliced her thigh and she fell. Suddenly, the world froze. Everything around her, including her enemies, stood encased in a layer of ice and frost. Leaning against one of the nearby Juggernauts, she found herself able to reach within its mind. She reactivated its cortex by mimicking the arcane sequence her untrained vision had perceived from her kommander. Sent forth at her bidding, this warjack charged into the nearby enemies.

Days later Sorscha Kratikoff stood before her queen in Korsk. Her new talents were quickly put to the test, and she began to learn to control her sorcery and warcaster ability from the enigmatic and gifted Umbrean prince, Vladimir Tzepesci. In her year of study with the nobleman, she fell in love. She saw in him ancient nobility, a sense of profound duty, and devotion to the memory of his ancestors. They had a brief romance before duty called her away to service at the height of their passion. Since their parting she seems to have become more embittered and pours her strength into the tasks at hand. Those who see her now would never suspect any ardor lingering beneath her iron discipline and unfaltering dedication to Khador.

Only the infrequent presence of Dark Prince Vladimir can thaw her soul, if but for a moment. "Fiery rage and icy hatred!" she was once heard to say. "These things a good soldier makes, not warmth and comfort." Despite these words, there are those who believe her fate is tied to Tzepesci by a cord that will not be easily broken.

VLADIMIR TZEPESCI, THE DARK PRINCE
KHADOR WARCASTER

Not long will any Tzepesci sit upon the throne, yet their blood nourishes the soil of the land. When the last perishes, so too shall a darkness descend without dawn, and a winter come where ash falls like snow.

—The Tzepesci Prophecy, spoken to King Vladin Tzepesci in 210 AR

VLADIMIR						
SPD	STR	MAT	RAT	DEF	ARM	CMD
6	6	7	5	15	16	9

SKIRMISHER	
POW	P+S
7	13

RUIN	
POW	P+S
4	10

FOCUS	7
DAMAGE	18
FIELD ALLOWANCE	C
WARJACK POINTS	+5
SMALL BASE	

FEAT: FORCED MARCH

The strategic and tactical prowess of the Dark Prince of Umbrey is legendary throughout the Motherland as well as any land he has touched. Vladimir carefully conserves the power of his warjacks to expend it in one great battlefield maneuver.

Warjacks in Vladimir's battlegroup beginning their activations in his control area double their base SPD and can run or charge without spending focus. Forced March lasts for one turn.

VLADIMIR
Parry – This model cannot be targeted by free strikes.

SKIRMISHER
⊘ **Magical Weapon**

Blood Boon – Once per activation, immediately after resolving an attack in which it destroyed a living enemy model with this weapon, this model can cast a spell with COST 3 or less without spending focus.

RUIN
⊘ **Magical Weapon**

SPELLS	COST	RNG	AOE	POW	UP	OFF
BLOOD OF KINGS	4	SELF	–	–	NO	NO

Vladimir gains +3 SPD, STR, MAT, DEF, and ARM for one round.

BOUNDLESS CHARGE	2	6	–	–	NO	NO

During its activation, target friendly model can charge without spending focus or being forced and gains +2" movement and Pathfinder ⊙ when it charges. Boundless Charge lasts for one turn.

RAZOR WIND	2	10	–	12	NO	YES

A blade of wind slices through the target model.

SIGNS & PORTENTS	4	SELF	CTRL	–	NO	NO

While in this model's control area, friendly Faction models gain an additional die on attack and damage rolls. Discard the lowest die in each roll. Signs & Portents lasts for one turn.

WIND WALL	3	SELF	–	–	NO	NO

This model cannot make ranged attacks, and non-magical ranged attacks targeting it automatically miss. While completely within 3" of this model, models cannot make ranged attacks and non-magical ranged attacks targeting them automatically miss. Wind Wall lasts for one round.

Even in times of old before the Iron Kingdoms, when certain lands in Khador were the provinces of barbaric tribes, among those who rode to battle were some possessed of rugged honor who united their people with a clarity of vision. Chieftains ruled these hordes, and horselords ruled the chieftains. Of noble stock, horselords ruled for generations with oppressive strength, calculated cruelty, and a will to organize the chaos of the world. The Tzepesci, one of the strongest families to rule the provinces of Old Umbrey, are among the last of the great families. Indeed, a millennia ago the Tzepesci were the governors of Old Korska before it fell into ruin, and they even controlled the throne of Khador for a time. Though reduced in influence, the Tzepesci name still resonates with Khador's eastern people.

Vladimir Tzepesci is the Great Prince of Korskovny Volozkya, one of the eighteen great houses that govern Khador, yet he represents much more. The ruling families of Umbresk and southern Gorzytska owe his family fealty from old oaths set in bone and blood. The influence he wields in this region is enough to stir uneasy rumors in the capital. He is a living relic of past glories and bloody deeds, and his noble bearing is testimony of an ancient lineage. A prophecy delivered to the Tzepesci kings of old tells of a great doom to befall Khador when the Tzepesci line comes to an end. Those who know of this legend call Vladimir Tzepesci the Dark Prince. So powerful is the blood in his veins that men shy from his gaze. He is a man of few words, accustomed to being heard when he speaks.

As some are born to capture strength and beauty with paints or to write great works of poetry, Vladimir was born to make war. He has waged many campaigns in the service of his nation as a brilliant tactician as well as a potent warcaster. A swordsman with few equals, he brings swift death to all who dare cross blades with him. Worthy opponents are treated to longer duels, but most enemies are dispatched with little consideration.

Vladimir takes great pride in wearing the ancient plate of his forefathers. Although it has seen some sorcerous repair over the centuries, it is the same suit of crimson mail his ancestor, Prince Buruvan Tzepesci, wore in battle against the Orgoth.

Vladimir has trained other warcasters, and it is no great secret that he became intimately acquainted with the promising young Sorscha Kratikoff during her mentoring. Little is known of the affair other than it ended quite abruptly and left Sorscha distinctively changed. There is some speculation that she was rebuffed due to her lowly heritage, but those who know Vladimir cannot credit such a motive and believe the situation may have been more complicated than it appeared. Whatever the case, he seems determined to stay true to the legacy of his forefathers, who were always strong and faithful in their duties even at the expense of their own happiness. There are those who call such notions—and his adherence to ancient tradition—exercises in vanity, but for Vladimir Tzepesci it is part of a code that defines him and connects him to his past.

Though Vladimir is respected for his great accomplishments, not all who meet him love him. It is whispered in secret among the courts that the time of the Tzepesci has passed, and Vladimir is but an unpleasant reminder of a vanished era. These conspirators anticipate the day when the Dark Prince falls and the vast treasures of the Tzepesci family are annexed into the vaults of the Khadoran Treasury.

BERSERKER
KHADOR HEAVY WARJACK

Respectfully, Kommandant, I must submit that even Zoktavir has questioned the Berserkers' stability. Need there be more evidence they are too dangerous to remain in service?

—*Excerpt from a report to Kommandant Gurvaldt Irusk*

BERSERKER						
SPD	STR	MAT	RAT	DEF	ARM	CMD
4	11	5	3	11	18	—

WAR AXE		
L	POW	P+S
	5	16

WAR AXE		
R	POW	P+S
	5	16

DAMAGE

1	2	3	4	5	6
		L		R	
L	L	M	C	R	R
	M	M		C	

FIELD ALLOWANCE	U
POINT COST	6
LARGE BASE	

BERSERKER

Aggressive – This model can run or charge without spending focus or being forced.

Unstable – At the end of any activation in which this model spent 1 or more focus points, roll a d6. If the roll is equal to or less than the number of focus points spent, this model explodes and models within 3" of it suffer an unboostable POW 14 blast damage roll. Remove this model from play.

WAR AXE

Chain Attack: Brutality – If this model hits the same model with both its initial attacks with this weapon, after resolving the attacks it can immediately make one head-butt power attack against that model.

HEIGHT/WEIGHT:	10'11" / 8.4 TONS
ARMAMENT:	TWIN WAR AXES (LEFT AND RIGHT ARMS)
FUEL LOAD/BURN USAGE:	715 LBS / 5 HRS GENERAL, 55 MIN COMBAT
INITIAL SERVICE DATE:	430 AR
CORTEX MANUFACTURER:	GREYLORDS COVENANT
ORIG. CHASSIS DESIGN:	KHADORAN MECHANIKS ASSEMBLY

TACTICAL TIPS

AGGRESSIVE – Yes, this rule is HORDES friendly.

UNSTABLE – Do not replace this model with a wreck marker.

CHAIN ATTACK: BRUTALITY – A model with a crippled weapon system cannot use it to make chain attacks or special attacks, including power attacks.

CORTEX SYSTEM – Due to extreme age and cortex decay, a Berserker has only two boxes in its Cortex system.

There is something uniquely terrifying about the Berserker. The oldest of Khadoran warjacks still in service, it is also among the oldest relied upon by any modern nation. Some proudly view this fact as proof of both the genius of Khadoran engineering and the timelessness of their weapons of war.

Berserker cortexes have become unstable in the years since their first manufacture well over a century ago, and the 'jacks are prone to charge without orders when near the frenzy of combat. The bloodthirsty manner with which they slaughter enemy infantry has long been legendary. Worse yet, their cortex alloys and the alchemical mixtures in which their cortexes bathe have become critically compromised by decay and are prone to massive concussive overload if stimulated with too much arcane energy.

Those who know their merits make excellent use of these brutal machines. Armed with a pair of immense axes, Berserkers are ruthless in close combat, and their volatile cortexes and propensity for violence become assets when facing their iron and steel counterparts from other nations. A Khadoran general with one in his army views it as a rampaging force of destruction to be unleashed at the right moment and expended in battle.

DECIMATOR
KHADOR HEAVY WARJACK

Subtlety is a word for strategy; brutality, for tactics. Even the most complex battle plans eventually require the application of brute force. This is where the Decimator excels.
—Kommandant Gurvaldt Irusk

HEIGHT/WEIGHT:	11′7″ / 9.8 TONS
ARMAMENT:	DOZER (LEFT ARM), RIP SAW (RIGHT ARM)
FUEL LOAD/BURN USAGE:	783 LBS / 4 HRS GENERAL, 45 MIN COMBAT
INITIAL SERVICE DATE:	587 AR
CORTEX MANUFACTURER:	GREYLORDS COVENANT
ORIG. CHASSIS DESIGN:	KHADORAN MECHANIKS ASSEMBLY

TACTICAL TIPS

BEAT BACK – The attacking model can advance even if the enemy model is destroyed by the attack.

As the Khadoran Empire has expanded its borders and come up against the toughest defenses of its enemies, it has needed increasingly powerful tools to sow destruction. Enter the Decimator, which Khador engineered to annihilate well-armored targets with powerful direct fire. The 'jack's thunderous cannon smashes its victims to the ground before it closes and tears them to unrecognizable scrap with its mighty saw.

The heart of the Decimator's dozer repeating cannon is a revolving chamber housing the weapon's oversized ammunition. The impact of one of these massive slugs smashes its unfortunate target backward—if not annihilating it outright—and punches a hole in the enemy line. In close combat, the Decimator relies on its massive rip saw, a wicked weapon capable of shredding anything in its path. The 'jack has been used extensively in recent years to assault the most impregnable fortifications of Khador's enemies, where it deals staggering punishment to their heaviest defenders.

DOZER

Beat Back – Immediately after a normal attack with this weapon is resolved during this model's combat action, the enemy model hit can be pushed 1″ directly away from the attacking model. After the enemy model is pushed, the attacking model can advance up to 1″.

RIP SAW

Sustained Attack – During this model's activation, when it makes an attack with this weapon against the last model hit by the weapon this activation, the attack automatically hits.

DECIMATOR

SPD	STR	MAT	RAT	DEF	ARM	CMD
4	12	6	4	10	20	—

DOZER

	RNG	ROF	AOE	POW
L	10	2	—	15

RIP SAW

	POW	P+S
R	6	18

DAMAGE

1	2	3	4	5	6
		L		R	
L	L	M	C	R	R
	M	M	C	C	

FIELD ALLOWANCE	U
POINT COST	9
LARGE BASE	

DESTROYER
KHADOR HEAVY WARJACK

Let the Cygnaran dogs hide in their trenches. Our Destroyers will flush them out like frightened hares and chop them into stew meat!

—Harisc Vokmir, Khadoran Mechaniks Assembly

DESTROYER						
SPD	STR	MAT	RAT	DEF	ARM	CMD
4	12	6	4	10	20	—

BOMBARD			
RNG	ROF	AOE	POW
14	1	3	14

EXECUTIONER AXE	
POW	P+S
5	17

DAMAGE

1	2	3	4	5	6
		L		R	
L	L	M	C	R	R
	M	M	C	C	

FIELD ALLOWANCE	U
POINT COST	9
LARGE BASE	

BOMBARD

Arcing Fire – When attacking with this weapon, this model can ignore intervening models except those within 1" of the target.

EXECUTIONER AXE

Critical Amputation – On a critical hit, warjack arms and weapon systems that suffer damage from this attack are crippled.

HEIGHT/WEIGHT: 11′7″ / 9.5 TONS
ARMAMENT: BOMBARD (LEFT ARM), EXECUTIONER AXE (RIGHT ARM)
FUEL LOAD/BURN USAGE: 815 LBS / 4 HRS GENERAL, 50 MIN COMBAT
INITIAL SERVICE DATE: 537 AR (ORIGINAL CHASSIS 480 AR)
CORTEX MANUFACTURER: GREYLORDS COVENANT
ORIG. CHASSIS DESIGN: KHADORAN MECHANIKS ASSEMBLY

TACTICAL TIPS

CRITICAL AMPUTATION – After marking regular damage, mark their remaining system boxes as well.

Compared to that of other nations, technological advancement of warjacks in Khador has been slow—mostly because the country's mechaniks build their warjacks to last. A prime example is the Destroyer, which has served in various iterations as the premier Khadoran siege-assault warjack for almost a hundred years, gaining particular fame in the First Thornwood War. The whistling of its shells arcing overhead is a prelude to destruction, heralding the thunderous blasts that tear apart everything in the target vicinity.

The Destroyer's current design has not changed in nearly 70 years, but the series goes back as far as 480 AR. Even with antiquated armament, those impressive early 'jacks shelled Cygnaran fortifications from across the Dragon's Tongue River. Improvements to the bombard cannon in 537 AR cemented the Destroyer as the centerpiece of Khadoran war engineering.

Though most famous for its role in delivering a punishing bombardment, the Destroyer is no less formidable when engaged in close combat. Its designers did not skimp on armor: its iron-plated chassis is as heavy as the Juggernaut's and provides formidable protection. One mighty stroke from a Destroyer can shear entire limbs from an enemy warjack.

JUGGERNAUT
KHADOR HEAVY WARJACK

You can't ignore a Juggernaut. It just keeps coming, shrugging off everything you throw at it. The only way to deal with one is heavy and unrelenting concentrated fire.
—*Major Markus "Siege" Brisbane*

HEIGHT/WEIGHT:	11'7" / 9 TONS
ARMAMENT:	ICE AXE (RIGHT ARM)
FUEL LOAD/BURN USAGE:	798 LBS / 4.5 HRS GENERAL, 50 MIN COMBAT
INITIAL SERVICE DATE:	516 AR (ORIGINAL CHASSIS 465 AR)
CORTEX MANUFACTURER:	GREYLORDS COVENANT
ORIG. CHASSIS DESIGN:	KHADORAN MECHANIKS ASSEMBLY

Bigger is usually better in Khador, and the country's mechaniks employ this principle with each successive warjack they design. As brutally efficient in modern warfare as when it was first conceived, the Juggernaut is a mammoth of plated armor regarded as the embodiment of Khadoran temperament and an example of the supremacy of the Khadoran martial warjack. Fewer Juggernauts come off the assembly lines today than in past decades, but they can endure brutal punishment and be rebuilt and repaired countless times before being scrapped. Some Juggernauts serving on the front lines have persisted for more than a hundred years.

OPEN FIST
👊 Open Fist

ICE AXE
Critical Freeze – On a critical hit, the model hit becomes stationary for one round unless it has Immunity: Cold ❄.

JUGGERNAUT						
SPD	STR	MAT	RAT	DEF	ARM	CMD
4	12	6	4	10	20	—

OPEN FIST	
L POW	P+S
3	15

ICE AXE	
R POW	P+S
7	19

DAMAGE

1	2	3	4	5	6
		L		R	
L	L	M	C	R	R
	M	M	C	C	

FIELD ALLOWANCE	U
POINT COST	7
LARGE BASE	

The current Juggernaut's armament and chassis date to 516 AR, but its original chassis is older, having been designed in 465 AR to replace the aging Berserker model. In fact, this chassis design is the basis for those in the majority of today's Khadoran warjacks. The Juggernaut combines the most powerful steam engines her mechaniks can design with as much armor as its chassis can carry.

Inspired by Greylords Covenant mechanikal techniques, the Mechaniks Assembly created the ice axe for the Juggernaut in 517 AR. This weapon encases its target in a layer of ice, causing it to seize up. Even glancing blows can freeze enemy warjacks in their tracks and cause their engines to screech protest against their frozen limbs.

Khadorans respect power, and there is not a soul in the Motherland who does not admire the storied Juggernaut and its endless list of accomplishments in battle.

MARAUDER
KHADOR HEAVY WARJACK

Praise to the Creator, who has sheltered our cities and delivered unto us such a weapon to shatter the fortifications of our enemies!

—Visgoth Ruskin Borga of the Old Faith blessing a Marauder being sent to battle

MARAUDER						
SPD	STR	MAT	RAT	DEF	ARM	CMD
4	12	6	4	10	20	—

RAM PISTON (L)	
POW	P+S
4	16

RAM PISTON (R)	
POW	P+S
4	16

DAMAGE

1	2	3	4	5	6
		L		R	
L	L	M	C	R	R
	M	M	C	C	

FIELD ALLOWANCE	U
POINT COST	7
LARGE BASE	

RAM PISTONS

Combo Smite (★Attack) – Make a melee attack. On a hit, instead of making a normal damage roll the target model is slammed d6″ directly away from this model and suffers a damage roll with POW equal to the STR of this model plus twice the POW of this weapon. The POW of collateral damage is equal to this model's STR.

HEIGHT/WEIGHT:	11′7″ / 10.25 TONS

ARMAMENT: TWIN RAMS (LEFT AND RIGHT ARMS)

FUEL LOAD/BURN USAGE: 860 LBS / 4 HRS GENERAL, 45 MIN COMBAT

INITIAL SERVICE DATE: 522 AR

CORTEX MANUFACTURER: GREYLORDS COVENANT

ORIG. CHASSIS DESIGN: TARGH FEDRO (CREDITED), KHADORAN MECHANIKS ASSEMBLY

TACTICAL TIPS

COMBO SMITE – This ability cannot be used while either of this model's arm systems is locked. A model with a crippled weapon system cannot use it to make chain attacks or special attacks, including power attacks.

Designed to pulverize buildings and armored warjacks with equal ease, the Marauder is armed with a pair of pneumatically driven battering rams. Though originally developed to aid in siege warfare, these crushing rams are even more useful for obliterating or displacing enemy warjacks, and they provide unsurpassed tactical control to their commanding warcasters. The Marauder can hurl ten tons of enemy warjack to the side with no more difficulty than a rampaging bear knocking aside a man.

An industrial mechanik named Targh Fedro was inspired to try this design after observing stonemasons in a quarry. After replacing an old laborjack's broken arms with battering rams, he tested it against the quarry walls and nearly brought down the entire face with a single blow. Excited at the military potential, he took the design to the Mechaniks Assembly to build a prototype using the ubiquitous Juggernaut chassis. Those who witnessed trials against similarly heavy Khadoran 'jacks were astonished at the power wielded by the piston-driven rams.

Though any warjack can knock away an adversary if it has sufficient distance for a full charge, the Marauder can achieve similar results standing still. With the devastating power of its ram pistons, a Marauder can send lesser machines flying through stone walls to become mere wrecks of torn metal and shattered pistons.

Get ready to have burns on your burns and calluses on your calluses. You'll be covered in oil and grime with nothing but a wrench and your wits to get the job done.

—Battle Mechanik Chief Usten Magrechev to trainees

No matter how heavily armored the great Khadoran warjacks are, even they are eventually worn down and sometimes wrecked in the crush of battle. Battle mechaniks are the skilled and brave individuals who dodge bullets and evade explosions to get the huge battle machines back into the fight. These loyal brothers of the Khadoran Mechaniks Assembly are patriots equal to any fighting soldier and often must withstand even heavier fire in the execution of their duties. Steadfast at the sight of spilled blood or oil, they are willing to put themselves in harm's way to conduct repairs.

Before proving their knack with a wrench and being redeployed as battle mechaniks, many of these skilled workers served their expected time in the Winter Guard, so they are often older and more seasoned than the freshly recruited youths bearing blunderbusses next to them. Few enemies are foolish enough to underestimate battle

LEADER & GRUNTS
⊛ 'Jack Marshal

Assist Repair (★Action) – This model can make this special action only when B2B with a friendly Faction warjack. When this model makes an Assist Repair special action, choose another model in this unit with the Repair ability also B2B with that warjack. The chosen model gains a cumulative +1 to its Repair skill on its next Repair skill check to repair that warjack this activation. If it passes the Repair check, remove 1 additional damage point from the warjack for each model that used Assist Repair on the chosen model.

Iron Sentinel – While B2B with a friendly Faction warjack, this model gains +2 DEF and ARM and cannot be knocked down.

Repair [7] (★Action) – This model can attempt repairs on any damaged friendly Faction warjack. To attempt repairs, this model must be B2B with the damaged warjack and make a skill check. If successful, remove d6 damage points from the warjack's damage grid.

LEADER & GRUNTS						
SPD	STR	MAT	RAT	DEF	ARM	CMD
5	6	5	4	13	12	8

MONKEY WRENCH	
POW	P+S
2	8

FIELD ALLOWANCE	3
LEADER & 3 GRUNTS	2
LEADER & 5 GRUNTS	3
SMALL BASE	

mechaniks bearing wrenches—implements as capable of crushing skulls as they are of loosening oversized and stubborn warjack bolts.

Chiefs are the hearts of battle mechanik teams. Sometimes the old vets get injured on the battlefield, but a Khadoran does not let a simple thing like a shorn-off limb get him down! Injured mechaniks repair their own broken bodies with cleverly improvised mechanikal limbs, often salvaging finer gears and mechanisms from the detritus of the battlefield. This indomitable ingenuity shows the same spirit and optimism as the battle mechaniks apply to the 'jacks they tend, finding ways in the most challenging circumstances to engineer machinery that can outlast any one battle and stand ready for the next.

TACTICAL TIPS

Repair – A wreck marker cannot be repaired.

DOOM REAVERS
KHADOR UNIT

I am not sure of the wisdom of employing such madmen. Our control over them seems tenuous at best.

—Great Prince Vladimir Tzepesci

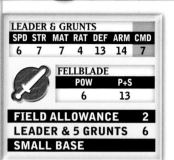

LEADER & GRUNTS						
SPD	STR	MAT	RAT	DEF	ARM	CMD
6	7	7	4	13	14	7

FELLBLADE		
	POW	P+S
	6	13

FIELD ALLOWANCE	2
LEADER & 5 GRUNTS	6
SMALL BASE	

LEADER & GRUNTS

- **Abomination**
- **Advance Deployment**
- **Fearless**

Berserk – When this model destroys one or more models with a melee attack during its combat action, immediately after the attack is resolved it must make one additional melee attack against another model in its melee range.

Spell Ward – This model cannot be targeted by spells.

FELLBLADE

- **Magical Weapon**
- **Reach**
- **Weapon Master**

TACTICAL TIPS

Spell Ward – This model is shielded from friendly and enemy spells alike.

Berserk – Spread them out if you do not want them killing each other.

battle by their urges. The maddened swordsmen can be only nominally controlled in conflict, though the Khadoran wizards have done what they can to restrain them. Doom reavers undermine the morale of even the stoutest veterans, but despite this they have earned their share of bloody victories. So long as they persevere they will continue to be employed despite the argument that fellblades are too dangerous and should never have been unleashed in the first place.

Khador is dotted with ancient ruins from the Orgoth era, and many of the black stone temples, fortresses, and hidden catacombs are now buried below ground. Occult scholars have picked through several of these sites, such as the ones below the great city of Khardov. It was there the Greylords Covenant unearthed a large cache of the infamous fellblades, swords adorned with howling faces that shift eerily at the fringes of vision and are painful to the sight. Saturated with tainted magic, the dark blades seem to come alive when wielded.

Swordsmen unfortunate enough to pick up these powerful weapons descended into savage and homicidal madness as they experienced incomprehensible whispers in their minds. Even in their sleep the swordsmen heard foreign babbling stoking them to acts of bloodshed. These men lashed out with berserk abandon and doubled strength, killing anything that crossed their paths.

To assist in the war effort, the crown decided to bind the blades to wayward prisoners, particularly soldiers who had been found guilty of gross insubordination or other military crimes. The Greylords turned these men into doom reavers chained to their fellblades and directed in

168

IRON FANG PIKEMEN
KHADOR UNIT

*We have been wielding our long spears to bring down the fiercest creatures of the mountains for a thousand years. Iron Fangs do not quail in the face of the enemy—even if it **is** six tons of iron and steel.*

—Dhurgo Bolaine, decorated Iron Fang Kapitan

The Iron Fangs are proud examples of the Khadoran fighting spirit. They stand toe-to-toe against six-ton, steam-powered machines that can crush the life out of them in a single blow. These hardened soldiers are part of an ancient tradition of spearmen who once fought the northern bear and later evolved into pikemen deployed by settled Khards to stand against the roving horse lords who dominated the southern plains and eastern hills of their empire. Just as they stood firm against the seemingly unstoppable tide of warlords on muscled horses, they now form up behind their shields and bring weapons to bear against the warjacks that dominate the modern battlefield. Their pikes tipped with powerful explosive charges, Iron Fangs can blast through infantry and heavy warjack armor with equal success.

LEADER & GRUNTS
⊘ Combined Melee Attack

Shield Wall (Order) – For one round, each affected model gains a +4 ARM bonus while B2B with another affected model in its unit. This bonus does not apply to damage originating in the model's back arc. Models in this unit can begin the game affected by Shield Wall.

BLASTING PIKE
⊘ Reach

Critical Knockdown – On a critical hit, the model hit is knocked down.

LEADER & GRUNTS						
SPD	STR	MAT	RAT	DEF	ARM	CMD
6	6	6	4	13	14	9

BLASTING PIKE	
POW	P+S
7	13

FIELD ALLOWANCE	2
LEADER & 5 GRUNTS	5
LEADER & 9 GRUNTS	8
SMALL BASE	

Behind their tower shields, Iron Fangs are notoriously difficult to kill; even coordinated rifle fire sometimes bounces off their armored frames as they continue their implacable advance. They have trained to regard their heavy armor as a second skin, able to ignore its weight and even sleep comfortably in it. In battle they move with military precision, interlocking their shields to form a nearly impenetrable mobile wall.

After centuries of service, the Iron Fangs have become a heralded tradition of the Khadoran Army, their fraternal bond legendary. Upon acceptance into the legion of Iron Fangs, a soldier swears a blood oath, casts off the life he lived before, and dedicates himself to his fellow soldiers, his country, and the art of war.

MAN-O-WAR SHOCKTROOPERS
KHADOR UNIT

Soldiers who retire from battle become no more than old, sad men. They shrivel away to nothing and huddle by their hearths to await death's release. I will not fade like that. When the time comes, I will die in steam!
—Deidric Harkinos, veteran man-o-war shocktrooper

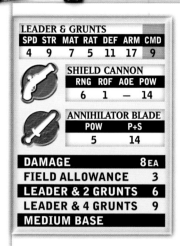

LEADER & GRUNTS						
SPD	STR	MAT	RAT	DEF	ARM	CMD
4	9	7	5	11	17	9

SHIELD CANNON			
RNG	ROF	AOE	POW
6	1	—	14

ANNIHILATOR BLADE	
POW	P+S
5	14

DAMAGE	8 EA
FIELD ALLOWANCE	3
LEADER & 2 GRUNTS	6
LEADER & 4 GRUNTS	9
MEDIUM BASE	

LEADER & GRUNTS
⚔ Combined Melee Attack

✤ Fearless

Shield Wall (Order) – For one round, each affected model gains a +4 ARM bonus while B2B with another affected model in its unit. This bonus does not apply to damage originating in the model's back arc. Models in this unit can begin the game affected by Shield Wall.

ANNIHILATOR BLADE
⟳ Reach

Man-o-war shocktroopers wield powerful annihilator blades, one stroke of which can split the armor of a light warjack or wholly eviscerate a mere man. As with more traditionally armored heavy infantry, they can file into ranks and lock their shields in formation, but each shield also boasts a powerful short-range cannon. Though the shocktroopers prefer to rely on their blades, the cannon blast gives them added reach and versatility on the battlefield.

Only the most steadfast soldiers earn the right to join the men-o-war, though many jump at the opportunity. After all, it is not every day that one can experience the world from a warjack's perspective.

Because fabricating warjack cortexes in Khador requires rare materials in short supply, the Khadoran Mechaniks Assembly had long sought a viable supplement to these expensive and precious weapons. In 470 AR Jachemir Venianminov came upon a solution that was simplicity itself: transforming men into steam-powered wrecking crews called men-o-war.

The suit of armor worn by a man-o-war is a miraculous creation imbuing the soldier with almost the same strength, durability, and protection against the elements as a warjack. There are drawbacks to wearing heavy battle armor powered by a steam boiler, however. Men-o-war are susceptible to heat stroke, exhaustion, and the occasional steam leak that can cook them alive in minutes. Despite these possibilities, one will never hear a man-o-war complaining or asking for comfort, for they are proud of their tradition and willingly embrace the risks in the service of the military.

WIDOWMAKERS
KHADOR UNIT

With every bullet you carry death.
—Widowmaker Kapitan Govoyen Krinevich

Widowmakers are the elite scout-sniper division of the Khadoran military, which has embraced and elevated them to the status of national heroes. The standards to join the Widowmakers are among the most exacting of all Khador's specialist forces, and only those riflemen who demonstrate peerless skill with the rifle are accepted. Because the Widowmakers are first and foremost a merit-based corps, membership is open to any who aspires to bring death from afar, whether peasant-born, rural hunter, or of noble blood. Widowmakers wield their long-barreled hunting rifles with skill that cannot be overstated, able to take apart incoming warjacks piece by piece with well-placed shots. Killing a man is as automatic as drawing breath.

LEADER & GRUNTS

◉ **Advance Deployment**

◔ **Pathfinder**

Camouflage – This model gains an additional +2 DEF when benefiting from concealment or cover.

Sniper – When damaging a warjack or warbeast with a ranged attack, choose which column or branch suffers damage. Instead of rolling damage on a ranged attack, this model can inflict 1 damage point. A model that participates in a combined ranged attack loses Sniper until the attack is resolved.

LEADER & GRUNTS						
SPD	STR	MAT	RAT	DEF	ARM	CMD
6	5	4	7	14	11	8

HUNTING RIFLE			
RNG	ROF	AOE	POW
14	1	—	10

SWORD	
POW	P+S
3	8

FIELD ALLOWANCE	1
LEADER & 3 GRUNTS	**4**
SMALL BASE	

A Widowmaker's primary role is to neutralize officers to facilitate chaos among the enemy. They frequently advance ahead of the main battlegroup, their arrival indicated by enemy officers abruptly falling dead before the report of rifle fire can be identified. They also support strategic withdrawals by ensuring their own wounded do not become prisoners. If a downed officer cannot be retrieved, Widowmakers make sure he does not fall into the wrong hands for interrogation. A true patriot knows it is better to die by a comrade's bullet than to be placed in irons on an enemy's torture rack.

Widowmakers know that inspiring fear and hatred come with the territory. Officially, Widowmakers are not used in domestic conflicts, but it is rumored that their talents have been used to pick off dissenters, rabble-rousers, or corrupt kayazy suspected of disloyalty to the crown. Widowmakers expect little charity from their enemies if captured; indeed, Cygnarans often hang them without trial.

TACTICAL TIPS

Camouflage – If a model ignores concealment or cover, it also ignores concealment or cover's Camouflage bonus.

WINTER GUARD INFANTRY
KHADOR UNIT

It is the joy of every son and daughter of the Motherland to take up arms and defend her to the death. He who would avoid this service does not deserve to breathe the same air as the patriot who stands next to him.

—Lord Regent Velibor

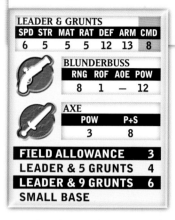

LEADER & GRUNTS						
SPD	STR	MAT	RAT	DEF	ARM	CMD
6	5	5	5	12	13	8

BLUNDERBUSS			
RNG	ROF	AOE	POW
8	1	—	12

AXE	
POW	P+S
3	8

FIELD ALLOWANCE	3
LEADER & 5 GRUNTS	4
LEADER & 9 GRUNTS	6
SMALL BASE	

LEADER & GRUNTS
Combined Ranged Attack

When a Khadoran male reaches seventeen winters, he is conscripted into the Winter Guard. Women are also accepted into the ranks, though they are discouraged from volunteering if they have children in their care. Some conscripts are assigned to police forces that patrol the towns and cities of Khador, while others are sent to the front lines. As the war escalates and unexpected threats manifest even within Khador's borders, the people increasingly look to the Winter Guard for protection.

Winter Guard equipment has changed only slightly since their inception. Their battle axes are stout and well suited for mundane tasks in the field—as well as for hacking into the enemy should they close. Most infantry, however, rely on the blunderbuss, a powerful if somewhat inaccurate weapon that uses a hefty blast of powder to fire a heavy slug capable of penetrating the armor of a warjack. Though southern riflemen disdain the short range of these squat weapons, there is no doubt they pack a powerful punch, particularly when Winter Guard concentrate fire. Relatively cheap to manufacture and using ammunition that can be produced in bulk, these guns place little strain on the Khadoran treasury.

The Winter Guard make up the majority of the Khadoran military and are found at the core of every garrison and substantial combat force. Their training is designed to get the young soldiers immediately into battle. Empress Ayn Vanar has been able to maintain constant reinforcements and field a formidable army at an affordable cost by running many Winter Guard training camps across Khador, from the largest complexes at Volningrad to the rural outposts near Uldenfrost. Through their training, members of the Winter Guard learn what it means to be truly Khadoran: to love their nation by risking death in battle.

MANHUNTER
KHADOR SOLO

Blood is the coin of this realm now, and he is the paymaster.
—Kommander Sorscha Kratikoff

Fishing and hunting are significant sources of food for many rural areas of Khador. Khadoran hunters tend to be held in higher regard than those of other kingdoms, particularly in the cold and rugged northern mountains and forests. Experts at tracking and killing dangerous game, some have moved on to the most cunning prey of all: man.

First and foremost, manhunters are trackers skilled at traversing the hostile wilderness. Lowland brush, forests, and snow are all as well-paved roads to a manhunter. Long years of harsh life in the Khadoran wilds have hardened their bodies, darkened their skin, and refined their skills. Masters of camouflage and hiding in plain sight, manhunters are scouts, and sometimes assassins, for the right price.

Manhunters often accompany reconnaissance groups of Widowmakers and their Kossite peers to strike at the enemy from unexpected directions, usually operating behind enemy lines. Whether stalking prey in silence or swinging

MANHUNTER

- Advance Deployment
- Fearless
- Pathfinder
- Stealth

Camouflage – This model gains an additional +2 DEF when benefiting from concealment or cover.

AXES
- Weapon Master

MANHUNTER						
SPD	STR	MAT	RAT	DEF	ARM	CMD
6	8	8	4	14	14	9

AXE		
×2	POW	P+S
	3	11

DAMAGE	5
FIELD ALLOWANCE	2
POINT COST	2
SMALL BASE	

TACTICAL TIPS

CAMOUFLAGE – If a model ignores concealment or cover, it also ignores concealment or cover's Camouflage bonus.

their twin hand axes with blinding efficiency, they are frightful killers. The hiring of such men by the Khadoran Army is an old tradition, and their value on the fringes has been exploited in many wars. In exchange for their services, they are well provided for by the armies that hire them.

There are dark whispers of manhunters who enjoy the hunt too much and give in to their animal urges and the euphoria of the kill. These hunters often possess track records good enough to offset the dark rumors, however—and there are none better at chasing an enemy to ground.

CRYX

DEATH DENIED
HISTORY OF THE NIGHTMARE EMPIRE

Your claim to power is meaningless. There is only servitude or annihilation. Make your choice.

—Emissary of Lord Toruk to the fourteen pirate kings of the Scharde Isles

The following is a treatise on the Cryxian mission written by Darragh Wrathe, winter 607 AR.

I will endeavor to chronicle Cryx's origins with special attention to the crucial events of recent years as we enter what might be the final stages of Lord Toruk's great plans. In the coming days we must act swiftly if we are to capitalize upon opportunities that have arisen even as we acknowledge that the vision of our most revered Dragon God is everlasting and patient and can penetrate the future beyond mortal reckoning.

The task set before us is neither simple nor easy, but the outcome is nevertheless inevitable. This world *will* fall to the Dragonfather, Lord Toruk. Our true strength has remained shrouded for a millennium, lest mankind unite against us and delay his everlasting dominion. Better to seem a remote nightmare, a threat to the shoreline hamlets and nothing more. Our enemies naively think themselves safe in the heartland; far from the oceans, they feel secure among the trappings of civility. Only when our innumerable legions set upon them and consign their fragile nations to ruin will they see the truth.

With every gunshot, sword stroke, and rending claw, our numbers grow. Death strengthens us even as it saps our enemies. Hiding will not avail them, nor resistance, nor any effort put forth by their weak and distant gods. We shall unleash oceans of blood, and our ships shall go forth on the tide with a plague wind filling our sails. Lord Toruk will not be denied, and all will have to choose: slavery in life or servitude in death. Every village that falls brings us another legion. Every city slaughtered becomes another fortress. There is no army in all of Caen more loyal. Our enemies would be made even more fearful were they to realize that their subjugation is not our true goal but simply an expedience.

We do not wage war for the sake of conquest. We care little for the land or resources that consume the petty politics of the kingdoms of men. We know nothing of true or lasting defeat. The loss of countless minions means nothing if it furthers our master's designs. Every ship, every army, every soul at our disposal is a weapon to be expended in his name. This is our strength. We will commit every resource toward total victory.

Serve well and the rewards may surpass your life's extinction. Betrayal is not an option, for our master sees and knows all. If there is strength in you, prove it. Your mortal flesh is but untested clay, and it will fail. When at last you are drowning in your own blood, you will be judged according to your capabilities. Should you be found worthy, you will be transformed into an eternal being so as to bear witness to his ultimate triumph. More likely you will pass ignominiously and your flesh will be torn from your bones and rendered in our necrofactoriums. If you have displeased Lord Toruk or our lich lord masters, death will not grant an escape from punishment. Your soul will be submitted to agonies beyond description as our masters consume the scant energies of your pitiful immortal essence.

To evade such a fate you must use whatever wit, talents, and power you possess to deliver death to those who would resist us. Set the machines created by our ceaseless industries loose upon our enemies. Let them receive no respite and no mercy.

Look to the ancient origins of our empire, and you will begin to understand the immortal glory that is the Dragonfather. The origins of Lord Toruk himself are beyond comprehension. We mortals only need know he is everlasting and beyond the strength of even the mightiest armies.

Nonetheless there are those who seek to oppose him.

The only creatures worthy of our lord's attention are his progeny, who alone possess the power to hinder our god and master. In a time forgotten by all that live, Lord Toruk was alone in strength and might and therefore sought to duplicate his perfection by creating a brood that would serve him. He divided his essence—his heart-stone, the primal athanc—and from these slivers of living crystal the dragons were born. Each was a shadow of his might, a reflection of his power, wrath, and ambition. The essence of these wyrms was too pure, however, for the lesser dragons were not capable of humbling themselves, even before their creator. Each considered itself a god in turn and refused to bow to the glory of the Dragonfather. Instead they turned on him who had made them. Lord Toruk realized his first and only mistake too late and was beset by the fury of fang and claw.

> **FOR SIXTEEN CENTURIES CRYX HAS EVOLVED WHILE LORD TORUK SHAPED EVERY ASPECT OF LIFE AND DEATH.**

Thus began the War of the Dragons, a relentless battle of wills and wits that has persisted for thousands of years. Over the centuries the Dragonfather has slowly annihilated his children, with each kill restoring a fraction of his athanc. We know not the names of all the fallen, for we are not privy to every detail of our master's hunts. We know of the death of Shazkz over the island that became Satyx and of the perishing of Gaulvang, but there have been many others. Each was a great and mighty serpent that perished beneath Lord Toruk's claws, leaving trails of searing blood that mark the land and serve to remind the others of their folly.

Those dragons that remained realized the inevitability of their destruction. Even the mightiest of them could not stand against our lord alone. Sixteen centuries ago the survivors put aside their sibling hatred to create a tenuous alliance. Acting with one will, they struck, and the skies burned with their fires. Our master is imperishable, but against so many he could gain no advantage. While they could not defeat him, neither could he vanquish them. At last he conceded and withdrew. He descended on the Scharde Islands, and there he built an empire.

For sixteen centuries Cryx has evolved while Lord Toruk shaped every aspect of life and death. Our nation has been forged into a weapon to conclude a war between immortal powers.

Lord Toruk is not alone in his timeless vision, for there exist among us his greatest servants who have been witness to the entirety of our history. No other nation can boast such perspective. A mortal lifetime offers no parallel to the experience of our immortal host.

As the duties of rule are beneath the Dragonfather, he has left the governance of Cryx to his twelve lich lords. They are exalted above all others. Though chosen to oversee his domain and carry forth his works, they are as far removed from their master as we their servants are from them.

Long ago, fourteen pirate kings held sway over the Scharde Islands. When first Lord Toruk made his presence known, these mortal fools could not recognize his true power. Each considered himself a master of a great fleet, and together they had yet to meet a threat they could not vanquish. They lived with ties to nothing except greed and excess and were not prepared to bow, each proud as a mighty king with his own army, court, and vassals, blood-bathed and battle-tested.

Lord Toruk could have simply annihilated them but knew the seeds of empire must be planted somewhere. He sent an emissary to reveal his demands. Ignorant of the tremendous honor and opportunity offered them, the pirate kings slew the messenger rather than answer. The mightiest of these doomed kings was Threnodax, and it was he who roused the others to defiance and convinced them to muster their armies and prepare to battle our god.

Among the pirate fleets one ship stood mightier than the rest. The *Atramentous* was a dirgenmast ship once of the nation of Tordor stolen by Threnodax for his flagship. Even in those ancient days it had earned a reputation as a terror on the seas, feared by all coastal dwellers for when its merciless crew would sail forth to pillage. Proving his capacity for bitter irony and measured vengeance, Lord Toruk chose to seize that vessel and turn its crew against their arrogant king.

The Dragonfather came to the *Atramentous* and obliterated its crew and captain in a breath of consuming fire. He extinguished their lives, collected their souls, and gave them new birth in death. They became revenants, dead spirits bound to their ship so tightly it could retain them even past the destruction of their flesh.

This was Lord Toruk's lesson regarding the futility of resistance. The ghost ship *Atramentous* came upon the pirate kings who had gathered at Threnodax's fortress in Darkmoor in the shadow of a long-dormant volcano. The unliving crew poured forth across the piers to light the ships of the harbor ablaze and sweep through the mortal crews like a culling wind. Each fresh corpse added to their number.

Thirteen of the kings gathered in a fortress tower and watched in horror as all they had built burned. Only King Moorcraig absented himself. Perhaps some oracle had warned him to seek hiding, but his time would come. The Dragon God descended upon the fortress, crumbling it to ruin beneath his terrible weight, and the once-proud kings prostrated themselves in the surviving tower. Stubborn to the end, King Threnodax kept his feet, continuing to speak defiance. Lord Toruk annihilated all thirteen in a single breath, but the twelve who had bowed were reborn. Their souls were enslaved and they would become the first lich lords, chosen by him as vassals to rule over a new empire. Threnodax he consumed for special torment, and perhaps that disgraced former king still dances in endless agony.

King Moorcraig hid within his castle and hoped his collection of ancient relics would protect him. His doom came on black wings. The Dragonfather flew over the castle and unleashed unquenchable fire. All of Moorcraig's plans and schemes burned and were buried in rubble.

The lich lords wasted no time or effort in founding Lord Toruk's empire and were privy to secrets and powers known previously only to the Dragonfather. Their tireless efforts gave rise to a nation and an army like none other—one worthy of our master and capable of bringing to heel the progeny that had betrayed him. Few of the original lich lords remain today, yet Lord Toruk has ever kept them twelve in number. The Dragonfather allows his servants to rise and fall by their virtues and ambitions, with the weak culled by the strong, who are elevated to replace them.

In those early centuries the lich lords divided the governance of Cryx among themselves, each finding his role in the construction of the empire. They gathered and united their servants and demonstrated their freshly awakened powers. They brought each scattered village and pirate hold to heel and made brutal examples of those who resisted, teaching the importance of obedience by blood and lash. They crushed whatever petty faiths the people clung to and gave them the choice of servitude in life or in death unending. Lord Toruk became the sole god and master of these islands.

The systematic organization and instruction of occult lore began in this era and grew into a tradition passed down through the centuries. We are the recent inheritors of secrets known only to the Dragonfather and translated for lesser minds by puissant undead masters such as Daeamortus, Asphyxious, Tenebrus, Fulmenus, Venethrax, Morbus, Corripio, and others. We have mastered the industry of reanimation and soul extraction that would become the wellspring of our strength. The powerful energies pouring forth from our lord himself have shaped the very land and its people. What some call the "blight" seeps inevitably into all things. This is the shadow of the Dragon God and his brand upon all in his domain.

Additional servants were selected for their knowledge, potential, and martial ingenuity. Among them were those chosen to aid the lich lords in building armies and initiating campaigns of conquest and exploration.

One of the first sent to the mainland was the iron lich Asphyxious, who demonstrated an unusual aptitude in the manipulation of death-born power. He was not one of the original pirate kings, but his origins stretch back to that same era and Lord Toruk saw his potential as a peerless weapon. By compact with the Dragonfather, Asphyxious was granted a form like that of the lich lords to lend strength to his mission.

Even as the moment arrived when Cryxian armies were ready to crush the petty kingdoms across the waters and thereby raze the path to Lord Toruk's progeny, the arrival of the Orgoth made the lich lords pause. Our masters decided to bide their time and observe, consolidating our nation's strength while the Orgoth broke the will of the people of the Thousand Cities. The raiders' ships came once to our shores, but our master disabused them of their ambitions. With his fiery breath he sent their ships twisting into the deep, still blazing as the ocean tried and failed to quench his flames. The Dragon's plans are adaptable, and he instructed his minions that they should deal with the Orgoth at a time of his choosing. The invaders were allowed to occupy the northern island of Garlghast, but any ship that dared Windwatcher's Passage was destroyed.

The Orgoth were worthy adversaries, and our agents sent to observe their progress learned why the Dragonfather acted with patience rather than attempting their immediate destruction. For over two centuries rebellions flared and failed: one futile attack after another, time and time again. Slowly the people rose against the Orgoth in ever-greater numbers, and our lords learned much from observing these battles. The mortals spent their blood without reservation to win victories inch by inch, inadvertently providing us insight into their tactics and potential use.

Inevitably, out of struggle and strife arises advancement and invention. Even though the lich lords of Cryx had created an entire occult science and applied its mechanisms to perfect our industries of war, they were not so arrogant as to refuse to acknowledge useful innovations or to seize them. It has long been our philosophy to turn the tools of our enemies against their makers. Where the great, hulking colossals fell against the Orgoth, Cryxian agents arrived to salvage debris and reclaim the corpses of those who had worked to maintain and control them in battle. By such measures we learned all that was necessary to construct our own engines of war.

We have since fueled our industries with every advancement made by the short-lived mechaniks of the mainland. When one of their great minds takes his last breath, our agents are there to unearth his grave, recover his remains, and plumb his soul for its secrets. Through the application of necromechanikal principles we have constructed vast numbers of helljacks, bonejacks, and thralls. To fuel our industries we mine necrotite from those places that have seen mass torture and death and where life energy bleeds into mud and ash to saturate the stones beneath the soil. It is a great resource, but we have another even more powerful one in the souls of the living. We who master the arts of necromancy can feed upon these souls and use them as fuel for the marshalling of our power.

When they were finally driven from their fortresses, the Orgoth retreated to their first and mightiest stronghold in our lands, the castle known as Drer Drakkerung on Garlghast Island. Lord Toruk was ready, having anticipated this eventuality. For years the necrotechs of Skell, Dreggsmouth, and Blackwater had slaved to craft weapons the equal of those possessed by the Orgoth. The invaders had an impressive mastery of the arcane, and their corpses had proven resistant to initial attempts to unravel their secrets. Raw force, not subtlety, would be required to crush them.

The Dragonfather gave his approval to commence the great attack, and the lich lords sent forth armies such as few have seen even in their most terrifying nightmares. The mainlanders ignorantly believe their rebellion had sent the Orgoth vessels fleeing across the Meredius, but theirs was merely the first blow. The ultimate victory belonged to Cryx. Our forces sailed against Garlghast led by five lich lords, each a master of warfare, boasting armies tens of thousands strong. It was a battle beyond imagining, with invoked powers that shook the surface of Caen, brought blood raining down, and boiled the ocean to froth.

Bitter in their disappointment, the Orgoth were determined to leave only ruin in their wake so that none would profit from the spoils of their defeat. When they saw Cryx would be triumphant, their warwitches invoked a final conflagration to obliterate both themselves and our army in a show of reckless, self-destructive power. They blasted the great city of Drer Drakkerung to ruin in an eruption of fire and ash. Three lich lords were in an instant erased from the face of Caen. The two who survived were forever changed. Forced into somnolent recovery after the near disintegration of their physical forms, their minds were thereafter unsuited to the chaos of war. They serve the Dragonfather still but do so from within Skell, where their minds, untethered from the distractions of the corporeal world, contemplate deeper mysteries.

Our master deemed the price fair. Even the loss of an army as great as this proved inconsequential next to ultimate victory. In the wake of the tremendous battle, Cryx's war industry required time to recover its strength—yet time is meaningless to us. An age to mortals is as the blink of an eye to the deathless. The staggering losses amount to nothing compared to the bounty reaped in the wake of the fall of the Orgoth. Their knowledge fell into the hands of the lich lords in the form of handful of living prisoners and countless blackened corpses.

Through the application of necromantic arts, many slain Orgoth finally spoke from beyond death to reveal their secrets. My master, the lich lord Terminus, personally extracted the methods of constructing their blackships, lore that revolutionized shipbuilding at Dreggsmouth and gave birth to the Black Fleet. Even now the transient nations remain ignorant of the full strength of our naval power. The ragtag pirate vessels that threaten their coasts have confused their assessment of our true capabilities. In time we will attack in such numbers they will think the sea boiling with the walking dead as we rise from the deeps to assail them.

> ## TIME IS MEANINGLESS TO US. AN AGE TO MORTALS IS AS THE BLINK OF AN EYE TO THE DEATHLESS.

After the fall of Drer Drakkerung, Lord Toruk gave his leave for additional forces to emerge from the inner island and extend our tendrils deeper into the continent. He needed generals to replace those destroyed on Garlghast, and for this task he chose Daeamortus and Terminus. Lich Lord Daeamortus had been responsible for necromantic research in Skell for centuries immemorial. Under the supervision of these two great lords, Cryxian influence and power were extended. In the aftermath of the destruction of the Orgoth, our armies were able to take the first great steps to locate the Dragon's children. Even as his minions were distracted by duty and lesser concerns, our master's mind remained fixed upon this objective, the ultimate purpose toward which all our strength is set.

Our agents have penetrated the cities of man. Our fleets have probed the mainland to find the easiest routes to the dragons' lairs. Even apparent defeats at Highgate, Ceryl, and Westwatch were part of his design. Lord Toruk indifferently discards one army as a feint to deliver another. Through such measures, the world bends to his schemes.

Lord Toruk's brood is arrogant yet shrewd and cautious. They dare not reveal themselves openly. They hide among the nations of mankind while lashing out against any who venture close. Cowards they may be, but each holds a sliver of our master's power, and their disregard for the passage of time gives them inhuman perspective. Do not underestimate them. Even the least dragon is the equal of legions—yet legions we have in ample supply.

We have identified the general locations of several of our masters' progeny, although their power and paranoia has made gathering details a challenge. Blighterghast is the nearest of these great enemies, a brazen foe that taunts our lord with its proximity. This dragon haunts the southern Wyrmwall, Cygnar's long chain of towering mountains. From the highest peaks, it keeps its eyes forever fixed on the movements of our nation. It was Blighterghast that first organized the lesser spawn into their alliance against the Dragonfather; even now the creature maintains a constant vigil for any sign that the great lord stirs so it can put forth the call to summon the others to battle.

> **EVEN THE LEAST DRAGON IS THE EQUAL OF LEGIONS—YET LEGIONS WE HAVE IN AMPLE SUPPLY.**

Although we know the mountains Blighterghast calls home, we have had only limited success finding its myriad lairs, and it slyly uses the movements of Cygnar's navy and coastal army forces for protection. Blighterghast knows the forces of Cygnar are inclined to destroy our minions whenever they are sighted, and thus the dragon has not interfered with that nation. Before we can expect to make progress toward Blighterghast's destruction, we must obliterate Cygnar's strongest fleets and their outlying coastal fortresses.

Our agents have made recent forays deep into the Wyrmwall Mountains and seeded them with unliving thralls that wait in deathless torpor to be mobilized by our masters. These forces are yet inadequate for our needs and must be reinforced considerably before we can expect to make substantial progress in rooting out Blighterghast. Despite its nearness, that foe may not be the best initial target of our wrath.

Lord Toruk's other spawn hide much farther away, as if distance were a barrier to the Dragonfather. These include Scaefang and Halfaug, which roam far to the frozen north of the nations of Khador and Rhul. Others dwell on the remote side of the Abyss. While such expanses of land and mortal armies between them are just annoyances to our lord, they are formidable obstacles for our legions. Diversionary attacks along Khador's coasts have allowed furtive movements inside the interior that will ultimately bring these enemies within reach. The last several years have tremendously magnified the scope of our operations on the mainland, and one of the primary reasons for this is to improve our intelligence gathering and access to dragons such as the pair hiding in the distant north.

Another such diversion was a string of raids Cygnar remembers as the Scharde Invasions. These operations were orchestrated solely to lay the foundation for our future conquest of Immoren. From 584 to 588 AR Lich Lords Terminus and Daeamortus directed a campaign of escalating attacks along the Cygnaran coast for the purpose of diverting their forces from our true objective, the establishment of permanent bases on the continent. We confounded them by striking minor villages while leaving major cities untouched and passing by one town to strike another. Once our forces had landed and our supply lines were established or no longer necessary, the raids ceased.

Cygnar counted themselves the victors of the Scharde Invasions and believed their reprisal strikes on the fringes of our outer islands were the cause of our defeat. Finding no pattern in our assaults, the mainlanders were duped into underestimating both our strength and our organization, a critical mistake they have only just begun to realize.

For many decades our agents deeper inland had been forced to rely on sporadic support delivered from Skell, Blackwater, and Dreggsmouth. Such supply lines were too distant to react to the chaos of war and too vulnerable to disruption. Under the cover of the Scharde Invasions, Asphyxious was tasked to initiate an ambitious plan to provide a self-sustaining infrastructure on the mainland, a reliable support network that could operate autonomously.

At his behest in the years that followed, our agents scouted necrotite harvesting sites, began scavenging corpses from mortal battlefields deeper inland, and constructed extensive underground networks housing secret necrofactoriums. By these underground tunnels our freshly created machines and soldiers could move undetected throughout the lands of men, and we began to accumulate undying armies beneath the soil to await the call to battle.

The Scharde Invasions ended, and our larger operations became hidden for a time. We awaited a properly large diversion, a time of conflict between the mortal armies when they would become too caught up in their own squabbles to notice our legions at their gates.

We did not have long to wait. Our opportunity arrived at the end of 604 AR with Khador's invasion of the Kingdom of Llael. Cygnar responded predictably by sending a large number of soldiers to bolster the Llaelese defenses. Given the speed and success of Khador's campaign, Cygnaran intervention could only forestall the inevitable. Our agents were there to pick clean the battlefields of their dead and dying.

Asphyxious' army gathered in subterranean strongholds below the Cygnaran Thornwood Forest, an intractable wilderness ideally suited for such purposes. Under his guidance they penetrated the forest and swept into the heart of the conflict. Corpses and hardware scavenged from these battles provided raw materials for industrious expansion. Our fortunes grew when forces from the Protectorate of Menoth became embroiled in the expanding war in western Immoren, unexpectedly aiding our plans by adding their own corpses to the fertile harvest.

The Menites represented a unique obstacle to our master's plans, however. Cryx requires unlimited access not only to the unsanctified dead but also to the tortured souls of the slain, and those who serve mankind's Creator would interfere with our operations through the intervention of their god. Lest the efforts of the Menites interfere with our vital industries, the lich lords have taken measures to dull their holy might.

Accordingly, we have waged a number of clandestine operations against the Menite faith, including the desecration of tombs, the pilfering of sacred relics, and the assassination of key elements of their leadership. One audacious plan focused on the corruption of the spiritual entity known as the Harbinger of Menoth. The Protectorate draws much strength from this supernatural emissary of their wrathful god, and her emergence prompted the lich lords to initiate several attempts to divert or undermine her power to our own ends. She has thus far evaded these attempts, which underscores the difficulty of reaching those shielded by divine providence. It is clear we need to erase this emissary and those who obey her.

Recent years have brought intelligence regarding the puzzling movements of one of Lord Toruk's lesser progeny. The unusual behavior of this single dragon has suggested that the subtle war between the Dragonfather and his spawn may soon enter into open and violent conflict. This is a reminder that we must never underestimate even the least of our lord's brood.

For some time our masters have known of the dragon named Everblight, recorded as one of the least powerful of the Dragonfather's spawn. Those who maintain the annals of our lord's accomplishments from before the founding of our nation relate that he nearly devoured Everblight almost four centuries before Cryx came to exist. The cowardly creature escaped by fleeing toward the lair of another of its siblings, the dragon Gaulvang, which was consumed in Everblight's place.

Little was heard of this dragon again until it emerged from hiding in 390 AR to obliterate the Iosan city of Issyrah. The creature was subsequently defeated by the massed military might of Ios. Despite Everblight's apparent destruction, in their ignorance the Iosans failed to achieve lasting victory. Every dragon holds a piece of the imperishable Lord Toruk, and therefore only a dragon can eliminate another. They will arise from any mortal injury, even complete destruction of the flesh. It was inevitable Everblight would return despite its apparent annihilation. Our understanding of its recent actions is woefully incomplete, as the dragon has become doubly elusive and unpredictable. That it exists and is gathering its might is certain, for its minions have begun to proliferate and in doing so have drawn the attention of the mortal nations.

Everblight took no part in the alliance of lesser dragons. It has instead gone so far as to prove itself their enemy by attacking and consuming one of its siblings, the convalescing dragon Pyromalfic that once dwelled beneath the Castle of the Keys. To further complicate matters, it seems Everblight has raised its own army, though it is a crude and pathetic force compared to those at our master's disposal. While no doubt Everblight was strengthened by its victory over Pyromalfic, this act made it an enemy of Lord Toruk's other progeny and may well lure them to retaliate. They cannot do so without turning away from their constant vigil, and our lord may gain the opportunity he needs to destroy them all.

Our patience must be eternal and unwavering. Though our legions appear ready to conquer all who would stand against the will of our master, his plans move with immortal precision. Ultimate victory could come tomorrow or be postponed for hundreds of years. For my part, I hope to witness the shadow of Lord Toruk sweep across this world to his illimitable glory.

While our enemies must succeed in defending against us on every occasion, our forces need only a single success to lay waste to their temporal kingdoms. Yet even the deaths of nations are but stepping-stones along our true path toward his eternal dominion.

IRON LICH ASPHYXIOUS
CRYX WARCASTER

I grant you new flesh, a form worthy to serve a god.

—Attributed to Lord Toruk

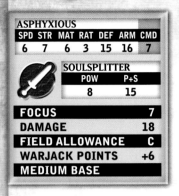

ASPHYXIOUS						
SPD	STR	MAT	RAT	DEF	ARM	CMD
6	7	6	3	15	16	7

SOULSPLITTER		
	POW	P+S
	8	15

FOCUS	7
DAMAGE	18
FIELD ALLOWANCE	C
WARJACK POINTS	+6
MEDIUM BASE	

FEAT: CONSUMING BLIGHT

Constant death follows in the wake of the iron lich as flotsam behind a raging leviathan, and it is on this death that Asphyxious feeds. In a horrific demonstration of necromancy, this terrible undead warcaster may leech the life from the earth itself as well as all those upon it.

Living enemy models currently in Asphyxious' control area suffer an unboostable POW 5 damage roll. Asphyxious gains up to 7 focus points. He cannot have more focus points than his current FOCUS as a result of Consuming Blight.

ASPHYXIOUS

Terror

Undead

Cull Soul – This model gains one soul token for each living enemy model destroyed within 2″ of it. When this model replenishes its focus during your next Control Phase, replace each soul token on it with 1 focus point.

SOULSPLITTER

Magical Weapon

Reach

Sustained Attack – During this model's activation, when it makes an attack with this weapon against the last model hit by the weapon this activation, the attack automatically hits.

SPELLS	COST	RNG	AOE	POW	UP	OFF
BREATH OF CORRUPTION	3	8	3	12	NO	YES

Models hit suffer a POW 12 corrosion damage roll. The AOE is a cloud effect that remains in play for one round. Models entering or ending their activation in the AOE suffer 1 point of corrosion damage.

HELLFIRE	3	10	–	14	NO	YES

A model/unit hit by Hellfire must pass a command check or flee.

PARASITE	3	8	–	–	YES	YES

Target model/unit suffers –3 ARM and this model gains +1 ARM.

SCYTHING TOUCH	2	6	–	–	YES	NO

Target friendly model/unit gains +2 to melee attack damage rolls. Affected models gain Critical Corrosion on their normal melee attacks.

TELEPORT	2	SELF	–	–	NO	NO

Place this model anywhere completely within 8″ of its current location, then its activation ends.

TACTICAL TIPS

CULL SOUL – A model can have more focus points than its FOCUS as a result of Cull Soul.

BREATH OF CORRUPTION – Affected models do not also suffer blast damage.

TELEPORT – This model cannot be placed in an obstruction or in impassable terrain as a result of this spell.

Asphyxious has become the Dragonfather's chosen instrument on the mainland and the unholy general of the rapacious unliving army of Cryx. His campaigns have carved out a bastion for Cryxian forces in the depths of the Thornwood, where he excavates pits of evil and despair in old, deserted battlefields in order to spawn countless horrors.

The iron lich has almost forgotten the time he was alive; it was the blink of an eye compared to the sixteen centuries he has spent in his greater form. Yet once he was a powerful member of the enigmatic Circle Orboros, tasked to watch over the Scharde Islands. When he saw Lord Toruk flying across the ocean to seize the islands for himself, Asphyxious realized the true shape of ultimate power.

The mortal druid spent his days witnessing the seminal acts by which the Cryxian Empire was born. He saw the dread ship *Atramentous* sail into Darkmoor Harbor to greet the gathered pirate kings, exulted in the following slaughter, and watched with jealous hunger as the Dragon

obliterated the twelve pirate kings and remade them into undying lich lords.

Renouncing his ancient vows, Asphyxious went to Lord Toruk at the site that would become known as Dragon's Roost, in the shadow of a great volcano. The druid prostrated himself and offered his service in exchange for even a fraction of the Dragon's power. Toruk made no promises but challenged the mortal to prove his willingness to sacrifice everything.

Asphyxious did not flinch. He climbed atop the lip of the volcano and jumped into its depths. His horrific screams were swallowed by the magma as it stripped his flesh. Toruk scooped his bones from the caldera with one massive talon and blew a spark of unlife into them. The druid's dark soul lingered, agitated from torment, and was placed into a metal vessel of power so as to evade the greedy clutches of Urcaen. On that day, Asphyxious entered the Dragon's employ.

After the forges of Skell were completed and the industry of Toruk's new empire began to belch smoke and assemble the first weapons for his new army, the Dragon called forth the liches. To Asphyxious and the lich lords he gave the gift of steel, as brittle bones were wrapped in frames of dark metal and imbued with the strength and durability of alloyed iron. Among the first of these iron liches, Asphyxious was

sent forth to do Toruk's bidding and to master the great powers of necromancy.

For sixteen centuries he has gathered lore, mastered war and the arcane arts, and become as formidable a creature as has ever walked the face of Caen. He looks to orchestrate the will of Toruk, see the Dragon's empire encompass the mainland, drown its cities in blood, and release a never-ending tide of souls from which he can drink and draw power. Asphyxious leaves behind ashen fields of lifeless grasses and withered trees. Blackened corpses and bubbling pools of gore are all that remain of his victims. The demands of his iron body create a ravenous thirst for fresh souls. The powerful iron carapace grants great physical strength, and his iron talons wield the ensorcelled Soulsplitter—a twin-pronged spear bathed in raw entropy.

Asphyxious is a terrible foe crafty beyond measure and capable of any act in Toruk's name. A prime source of the cancer feeding upon western Immoren, he gleefully spreads the shadow of the Dragonlord's wings. It is a shadow that will one day, by his efforts, extend across all Caen.

WARWITCH DENEGHRA
CRYX WARCASTER

She is proof of the malleability of young flesh and minds, as well as its infinite potential. Asphyxious shaped what was once frail and gentle into a cruelly sublime weapon.

—Skarre Ravenmane

DENEGHRA						
SPD	STR	MAT	RAT	DEF	ARM	CMD
7	5	5	4	16	14	8

SLIVER		
	POW	P+S
	7	12

FOCUS	7
DAMAGE	16
FIELD ALLOWANCE	C
WARJACK POINTS	+5
SMALL BASE	

FEAT: THE WITHERING

Darkness and death obey the beck and call of the warwitch. With mere spoken words and an arcane gesture, Deneghra blankets an area with a web of debilitating despair.

Enemy models currently in Deneghra's control area suffer –2 to their SPD, STR, MAT, RAT, DEF, ARM, and FOCUS and cannot run or make special attacks. The Withering lasts for one round.

DENEGHRA

 Stealth

Cull Soul – This model gains one soul token for each living enemy model destroyed within 2″ of it. When this model replenishes its focus during your next Control Phase, replace each soul token on it with 1 focus point.

Parry – This model cannot be targeted by free strikes.

SLIVER

Magical Weapon

Reach

Shadow Bind – A model hit by this weapon suffers –3 DEF and when it advances it cannot move except to change facing. Shadow Bind expires after one round.

SPELLS	COST	RNG	AOE	POW	UP	OFF
CRIPPLING GRASP	3	8	–	–	YES	YES
Target model/unit suffers –2 SPD, STR, DEF, and ARM and cannot run or make special attacks.						
GHOST WALK	3	6	–	–	NO	NO
Target friendly model/unit gains Ghostly for one turn. (A model with Ghostly can advance through terrain and obstacles without penalty and can advance through obstructions if it has enough movement to move completely past them. An affected model cannot be targeted by free strikes.)						
INFLUENCE	1	10	–	–	NO	YES
Take control of target enemy non-warcaster, non-warlock warrior model. The model immediately makes one normal melee attack, then Influence expires.						
PARASITE	3	8	–	–	YES	YES
Target model/unit suffers –3 ARM and this model gains +1 ARM.						
SCOURGE	4	8	3	13	NO	YES
Models hit by Scourge are knocked down.						
VENOM	2	SP 8	–	10	NO	YES
Venom causes corrosion damage 🜔. Models hit suffer the Corrosion continuous effect 🜔.						

TACTICAL TIPS

THE WITHERING – Because The Withering affects SPD, affected models cannot charge. Power attacks are special attacks.

CULL SOUL – A model can have more focus points than its FOCUS as a result of Cull Soul.

CRIPPLING GRASP – Because Crippling Grasp affects SPD, affected models cannot charge. Power attacks are special attacks.

SCOURGE – This means every model in the AOE is knocked down, friendly and enemy alike.

Wherever she travels, Deneghra leaves a scorched path of devastation. On the battlefield she is a beautiful terror single-mindedly stalking each victim. Perversely angelic in her wicked beauty, Deneghra drifts like a phantom through trees and walls whenever she wills it. She need but whisper and men claw at their skulls in vain attempts to silence the voice inside their minds. Those wretches who fall to her spell would slit a familiar throat—comrade, brother, or beloved wife—at her command.

The few who succeed in staving off her seductions become her reluctant prey. She twirls, leaps, and laughs while enemy soldiers weep and blades slash air or strike harmlessly off her bladed armor. Then she ends the game with a single sweep of her mechanikal spear Sliver. In Deneghra's hand the weapon turns her foe's shadow against him by entwining him in a writhing mass of umbral coils. Rather than being a release, death traps her victim's soul in the cages dangling at her side.

The Cryxian warwitches are cruel beyond comparison and willing to commit any act, no matter how depraved, in their lord's name. Adept at necromancy and blade, they are cunning, adaptable, and unpredictable. The witches have

been so warped by Toruk's influence that some suspect they have been drained of all humanity.

None who knew Deneghra as a youth could have anticipated she would become a merciless killer. She and her twin began life in a fishing village on the western coast of Cygnar. Occult portents unveiled by Skarre Ravenmane indicated a mortal birth of a sorceress with unbridled potential. After informing her master Asphyxious of this presaged birth, the pirate queen was dispatched to ensure the procurement of this precious asset personally. Skarre returned with her captive, believing herself successful. The auguries had been vague, however, and she was unaware the power foretold was manifest in a pair of twins, not in a single birth. Asphyxious discovered the nature of these misread signs later, too late to rectify the situation easily.

Deneghra proved an apt pupil. Asphyxious took her personally under his wing and twisted the young woman into a phantasmal temptress—body, mind, and soul. She excelled at the arcane arts, and even the terrifying helljacks bowed to her will. When the iron lich judged her ready, he unveiled the darkest secret: she had a twin sister who possessed the other half of her soul. Asphyxious spoke of a Cygnaran sorceress who had stolen her essence while sharing a womb, preventing her from reaching her potential. In a murderous rage Deneghra petitioned to join the incursion of the mainland in order to find this twin and reclaim the stolen power. Pleased with his machinations, the iron lich sent forth his protégé as a lieutenant in his army.

Some scream in horror at her approach and others beg her for salvation, but Deneghra yearns for one sound alone—the throttled gurgle of her sister's death rattle. That alone would be the sweet music of victory to her black soul.

PIRATE QUEEN SKARRE
CRYX SATYXIS WARCASTER

She's the drowning tide, the black wave that sends all hands to the deep.

—Satyxis raider on the **Widower**

SKARRE						
SPD	STR	MAT	RAT	DEF	ARM	CMD
7	6	7	4	16	15	9

TAKKARYX	
POW	P+S
7	13

BLOODWYRM	
POW	P+S
3	9

GREAT RACK	
POW	P+S
4	10

FOCUS	6
DAMAGE	16
FIELD ALLOWANCE	C
WARJACK POINTS	+6
SMALL BASE	

FEAT: BLOOD MAGIC

As the dark queen of the Broken Coast, Skarre Ravenmane wields her natural powers of the ancient, island-born black magic with ease. She hesitates at nothing, even sacrificing her own blood to imbue her followers with dark power to enhance their abilities.

Skarre suffers up to 5 damage points. While in her control area, friendly Faction models gain +1 STR and ARM for each damage point she suffers as a result of Blood Magic. Blood Magic lasts for one round.

SKARRE

Sacrificial Strike (★Action) – RNG CMD. Target a model in this model's LOS. If that model is in range, remove one friendly Faction trooper model within 1" of this model from play. The target model suffers a magical damage roll with POW equal to the base ARM of the removed model.

TAKKARYX

⊘ Magical Weapon

Life Trader – When an attack with this weapon hits, this model can suffer 1 damage point to gain an additional die on the damage roll against the model hit. Life Trader can be used once per attack.

BLOODWYRM

⊘ Magical Weapon

Life Drinker – When it destroys a living enemy model with this weapon, immediately after the attack is resolved this model heals d3 damage points.

GREAT RACK

Knockdown – When a model is hit by an attack with this weapon, it is knocked down.

SPELLS	COST	RNG	AOE	POW	UP	OFF
BACKLASH	3	8	–	–	YES	YES

When target enemy warjack that is part of a battlegroup is damaged, its controller suffers 1 damage point.

BLOOD RAIN	3	8	3	12	NO	YES

Blood Rain causes corrosion damage ⚗. Models hit suffer the Corrosion continuous effect ⚗.

DARK GUIDANCE	4	SELF	CTRL	–	NO	NO

While in this model's control area, friendly Faction models gain an additional die on their melee attack rolls this turn.

HELLFIRE	3	10	–	14	NO	YES

A model/unit hit by Hellfire must pass a command check or flee.

RITUAL SACRIFICE	2	6	–	–	NO	NO

Remove target friendly warrior model from play. Skarre gains d6 additional focus points during your next Control Phase. Ritual Sacrifice can be cast only once per turn.

TACTICAL TIPS

SACRIFICIAL STRIKE – This special action is not an attack. The damage roll is boostable.

Without warning she disgorges undead forces and helljacks from the black hull of her vessel to obliterate any resistance. She withdraws with equal speed and leaves ruin and chaos as her legacy. Even the Orgoth feared the Satyxis reaver witches. Few know better than she the power of shed blood, for she is able to invoke acidic rains and project gouts of hellfire from her fingertips.

Sacrifice is vital to Skarre's dark magic. She carries with her a millennia-old ritual dagger she uses to drain the energies binding her comrades together—living or dead, willing or captive—to fuel its enchantments. Alive with stolen essence, the blade can unleash a powerful curse upon Skarre's foes. She is swift to employ her dagger to wrack her victims with gut-wrenching pain that leaves behind twisted, broken corpses.

Skarre seized dominion over the Satyxis through strength and cunning. Her bloodline is famed among them, as her mother ruled before her, but for the Satyxis the right to lead is proven in battle and not inherited. Even as a youth she took to the waves and dominated her kind through the power of her magic and the strength of her will. She has the power to see patterns in the spray of freshly spilled blood, visions granted by sacrifice and pain.

She has made a point of destroying any who would dare plot against her. Cryxian intrigues have occasionally caught her in the subtle and dangerous games of the lich lords, who view her as an effective weapon and a living pawn. Her true loyalty has always been to the Dragonfather, not to any single lich lord.

Skarre Ravenmane, called the Pirate Queen, is the bloodthirsty ruler of the Satyxis, the warrior women of the island of Satyx blighted by ancient dragon blood to become something more than human. Her ship, the *Widower*, strikes along the western coast frequently and without apparent rhyme or reason. Following the guidance of mystical omens revealed to her through rites of slaughter and bloodletting, she braves the storm and lands ashore to deliver panic and grief. For decades anxious mainland admirals and captains entrusted to guard the coastline have tried and failed to predict her movements. Any foolish enough to confront her directly have been destroyed to fuel her legend.

Skarre reads portents and auguries in every kill and claims Lord Toruk speaks to her through the entrails of her victims. Through these signs she steers the Widower to private ports of call to trade blood, steal coin, and sell depravity. Children cling tightly to their mothers when the fog thickens along the Broken Coast, for the dreaded pirate queen may be hiding within.

DEATHRIPPER
CRYX BONEJACK

Something primal in us fears the skulls and jaws of untamed beasts. It is singularly frightening to be confronted by a fiend with bones stripped of flesh, fangs bared, and empty eye sockets staring into your soul.

—Professor Viktor Pendrake, Corvis University

DEATHRIPPER						
SPD	STR	MAT	RAT	DEF	ARM	CMD
7	7	6	5	15	14	—

MANDIBLE		
	POW	P+S
H	6	13

DAMAGE

1	2	3	4	5	6

| H | H | C | A | A | M |
| H | C | C | M | M | M |

FIELD ALLOWANCE	U
POINT COST	4
MEDIUM BASE	

DEATHRIPPER
⊕ Arc Node

MANDIBLE

Sustained Attack – During this model's activation, when it makes an attack with this weapon against the last model hit by the weapon this activation, the attack automatically hits.

The Deathripper, the quintessential Cryxian bonejack, is a terrifying weapon of surprising speed and bestial ferocity that charges forward to tear apart its enemies while serving as a magical conduit for the horrifying spells of its master. These 'jacks skitter across the battlefield pouring forth poisonous smoke and steam from wickedly efficient, necrotite-fueled engines. The high-pitched keen of the Deathripper venting steam has been written about for decades in fevered war journals. It is a sound rarely forgotten.

The Deathripper is built of blackened iron and steel fused with the skulls and fangs of fearsome, blighted beasts. Powered by steam engines driven by necrotite—coal laced with death energy—a Deathripper's jaws leverage enough power to sever limbs and shear through armored

HEIGHT/WEIGHT:	6′4″ / 2.5 TONS
ARMAMENT:	MANDIBLE (HEAD), ARC NODE
FUEL LOAD/BURN USAGE:	44 LBS NECROTITE, 88 LBS COAL / 18 HRS GENERAL, 3 HRS COMBAT
INITIAL SERVICE DATE:	UNKNOWN, first reported in 502 AR
CORTEX MANUFACTURER:	UNKNOWN
ORIG. CHASSIS DESIGN:	UNKNOWN

plates. In a blur of billowing smoke, wailing metal, and bleeding hydraulics, just a few Deathrippers can strip a light warjack down to its components within minutes.

Arc node technology was the pride of Cygnar when initially developed, but before long Cryx had unraveled the puzzle in their particular, twisted way: defiling the tombs of innovative engineers and pulling forth their secrets through necromantic rituals, necrotechs soon learned how to create arc nodes of their own. They improved upon the foreign process by using profane materials and unholy techniques to cheapen and accelerate manufacturing. Now Cryxian warcasters enter the field with a small swarm of arc node–equipped bonejacks, each a conduit for the devastating arcane power wielded by its controlling warcaster.

DEFILER
CRYX BONEJACK

'Tis a shame they are so effective. They leave so little for us to salvage.
—Warwitch Deneghra

HEIGHT/WEIGHT:	6'4" / 2.6 TONS
ARMAMENT:	SLUDGE CANNON (HEAD), ARC NODE
FUEL LOAD/BURN USAGE:	44 LBS NECROTITE, 88 LBS COAL / 17 HRS GENERAL, 2.75 HRS COMBAT
INITIAL SERVICE DATE:	UNKNOWN, first reported in 512 AR
CORTEX MANUFACTURER:	UNKNOWN
ORIG. CHASSIS DESIGN:	UNKNOWN

No two bonejacks are exactly the same, with variations in form and weaponry commonly noted. Mainlanders often wonder how the Nightmare Empire can produce such a swarming profusion of fast and deadly constructs. Whereas other nations allocate each precious warjack cortex carefully, fabrication in Cryx proceeds unhindered by any limits. The chief architects of the Cryxian engines of war are necrotechs—mad, unliving geniuses capable of seemingly endless innovation even as they hoard secrets and compete with one another for the favor of their unforgiving masters. Running day and night, their factories produce a near-endless supply of nightmarish fabrications.

DEFILER
🜨 Arc Node

SLUDGE CANNON
🜨 Continuous Effect: Corrosion

🜨 Damage Type: Corrosion

The Defiler has proved its worth as a light assault bonejack. Fast and mobile, it can lope across the battlefield in a few long strides and fix an enemy warcaster in its sights before the fight has scarcely begun. Its arc node remains ever ready to deliver arcane death.

Unlike the Deathripper, the Defiler avoids close combat. Instead it fires on the enemy from a distance with its sludge cannon, which spews a concentrated, caustic poison that consumes metal and stone more easily than flame eats wood. Faced with the potential of its arc node and the horrendous wounds caused by its sludge cannon, enemies often desperately try to close and deal with this bonejack before their allies are torn apart.

DEFILER

SPD	STR	MAT	RAT	DEF	ARM	CMD
7	7	6	5	15	14	—

SLUDGE CANNON

RNG	ROF	AOE	POW
SP 8	1	—	12

BASH

POW	P+S
0	7

DAMAGE

1	2	3	4	5	6
	H	C			
	C	A	A	A	
H	H	C	A	A	M
H	C	C	M	M	M

FIELD ALLOWANCE	U
POINT COST	5
MEDIUM BASE	

NIGHTWRETCH
CRYX BONEJACK

I wish I could say I'm happy to see them using something that doesn't burn us, dissolve us, or chew us to bits—but I'm not.

—Captain Aleksandr Radu, Skrovenberg militia

NIGHTWRETCH						
SPD	STR	MAT	RAT	DEF	ARM	CMD
7	7	6	5	15	14	—

DOOMSPITTER			
RNG	ROF	AOE	POW
6	1	—	14

BASH	
POW	P+S
0	7

DAMAGE

1	2	3	4	5	6
H	H	C	A	A	M
H	C	C	M	M	M

FIELD ALLOWANCE	U
POINT COST	4
MEDIUM BASE	

NIGHTWRETCH
Arc Node

DOOMSPITTER

Blaster – When this model makes an attack with this weapon, before the attack roll it can spend 1 focus point to give the attack a 3˝ AOE.

HEIGHT/WEIGHT:	6´4˝ / 2.75 TONS
ARMAMENT:	DOOMSPITTER (HEAD), ARC NODE
FUEL LOAD/BURN USAGE:	44 LBS NECROTITE, 88 LBS COAL / 17 HRS GENERAL, 2.5 HRS COMBAT
INITIAL SERVICE DATE:	UNKNOWN, FIRST REPORTED IN 590 AR
CORTEX MANUFACTURER:	UNKNOWN
ORIG. CHASSIS DESIGN:	UNKNOWN

For centuries Cygnar has had the dubious privilege of being the testing ground for Cryxian innovation. The Third Army out of Highgate and Westwatch has had to face the unveiling of weapons too dreadful to be imagined. None who serve along this stretch of open coastline consider the undead lacking in cunning. They have witnessed an endless variety of nightmares, of which the Nightwretch is one example.

When a dispatch arrived from New Larkholm saying that a Cryxian landing party had been sighted two leagues south of the city, the nearby coastal fort of Westwatch immediately sent out a company of long gunners, each eager to put a few bullets in Cryxian raiders. Unaware that they faced a new weapon, they stood shoulder to shoulder as they had been trained. Their disciplined shots dropped several of the incoming bonejacks— but not enough.

These men had only a moment to consider the unfamiliar look of the new Nightwretch bonejacks before small cannons set into the head of each fired in their direction. Carrying a particularly volatile mixture of lead shot and alchemical waste by-products, the projectiles exploded with a concussive blast that could be heard for miles. No one escaped to tell of the Cygnaran failure: in seconds the entire company was reduced to a smoldering heap of flesh flayed from bone. The 'jacks turned and followed their master back to the landing skiff on the rocky beach, their testing mission a success. Necrotechs soon began mass production.

CORRUPTOR
CRYX HELLJACK

To kill is simple, but to turn the enemy's flesh against him is divine.
—Necrosurgeon Fylis

HEIGHT/WEIGHT:	12′ / 6.7 TONS
ARMAMENT:	NECROSLUDGE CANNON (LEFT ARM), NECROJECTOR (RIGHT ARM)
FUEL LOAD/BURN USAGE:	91 LBS NECROTITE, 203 LBS COAL / 9.8 HRS GENERAL, 1.2 HRS COMBAT
INITIAL SERVICE DATE:	UNKNOWN, first reported in 606 AR
CORTEX MANUFACTURER:	UNKNOWN
ORIG. CHASSIS DESIGN:	UNKNOWN

Longstanding pioneers in the development of caustic compounds and necrotic poisons, enterprising necrotechs have reaped a great harvest of alchemical knowledge from the escalating warfare on the mainland. The Corruptor is the culmination of this dark knowledge, a helljack armed with venomous weapons designed to consume both body and soul.

The fiendish warjack was created specifically to deliver these venomous distillates. Both its necrosludge cannon and insidious necrojector drip with toxic alchemical sludge. These horrific poisons can cause the human body to explode in a torrent of acidic filth and strip a victim's soul, restoring vitality to the Corruptor's warcaster or increasing the bond through which his dark powers can manifest.

CORRUPTOR

Immunity: Corrosion

Attack Type – Each time this model makes a normal melee or ranged attack, choose one of the following abilities:

- **Burster** – When this attack boxes a living model, center a 3″ AOE on that model, then remove the model from play. Models in the AOE are hit and suffer an unboostable POW 10 corrosion damage roll.

- **Distillation** – When a living enemy model is destroyed by this attack while this model is in its warcaster's control area, immediately after the attack is resolved the warcaster heals d3 damage points.

- **Psycho Venom** – When a living enemy model is boxed by this attack, it heals 1 damage point. For the rest of the turn, this model's controlling warcaster can channel spells through the enemy model as if it were a model in his battlegroup with the Arc Node ability. At the end of the turn, the enemy model is destroyed.

NECROJECTOR
Open Fist

CORRUPTOR						
SPD	STR	MAT	RAT	DEF	ARM	CMD
6	10	7	5	13	17	—

NECROSLUDGE CANNON			
RNG	ROF	AOE	POW
12	1	—	14

NECROJECTOR	
POW	P+S
5	15

DAMAGE

1	2	3	4	5	6
		□		□	
	□	□	□		
□		□		□	
	L			R	
L	L	M	C	R	R
	M	M	C	C	

FIELD ALLOWANCE	U
POINT COST	8
LARGE BASE	

TACTICAL TIPS

BURSTER – Because the boxed model is removed from play before being destroyed, it does not provide a soul or corpse token.

REAPER
CRYX HELLJACK

When that thing reeled in a six-ton Ironclad like a dragonfish on a line, all bets were off.

—Commander Coleman Stryker

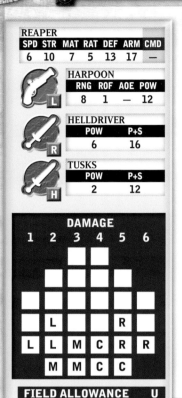

REAPER						
SPD	STR	MAT	RAT	DEF	ARM	CMD
6	10	7	5	13	17	—

HARPOON			
RNG	ROF	AOE	POW
8	1	—	12
L

HELLDRIVER	
POW	P+S
6	16
R

TUSKS	
POW	P+S
2	12
H

DAMAGE

```
        1   2   3   4   5   6
                □   □
            □   □   □   □
        □   □   □   □   □
            L           R
        L   L   M   C   R   R
            M   M   C   C
```

FIELD ALLOWANCE	U
POINT COST	7
LARGE BASE	

HARPOON

Drag – If this weapon damages an enemy model with an equal or smaller base, immediately after the attack is resolved the damaged model can be pushed any distance directly toward this model. After the damaged model is moved, this model can make one normal melee attack against the model pushed. After resolving this melee attack, this model can make additional melee attacks during its combat action.

HELLDRIVER

⊘ **Reach**

Sustained Attack – During this model's activation, when it makes an attack with this weapon against the last model hit by the weapon this activation, the attack automatically hits.

HEIGHT/WEIGHT: 11′10″ / 6.5 tons
ARMAMENT: HARPOON (LEFT ARM), HELLDRIVER (RIGHT ARM), TUSKS (HEAD)
FUEL LOAD/BURN USAGE: 88 LBS NECROTITE, 196 LBS COAL / 10 HRS GENERAL, 1.5 HRS. COMBAT
INITIAL SERVICE DATE: UNKNOWN, FIRST REPORTED IN 557 AR
CORTEX MANUFACTURER: UNKNOWN
ORIG. CHASSIS DESIGN: UNKNOWN

or steel. With frightening speed, it reels its victim to within striking range of its helldriver—a vicious mechanikal spike of tempered steel driven by a wickedly powerful piston. Capable of punching through iron plate, the helldriver generates enough force to pierce boiler casings, rend gears, and reduce enemy warjacks to scrap.

Cryxian helljacks are disturbingly similar to living creatures, perverse amalgams of enormous insects fused with the implements of industrialized slaughter. A hulking creature of bone and steel with blackened armor plating that houses a cortex thirsting for death, the Reaper helljack is one of the most terrible inventions to emerge from the necrofactoriums of Cryx.

The Reaper stalks the battlefield with the single-minded determination of a vicious hunter. With a thunderous report and the grinding peel of rapidly uncoiling chain, the horrific 'jack fires its harpoon to sink deep into flesh

SLAYER
CRYX HELLJACK

I do not credit that thing is a machine. It was as if I stared into the face of death itself.
—Unnamed survivor of an attack on Southshield

HEIGHT/WEIGHT:	11´10˝ / 6.25 TONS
ARMAMENT:	TWIN DEATH CLAWS (RIGHT AND LEFT ARMS), TUSKS (HEAD)
FUEL LOAD/BURN USAGE:	100 LBS NECROTITE, 200 LBS COAL / 12 HRS GENERAL, 2 HRS COMBAT
INITIAL SERVICE DATE:	UNKNOWN, first reported in 531 AR
CORTEX MANUFACTURER:	UNKNOWN
ORIG. CHASSIS DESIGN:	UNKNOWN

The Slayer is a swift, hulking beast of bone and black iron that seeks to murder anything in its path. Its soulfire furnace blazes with a savage intensity that pushes the helljack to ever-greater feats of destruction. The Slayer exists to sow destruction, cleave through bodies with its great claws, and soak the earth with the spent vitality of its broken victims.

An eerie green glow pulsates from the Slayer's furnace, a frightful light illuminating even its eye sockets, suggesting some greater intelligence. After decades of Cryxian terror along the coasts, any greenish lights—like those found floating in the bogs and fens of Immoren—are often called "Cryxlight" by superstitious travelers.

DEATH CLAW
✊ **Open Fist**

Combo Strike (★Attack) – Make a melee attack. Instead of making a normal damage roll, the POW of the damage roll is equal to this model's STR plus twice the POW of this weapon.

The Slayer's tempered metal claws are powerful enough to rend metal and powder bone on impact. It is further armed with cruelly curved tusks amputated from great beasts and bolted crudely onto its armored skull for use in vicious charges. The helljack's furnace is powered by the remnants of life trapped within its necrotite fuel. Those who tend to these murderous machines insist they run best on necrotite scavenged directly from the field of slaughter.

SLAYER

SPD	STR	MAT	RAT	DEF	ARM	CMD
6	10	7	5	13	17	—

DEATH CLAW (L)

POW	P+S
6	16

DEATH CLAW (R)

POW	P+S
6	16

TUSKS (H)

POW	P+S
2	12

DAMAGE

1	2	3	4	5	6
		□	□		
	□	□	□		
	□	□	□	□	
		L		R	
L	L	M	C	R	R
	M	M	C	C	

FIELD ALLOWANCE	U
POINT COST	6
LARGE BASE	

TACTICAL TIPS

COMBO STRIKE – This ability cannot be used while either of this model's arm systems is locked. A model with a crippled weapon system cannot use it to make chain attacks or special attacks, including power attacks.

BANE THRALLS
CRYX UNIT

Our scout's torch and lantern went black, and we heard him scream. A moment later a horrible chill washed over us. We could feel them before we could see them.

—Swift Sergeant Tyrell Forlaine, Cygnaran Reconnaissance Service

LEADER & GRUNTS						
SPD	STR	MAT	RAT	DEF	ARM	CMD
5	7	6	4	12	15	8

WAR AXE		
	POW	P+S
	4	11

FIELD ALLOWANCE	3
LEADER & 5 GRUNTS	5
LEADER & 9 GRUNTS	8
SMALL BASE	

LEADER & GRUNTS

Stealth

Undead

Dark Shroud – While in this model's melee range, enemy models suffer –2 ARM.

WAR AXE

Weapon Master

Bane thralls—cunning undead warriors inscribed with countless runes and sigils of their dark rebirth—are versatile and deadly soldiers among more mindless undead. Wickedly proficient at killing, they host a darkness that both permeates their being and seeps into the world of the living. Few know the means by which these potent creatures are created, and only the most depraved masters of necromancy can begin to understand the nature of the malignant power from whence they arise.

Bane thralls are enshrouded in a cold, preternatural darkness that siphons the very light from the air and is utterly inimical to living flesh. It obscures their forms even in bright daylight and makes fighting them difficult, as tendrils of this darkness reach out hungrily to choke the living. In addition to this gloom, bane thralls display a malevolent glimmer in their eyes that reveals a hateful intelligence. The foul creatures delight in slaughter and seek any opportunity to charge into battle and sow death. Sometimes they can even be heard whispering to each other in ancient tongues, as if coordinating a plan of attack. They march into battle with the discipline and inexorable confidence that only soldiers with no fear of death can possess.

Bane thralls are a profane clue that Cryxian necromancers have unlocked dimly understood horrors, as if connected to some force beyond Caen that thrives on extermination. Some darkness never goes away, no matter what the stories might say, and the bane thrall is a testament to ancient blasphemies.

BILE THRALLS
CRYX UNIT

Dead flesh is more versatile than machinery alone. With the proper application of our art, even the wreckage of battle can rise to serve us once more.
—Master Necrotech Mortenebra

Disgorged from the hellish workshops of Cryx, bile thralls are noted for their bloated and distended bodies and the gurgling noises heard as pumps and siphons perform unspeakable mockeries of biological processes within them. Bile thralls store volumes of corrosive digestive and decomposition agents, with hoses and tubes leading from their distended mouths and fabricated orifices to crude firing mechanisms. With a lurching spasm, each bile thrall can force a startling volume of caustic fluid out of the nozzle over a wide area to dissolve flesh and devour tempered metal.

In the midst of enemy troops, a bile thrall can force itself to perform a particularly powerful explosive discharge. It compresses its overpressurized intestines in a massive purge that creates a grisly shower of fluid, flesh, and metal. Anything caught in the foul blast quickly corrodes beneath the potent dissolving agents. Metal melts into slag while skin and organs painfully liquefy into a bloody, unrecognizable mess.

LEADER & GRUNTS
☠ **Undead**

BILE CANNON
⚗ **Continuous Effect: Corrosion**

⚗ **Damage Type: Corrosion**

Purge (★Attack) – Each model within 6″ of this model that is in its front arc is automatically hit unless this model's LOS to it is blocked by terrain. Models hit suffer a POW 12 corrosion damage roll ⚗ and the Corrosion continuous effect ⚗. After this attack is resolved, remove this model from play. Purge is a ranged attack.

LEADER & GRUNTS						
SPD	STR	MAT	RAT	DEF	ARM	CMD
5	4	2	3	10	13	7

BILE CANNON			
RNG	ROF	AOE	POW
SP 8	1	—	12

FIELD ALLOWANCE	3
LEADER & 5 GRUNTS	**5**
LEADER & 9 GRUNTS	**8**
SMALL BASE	

Cryxian commanders unleash dozens of bile thralls at a time. Powered by their sloshing and throbbing internal mechanisms, they waddle sluggishly across the battlefield until just the right moment to disgorge their innards. Bile thralls serve as much to obliterate an enemy's morale as to destroy its soldiers. Those who have seen the creatures in action have been known to go days without eating, and most who have risked going toe-to-toe with them cannot forget the putrid stench.

MECHANITHRALLS
CRYX UNIT

The Dragon feeds on our wars. Every dead soldier is another weapon in the hands of our enemy. While we weaken, Cryx grows stronger.

—King Leto Raelthorne

LEADER & GRUNTS						
SPD	STR	MAT	RAT	DEF	ARM	CMD
6	7	5	4	12	12	6

x2

STEAMFIST		
	POW	P+S
	4	11

FIELD ALLOWANCE	3
LEADER & 5 GRUNTS	3
LEADER & 9 GRUNTS	5
SMALL BASE	

LEADER & GRUNTS
☠ Undead

STEAMFIST
Combo Strike (★Attack) – Make a melee attack. Instead of making a normal damage roll, the POW of the damage roll is equal to this model's STR plus twice the POW of this weapon.

Favored tools of dark warcasters only too eager to set packs of the creatures upon their foes, mechanithralls were among the first horrors Cryx unleashed on the mainland. Their powerful fists crush the skulls of coastal defenders and innocent villagers with equal disregard, and there is no end to their reserves. The Nightmare Empire rebuilds their ranks from the corpses of the slain—soldiers who survive an engagement may well experience the horror of seeing their fallen friends among the next wave of attackers. The lifeless eyes of their former companions stare from behind rotting flesh, while steam-powered pistons promise an impending and brutal death.

Necrotechs and stitch thralls pick through ravaged battlefields even as battle rages, scavenging for friendly and enemy corpses alike as well as for salvageable pipes and steam engines to integrate into them. Inscribed with basic runes and animated by dark energies, the remade bodies become fresh reinforcements for the Cryxian army. Mechanithralls are further augmented with two heavy gauntlets powered by dark energies and steam pressure coursing through the conduits and pipes that weave throughout their cadaverous bodies. These gauntlets greatly enhance their unliving strength; indeed, a mechanithrall's strike is nearly as powerful as the impact from a steamjack.

Mechanithralls charge heedlessly into destruction, climbing over bodies with as little concern as over any other terrain to strike at the enemy. They follow orders blindly and have been seen using cover and lying in ambush—perhaps tactical habits from their former lives reappearing in endless echoes, much like the vile creatures themselves.

Like the poisonous Morovan tiger vine, Satyxis look fair from a distance but bring nothing but agony and swift death. Steer well clear, lads.
—Captain Halford Bray of the Palaxis

The waters of the Meredius can be terrifying, with names reflecting a legacy of shattered hulls and sunken vessels. The Sea of a Thousand Souls, the Windless Waste, the Wailing Sea, the Dying Strands, Sailor's Lament—these are the waters sailed with impunity by the Satyxis raiders. Even in a region known for its terrifying pirates, the Satyxis stand above the rest. Belonging to an ancient tradition in which sailing is as natural as breathing, these fierce warrior women believe nothing in life to be sweeter than plunder and slaughter.

Even in the days they were still human, by mainlander standards the Satyxis were always brutal, known for blood magic and the inventive cruelty of their wickedly barbed weapons. In 1640 BR, the Satyxis were changed forever when the white dragon Shazkz clashed with Toruk in the skies above their island, spilling blighted blood like rain. That blight withered their men into husks but transformed the women into something other than human as horns grew from their skulls and their cruelty magnified.

LEADER & GRUNTS

⬤ **Advance Deployment**

⊘ **Combined Melee Attack**

LACERATOR

⟳ **Reach**

Chain Weapon – This attack ignores the Buckler and Shield weapon qualities and Shield Wall.

Critical Knockdown – On a critical hit, the model hit is knocked down.

Feedback – If this weapon damages a warjack that is part of a battlegroup, its controller suffers 1 damage point.

LEADER & GRUNTS						
SPD	STR	MAT	RAT	DEF	ARM	CMD
7	5	6	4	14	12	8

LACERATOR	
POW	P+S
4	9

HORNS	
POW	P+S
3	8

FIELD ALLOWANCE	2
LEADER & 5 GRUNTS	5
LEADER & 9 GRUNTS	8
SMALL BASE	

Over the next 600 years, the island slipped into mainland legend. When Toruk arrived to claim the island as part of his empire, the Satyxis queen bowed to the Dragonfather, having foreseen his coming. She offered a regular tithe in soldiers to serve at the whims of the lich lords who rule in his name.

Foremost among these soldiers are the raiders born to ride the waves, versed in barbed whips and other weapons crafted to elicit pain and flay flesh from bone. Mainlanders have come to know the Satyxis by the acts of these raiders and to dread the terrible sound of their war horns as they land ashore to deliver Toruk's wrath.

TACTICAL TIPS

FEEDBACK – Combined attacks cause only 1 point of feedback damage.

NECROTECH & SCRAP THRALLS
CRYX SOLOS

They are mad, secretive, and dangerous, but they are industrious. They spawn our every helljack, bonejack, and thrall, sculpting steel and bone into the death that walks.

—Lich Lord Thalassina

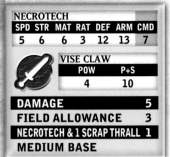

NECROTECH						
SPD	STR	MAT	RAT	DEF	ARM	CMD
5	6	6	3	12	13	7

VISE CLAW		
	POW	P+S
	4	10

DAMAGE	5
FIELD ALLOWANCE	3
NECROTECH & 1 SCRAP THRALL	1
MEDIUM BASE	

NECROTECH
💀 Undead

Create Scrap Thrall [8] (★Action) – To use this special action, this model must be in base contact with a wreck marker. Make a skill check. If it passes, d3 Scrap Thralls are created from a light wreck marker or d6 from a heavy wreck marker. Remove the wreck marker from play and place the Scrap Thralls within 3″ of this model. Placed Scrap Thralls cannot activate this turn.

Repair [8] (★Action) – This model can attempt repairs on any damaged friendly Faction warjack. To attempt repairs, this model must be B2B with the damaged warjack and make a skill check. If successful, remove d6 damage points from the warjack's damage grid.

Steady – This model cannot be knocked down.

VISE CLAW
⟳ Reach

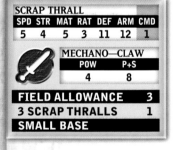

SCRAP THRALL						
SPD	STR	MAT	RAT	DEF	ARM	CMD
5	4	5	3	11	12	1

MECHANO–CLAW		
	POW	P+S
	4	8

FIELD ALLOWANCE	3
3 SCRAP THRALLS	1
SMALL BASE	

SCRAP THRALL
💀 Undead

Thrall Bomb – When this model is disabled, center a 4″ AOE on it and then remove this model from play. Models in the AOE are hit and suffer a POW 8 blast damage roll.

MECHANO-CLAW

Death Burst (★Attack) – This model makes a melee attack. If that attack hits, instead of dealing damage normally, center a 4″ AOE on the model hit and remove this model from play. The model hit suffers a POW 16 damage roll. If the attack misses, center the AOE on this model and remove this model from play. Models in the AOE other than the model directly hit are hit and suffer a POW 8 blast damage roll. Blast damage from this attack is not considered to have been caused by a melee attack.

Part necromancer and part evil genius—spiced with a dash of deranged lunatic—Lord Toruk's necrotechs blend talent and terror. Tasked with the details of constructing the undead soldiers and machines of the Cryxian army, they deliver steady reinforcements to the lines and do not hesitate to use their own dead flesh to test ingenious attachments and necromechanikal augmentations.

TACTICAL TIPS

CREATE SCRAP THRALL [8] – The number of Scrap Thralls that can be created is not limited by FA.

REPAIR – A wreck marker cannot be repaired.

DEATH BURST (★ATTACK) – This model can make a Death Burst special attack even if it charges.

When not designing the next wave of horrors, necrotechs skitter into battle with their "pretty little children." They are quickly able to repair their infernal constructs using whatever materials fate and carnage provide.

Necrotechs improvise scrap thralls from heaps of bone and metal taken from corpses and destroyed 'jacks. Once animated, these thralls shamble forth as delivery vehicles for necrotite-enhanced bombs. Likely to explode when struck by shrapnel or a wayward bullet, each ramshackle undead seeks to grab and hold an enemy in its unrelenting clutch until the bomb detonates in a shower of metal-and-bone destruction. These hastily contrived creatures suggest the hideous potential a necrotech can unleash with enough time, the necessary materials, and a proper workshop.

SKARLOCK THRALL
CRYX SOLO

As thou art an extension of my will and power, so wilt this thrall become an extension of thine.
—Iron Lich Asphyxious instructing young Deneghra

The skarlock thralls are insidious creatures of blackest sorcery. Linked to their warcasters by bonds so powerful they can act in their masters' stead, skarlocks move against enemies with confidence born of a hateful intelligence that shines from their eye sockets.

Unique beings, skarlock thralls can possess extensive personalities and agendas. More than any other constructed thrall, skarlocks retain the memories and lore they gained during life in addition to knowledge absorbed during the inscription of their animating runes. From its very fabrication, each skarlock is inextricably bound to its master and is incapable of disloyalty. A dense inlay of dark sigils blackens their bones and desiccated flesh, instilling tremendous necromantic power and sorcerous potential into their physical forms.

SKARLOCK THRALL
☠ Undead

Attached – Before the start of the game, attach this model to a friendly Faction warcaster for the rest of the game. Each warcaster can have only one model attached to it.

Soul Taker – This model gains one soul token when a living enemy model is destroyed within 2″ of it. This model can have up to three soul tokens at a time. During its activation, this model can spend soul tokens to gain additional attacks or to boost attack or damage rolls at one token per attack or boost.

Spell Slave (★Action) – This model must be in its warcaster's control area to make the Spell Slave special action. When it does, it casts one of its warcaster's spells with a COST of 3 or less. The warcaster is considered to have cast that spell but this model is its point of origin. When making a magic attack roll, this model uses its warcaster's FOCUS. This model cannot cast spells with a RNG of SELF or CTRL.

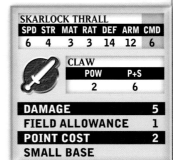

SKARLOCK THRALL						
SPD	STR	MAT	RAT	DEF	ARM	CMD
6	4	3	3	14	12	6

CLAW		
	POW	P+S
	2	6

DAMAGE	5
FIELD ALLOWANCE	1
POINT COST	2
SMALL BASE	

As part of the bonding process, skarlocks become conduits for the unique arcane abilities of their warcasters, who often send them forth to unleash this power from a distance. Lesser minions make every effort to appease the creatures, knowing that each represents the eyes and ears of a malevolent and powerful master.

TACTICAL TIPS

ATTACHED – This model cannot be reassigned if its warcaster is destroyed or removed from play.

SPELL SLAVE – This model cannot cast spells if its warcaster is destroyed or removed from play. The Skarlock cannot channel spells because it does not control warjacks.

MERCENARIES

GLORY AND COIN
MERCENARIES OF THE IRON KINGDOMS

My favorite two colors are blood and gold, and on a good day I see a lot of both.

—Herne Stoneground

The following is from an anecdotal conversation between Greygore Boomhowler and a new recruit.

Aye, I met many an army sod what turns his nose up at mercs. As if their own coin spends better. They got fancy uniforms t'be sure, but what else they got t'be so proud about? Most never seen battle afore. A bunch o' milk-drinkin lads barely to manhood cannae tell one end of a rifle from the other. Sneeze too loud and them baby-faced recruits soil their britches and drop their weapons.

Take yer average merc. We been in scraps every chance we could just to get by. Need coin for payin the boys, coin for supplies and ammo, coin for drinkin. If we cannae hold our own in a fight we dinnae get paid. It's honest work, na mistake. It's a hard livin, with ever day the risk o' bein put down for good. Only thing'll keep you alive is skill with blade or gun. Ne'er know where a job'll take you. Might be up to the frozen north where spit'll freeze afore it leaves yer mouth or down in the Marches sloggin through dust storms and eatin sand. Bein a merc is tough. If you want to kick up yer heels and get paid yer better off takin a job in town. Ever day with my company ye best be ready to hunker down while bullets are flyin overhead and split some skulls with that axe at yer belt.

What ye most gotta understand is we got rules we follow. Tis my name on the company and my name on our charter, and yer actions in battle'll come back to me. Make me regret hirin you and I'll tear yer arm off and cram yer own fist down yer gullet. Bein a proper merc ain't like bein a bandit. We live by the Charter set up in ancient days like any good company. When we hire on we see the course. It dinnae matter if the fightin gets rough, we stick in there. There's na turnin about and sellin ourselves to the other side cause they offered a few more coins. There are criminals and bandits what work like that and it's a quick way to get strung up on the gallows. We dinnae put up with that. My name is known from Caspia to Blackwater cause my word is good and I give what service I promise. When Boomhowler signs his mark on the page, he puts his gun and his axe where they tell him. If ye dinnae like it, hire on to a pirate ship and leave me be.

I'm the boss, so dinnae worry about anyone else here. In the regular army ye'd have to watch all the officers up the ranks from ye, know which ones to salute and which ones yer na supposed to look at, and hope na to run into em what with too many mugs under yer belt. We got freedom. We spend our money how we want and we have a good time when we're na in battle. This company plays as hard as we fight. What good is clink squirreled away if ye cannae spend and enjoy it?

There are lots o' mercs and we compete with em all. Each has his own bag o' tricks, and it's good to know what to expect. Some'll pretend t'be yer best friend so keep yer wits. We all earn our pay the same way, but every company's got their own contracts. Each of em would as soon see ye in a ditch bleedin fer takin a job they want. We work alongside some companies when the contract calls fer it, but dinnae trust em beyond that. Some mercs just want coin. Others got their own axe to grind. Maybe they're holdin some past job we took against us and are lookin fer a scrap. Some pretend t'be proper mercs but dinnae even wear the company ink. They got na scruples and are just assassins. Watch yer back and keep yer axe at the ready.

Ye seem to have a good head on yer shoulders. Follow my lead and duck when I say and we'll all be rollin in gold afore ye know it.

GREYGORE BOOMHOWLER & CO.
MERCENARY MINION TROLLKIN CHARACTER UNIT

That sound! Like a lion riding a church bell in the middle of a landslide. I covered me ears in time, but not all me mates were fast enough. Some of 'em ain't heard a sound since.

—Reid Markus, Cygnaran long gunner

BOOMHOWLER						
SPD	STR	MAT	RAT	DEF	ARM	CMD
6	7	7	5	12	16	9

BLUNDERBUSS			
RNG	ROF	AOE	POW
8	1	—	12

GREAT AXE	
POW	P+S
5	12

GRUNT						
SPD	STR	MAT	RAT	DEF	ARM	CMD
6	7	6	4	12	16	8

BLUNDERBUSS			
RNG	ROF	AOE	POW
8	1	—	12

GREAT AXE	
POW	P+S
5	12

BOOMHOWLER'S DAMAGE	8
FIELD ALLOWANCE	C
BOOMHOWLER & 5 GRUNTS	6
BOOMHOWLER & 9 GRUNTS	9
MEDIUM BASE	

Mercenaries – These models will work for Cryx, Cygnar, and Khador.

Minions – These models will work for Trollbloods.

BOOMHOWLER
- Ⓦ **Combined Melee Attack**
- Ⓧ **Officer**
- Ⓨ **Tough**

Fell Howl – This model can make one of the following fell calls anytime during its unit's activation. A friendly Faction model/unit can be affected by only one fell call each turn.

- **Call of Defiance** – When a model in this unit that is in formation makes a Tough roll of 4, 5, or 6, it heals 1 damage point and is knocked down. Call of Defiance lasts for one round.

- **Call to Action** – Knocked down models in this unit in formation immediately stand up.

- **Rage Howler** – Enemy models/units currently in this model's command range must pass a command check or flee. Warjacks and warbeasts currently in this model's command range suffer –2 to attack rolls for one round.

GRUNT
- Ⓦ **Combined Melee Attack**
- Ⓨ **Tough**

TACTICAL TIPS

BOOMHOWLER – Because Boomhowler is an Officer, when he is destroyed he does not replace a Trollkin in his unit. Instead a Trollkin in the unit becomes the new unit commander.

double fees to stop singing and cavorting at all hours of the day and night. When Boomhowler is not singing, drinking, or fighting, he is involved in Bragg's favorite activity: procreation. The trollkin's legendary voice has entranced females of all races throughout the Kingdoms. Indeed, he is quite the handful off the battlefield, but his antics are well worth it once the battle has been joined.

Boomhowler is proficient with both blunderbuss and axe, but his rumbling voice is his most powerful weapon. A single bellow sends forth a heavens-shaking cry—a rolling reverberation that rises above the clash of swordplay and the crack of gunfire. Felt as much as heard, this sonic tsunami shatters glass, splinters wood, and rips gashes in the metal hides of warjacks. The sensitive inner workings of the mechanikal giants are susceptible to this swell of sound, which rattles loose cogs and unbalances essential fluids. Truth be told, Boomhowler's wail taxes him a great deal, and he cannot sustain it for extended amounts of time.

Some soldiers claim Greygore's voice was key in winning battles even before the first drop of blood was spilled. His mere presence has more than once caused entire hordes to flee, while at other times his stirring chants have kept his comrades fighting despite their most grievous wounds. Among those who appreciate his unique talents is the outlaw warcaster Asheth Magnus, and the two seem to have come to an equitable arrangement.

Boomhowler's company of trollkin fights with a combination of axe and blunderbuss, though some traditional trollkin dislike the fell caller's influence over the many young who have given up their tribal ways to join him abroad. Greygore is without question more comfortable in the cities than in the wilds, but he occasionally forays into the ancestral homes of his people to recruit for his unique mercenary company. The number of these volunteers waxes and wanes, but Boomhowler is never found without at least a few loyal followers.

Whether Greygore Boomhowler is truly the reincarnation of the legendary Bragg or just a self-important merc with a bloated ego matters little to his employers. He and his trollkin company are an impressive addition to any army, and between bouts of drunken revelry he has a wealth of talent and experience to spread among his troops.

The legendary trollkin fell caller Bragg was quite virile and supposedly irresistible in his day, spreading progeny bestowed with his peculiar talents across Immoren. These special folk, known as "fell callers," command a power of voice that staggers the imagination. One of the more notable examples is Greygore Boomhowler, a crass axe-for-hire with a great command of the Gift of Bragg. Those who have heard his vocal prowess are generally divided on whether the experience was positive or negative, but without exception they recount it with strong emotion.

Boomhowler proclaims himself the reincarnation of Bragg. An admitted outcast among the wild trollkin tribes, he chooses to wear garish strips of colorful cloth in a style of his own design not related to any true *quitari* tartan patterns of his people. He also refuses to be quiet, even in ambush. Indeed, some commanders have paid him and his mercs

HERNE & JONNE
MERCENARY RHULIC CHARACTER UNIT

Eighteen degrees left! Seven degrees skyward! Three degrees for wind!
This one's going to kick them in the shorts.

—Herne Stoneground to Arquebus Jonne in battle

HERNE						
SPD	STR	MAT	RAT	DEF	ARM	CMD
4	6	6	6	12	13	9

PISTOL			
RNG	ROF	AOE	POW
8	1	—	10

AXE	
POW	P+S
3	9

JONNE						
SPD	STR	MAT	RAT	DEF	ARM	CMD
6	8	6	4	12	15	9

BARRAGE ARQUEBUS			
RNG	ROF	AOE	POW
12	1	—	14

GREAT AXE	
POW	P+S
5	13

HERNE'S DAMAGE	5
JONNE'S DAMAGE	8
FIELD ALLOWANCE	C
POINT COST	3
HERNE SMALL BASE	
JONNE MEDIUM BASE	

Mercenaries – These models will work for Cygnar, Khador, and the Protectorate.

HERNE
⬡ Officer

BARRAGE ARQUEBUS
Range Finder – While B2B with Herne, Jonne gains +2 to attack rolls with this weapon.

Scattershot (★Attack) – To make a Scattershot special attack, Herne and Jonne must be B2B. Make a normal attack with this weapon. After determining point of impact for that attack, roll deviation for two additional 3" AOEs centered on that point. Models in an AOE are hit and suffer a POW 7 blast damage roll.

TACTICAL TIPS

SCATTER SHOT - The additional shots deviate the full d6" regardless of range. A model in more than one AOE suffers a damage roll for each of them.

HERNE - Because Herne is an Officer, when he is destroyed he does not replace Jonne. Instead Jonne becomes the new unit commander.

Herne Stoneground spent his younger days as a traveling alchemist's assistant. As he roamed from stronghold to stronghold learning his mentor's trade, he became increasingly curious about the sciences involved in gunsmithing, cannoneering, and demolition. By his second decade he had already mastered the manufacture of double-barreled firearms, and his creations earned him a reputation among traders and military merchants alike. The Stoneground mark is hailed in some parts as a sign of the highest quality in firearms.

Mistrustful of messengers, Herne has always insisted on delivering his wares personally. A Stoneground original can fetch a thousand Cygnaran crowns on the open market—and a select few sell at a much higher price behind closed doors—so Herne typically kept several bodyguards in his employ. That changed when he encountered a well-respected ogrun named Jonne.

Jonne was born and raised in Rhul, where for centuries most of his conclave have served as guards and smith hands for the Rhulfolk. Growing up quickly on the trade-rich border of Llael, Jonne became used to the flash and pomp of Llaelese merchants. It did not take long for the adolescent ogrun to make a name for himself on the Black River loading docks, where merchants came to ask for him by name. This slight taste of fame went right to Jonne's head, and he soon signed on with a Rhulic mercenary group called the Emberhold. While in the company he practiced his martial skills and worked as a sword-for-hire for any who might be in need of his muscle.

One day during the delivery of a pair of Stoneground originals to one such employer, Jonne met Herne Stoneground himself. A pair of ill-fated brigands picked that time to interrupt the sale. Moving instinctively, Jonne snatched up the two bandits and restrained them until the watch arrived. So fast was his reaction and effective his skill, the surrounding folk broke into applause as the ogrun handed over the brigands. Herne offered Jonne a lucrative contract on the spot, and from that day forth the two were fated to become one of the most famous mercenary teams in all the Iron Kingdoms.

Though that was nearly fourteen years ago, Jonne remains bound to Herne in friendship built through many shared adventures. The ogrun has gone far beyond the call of duty for his charge by saving Herne time and again, and the dwarf feels safe under Jonne's watchful eye. Though some less scrupulous employers might allow their hired muscle to perish in order to save their own skin, Herne would not think of it, leaping to aid his ogrun friend without thinking of his own safety.

Some years ago, after months of Jonne's grumbling, the duo agreed that small arms manufacturing was not the lucrative business it once had been and that true wealth lay in large ordnance. Herne put his mind and gunwerks skills to the task and soon unveiled the Stoneground barrage arquebus. In an effort to market the new creation, Herne and Jonne took to the road, hiring themselves out to potential customers in order to demonstrate the gun's effectiveness firsthand.

The arquebus, a triple-barreled contraption that launches three cannonballs at once, is a beautifully crafted weapon so massive that only the bulging muscles of Jonne—or "Arquebus Jonne," as he has come to be called—can possibly hold it aloft. For his part, Herne uses his shrewd judgment and mathematical skill to help refine the weapon's trajectories. With its weight and kick, the barrage arquebus is difficult to aim, but this shortcoming is balanced by its fragmenting ammunition. The arquebus is devastating at a respectable range, and Jonne is just as deadly in close combat with his mighty axe. Foes who survive the shelling long enough to close also risk facing Herne's axe and pistol—neither of which he is reluctant to employ.

Herne Stoneground and Arquebus Jonne have argued payment options with Khadoran kommandants, joined Cygnaran officers in after-battle victory toasts, and witnessed the prebattle prayers of Menite priests. They have earned a reputation as consummate professionals, and their fees are considered entirely reasonable for those in need of the kingdoms' premier walking artillery platform.

EIRYSS, MAGE HUNTER OF IOS
MERCENARY CHARACTER SOLO

It's a shame there's not more mercenaries like her. What Eiryss hunts, dies. She's as reliable as the setting sun.

—Cygnaran Captain Morris Beaumayne

EIRYSS						
SPD	STR	MAT	RAT	DEF	ARM	CMD
7	4	6	9	16	12	9

CROSSBOW			
RNG	ROF	AOE	POW
12	1	–	10

BAYONET	
POW	P+S
2	6

SABER	
POW	P+S
3	7

DAMAGE	5
FIELD ALLOWANCE	C
POINT COST	3
SMALL BASE	

Mercenary – This model will work for Cygnar, Khador, the Protectorate, and the Retribution.

EIRYSS

⊙ Advance Deployment

✪ Fearless

◐ Pathfinder

▤ Stealth

Attack Type – Each time this model makes a normal ranged attack, choose one of the following abilities:

• **Death Bolt** – Instead of rolling damage, a model hit suffers 3 damage points. When damaging a warjack or warbeast, choose which column or branch suffers the damage.

• **Disruptor Bolt** – A model hit loses all focus points. A model hit with the Focus Manipulation special rule does not replenish focus points next turn. A warjack hit suffers Disruption for one round. (A warjack suffering Disruption loses its focus points and cannot be allocated focus or channel spells for one round.)

• **Phantom Seeker** – This model ignores LOS when making ranged attacks. This model ignores concealment and cover when resolving ranged attacks.

Camouflage – This model gains an additional +2 DEF when benefiting from concealment or cover.

Retribution Partisan – When included in a Retribution army, this model is a Retribution model instead of a Mercenary model.

Technological Intolerance – When this model ends its normal movement within 5″ of a friendly non-myrmidon warjack, its activation ends immediately.

TACTICAL TIPS

Disruptor Bolt – Just as with Disruption, Disruptor Bolt does not prevent a model from gaining focus in other ways. A warcaster can still gain focus from soul tokens, for example.

Phantom Seeker – Keep in mind that Phantom Seeker does not ignore Stealth.

Camouflage – If a model ignores concealment or cover, it also ignores concealment or cover's Camouflage bonus.

Iosans have long been mysterious—doubly so since their nation isolated itself from outside contact in 581 AR. Any who have ventured uninvited into that territory have vanished. Neither humans nor Rhulfolk comprehend the power of the elves, nor do they understand Iosan technology and magic, but one Iosan hunter has risen to leave her mark on the wars of man: Eiryss has earned a reputation as one of the most reliable and formidable of lone mercenary operatives, a peerless hunter and shooter.

Despite several decades of offering her skills for hire and earning her reputation through word of mouth, Eiryss is still largely a mystery among the mercenary community, as enigmatic as her Iosan people. The mercenary tradition is deeply ingrained in western Immoren, a part of the fabric of both the human nations and Rhul. Carefully observed

mercenary rules of procedure date back to the ancient days of the Thousand Cities Era, when every township was inclined to hire sell-swords to fight their wars. Yet Ios has stood aloof from this trade, making Eiryss an aberration among her own kind.

This aura of mystery combined with her reputation as a ruthless and efficient killer has led to cool relations between Eiryss and others in the trade. A variety of suspicious rumors circulate among the various smoky halls, but most people dismiss them as a natural consequence of her successes. Without question there are other skilled bounty hunters and assassins who feel Eiryss has stolen work from them.

To those employing such soldiers, among a bewildering array of disreputable murderers-for-hire, Eiryss' reputation is golden and her services always in demand. Despite this, she is not one to haggle like a fishmonger over her rates; some captains privately admit the very modest fees she sets are far below her worth. They speculate that perhaps human currency means less to her kind—but whatever her reasons, they are happy enough to leave their coin in their pouches and their curiosity unsatisfied.

Eiryss is prompt and professional, often arriving to a prospective battlefield before the rising sun to learn the lay of the land; thus, she often knows the ground better than the commanders themselves. She interacts with all officers, from the lowest to the highest ranks, with the same polite respect and quiet deference, often so unobtrusively that her employers nearly forget she is present during deliberations of plans and tactics. Even from the shadows, her ears and eyes miss nothing; she can memorize a plan of battle in an instant and later perfectly recall the disposition of allied squads and officers. Once battle is joined she needs no instruction, vanishing into the undergrowth with her crossbow in hand to await the opportunity to kill.

The one group that finds Eiryss' skill unnerving—regardless of the glowing reports of hiring bursars—is military arcanists. Hunting and slaying sorcerers and warcasters is a peculiar specialty, and the Iosan offers her services in this area as well as for less arcane targets. She has never explained her skill as a hunter of spell-slingers but clearly has much experience.

Given the relative importance of wizards and warcasters in every western Immoren army, Eiryss' ability to strike decisive blows against enemy arcanists multiplies her worth. Cygnaran officers task her to slay members of Khador's Greylords Covenant, and Khadoran officers are eager to see her assassinate Cygnaran gun mages. Being in the rare position to exterminate a ranking warcaster can completely change the fortunes of battle. Given that she has no particular loyalty to one side or the other, her talent in this regard is seen by members of these hunted professions as a matter of no small concern.

REINHOLDT, GOBBER SPECULATOR
MERCENARY CHARACTER SOLO

What d'ye mean ye don' know who I am? I'm famous, I am! Bloody famous!

—Reinholdt, self-proclaimed world traveler

REINHOLDT						
SPD	STR	MAT	RAT	DEF	ARM	CMD
7	2	2	2	16	9	4

FIELD ALLOWANCE	C
POINT COST	1
SMALL BASE	

Mercenary – This model will work for Cygnar and Khador.

REINHOLDT

Warcaster Benefits – While this model is B2B with a friendly warcaster, this model can use one of the following special abilities:

- **Lucky Charm (★Action)** – During his activation this turn, the warcaster can gain an additional die on an attack or damage roll. Discard the lowest die.

- **Reload (★Action)** – During his activation this turn, the warcaster can make one additional ranged attack ignoring ROF.

- **Spyglass (★Action)** – Measure the distance between two models within the warcaster's LOS.

Few men can claim they have ventured from one end of the Iron Kingdoms to the other and back, and even fewer gobbers can make such a bold statement. One of these diminutive creatures does more than just suggest, however; he downright insists he has been everywhere at least twice and seen it all at least once.

Reinbaggerinzenholdt, or Reinholdt for short, claims to have seen many wondrous sights, from the throne room of Stasikov Palace to the glowing walls of Shyrr. He sports strange trinkets and baubles from all over Immoren, and his accent is nearly indistinguishable from that of the natives of wherever he happens to be at the time. Whatever the cause or source, Reinholdt is an endless font of esoteric facts and sometimes useful advice. Not an expert at anything in particular, he seems at least partially versed in whatever comes up at the moment.

Even with the veracity of his claims in question, a number of warcasters and other military officers throughout western Immoren are willing to indulge him and periodically hire his services. Although he claims to have once worked as a bodger, Reinholdt has demonstrated little aptitude or interest in fixing things. In some cases it seems likely he is allowed to accompany those who hire him more for his conversational oddities than for any practical purpose. All the same he has proven his worth at unexpected times and places and has demonstrated a skill at several tasks that recommend him to his employers.

Among the gobber's skills is a knack for speedily reloading firearms. In fact, Reinholdt is entirely at ease manipulating volatile ammunition cartridges packed with explosive powder. Those officers who count themselves as riflemen or pistoleers have found this ability alone enough to make hiring him worthwhile.

Reinholdt carries a host of trinkets and artifacts and makes great use of these "tools." His brass Ordic spyglass with its fine lenses—which he says he received for helping beat back a Cryxian pirate invasion near Berck—is one of his favorites. The glass allows him to spot potential dangers from afar and estimate just how long it will take for those perils to cause him personal harm. Though it might take an employer a while to adjust to this seconds-to-impact method, Reinholdt is rarely off by much—and even then it is usually on the conservative side. Some claim Reinholdt's mere presence has brought them luck, though proving such claims is difficult.

Whatever luck he brings to others, Reinholdt seems to have led a charmed life. Despite his presence at countless battlefields across Immoren, he has never suffered a serious injury. He once sneezed himself out of a moving carriage into a patch of thornbriar bushes just before the carriage burst into flames upon hitting a powder trap set by brigands. Another time a blunderbuss shot deflected harmlessly off of a silver soup spoon in his pocket that he had "acquired" earlier that same day. Most often his survival has been the result of anticipating a threat and heading in the opposite direction.

Reinholdt is not what one would call a hero. He is far more likely to run and hide than stick around if a situation gets too hairy. Indeed, he has been known to vanish from sight in typical gobber fashion when an enemy comes too close. If left with little choice, the resourceful chap searches his pockets and pouches for anything that might aid his escape. Few have the heart to hold these habits against him. Those who have become fond of his eccentricities often welcome him back to the table the next campaigning season.

**COMMANDER
COLEMAN STRYKER**
Warcaster

**COMMANDER
COLEMAN STRYKER VARIANT**
Warcaster

**CAPTAIN
VICTORIA HALEY**
Warcaster

**CAPTAIN VICTORIA
HALEY VARIANT**
Warcaster

**LIEUTENANT
ALLISTER CAINE**
Warcaster

**JOURNEYMAN
WARCASTER**
Solo

**JOURNEYMAN
WARCASTER VARIANT**
Solo

IRONCLAD
Heavy Warjack

FIELD MECHANIKS
Unit

ARCANE TEMPEST GUN MAGES
Unit

STORMBLADE INFANTRY
Unit

CYCLONE
Heavy Warjack

DEFENDER
Heavy Warjack

LONG GUNNER INFANTRY
Unit

LANCER
Light Warjack

CHARGER
Light Warjack

SENTINEL
Light Warjack

TRENCHER INFANTRY
Unit

**CLASSIC COMMANDER
COLEMAN STRYKER**
Warcaster

**CLASSIC LIEUTENANT
ALLISTER CAINE**
Warcaster

CLASSIC IRONCLAD
Heavy Warjack

CLASSIC DEFENDER
Heavy Warjack

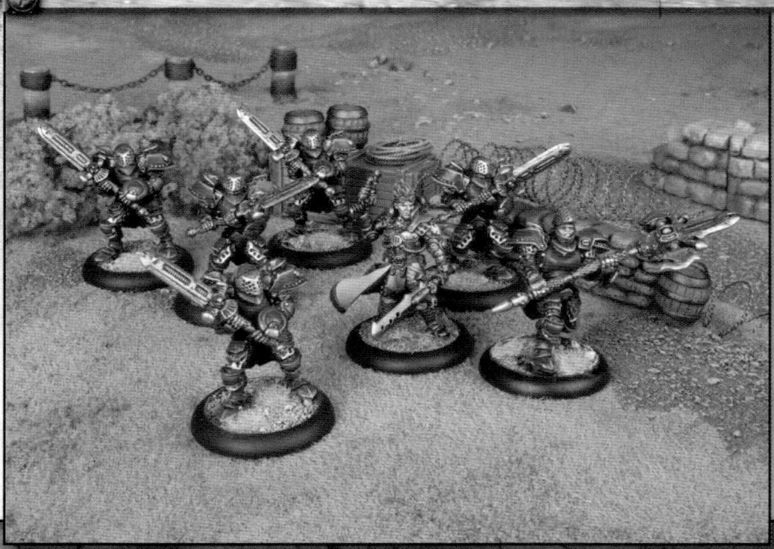

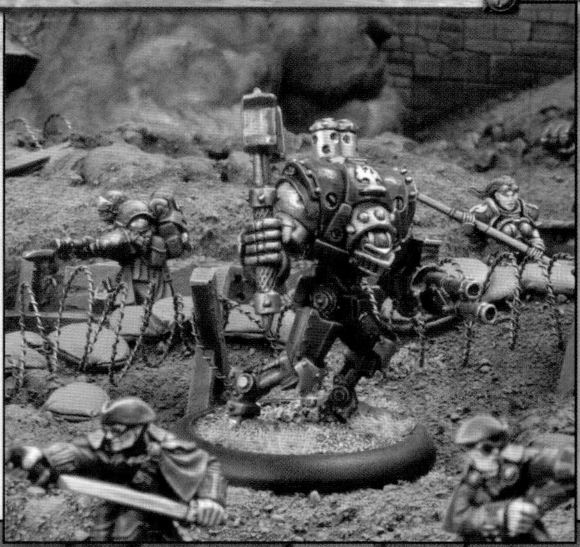

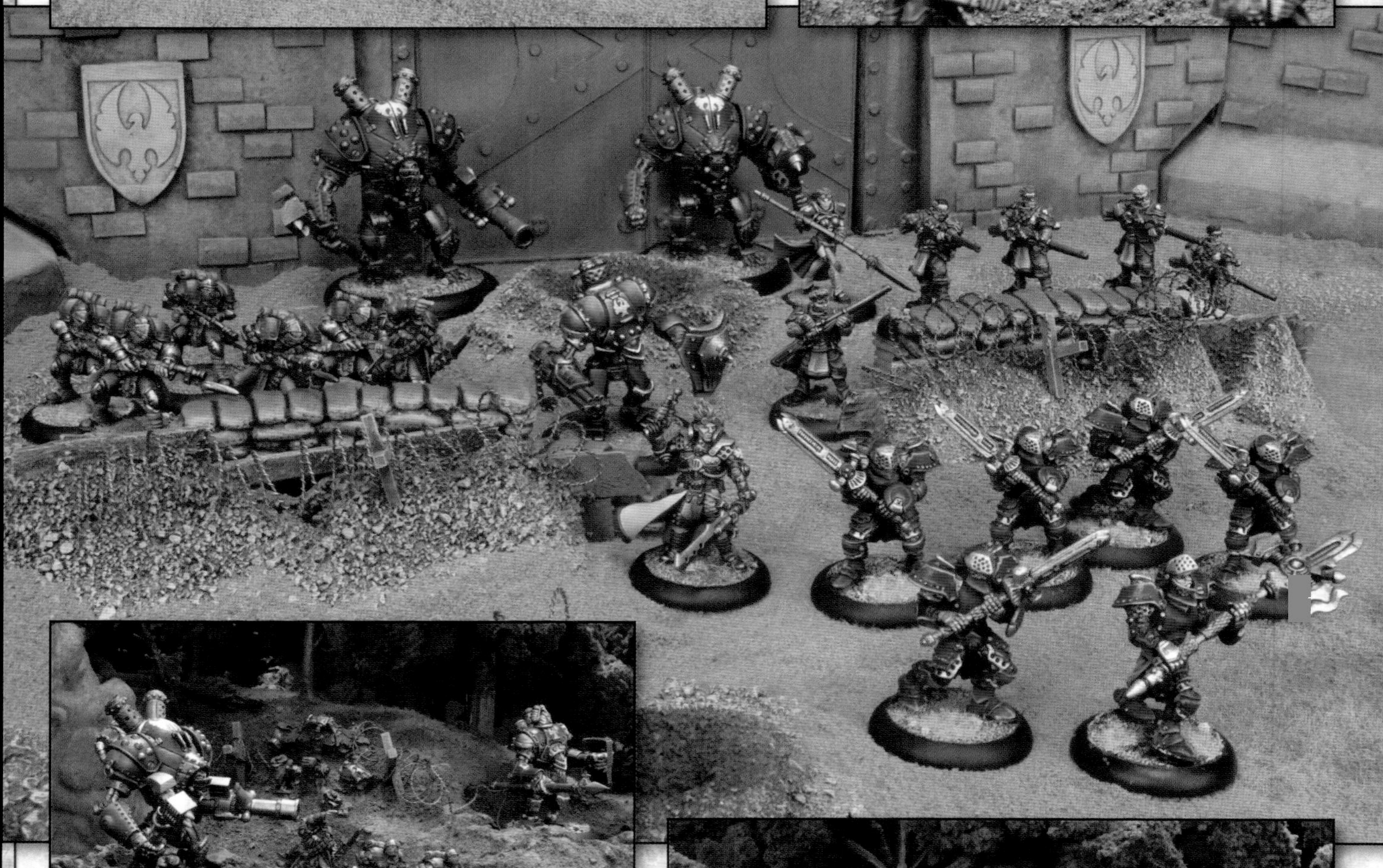

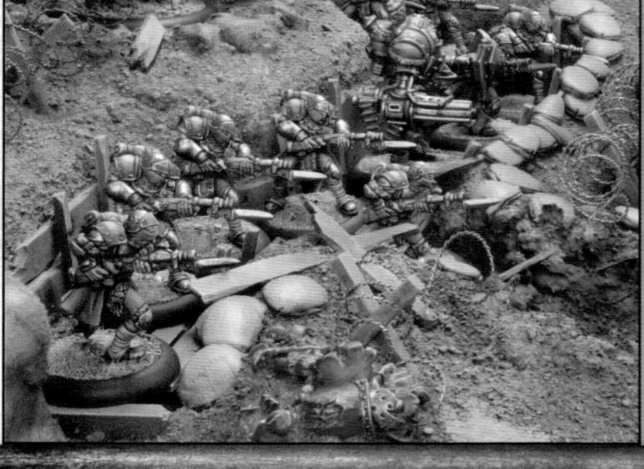

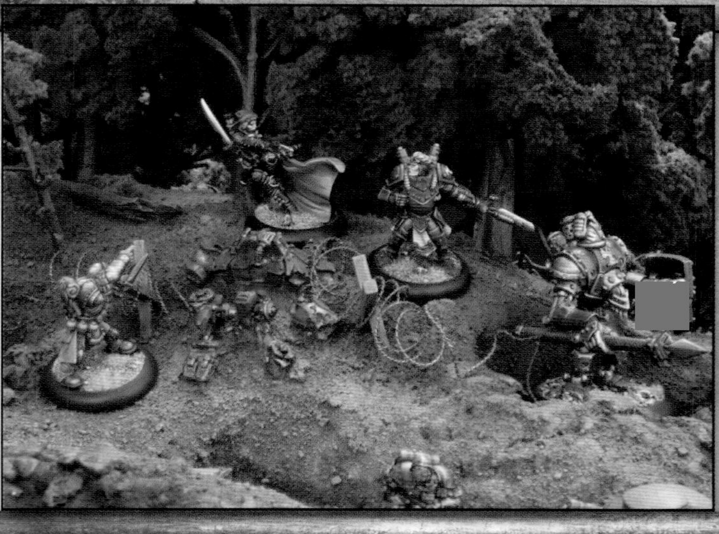

**HIGH EXEMPLAR
KREOSS**
Warcaster

**HIGH EXEMPLAR
KREOSS VARIANT**
Warcaster

**THE HIGH
RECLAIMER**
Warcaster

**GRAND SCRUTATOR
SEVERIUS**
Warcaster

**PALADIN OF THE ORDER
OF THE WALL**
Solo

CRUSADER
Heavy Warjack

**PALADIN OF THE ORDER
OF THE WALL VARIANT**
Solo

KNIGHTS EXEMPLAR
Unit

TEMPLE FLAMEGUARD
Unit

CHOIR OF MENOTH
Unit

TEMPLAR
Heavy Warjack

VANQUISHER
Heavy Warjack

HOLY ZEALOTS
Unit

DELIVERERS
Unit

REVENGER
Light Warjack

REDEEMER
Light Warjack

REPENTER
Light Warjack

CLASSIC HIGH EXEMPLAR KREOSS
Warcaster

CLASSIC VANQUISHER
Heavy Warjack

CLASSIC CRUSADER
Heavy Warjack

**KOMMANDER
SORSCHA**
Warcaster

**KOMMANDER
SORSCHA VARIANT**
Warcaster

**VLADIMIR, DARK PRINCE
OF UMBREY**
Warcaster

**VLADIMIR, DARK PRINCE
OF UMBREY VARIANT**
Warcaster

**ORSUS ZOKTAVIR,
THE BUTCHER OF KHARDOV**
Warcaster

IRON FANG PIKEMEN
Unit

DECIMATOR
Heavy Warjack

JUGGERNAUT
Heavy Warjack

MAN-O-WAR SHOCKTROOPERS
Unit

MANHUNTER
Solo

MANHUNTER VARIANT
Solo

DESTROYER
Heavy Warjack

223

BERSERKER
Heavy Warjack

BATTLE MECHANIKS
Unit

DOOM REAVERS
Unit

MARAUDER
Heavy Warjack

WIDOWMAKERS
Unit

WINTER GUARD INFANTRY
Unit

**CLASSIC KOMMANDER
SORSCHA**
Warcaster

**EXTREME
JUGGERNAUT**
Heavy Warjack

CLASSIC DESTROYER
Heavy Warjack

CLASSIC MARAUDER
Heavy Warjack

CLASSIC JUGGERNAUT
Heavy Warjack

**WARWITCH
DENEGHRA**
Warcaster

**WARWITCH
DENEGHRA VARIANT**
Warcaster

PIRATE QUEEN SKARRE
Warcaster

**IRON LICH
ASPHYXIOUS**
Warcaster

CORRUPTER
Helljack

**SKARLOCK
THRALL**
Solo

REAPER
Helljack

SLAYER
Helljack

BANE THRALLS
Unit

MECHANITHRALLS
Unit

NIGHTWRETCH
Bonejack

DEATHRIPPER
Bonejack

DEFILER
Bonejack

NECROTECH AND SCRAP THRALLS
Solos

SATYXIS RAIDERS
Unit

BILE THRALLS
Unit

**CLASSIC WARWITCH
DENEGHRA**
Warcaster

CLASSIC SLAYER
Helljack

CLASSIC REAPER
Helljack

**EIRYSS,
MAGE HUNTER OF IOS**
Solo

**REINHOLDT,
GOBBER SPECULATOR**
Solo

**HERNE STONEGROUND
& ARQUEBUS JONNE**
Unit

GREYGORE BOOMHOWLER & CO.
Unit

The goal on the battlefield is to crush your enemy, and doing it with a painted army gives you both a banner of pride to carry and a way to inspire fear in your opponent. Fielding a well-painted army shows you mean business. This guide will introduce the simplest and fastest way to paint your miniatures to a level that will make you proud. We will describe tools and techniques you can use from the moment you open the model package through the stages of painting and on to decorating the base for the finished piece. This guide will teach you how to get your army painted and onto the field in a way that is as satisfying as it is quick and easy.

Painting miniatures is very rewarding, from the day you start into years later. Like many skills, the more you do it the better and faster you will become. The time you spend doing it, or "brush time," will be your greatest teacher. With a little guidance and brush time, before long you will knocking out models left and right—just like on the field.

There are a couple of points to keep in mind when working. First, some of these models are huge! When painting a big machine, just think of it in smaller parts. Isolate the areas as you paint, dividing and conquering, and it's the same as painting a smaller model. Second, the fine details are important; make them work to your advantage. Soon you will know the tricks to painting these details fast while keeping them looking good.

Let's get started!

Formula P3 Hobby Tool and Paint Racks

Formula P3 Paints

Formula P3 Super Glue

FINE STUDIO BRUSH   PIP 93088

WORK STUDIO BRUSH   PIP 93087

BASE HOBBY BRUSH   PIP 93009

Formula P3 Paint Brushes

WORTH A THOUSAND WORDS

To learn more about painting and using tools and to pick up a multitude of tricks and techniques, check out the Formula P3 hobby DVD *Modeling & Painting, Vol. 1: Core Techniques*. It provides a solid visual databank of useful information for both new and experienced hobbyists.

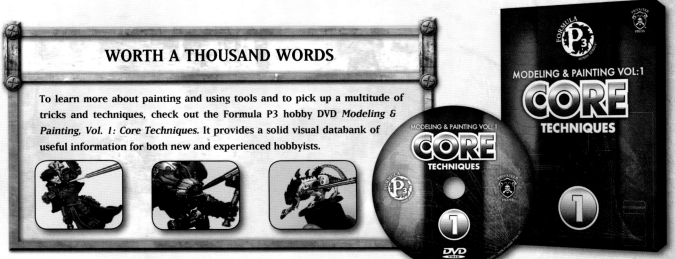

MODELING & PAINTING VOL:1

CORE TECHNIQUES

PREPPING YOUR MODEL

Using the right tools will make it much easier to achieve your goal. Take a moment to look over the list of tools and supplies and the picture of the tool and supply layout on the facing page. The majority of these tools made by Privateer Press you can get at your local hobby store; the others you can find at any general store if you don't already have them.

Start with your work area. Besides a table and chair, you will need a good light source; a swing-arm lamp that clamps onto the side of your table will work fine. Also have a self-healing mat or a piece of masonite available to protect the table surface when you are cutting.

When you first open your box set or blister pack, take some time to get to know your miniature. Locate all the parts and determine what they are and what they will be doing in the final model. It may help to dry fit them, which is holding each piece in place as you expect it will appear in the final assembly. Using files, a hobby knife, and clippers, begin to clean the miniature. Carefully remove the mold line with a file and the hobby knife. This is the fine line wrapping around the miniature that is created when the two halves of the mold come together when the miniature is cast. Clean off any slivers and small chunks of metal with the clippers, a little at a time. When you're confident the model is clean, fix the parts together using super glue, then glue the model to its base. Don't use too much, and don't glue your fingers together!

After the miniature is cleaned and assembled, it's time to prime it for painting. This step may not seem as exciting as applying color, but it's necessary: the primer provides a surface coat for the acrylic Formula P3 paint to adhere to. This is a simple process; just secure the model to the outside of a box with masking tape and go outside or to a well-ventilated area to spray it with primer. Be sure to follow the directions on the primer can. Spray from several angles so that the primer covers the entire model, but be sure to spray lightly so that the model details are preserved. You have the choice of black or white primer. In general, if the miniature is going to be dark overall with a lot metal, it's best to prime it in black. If the miniature is going to be painted in brighter colors, prime it in white.

Allow the primer to dry for a couple of hours. You can speed this up a bit with a hair dryer if you want to, but be careful when doing this with plastic models so that they do not bend or warp. When the primer is dry, it's time to paint.

1. Clipping extra pieces from the model's body.

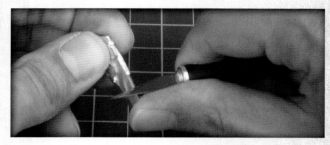

2. Using a hobby knife to scrape mold lines off the shield.

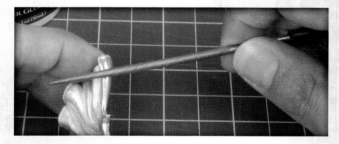

3. Filing mold lines off the cape.

4. Gluing the shield together.

5. Priming the model (black) that is mounted on the box.

THE TOOLS FOR PAINTING

The most important tools you need before beginning to paint are the brushes. A couple of brushes in different sizes will work just fine at first; you can add to your collection as you paint more and more models and want more specialized brushes. Privateer Press makes a range of Formula P3 Brushes that will cover all your needs. In addition, you need two pots of water. Use one for cleaning your bushes and another for thinning your paints—be sure to keep this water clean! Lastly, you need paper towels for general use and some type of palette to mix your paints on; this can be a sheet of plastic card, a piece of porcelain, or some glossy card stock.

BASIC PAINTING ORDER AND TRICKS

Now that you have all the tools you need to get started, let's talk a bit about the way and order in which to paint. To make the paints easier to work with, try thinning them just a touch on the palette; 8 parts paint to 1 part water is enough. This will allow them to brush on significantly smoother and cleaner. You will need to apply a couple of coats to completely cover a surface—this is entirely natural—but with slightly thinned paint the end result will be even, not chunky.

A large part of painting a miniature is defining the shadows and highlights. You are also giving it color, of course, but the real impact comes from representing the way light hits its surfaces. This gives the eye information not only about the shape of the model but also about the material of the surface: whether it is flesh or metal, smooth or textured, polished or dull. In a sense, you are exaggerating what you would see in real life. This will make the miniature look downright cool on a table, simple as that.

The steps for model painting are pretty straightforward:

- First you will lay down the basecoat. This takes the most time and is a very important stage.

- Next you will apply any washes and shading you want.

- After this, you will highlight the miniature.

- Lastly, you will give it the final touches and details.

When laying down the basecoat start with the area that will be the messiest and then move on to the areas that will be easier, considering the shape, size, and location of each. How difficult will it be to paint without messing up other areas? With a little brush time, you will be able to make this assessment almost automatically.

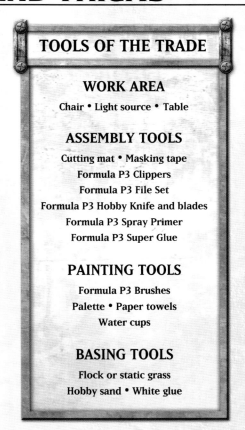

TOOLS OF THE TRADE

WORK AREA
Chair • Light source • Table

ASSEMBLY TOOLS
Cutting mat • Masking tape
Formula P3 Clippers
Formula P3 File Set
Formula P3 Hobby Knife and blades
Formula P3 Spray Primer
Formula P3 Super Glue

PAINTING TOOLS
Formula P3 Brushes
Palette • Paper towels
Water cups

BASING TOOLS
Flock or static grass
Hobby sand • White glue

Each faction has its own identifying colors; you can see them in the artwork throughout this book as well as on the painted miniatures in the gallery. This will give you an idea of what colors you will want. The sections on painting each faction include lists of the paints used. And you can always decide on a palette of colors that's all your own!

PAINTING TUTORIAL

Let's paint a Protectorate of Menoth Paladin of the Order of the Wall from start to finish.

PRIMER

The extensive metal on the model will look best over dark primer, so prime him in black. The Protectorate colors will cover the black on the non-metal areas without a problem.

BASECOAT

Use Cold Steel for the metal areas, Rhulic Gold for the gold areas, Sanguine Base for the burgundy areas, and Menoth White Base for the cream areas. Use Skorne Red for the gems and Thamar Black for the sword grip.

WASHING AND SHADING

A good, simple, and fast way to paint is to wash the metals for shading, then highlight everything else. For this model, mix some Umbral Umber and Bloodstone with Armor Wash and wash the gold with the mixture.

THE FIRST HIGHLIGHTS

Highlight in two stages for more impact. First, highlight the gold with Solid Gold, the metal with Quick Silver, the cream with Menoth White Highlight, the burgundy with Sanguine Highlight, the gems with Khador Red Base, and the black with a bit of Coal Black. Leave some of the basecoat showing for depth.

THE SECOND HIGHLIGHTS

Use colors of brighter values in this step—it's good to exaggerate on a model. Highlight the edges of the cream with Morrow White and the burgundy with a mix of Menoth White Highlight and Sanguine Highlight. Leave some of the first highlight color showing. Finish the gem by painting a bit of Khador Red Highlight under it and adding a dot of Morrow White to the top and bottom. Finish the sword handle with a mix of Menoth White Highlight and Coal Black. Finally, paint Midlund Flesh on the paladin's face.

FINISHED

Ready for battle! The entire fast and simple process took just a couple of hours. Nothing fancy—just a basecoat, a wash on the metals, and a couple of highlights—but he's looking great.

Notice how his base is finished. See "Basing Your Model" on p. 241 for how to do this.

PAINTING THE FACTIONS

Each faction has a unique palette of "team colors." Color choices can convey the tone or alignment of a miniature and lend a particular feel to the model and its army. To see how this works, take a look at the WARMACHINE factions: Cygnar displays the collegiate and militaristic colors of bright blue, white, and gold. The Protectorate features the traditional religious and royal colors of burgundy and linen along with fiery metallics. Khador's combination of red, steel, and gold is both strong and aggressive. Finally, Cryx carries a dark aura with blighted green-grey, gold, and the eerie glow of necrotite. This section will give you a basic approach to painting these colors for the four factions. We painted these models using exactly the colors and techniques described, and you can, too!

PAINTING TERMINOLOGY

BASECOAT
The initial coat of paint on which everything else will be built. It is important that the basecoat is very clean and every color is where it should be. Your shades and highlights will coordinate with the basecoat and main color choices.

DRYBRUSHING
The quick way to highlight a textured surface. Use a lighter color, but remove most of the paint from your brush by stroking the bristles on a paper towel until the paint is almost gone. Then carefully and quickly move the brush back and forth across the surface of the miniature.

HIGHLIGHTING
A lighter color applied to the basecoat in the raised areas of a miniature to create the look of light hitting the surface. When highlighting in multiple steps, keep a little bit of the underlying color showing, overlapping them like the shingles on a roof.

SHADING
A darker color applied to the basecoat in the recessed areas of a miniature to create shadows. Exaggerating the shade and highlight colors will add to the visual appeal of a model.

WASH
A tinted mix liberally applied to the basecoat to create detailed shading. The wash will run into the smallest crevasses on a model and dry as a shadow, so it needs to be a darker color than the basecoat. The wash mix works well as 4 parts Mixing Medium, 1 part paint/ink, and 3 parts water.

CYGNAR

● Cygnar Blue Base   ◐ Rhulic Gold   ◑ Cold Steel   ● Thamar Black

Use Cygnar Blue Base, Rhulic Gold, Cold Steel, and Thamar Black for the basecoat. Remember to make sure these basecoats are neat and in the correct areas. You will need to apply a couple of coats for solid coverage.

For shading, start by making a wash of Armor Wash mixed with a touch of Bloodstone and Umbral Umber. Apply this to the gold areas. Apply pure Armor Wash to the steel areas. Once the shading is done, highlight the edges of the blue armor with a layer of Cygnar Blue Highlight.

Paint Solid Gold on the raised edges of the gold areas and Quick Silver on the edges of the steel areas. Mix a little Morrow White with Cygnar Blue Highlight as a final highlight color and as apply it in a thin line on the uppermost edges of the blue armor. Finish by painting the eyes Khador Red Base.

KHADOR

● Khador Red Base   ○ Rhulic Gold   ● Pig Iron

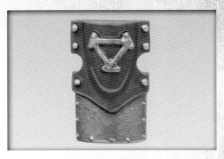

The basecoat for the Khador faction is Khador Red Base, Rhulic Gold, and Pig Iron. You will need to apply a few coats of the Khador Red Base to cover the area fully.

It's a good idea to paint an area black before you apply any metal colors to it, so blacken the rivets with Thamar Black to get them ready for the metal paint. Make a shading color by mixing Umbral Umber and Exile Blue with Khador Red Base. Paint this mix in the recesses and shadows of the red areas. Apply a little Armor Wash in between the red and metal areas.

Highlight the rivets with Cold Steel, the gold with a little Solid Gold, and the edges of the red areas with Khador Red Highlight.

THINNING PAINTS

Try thinning down paint with ink instead of water to achieve a thin consistency without diluting the color. A little Red Ink added to Khador Red Base will yield a nice, red, thinner paint. You can even mix up the ink and paint colors for custom shades just as you can with multiple paint colors.

THIN BLACK LINE

When two colors sit next to each other on a model, separating them with a thin dark line (either black or a very dark version of one of the adjacent colors) emphasizes them individually and helps the eye interpret the image more easily. In other words, it looks good!

CRYX

● Cryx Bane Base   ● Blighted Gold   ● Cold Steel   ● Gnarls Green   ○ 'Jack Bone

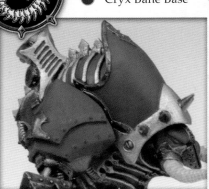

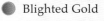

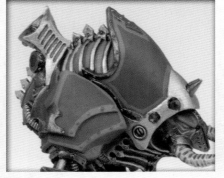

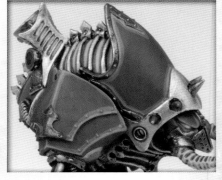

For the Cryx basecoat, use Cryx Bane Base for the hull, Blighted Gold and Cold Steel for the metals, Gnarls Green for the glowing areas, and 'Jack Bone for the tusks.

Wash the tusks with Battlefield Brown. Highlight the hull with a mix of Cryx Bane Base and Cryx Bane Highlight. Highlight the glows with Iosan Green.

The final highlights are Cryx Bane Highlight on the hull, Menoth White Base on the tusks, Necrotite Green on the glows, Quick Silver on the steel edges, and Cold Steel on the gold edges.

PROTECTORATE OF MENOTH

○ Menoth White Base   ● Sanguine Base   ◐ Rhulic Gold   ◑ Cold Steel   ● Thamar Black

For the basecoat, use Menoth White Base for the cream area, Sanguine Base for the burgundy area, Rhulic Gold and Cold Steel for the metals, and Thamar Black for the Menofix.

Begin by shading the metals with a wash of Armor Wash, then add some Bloodstone and Umbral Umber to the Armor Wash to make a shadow wash for the Rhulic Gold. Highlight the burgundy area with Sanguine Highlight and the cream area with Menoth White Highlight. Paint a thin line of Coal Black on the Menofix.

For the final highlight stage, use Solid Gold on the gold areas, a mix of Menoth White Highlight and Sanguine Highlight on the burgundy area, and Quick Silver on the metals. Apply a thin line of Morrow White on the cream area. Lastly, mix Coal Black and Menoth White Highlight together and apply a thinner line of this on the Menofix.

BASING YOUR MODEL

Decorating a miniature's base takes the model to a whole new level of realism and can significantly increase its "wow factor." It doesn't need to be elaborate, though; the step-by-step process described here is simple and quick. Other uncomplicated options include painting the sand a different color, using more (or no) static grass, and even using baking soda for snow. With a little practice and imagination, you will be able to create works of natural battlefield beauty on any base.

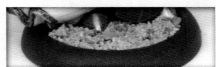

Begin by applying some white glue thinned with a little water. You can use a good brush for this—just make sure you use water-soluble glue and wash your brush thoroughly.

Swirl the base in a container of hobby sand until you have the coverage you want. Let dry.

Create a stain of water, Brown Ink, and Umbral Umber and paint the mix into the sand. Let this dry.

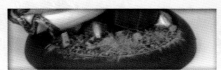

Drybrush the sand with Rucksack Tan. Drybrushing can be messy; be careful not to get Rucksack Tan on the feet of the miniature.

Using white glue, glue some static grass or flock onto the base and let dry.

Give the base and grass a final drybrushing of 'Jack Bone. Clean up any mess on the edge of the base, and you have a finished piece.

BUILDING TERRAIN

In addition to painted miniatures, nicely modeled terrain adds a great deal of character to your games of WARMACHINE.

A basic game board is simple enough to make. A 4´ x 4´ piece of plywood provides an ideal battlefield after being textured with sand, painted, and flocked. A sheet of green felt laid over some books to simulate hilly terrain can also be effective in a pinch.

Modular elements placed onto the game board make your battlefield tactically challenging and keep the terrain varied from game to game. In addition to focusing on their aesthetics, remember to consider the functionality of terrain elements during construction so they can comfortably accommodate models during play.

WOODS

Whether they take the form of a sprawling forest or a small copse of trees, woods are an integral part of any terrain library. They add tactical elements like concealment and difficult terrain to the battlefield. The necessity to define an area for the woods while simultaneously making the trees passable for large units of models makes the construction of an appropriately dense forest quite a challenge. The following method allows you to create realistic forests with movable trees to accommodate models.

Rather than place each tree on its own base within the forest template, place three or four trees on a large stand. Three of these tree stands will fit onto a larger flat template that defines the area of woods. Building forests this way means fewer components and makes game setup and cleanup much quicker. Most importantly, the woods will look like *woods* rather than a template with two or three trees on it.

TREE STANDS

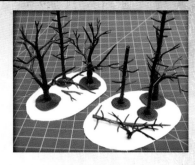

First, cut the tree stands out of foam core board, and bevel the edges. Next, use Formula P3 Super Glue to attach the plastic tree armatures (available from a variety of manufacturers and found at most hobby stores) onto to the stand. For burned woods, be sure to attach a few broken and knocked down trees.

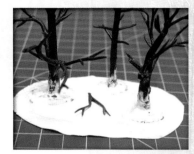

Next, use construction adhesive to fill in the seams where the plastic trees attach to their stands. Doing this allows you to apply the sand and flock more evenly.

After you complete the tree stands, cut the woods templates out of foam core. Ensure you cut them large enough to accommodate three of the tree stands. Bevel the edges as you did for the smaller stands.

FINISHING THE WOODS

Cover the bases with wood glue and add some sand. When that is dry, spray the piece with Formula P3 Black Primer. Drybrush the sand with three colors: Battlefield Brown first, then Moldy Ochre, and finally 'Jack Bone. Drybrush the trees with Battlefield Brown mixed with a little Bastion Grey. Apply some flock to the base. At this point you need to decide if your woods will be alive and lush or burned and blackened.

For lush woods, affix some foliage clusters to the tree armatures. There are a variety of spray adhesives and tacky glues that are specifically designed for foliage. If your trees will be handled a lot, super glue can provide a more durable bond.

For burned woods, affix small foliage clusters at the top or side of one or two of the tree armatures, but leave the rest bare. In short bursts, spray the tree trunks with black primer. Spray the edges of the foliage, the center of the stands, and the larger tree template as well. Drybrush some patches of Bastion Grey over the blackened areas for a charred, ashen look.

LINEAR OBSTACLES

No soldier wants to go into battle without solid cover, so it is fitting that walls and barricades are the staple terrain element for many tabletop battlefields. Structures of the Iron Kingdoms utilize a variety of building materials. Walls commonly consist of fieldstones with metal framing. The following techniques will allow you to build fantastic-looking linear obstacles for your battlefield.

WALL CONSTRUCTION

From a sheet of 1" insulation foam, cut a strip about 0.25" thick. Then cut the strip into 6" lengths. Each wall section should be 0.25" thick, 6" long, and 1" high. Take the strips

and press both sides on the sidewalk outside, a cinderblock, or anything that will give them a rough texture.

Draw horizontal lines along the length of the wall with a standard wooden pencil. (A mechanical pencil will tear the foam, and pen ink sometimes repels glue or paint.) Then draw the vertical separations of each brick. Vary the size and spacing of each block since Iron Kingdoms stonework does not use machine-made bricks and should not resemble a modern-day brick wall. The texture you pressed on the wall earlier will make the drawn-on stones look like textured rock. Cover the entire piece with a thin 60/40 wash of wood glue and water and let it dry.

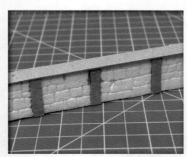

For the metal retainers, cut strips of cardboard 1" long by 0.25" wide. Superglue three of these strips vertically on each side of the wall. Then cut a strip 6" long by 0.5" wide and superglue it along the top of the wall.

Cut a small piece of foam core into roughly an oval shape. Bevel the edges and cut a groove in the center. Cut all the way down to, but not through, the bottom layer of card. Make the groove 0.25" wide to allow the foam wall to sit snugly inside.

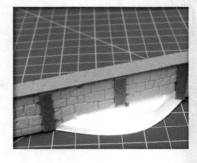

Place a bead of construction adhesive along the groove, and press the wall into it. Use the excess adhesive that squishes out to fill any gaps and smooth the join. Now the wall has a base that prevents it from tipping over. To avoid the "floating wall" effect, try to get the pink foam to sit flush with the bottom of the foam core base. To allow the wall sections to be positioned at 90-degree angles, make sure the base is centered and cut notches out of the corners of the top piece of card. As a final touch, add some rivets on the card strips.

FINISHING THE WALL

Glue some sand to the foam core base, and spray the wall with Formula P3 Black Primer. Drybrush and flock the base just as you did with the woods. Drybrush the stone with Ironhull Grey, then Trollblood Highlight, and finally with a 50/50 mix of Trollblood Highlight and Morrow White. (Make sure to keep the drybrushing very dry to avoid filling in the recesses between each stone.)

To give the wall a dirty and somewhat mossy appearance, apply a very thin wash of Umbral Umber to the bottom half; when this dries, drybrush the bottom third with Traitor Green. Basecoat the metal retaining strips with Pig Iron. Wash this with a very thin mix of Bloodstone and Khador Red Highlight to make the metal appear rusted.

CONCLUSION

You can add other terrain elements like hills, buildings, rivers, and lakes to create any battlefield you can imagine. Don't be afraid to experiment, and above all, have fun!

Every ability or effect that is not always "on" has conditions dictating when it begins and ends. Situations where multiple effects resolve at the same time are not uncommon, and it is important to be able to sort out the order effects resolve.

The rules on timing of abilities use the terms **active player** and **inactive player**. If a model is making an attack, its controller is the active player. If no model is making an attack, the active player is the player whose turn it is. In both cases, the other player is the inactive player. When resolving effects that occur "after the attack is resolved," the active and inactive players remain the same as during the attack until all effects triggered by the attack are resolved.

Some effects cause certain conditions of an attack, such as whether it hit or what models it boxed, to change during resolution. When resolving triggered effects, recheck trigger conditions as you resolve each ability. If a condition is no longer met, the effect does not resolve. Similarly, if an effect on one model causes a condition to change on another, effects triggered by that condition will resolve for each of those models.

EXAMPLE: *A Bloat Thrall has the Death Blast ability, which causes it to explode when disabled. If it is also affected by Terminus' Shadow of Death, which grants Tough ⊛ to undead ☻ models, when an enemy model disables it, both Tough and Death Blast need to resolve as inactive player effects. If you resolve Death Blast first, the Bloat Thrall will explode and be removed from play. Tough then does not resolve. If you resolve Tough first and pass the check, the Bloat Thrall regains one wound and so is no longer disabled. Death Blast then will not resolve, as its condition is no longer met. If you fail the Tough check, Bloat Thrall will remain disabled; the condition of a disabled model will still be met, and Death Blast will resolve.*

There are many times during an attack when abilities can resolve. The structure of an attack is outlined below. In most cases the exact sequence shown here does not need to be followed step by step, but this description will help you resolve complex interactions if they occur.

SIMULTANEOUS AND SEQUENTIAL

When an effect causes multiple attacks or damage against multiple models, the attacks and damage can be either simultaneous or sequential. These labels denote whether various effects can resolve before all the attacks or damage are resolved or if the effects can intercede, possibly changing the outcome of the original effect. When resolving simultaneous effects, completely resolve all attack and damage rolls before applying any of the target's special rules triggered by suffering damage, being destroyed, or being removed from play.

EXAMPLE: *When a model is slammed, the slam damage is simultaneous with the collateral damage, so first resolve the damage roll on every affected model. Then resolve effects triggered by a damage roll being sufficient or insufficient to damage them. Finally, apply damage to every affected model.*

EXAMPLE: *A Repenter makes a Flame Thrower spray attack against some Scrap Thralls. The attack generates several damage rolls that all resolve simultaneously. Scrap Thralls destroyed by the attack do not explode due to their Thrall Bomb ability until after all the attack and damage rolls generated by the spray attack are resolved.*

EXAMPLE: *Captain Haley targets a member of a unit of Knights Exemplar with Chain Lightning and hits three additional Knights. Resolve the damage rolls for the four Knights Exemplar hit by the spell before any of the Knights Exemplar gain the benefits of their Bond of Brotherhood ability.*

AT ANY TIME DURING THIS MODEL'S ACTIVATION

Many effects and rules state they resolve or can be used "at any time during this model's activation." This is not literally true. The resolution or opportunity for use does occur at any time during the model's activation—*except* when it or another model is resolving a movement, attack, or any other effect.

EXAMPLE: *Warcasters can cast spells "at any time during their activation." This means Goreshade the Bastard can cast a spell before and after moving, before and after an attack, before using his feat, and after placing all models from his feat. He cannot, however, cast a spell while he is moving, making an attack, or using his feat to place Bane Thralls into play.*

ACTIVATION TIMING

1. Resolve effects that occur before activating.

2. Resolve effects that occur at the beginning of activation.

3. Resolve all required forfeiture of movement and action.

4. If activating a unit, the unit commander can issue an order.

5. Resolve effects that occur before moving.

6. The model makes its normal movement.

7. Resolve effects that occur at end of normal movement.

8. If activating a unit, repeat steps 6 and 7 for all troopers, then resolve effects that occur at end of unit's movement.

9. The model makes its action.

10. Resolve effects that occur at end of action and at end of combat action.

11. If activating a unit, repeat steps 9 and 10 for all troopers, then resolve effects that occur at end of unit's actions.

ATTACK MAIN SEQUENCE

1. Determine what the attacker can target.
2. Resolve effects that occur before attacking.
3. Declare the attack and its target.
4. If the attack is a ranged or magic attack, check the range to the target. If the target is out of range, the attack automatically misses; do not make any attack rolls, and go to step 7.
5. Resolve effects that occur when a model is targeted by an attack, such as effects that cause an attack to hit or miss automatically.
6. Make all attack rolls as dictated by the type of attack and its special rules. For example, a spray attack would go through the attack roll sequence for each model in the template before proceeding to step 7.

ATTACK ROLL

1. Resolve effects that change the number of dice rolled, such as boosting the roll.
2. Roll the dice.
3. Resolve effects that allow a player to choose or remove dice from the roll.
4. Determine if the model would be hit or missed by the attack roll against it.
5. Resolve effects that cause the attack roll to be rerolled, returning to step 2.
6. The attack roll is complete. Return to the main sequence.

7. Resolve effects that cause the attack to hit a model other than the target automatically.
8. Resolve AOE hit or deviation. All models within the AOE at its final position are now hit by it. Remember that only the target of the AOE attack is directly hit, and then only if the attack roll against it succeeds. All other models are hit but not directly hit.
9. Resolve all other effects that are triggered by hitting or missing.
10. Roll all damage rolls against models that have been hit, or as specified by special rules.

DAMAGE ROLL

1. Resolve effects that change the number of dice rolled, such as boosting the roll.
2. Roll the dice.
3. Resolve effects that allow a player to choose or remove dice from the roll.

4. Determine if the roll would damage the model.
5. Resolve effects that cause the damage roll to be rerolled, returning to step 2.
6. Resolve effects triggered by a damage roll being sufficient or insufficient to damage a model.
7. The damage roll is complete. Return to the main sequence.

11. Apply all damage.

DAMAGE APPLICATION

1. Mark damage on the appropriate stat card.
2. Resolve effects triggered by a model suffering damage.
3. If the damage applied in step 2 fills the last damage box for a model, that model becomes disabled. Resolve effects triggered by the model becoming disabled.
4. If the model is still disabled, it becomes boxed. Resolve effects triggered by a model becoming boxed.
5. If the model is still boxed, it is destroyed. Resolved effects triggered by a model being destroyed.
6. Remove the destroyed model from the table, then return to the main sequence.

12. The attack is now resolved. After the attack is resolved:
    a. Resolve effects that automatically damage, destroy, or remove models from play.
    b. Resolve active player effects that do not involve making an attack.
    c. Resolve inactive player effects.
    d. Resolve active player effects that involve making an attack.

APPENDIX B: WARJACK BONDING
MAKING A BOND, BREAKING A BOND, AND BOND EFFECTS

The potent connection shared between a warcaster and his warjacks can evolve into a powerful bond over time. Bonding awakens a warjack's cortex, opens it more fully to its controlling warcaster, and infects it with limited self-awareness. As this connection grows stronger, the warjack begins to develop a rudimentary personality based on the characteristics of its warcaster. In essence, the personality of the warcaster is imprinted on the warjack's cortex.

Since this imprinting tends to take place in moments of extreme emotional duress such as in the heat of battle, the effects of bonding are unpredictable. While one bonded warjack might become protective of its warcaster or act like a faithful hound, another might take on darker aspects of its controlling warcaster's personality such as relishing the suffering of others.

Through continuous contact a warcaster learns the subtle intricacies of the warjack's unique cortex, allowing him to enhance his control over the machine. An open conduit, the bonded warjack is in turn able to receive greater amounts of focus from its controlling warcaster.

Bonding is an optional rule best suited to campaign or league play, as bonds require time to establish. If all players agree, however, each can begin a game with one or more bonded warjacks.

FORGING A BOND

After a player completes a campaign or league game, he can roll to determine if a bond forms between each warcaster he fielded who survived and each of the remaining warjacks in that warcaster's battlegroup. Warcasters who were destroyed or removed from play during the game cannot make bonding checks, but their existing bonds are unaffected.

The longer a particular warjack has served in a warcaster's battlegroup, the greater the chance a bond will be established after each game. During league or campaign play, players should track the number of consecutive battles in which an unbonded warjack has fought as part of the same warcaster's battlegroup without being destroyed or removed from play.

When determining if a **bond** is formed, roll a d6 and add 1 to the roll for each consecutive battle, including the one just completed, in which the warjack served in that warcaster's battlegroup. A bond is formed on a total roll of 7 or greater.

Established Bond = d6 + 1 for each qualifying battle ≥ 7

Failed Bond = d6 + 1 for each qualifying battle < 7

EXAMPLE: *After finishing a campaign battle, Mike rolls to see if The High Reclaimer's unbonded Crusader bonds to him. Since this was its third game under his control without being destroyed or removed from play, the bond forms on a roll of 4 or higher.*

A warcaster can bond more than one warjack, but each warjack can bond to only a single warcaster at a time. Furthermore, once a warjack becomes bonded to a warcaster, it remains bonded to him until being destroyed or removed from play; bonded warjacks do not participate in bonding checks. A bonded warjack not under the control of its bonding warcaster loses the benefits of its bond until coming under his control again, but the bond itself is not broken.

BREAKING A BOND

If a bonded warjack ends a game destroyed or removed from play, its bond is broken. A player can also choose to remove a bond from a warjack before any game: the warjack's controlling warcaster has had its cortex reinitialized. Its bond is broken, and the current game is counted as the first consecutive game for the warjack's bonding roll bonus.

EFFECTS OF BONDING

A bonded warjack can be allocated up to 4 focus points.

Bonding affects each warjack in a unique way as its personality develops. When a bond is established, roll 2d6 plus the warcaster's CMD and consult the corresponding faction table to determine the effects of the bonding. The player can modify his die roll by 1 (adding or subtracting) if he wishes.

Remember that a bonded warjack loses all benefits from its bond while not under the control of the warcaster to whom it is bonded.

Bond Effect = 2d6 + CMD (+/–1 if desired)

CYGNAR BONDS

2D6 + CMD	RESULT	2D6 + CMD	RESULT
10 or less	**Craven** – This warjack gains +2 DEF and can run without spending focus. It can advance into an enemy model's melee range only if that model is in the control range of this warjack's controlling warcaster.	16	**Anchor** – While this warjack is in its controlling warcaster's control area, this warjack and friendly warrior models B2B with it cannot be knocked down.
11	**Dominator** – When this warjack makes an attack against an enemy warjack or warbeast in the control area of this warjack's controlling warcaster, this warjack gains +2 to attack and damage rolls against the enemy model.	17	**Protective** – While B2B with this warjack, its controlling warcaster gains +2 DEF against melee attack rolls and cannot be knocked down. While B2B with its controlling warcaster, this warjack does not move when slammed.
12	**Invigorated** – When its controlling warcaster channels a spell through it, after the spell is cast this warjack can make a full advance.	18	**Psychically Attuned** – This warjack's controlling warcaster can upkeep spells cast on it without spending focus and ignores LOS when targeting it with spells.
13	**Combat Positioning** – At the end of any activation in which this warjack made at least one attack, it can advance up to 3″ toward its controlling warcaster.	19	**Nexus** – This warjack's controlling warcaster can allocate focus points to it during his activation. Additionally, during that warcaster's activation, you can remove any number of focus points from this warjack and place them on him. The warcaster cannot exceed his current FOCUS in focus points as a result of this bond.
14	**Marksman** – While in its controlling warcaster's control area, this warjack can reroll missed ranged attack rolls.	20+	**Extended Control** – This warjack gains Extended Control Range. (When checking to see if a model with Extended Control Range is in its controller's control area for focus allocation, double the area.)
15	**Heightened Awareness** – If this warjack begins its activation in its controlling warcaster's control area, it gains Eyeless Sight 👁 for one round.		

KHADOR BONDS

2D6 + CMD	RESULT	2D6 + CMD	RESULT
10 or less	**Bloodthirsty** – While in its controlling warcaster's control area, this warjack gains Berserk and cannot make Chain Attacks. (When a model with Berserk destroys one or more models with a melee attack during its combat action, immediately after the attack is resolved it must make one additional melee attack against another model in its melee range. During an activation that this model charges, it cannot gain additional attacks from Berserk until its charge attack is resolved.)	15	**Dominator** – When this warjack makes an attack against an enemy warjack or warbeast in the control area of this warjack's controlling warcaster, this warjack gains +2 to attack and damage rolls against the enemy model.
		16	**All Terrain** – If it begins its activation in its controlling warcaster's control area, this warjack gains Pathfinder 🌿 this activation.
11	**Appetite for Destruction** – If this warjack begins its activation in its controlling warcaster's control area, this activation it can make power attacks without spending focus and this warjack's first melee attack each activation must be a power attack. If this warjack cannot make a power attack, it must make initial melee attacks for its combat action instead.	17	**Rassler** – While in its controlling warcaster's control area, this warjack can make headlock/weapon lock, head-butt, throw, and double-hand throw power attacks without spending focus and cannot be knocked down or moved by a push or slam power attack made by a model with a smaller base.
12	**Irresistible Force** – Models slammed by this model are moved +2″. While in its controlling warcaster's control area, this warjack can power attack slam without spending focus.	18	**Unstoppable** – While in its controlling warcaster's control area, this warjack cannot be knocked down or made stationary. If it begins its activation in its controlling warcaster's control area, this activation this warjack can run or charge even if its Movement system is crippled.
13	**Indomitable** – If this warjack begins a charge or a power attack slam or trample in its controlling warcaster's control area, it gains Pathfinder 🌿 during its activation. While in its controlling warcaster's control area, this warjack gains +2 on trample attack rolls.	19	**Rain Shadow** – While this warjack is in its controlling warcaster's control area, friendly warrior models B2B with it do not suffer blast damage.
14	**Demolisher** – While in its controlling warcaster's control area, this warjack can reroll missed charge and power attack rolls.	20+	**Corrective Firing** – When AOE ranged attacks made by this warjack deviate while it is in its controlling warcaster's control area, it can reroll the direction and/or distance of deviation.

PROTECTORATE BONDS

2D6 + CMD	RESULT
10 or less	**Extended Control** – This warjack gains Extended Control Range. (When checking to see if a model with Extended Control Range is in its controller's control area for focus allocation, double the area.)
11	**Demolisher** – While in its controlling warcaster's control area, this warjack can reroll missed charge and power attack rolls.
12	**Corrective Firing** – When AOE ranged attacks made by this warjack deviate while it is in its controlling warcaster's control area, it can reroll the direction and/or distance of deviation.
13	**Wrathful** – When a model in its battlegroup is targeted by an enemy attack, this warjack gains +2 to attack and damage rolls for one round.
14	**Dominator** – When this warjack makes an attack against an enemy warjack or warbeast in the control area of this warjack's controlling warcaster, this warjack gains +2 to attack and damage rolls against the enemy model.
15	**Rain Shadow** – While this warjack is in its controlling warcaster's control area, friendly warrior models B2B with it do not suffer blast damage.
16	**Protective** – While B2B with this warjack, its controlling warcaster gains +2 DEF against melee attack rolls and cannot be knocked down. While B2B with its controlling warcaster, this warjack does not move when slammed.
17	**Arcane Defenses** – If it is in its controlling warcaster's control range during your Maintenance Phase, continuous effects and enemy upkeep spells on this warjack automatically expire.
18	**Anchor** – While this warjack is in its controlling warcaster's control area, this warjack and friendly warrior models B2B with it cannot be knocked down.
19	**Defensive** – This model gains Shield Guard. (Once per round, when a friendly model is directly hit by a ranged attack during your opponent's turn and this model is within 2″ of the friendly model hit, this model can become the target of the attack and be automatically hit instead. This model cannot use Shield Guard if it is incorporeal (⬣), knocked down, or stationary.)
20+	**Psychically Attuned** – This warjack's controlling warcaster can upkeep spells cast on it without spending focus and ignores LOS when targeting it with spells.

CRYX BONDS

2D6 + CMD	RESULT
10 or less	**Bloodthirsty** – While in its controlling warcaster's control area, this warjack gains Berserk and cannot make Chain Attacks. (When a model with Berserk destroys one or more models with a melee attack during its combat action, immediately after the attack is resolved it must make one additional melee attack against another model in its melee range. During an activation that this model charges, it cannot gain additional attacks from Berserk until its charge attack is resolved.)
11	**Man Killer** – While in its controlling warcaster's control area, this warjack can reroll missed attack rolls against living enemy models.
12	**Blood Hunter** – When this warjack destroys one or more living enemy models with a melee attack while in its controlling warcaster's control area, after the attack is resolved this warjack can advance up to 1″.
13	**Craven** – This warjack gains +2 DEF and can run without spending focus. It can advance into an enemy model's melee range only if that model is in the control range of this warjack's controlling warcaster.
14	**All Terrain** – If it begins its activation in its controlling warcaster's control area, this warjack gains Pathfinder (⬤) this activation.
15	**Hound** – When this warjack's controlling warcaster destroys one or more enemy models with melee or ranged attacks during its activation, at the end of its activation this warjack can immediately advance up to 3″.
16	**Invigorated** – When its controlling warcaster channels a spell through it, after the spell is cast this warjack can make a full advance.
17	**Nexus** – This warjack's controlling warcaster can allocate focus points to it during his activation. Additionally, during that warcaster's activation, you can remove any number of focus points from this warjack and place them on him. The warcaster cannot exceed his current FOCUS in focus points as a result of this bond.
18	**Predator** – If it begins its activation in its controlling warcaster's control area, this activation this warjack can charge, power attack slam, and power attack trample without spending focus. If it charges, power attack slams a living model, or power attack tramples during its activation it gains +2 SPD this activation.
19	**Prowler** – If this warjack begins its activation in its controlling warcaster's control area, it gains Prowl for one round. (While within a terrain feature that provides concealment, the AOE of a spell that provides concealment, or the AOE of a cloud effect, a model with Prowl gains Stealth (⬤).)
20+	**Heightened Awareness** – If this warjack begins its activation in its controlling warcaster's control area, it gains Eyeless Sight (⬤) for one round.

RETRIBUTION BONDS

2D6 + CMD	RESULT
10 or less	**Wrathful** – When a model in its battlegroup is targeted by an enemy attack, this warjack gains +2 to attack and damage rolls for one round.
11	**Demolisher** – While in its controlling warcaster's control area, this warjack can reroll missed charge and power attack rolls.
12	**Anchor** – While this warjack is in its controlling warcaster's control area, this warjack and friendly warrior models B2B with it cannot be knocked down.
13	**All Terrain** – If it begins its activation in its controlling warcaster's control area, this warjack gains Pathfinder ⓑ this activation.
14	**Protective** – While B2B with this warjack, its controlling warcaster gains +2 DEF against melee attack rolls and cannot be knocked down. While B2B with its controlling warcaster, this warjack does not move when slammed.
15	**Mage Killer** – While in its controlling warcaster's control area, this warjack can reroll attack and damage rolls against enemy spellcasters and models with enemy upkeep spells on them. Each roll can be rerolled only once as a result of this bond.

2D6 + CMD	RESULT
16	**Extended Control** – This warjack gains Extended Control Range. (When checking to see if a model with Extended Control Range is in its controller's control area for focus allocation, double the area.)
17	**Heightened Awareness** – If this warjack begins its activation in its controlling warcaster's control area, it gains Eyeless Sight ⓢ for one round.
18	**Arcane Defenses** – If it is in its controlling warcaster's control range during your Maintenance Phase, continuous effects and enemy upkeep spells on this warjack automatically expire.
19	**Psychically Attuned** – This warjack's controlling warcaster can upkeep spells cast on it without spending focus and ignores LOS when targeting it with spells.
20+	**Field Booster** – When this warjack spends focus to remove a damage point from its field damage track while in its controlling warcaster's control area, the warcaster heals 1 damage point. When its controlling warcaster spends focus to heal a damage point while this warjack is in his control area, this warjack removes 1 damage point from its field damage track unless its field generator is currently disabled.

MERCENARY BONDS

2D6 + CMD	RESULT
10 or less	**Bloodthirsty** – While in its controlling warcaster's control area, this warjack gains Berserk and cannot make Chain Attacks. (When a model with Berserk destroys one or more models with a melee attack during its combat action, immediately after the attack is resolved it must make one additional melee attack against another model in its melee range. During an activation that this model charges, it cannot gain additional attacks from Berserk until its charge attack is resolved.)
11	**Appetite for Destruction** – If this warjack begins its activation in its controlling warcaster's control area, this activation it can make power attacks without spending focus and this warjack's first melee attack each activation must be a power attack. If this warjack cannot make a power attack, it must make initial melee attacks for its combat action instead.
12	**Craven** – This warjack gains +2 DEF and can run without spending focus. It can advance into an enemy model's melee range only if that model is in the control range of this warjack's controlling warcaster.
13	**Hound** – When this warjack's controlling warcaster destroys one or more enemy models with melee or ranged attacks during its activation, at the end of its activation this warjack can immediately advance up to 3″.
14	**Dominator** – When this warjack makes an attack against an enemy warjack or warbeast in the control

2D6 + CMD	RESULT
	area of this warjack's controlling warcaster, this warjack gains +2 to attack and damage rolls against the enemy model.
15	**Demolisher** – While in its controlling warcaster's control area, this warjack can reroll missed charge and power attack rolls.
16	**All Terrain** – If it begins its activation in its controlling warcaster's control area, this warjack gains Pathfinder ⓑ this activation.
17	**Combat Positioning** – At the end of any activation in which this warjack made at least one attack, it can advance up to 3″ toward its controlling warcaster.
18	**Corrective Firing** – When AOE ranged attacks made by this warjack deviate while it is in its controlling warcaster's control area, it can reroll the direction and/or distance of deviation.
19	**Playin' Possum** – While in its controlling warcaster's control area, this model gains Feign Death. (A model with Feign Death cannot be targeted by ranged or magic attacks while knocked down.)
20	**Prowler** – If this warjack begins its activation in its controlling warcaster's control area, it gains Prowl for one round. (While within a terrain feature that provides concealment, the AOE of a spell that provides concealment, or the AOE of a cloud effect, a model with Prowl gains Stealth ⓢ.)

RULES INDEX

abilities, 36
   attack-generating, 60–61
   range of (RNG), 35

Abomination advantage, **33**, 84

actions, 48–49
   and fleeing, 85
   forfeiting, 65
   out of formation, 71
   and knocked down models, 63–64
   and stationary models, 64

Activation Phase, 42
   and channeling, 79
   forfeiting, 65
   timing, 244

active/inactive player, 244

additional attacks, **49**
   spending focus for, 49, 73, 75

additional dice, 28

advancing, 46–47: *charge, full advance, run*
   and entering an area, 64
   and fleeing, 85
   out of formation, 71
   and stationary models, 64

Advance Deployment advantage, **33**

advantages, 33–34: *Abomination, Advance Deployment, Arc Node, Combined Melee Attack, Combined Ranged Attack, Commander, Construct, Eyeless Sight, Fearless, Gunfighter, Incorporeal, 'Jack Marshal, Officer, Pathfinder, Standard Bearer, Stealth, Terror, Tough, Undead*

affinities, 82

aiming bonus, 57, 63

allies, 80

allocate, 74–75

animi, animus, 63, 64

> **Animi are the spell-like abilities utilized by warbeasts in HORDES.**

apocalypse encounter level, 38

arc nodes, *see also* channeling
   Arc Node advantage, **33**
   and battlegroup commanders, 74
   crippled, 66

arcs, front and back, 37

area of effect (AOE), 35
   of spells, 77

area-of-effect (AOE) attack, 58–60
   blast damage roll for, 59
   damage point of origin, 64
   deviation, 59–60
   direct hit, 59
   templates, 255–256

arm locks. *see* weapon locks

arm systems, and crippled, 66

Armor (ARM), 33

armies
   building, 38
   versions of models in, 83

army list entry, 32

army points, 38

attachments, 32, 71

attack rolls
   additional dice on, 28
   for AOE attacks, 59
   automatic hit/miss, 61
   and back strike, 61
   boosting, 73, 75
   for charges, 47, 82
   for combined attacks, 62
   for critical effects, 68–69
   vs. damage roll, 50
   and Gunfighter, 63
   and Incorporeal, 34
   for magic attacks, 77–78, 83
   for melee attacks, 33, 51
   for Mounts, 81
   for ranged attacks, 56–58
   for spray attacks, 60
   rerolling, 65
   timing, 245

attacks
   additional, 49, 73, 75
   AOE, 58–60
   combined melee or ranged, 62
   and fleeing, 85
   out of formation, 71
   impact, 82
   and knocked down models, 63
   magic, 75–79
   melee, 50–56, 81–82
   normal, 48–49
   power, 51–56
   ranged, 56–60
   ride-by, 81
   sequence of, 244
   special, **36**, 49, 61
   spray, 58, 60, 256
   timing, 245
   types, 50–60: *magic, melee, ranged*

automatic
   effects, 68
   hit/miss, 61

autonomous warjacks, 80

away from vs. directly away from, 48

B2B, 46

back arcs, 37

back strikes, **61**, 77

base stats, 33
   of knocked down models, 63

bases
   base-to-base, B2B, 46
   contact, 46
   overlapping, 64
   and replacing models, 64
   sizes, 37
   and volume, 43

battlefield, **40**, 86

battlegroups, 39

battlegroup commanders, 74
   reactivating inert warjacks, 68

battle royale encounter level, 38

beyond the play area, 64

blast damage
   roll, 59
   and structures, 89
   template, 255
   and trenches, 88

bonds, 82, **246**
   epic, 83

bonejacks, 31

bonuses
   aiming, **57**, 63
   back strike, 61
   Buckler, 35
   cavalry charge, 82
   for combined attacks, 62
   concealment, 57
   cover, 58
   and crippled system, 66
   and current stats, 63
   free strike, 51
   and inert warjack, 67
   overboosting power field, 74
   Shield, 36
   warjack points, 38

boosting rolls, 28, 73,75

boxed, disabled, and destroyed, 66–68

Buckler, **35**, 66

buildings, 89

can, cannot, must, 29

cavalry, 81–82
   charging with, 81–82
   dragoons, 82
   light cavalry, 82
   Mount weapon, 81
   special rules, 81: *ride-by attack, Tall in the Saddle*

channeling, 79, *see also* arc nodes
   and control area, 75
   and knocked down models, 63

characters, 39
   epic, 83
   units, 39
   warjacks, 82

charging, 46
   outside activation, 47
   attacks, 47
   with cavalry, 81–82
   successful/failed, 47

checks
   command, 71, **84**
   skill, 49
   warjack bonding, 246

cloud effects, **69**. 78

combat
   actions, 48
   and cloud effects, 69
   damage, 65
   melee, 51
   overview, 51
   ranged, 56
   special effects, 68
   special situations, 60

combined melee attacks, 62
   advantage, 33
   damage roll for, 62
   primary attacker, 62

combined ranged attacks, 62
    advantage, 33
    damage roll for, 62
    primary attacker, 62

Command (CMD), 33

command checks, 84
    out of formation, 71

Commander advantage, **33**, 74, 84

command range, 84

concealment, 57
    and cloud effects, 69
    and magic rolls, 78

conflicting rules, 29

Construct advantage, **33**, 73

contact, 46

continuous effects, 69
    immunities to, 34–35

control
    and affinities, 82
    and battlegroup commanders, 74
    of friendly and enemy models, 28
    and 'jack marshals, 80
    of mercenary warjacks, 83
    and weapon crews, 71

control areas, 75
    and AOE, 77
    and channeling, 79
    and focus point allocation, 74
    and RNG, 76
    and upkeep spells, 78

Control Phase, 42

Corrosion/Critical Corrosion, 69

Cortex and crippled Cortex, 66
    and focus allocation, 73

COST, 76

cover, 57–58
    and magic attack rolls, 78
    and wreck markers, 67

crippled/non-crippled systems, 66: *Arc Node, Cortex, Field Generator, Movement, Weapon, no longer crippled*

critical effects, critical hits, 68

current
    controller, 28
    stats, 33

d3, d6, 28

damage
    capacity, 36
    healing/removing/repairing, 68
    marking, 65
    point of origin of AOE, 59
    timing, 245
    types of, 68: *cold, corrosion, electrical, fire*

damage grid, 36–37, **65**, 73
    damage boxes, **36–37**, 65
        marking, 65
        system boxes, 36–37, 66
        unmarked, 66
    first "X" box on, 66
    force fields, 66
    wounds, **36**, 65

damage rolls
    additional die with, 53, 54, 63, 65
    boosted, 65

comparing to ARM, 65
    with crippled weapons systems, 66
    and critical effects, 68
    direct hit on, 59, 60
    multiple, 244
    rerolling, 65
    resolving with simultaneous effects, 244
    simultaneous, marking, 66

damage rolls, in specific cases
    for AOE attacks, 59
    blast, 59
    for collapsed structures, 89
    for collateral damage, slam, 53
    for collateral damage, throw, 55
    for combined melee attacks, 62
    for combined ranged attacks, 62
    for direct damage, 65
    for falling, 63
    for Fire continuous effect, 69
    for head-butts, 52
    and knocked down models, 63
    for magic attacks, 65, 77
    for melee, 65
    of a Mount, 81
    for pushes, 52
    for ranged weapons, 56, 65
    for slams, 53
    for spray attacks, 60
    for throws, 54
    for tramples, 56

Defense (DEF), 33

deployment, deployment zones, 40–41

destroyed
    boxed, disabled, and, 66–68
    and removed from play/the table, 67
    and returning to play, 68
    warcaster, 67
    warjacks and wreck markers, 67

deviation
    of AOE attacks, 59–60
    template, 255

dice, 28
    additional, 28
    d3 and d6, 28
    reroll, 65
    shorthand, 28

direct hits, 51, **64**, 77

directly
    away from and directly toward, 48
    facing, 37

disabled, boxed, and destroyed, 66
    healing while, 68
    and leaving play, 67
    no longer disabled, 66

dismounted, 82

disputes, resolving, 30

double-hand throw, 55
    being thrown, 54
    damage, 54
    and deviation, 55

dragoons, 82

drive, 80

duel encounter level, 38

duration, 29, 42

effects
    automatic, 68

continuous, 69
critical, 68
    targeting units, 72
    shaking, 73, 75

elevation
    elevated attacker, 78
    elevated target, 78
    and falling, 63
    hills, 88
    and line of sight (LOS), **43**, 44
    and melee range, 51

elite cadre, 82

encounter levels, 38: *apocalypse, battle royale, duel, grand melee, skirmish, war*

enemy vs. friendly, 28

engaged, engaging, 51
    channelers, 79
    and knocked down models, 63
    and stationary models, 64

entering an area, 64

entryways, 89

epic models, 82–83
    epic warcaster bonding, 83, 246

excuses, 5

Eyeless Sight advantage, 34

facing
    and directly facing, 37
    with rule of least disturbance, 64

Faction, 29

falling, 63
    damage roll, 63
    and overlapping bases, 64

Fearless advantage, **34**, 85

feats, 36
    and knocked down models, 63
    and stationary models, 64

field allowance (FA), 39–40

Field Generator system, and crippled, 66

field promotion, 72

Fire/Critical Fire, 69

first player, 40

fleeing, 85
    out of formation, 71

Focus Manipulation, 42

focus points
    allocating, 73, 74
    and autonomous warjacks, 80
    and bonded warjacks, 246
    and channeler, 79
    in teh Control Phase, 42
    and COST, 76
    and crippled Cortex, 66
    and crippled Field Generator, 66
    FOCUS stat, 33, 74
    how to represent, 75
    in the Maintenance Phase, 42
    manipulation, 74
    removing, 42
    replenishing, **42**, 74
    spending, 73, 75, 82
    unspent, 74

force fields, 66

Forces of WARMACHINE books, 80, 83

forfeiting, 64–65, 71

for one round, 42

forests, 87–88

formation
- and activating units, 42–43
- and cavalry attacks, 81–82
- and combined attacks, 62
- and command check, 84
- in/out formation, 71–72
- rand placement, 48
- and rallying, 85
- receiving orders, 72
- and standard bearer, 70

free-for-all games, 40

free strikes, 51
- and Gunfighter, 63
- resolving against trampler, 56

friendly vs. enemy, 28

front arc, 37

full advance, 46

gaining dice, 28

game rounds, 42

grand melee encounter level, 38

granted, 28

Grunts, 70
- field promotion, 72

Gunfighter advantage, 34, 63

half (of a stat), 28

hazards, 52, 88

Head system, and crippled, 66

head-butt, 52

headlock, 51–52
- and knocked down models, 63
- and Open Fist, 73

healing, 68

helljacks, 31

hills, 88

hit
- automatic, 61
- direct, **64**, 77

HORDES, 27, 31, 95

hulls, 66

immunities, 34–35, 68: *Cold, Corrosion, Electricity, Fire, continuous effects*

impact attacks, 81–82

impassable terrain, 86

imprints, 82

Incorporeal advantage, 34
- and magical weapons, 68

independent models, **31**, 74: *solos, warcasters, warjacks*

inert warjacks, 67–68, 80

initial attacks
- and Gunfighter, 63
- with light cavalry, 82
- and locked weapons, 52
- with melee weapons, 48, **50**
- with ranged weapons, 49, **56**

intervening models, 43
- and cavalry charge, 81
- and knocked down models, 63

intervening terrain, 45, 51
- obstructions, obstacles, 87

Iron Kingdoms, 27, 94–95

'jacks, *see* warjacks

'Jack Marshal advantage, **34**, 80
- and mercenary warjacks, 83
- reactivating inert warjacks, 68

knocked down, 63
- channeler, 79
- standing up, 64
- target, 78

Leader, 70
- field promotion, 72
- and unit commander, 71

least disturbance, rule of, 64

leave play, 67–68

light cavalry, 82

linear obstacles, 87

line of sight (LOS), 43–45
- and channeling spells, 79
- and cloud effects, 69
- and focus point allocation, 74
- and knocked down models, 63
- and point of origin, 64

living models, 31
- non-living (Construct, Undead), 34

location (L/R/H/–), 35

Magic Abilities, 83

magic attacks, 75–79

magic attack rolls, 77
- for Magic Ability special attacks, 83
- modifiers, 77–78: *back strike, cloud effect, concealment, cover, elevated target, elevated attacker, knocked down target, stationary target, target in melee*

magic damage, 65, 77

Magical Weapon, 36
- and Incorporeal, 68

Maintenance Phase, 42

markers, 67, 90

massive casualties, 84

materials needed for play, 27

maximum range, 30

measuring
- command range, 84
- control area, 75
- deviation, 59–60
- distance, 30
- melee range, 50
- movement, 46
- for ranged attack, 56
- spell range, 76, 77
- a throw, 54
- tools, 27
- within vs. completely within, 30

melee
- additional attacks, 50
- attack modifiers, 51
- attack rolls, **51**, 63
- and cavalry, 81

and cloud effects, 69
- damage rolls, 50
- and elevation, 51
- engaged, 51
- free strikes, 51
- and knocked down models, 63
- Melee Attack (MAT), 32
- power attacks, 51–56
- range, 50–51
- and stationary models, 64
- targeting a model in, 58, 78

mercenaries
- and allies, 80
- contracts, 38
- and field allowance (FA), 40
- warcasters, warjacks, 83

miss
- AOE attack, 59
- automatic, 34, 61, 77
- combined attack, 62
- melee attack, 51, 58
- and range, 35, 56–57
- rerolls, 65
- spells, 77–78
- spray attack, 60

models
- activating, 42
- entries, 32
- field allowance (FA), 39–40
- independent, 31
- intervening, 43–44
- living, 31
- point cost, 39
- stationary, 64
- types, 31: *solos, troopers, warcasters, warjacks*
- volume, 43
- warrior, 31

model statistics (stats), 32–33: *ARM, Armor; CMD, Command; DEF, Defense; FOCUS, Focus; MAT, Melee Attack; RAT, Ranged Attack; SPD, Speed; STR, Strength*

Mounts, 81

movement
- advancing, 46
- beyond the play area, 64
- and facing, 46
- forfeiting, 65
- and knocked down models, 63
- measuring, 46
- modifiers to, 46
- Movement system, and crippled, 66
- normal, 46
- penalties, 48
- restrictions, 48
- unit movement, 72

multiplayer games
- formats, 40: *free-for-all, team*
- scenarios:
  - *Basic Battle, 90*
  - *Mangled Metal, Mosh Pit, 92*

multiple spell effects, 79

must, 29

myrmidons, 31

names, **28–29**, 82, 83

objective markers, 90

obstacles, 87–89

obstructions, 87–89

offensive spells, 77

Officer advantage, 34
   and drives, 80
   and field promotion, 72
   issuing orders, 72

Open Fist, 36
   and locks, **51**, 73
   and power attacks, **51**, 73

open terrain, 86

orders, 36
   issuing orders, 72
   and fleeing, 85
   out of formation, 71
   and knocked down models, 63
   and ride-by attacks, 81
   and stationary models, 64

origin of damage, *see* point of origin

overboosting a power field, 74

Pathfinder advantage, 34

penalties
   and charging, 46
   movement, 48
   for obstacles, 87
   for rough terrain, 86
   with spray attacks, 60
   for targeting a model in melee, 58

phases of the turn, 42

placing, 48
   beyond the play area, 64

play materials, 27

point cost, 38–39

point of impact
   of AOE magic attacks, 77
   and deviation, 59–60
   of a throw, 54

point of origin
   of AOE damage, 59
   of attack or effect, 64

Power (POW), 35, 76

power attacks, **51–56**. 73

power fields, 74

Power plus Strength (P+S), 35

primary attacker of combined attacks, 62

priority, 29

push, being pushed, 52

rallying, 85

range
   measuring, 56
   and point of origin, 64
   Range (RNG) stat, **35**, 36, **76**

ranged attacks
   and concealment and cover, 57
   declaring target, 56
   maximum number in an activation (ROF), 56
   modifying ranged attack rolls, 57
   Ranged Attack (RAT), 33
   ranged attack rolls, 56–57
   targeting a model in melee, 78

ranged weapons, 56

rate of fire (ROF), **35**, 56

Reach, **36**, 50

reactivating warjacks, 68, 80, 82

record sharing, 30

reference objects for LOS, 43

removed from play, 67
   and returning to play, 68

removed from the table, 67
   and returned to play, 68

repairing warjacks, 68
   and wreck marker, 67

replacing models, 64

replenishing focus points, **42**, 74

rerolls, 65

resolving attack, 245

return to play, 68

ride-by attacks, 81

rough terrain, 86

rounds, 42

rounding, 28: *distances, numbers*

rule priority, 29

rule of least disturbance, 64

rules issues, resolving, 30

running, 46

scenarios, 40, **90–93**
   multiplayer, 90, 92
   objective markers, 90
   random determination of, 90
   specific
    Basic Battle, 90
    Break the Line, 91
    Killing Field, 91
    Mangled Metal, 92
    Mosh Pit, 92
    No Man's Land, 93
    Throw Down, 93

shake effects, 73, 75

sharing information, 30

Shield, 36
   and crippled system, 66
   on inert warjacks, 67

simultaneous, 244
   AOE attacks, 59
   continuous effects, 69
   damage to force fields, 66
   damage with slam, 53
   damage with throw, 54–55
   fall damage, 63
   multiple attacks/damage rolls, 65
   spray attack, 60
   trample attacks, 56

skill check, 49

skill value, 49

skirmish encounter level, 38

slam
   attack, 52
   being slammed, 53
   damage, 53
   damage, collateral, 53
   and knocked down models, 63
   and overlapping bases, 64
   successful, 52

solos, 31

special actions (★action), **36**, 49

special attacks (★attack), 36

special effects
   automatic, 68
   continuous, 69: *resolving, and upkeep, Corrosion, Fire*
   critical, 68–69: *and AOE attack, Critical Corrosion, Critical Fire, critical hit*

special rules
   precedence, 29
   of warcasters, 74–75
   of warjacks, 73–74

Speed (SPD), 32
   modifiers to, 46

spellcasters, 75

spells, 75–79
   Arc Node advantage, 79
   attacking a structure with, 77
   casting, 77
   casting while out of formation, 71
   channeling, 79
   and fleeing, 85
   magic attack, 77
   multiple effects, 79
   point of origin of channeled, 79
   point of origin of normal, 75
   range, measuring for, 77
   and stationary models, 64
   stats, 76–77: **, Area of Effect, COST, Offensive, Power, Range, Upkeep*
   targeting, 78
   targeting a model in melee, 58, 78
   targeting restrictions, 77, 78
   targeting units, 72
   upkeep, 78

sportsmanship, 5, 30

spray attacks, 60
   boosting, 60
   that miss, 58
   and terrain, 60
   template, 256

Stall, 33

Standard Bearer advantage, 34

standing up, 64

starting roll, 40

stats
   bars, 32–33
   base vs. current, 33
   cards, 32
   continuous effects, 69
   model, 32–33
   modifying, 33
   weapon, 35

stationary, 64
   channeler, 79
   targets, 78

steamjacks, 31, *see also* warjacks

Stealth advantage, 34

Strength (STR), 32

structures, 88–89

systems and crippled systems, 66: *Arc Node, Cortex, Field Generator, Head, Left Arm, Movement, Right Arm*

system boxes, 36–37

table, 40
   beyond the table edge, 64

tactics, 71

RULES INDEX

Tall in the Saddle, 81

targets
elevated, 78
stationary, 64, 78
switching, 65
unit vs. model/unit, 72

targeting a model in melee, 58
and point of origin, 64

team games, 40

templates, 255–256

terrain, 86–89
details to discuss, 86
elevated, attacker/target on, 78
as spell target, 77
types, 86: *impassable, open, rough*
wreck markers, 67

terrain features, 86–89
elevation, 43–44
entryways, 89
forest, 87–88
hills, 88
linear obstacles, 87
obstacles, obstructions, 87
structures, 88–89
trenches, 88
variably sized, 87
water (deep, and shallow), 88

terrifying entities, 84–85

Terror advantage, **34**, 84–85

theme forces, 83

throw
attack, 53–54
being thrown, 54
damage, 54–55
and overlapping bases, 64

timing, 244–245

tokens
for model destruction, 63
soul, 67

Tough advantage, 34

toward vs. directly toward, 48

trample, 55–56

trenches, 88

troopers, 31–32
activating, 42
cavalry, 81–82
charging, 47
combined attacks, 62
command check, 84
damage capacity, 36
fleeing, 85
in/out of formation, 72–72, 84
making a ride-by attack, 81
models, 70–71
movement, 72
orders, 72
placed, 48
rallying, 85
running, 46

turn order, 40

two-player games, 40
scenarios, 90–93

Undead advantage, 34

unit attachments, 32, **71**
tactics, 71

unit components, 31–32, **70**
attachments, 32: *unit attachments, weapon attachments*
Grunts, 32, 70
Leaders, 32, 70
Officers, 32, 70
standard bearers, 70
troopers, 31, 70
unit commanders, 32, 70
weapon crews, 71

units
activating, 31, **42**
in an army list, 38–40
cavalry, 81
character, 39
charging, 72
combined melee and ranged attacks, 62
command checks, 84
control, 28
deployment, 40
as effect/spell targets, 72
FA, field allowance, 39–40
fleeing, 85
in and out of formation, 32, **71–72**, 84
and 'Jack Marshal, 80
leader or unit commander replacement, 70
massive casualties, 84
moving, 72
multiple spells or animi, 79
orders, 72
point cost of, 32, 39
profile, 32
rallying, 85
returning models to play, 68
ride-by attack, 81
tactics, 71
targeting, 72
and terrifying entities, 84
in theme forces, 83
and upkeep spells, 78

upkeep spells, 67, 78

victory conditions, 41

volume, 43

warcaster special rules,
affinities, 82
allocating focus points, 74
Battlegroup Commander, 74
casting spells, 77
Commander, **33**, 74
control area, 75
destruction, 67
epic, 83
Fearless, **34**, 74
feats, **36**, 74
and focus, 74
FOCUS stat, **33**, 74, 75,
mercenary, 83
power field overboost, 74
special rules, 74–75
Spellcaster, 75
spending focus, 75
theme forces, 83
Warjack Bond, 83

war encounter level, 38

warjack bonds, 83, 246
Cryx, 248
Cygnar, 247
Khador, 247
Mercenary, 249
Protectorate, 248
Retribution, 249

warjacks, 73
autonomous, 80
base size, 31
bonding, 83, 246
channeling, 79
character, 82: affinities, bonding, imprints
Construct advantage, 73
damage grid, 36–37, 65–66
destruction, 67
force fields, 66
'jack marshals, 80
inert, 67
mercenary, 83
points, 38
reactivating inert, 68
repairing, 68
restarting, 88
special rules, 65, 73
systems, 66
and trample, 55–56, 73
types, 31: *bonejacks, heavy, helljacks, light, myrmidons*
volume, 43
in water, 88
warlocks, 31

warriors, 31
base size, 37
in deep water, 88
restarting warjacks, 88
volume, 43

water (deep/shallow), 88

weapon attachments, 71

weapon crews, 71

weapon locations, 35, 66

weapon locks, 51–52
and knocked down models, 63
and Open Fist, 73

Weapon Master, 36,

weapon qualities, 35–36: *Buckler, Continuous Effect: Corrosion, Continuous Effect: Fire, Critical Fire, Damage Type: Cold, Damage Type: Corrosion, Damage Type: Electricity, Damage Type: Fire, Magical Weapon, Open Fist, Reach, Shield, Weapon Master*

weapon statistics, 35
AOE, Area of Effect, 35
L/R/H/–, Location, 35
P+S, Power plus Strength, 35
POW, Power, 35
RNG, Range, 35
ROF, Rate of Fire, 35

weapon systems, 66
and Buckler, 35
crippled, 66
locked, 52
and Shield, 36

whining, 5

within vs. completely within, 30

wounds, 36, 65

wreck markers, 67

x2, 35

you and yours, 28

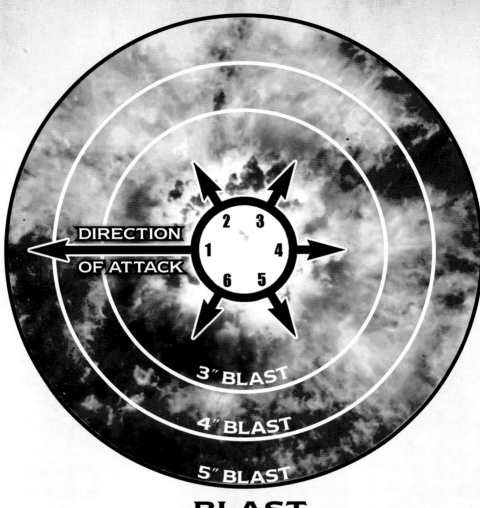

DIRECTION

OF ATTACK

2 3

1 4

6 5

3" BLAST

4" BLAST

5" BLAST

BLAST

WRECK MARKERS

Photocopy these templates for your personal use.

SPRAY

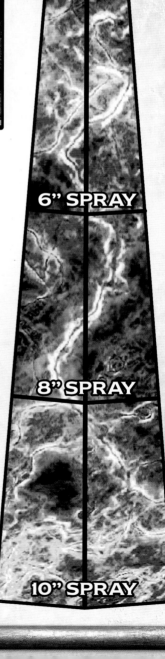

6" SPRAY

8" SPRAY

10" SPRAY

TRENCH

WALL

Photocopy these templates for your personal use.